WINNING
—THE—
GAME

WINNING
—— THE ——
GAME

MASTER YOUR POTENTIAL,
LEAD WITH PURPOSE, AND
LOVE THE PROCESS

CHRIS BALL

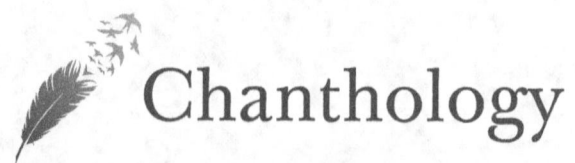

Chanthology

Chanthology Limited

© Copyright Chanthology Limited, 2025

Written by Chris Ball
www.chrisball.com

Chris Ball has asserted his rights under the Copyright, Designs and Patents Act, 1988, to be identified as the author of this work.

All rights reserved. No part of this publication may be copied, recorded, transmitted or reproduced in any way without prior permission in writing from the publisher.

ISBN: 978-1-915449-88-7 Paperback
ISBN: 978-1-915449-87-0 Hardcover
ISBN: 978-1-915449-99-3 Ebook

To find out more about our authors and books, visit www.chanthology.com and sign up for our newsletter.

Contents

Dedications vii
Preface ix
Introduction 1
Chapter 1: Game On! 5
Chapter 2: Rise Up Self 23
Chapter 3: Charting Course 59
Chapter 4: Eating the Elephant 99
Chapter 5: Setting the Sails 163
Chapter 6: Soar Higher! 203
Chapter 7: Weathering the Storms 227
Chapter 8: Being the Captain 267
Chapter 9: Final Words: A Blueprint for
              Transformational Success 331
Acknowledgements 339

Dedications

This book is warmly dedicated to my son, Josh, whose perseverance and determination inspire me to strive harder and reach further every day. To my daughter, Emy, whose encouragement and heartfelt recommendations have fuelled my journey with endless inspiration. Elena, Isabel, and Olivia introduced a new level of challenges and joys into my life. To Aline, my loving and highly supportive wife, whose unwavering belief has been my anchor. To my five brothers, who each, in their own way, have taught me to play, win and lose, and get up and play again. Each of you has played a pivotal role in this journey, and for that, I am eternally grateful.

Preface

I wonder what has compelled you to get this book?

As you stand on the threshold of diving into this book, I wanted to take a brief moment to set the stage and share a few important aspects of the journey we're about to embark on together.

Writing "Winning the Game" wasn't a spontaneous decision but rather the culmination of three distinct motivations.

I've always been someone who craves learning. Life has been an incredible classroom, and I was fortunate enough to have countless mentors offering lessons at every turn. This book draws upon these lessons, condensing what I've found most impactful into guiding principles. They've been the backbone of my own journey to success, and I'm hoping they might light the way for you too.

Also, I wish I had a pound for every time someone asked how I managed to have success in business and in life. Such questions highlight a genuine curiosity. Instead of sharing my thoughts in sporadic conversations, which I actually really enjoy, it made sense to compile them in one accessible place.

Lastly, there seemed to be a missing link in literature: combining the fun and strategy of gameplay with real-life success tactics. I've always felt that the strategies we use in games aren't too distant from those we apply in our professional lives. This fusion of game and life strategies, which has been somewhat of a personal formula for me, became an inspiration for the book.

So, there you have it—the three main reasons that brought "Winning the Game" to life.

The pages you're about to turn are a collection of stories—narratives that speak of human resilience, of humbling failures, of monumental transformations, and also soaring successes. Each of these tales holds a mirror to the myriad of emotions, challenges, and breakthroughs that we, as individuals, encounter in our quest for success.

While every single story finds its roots in genuine experiences and raw truths, I've made a conscious decision to change certain names. This is not to dilute the authenticity but rather to protect the privacy of those who were kind enough to share their personal journeys with me. It's a testament to the respect I hold for each individual and the trust they placed in me to uphold the sanctity of their life stories.

In some instances, I choose to blend some stories into one another to form a composite tale. This amalgamation is intentional. By weaving together strands from different narratives, I sought to craft a richer, more vivid, and all-encompassing tapestry that embodies the true essence of personal transformation and the intricate dance of success and setbacks.

While certain details in these stories have been tweaked to create a cohesive narrative, the core lessons—the heart and soul of each tale—remain untouched, unaltered, and undeniably real. They are the distilled wisdom of genuine experiences, ready to inspire, guide, and enlighten.

As you turn the pages, I hope you find a mix of inspiration, strategy, and fun. Thank you for trusting me with your time and mind. Let's start "Winning the Game."

Introduction

Life is a game—a complex, ever-evolving game where the rules aren't always clear, the stakes are high, and the playing field can shift without warning. Some people stumble through, trying to keep up with the pace, while others master the art of the game, turning every challenge into a stepping stone toward success. But what if you could be the one who not only plays the game but rewrites the rules, changes the odds, and creates a life that's not just successful, but truly fulfilling?

This book has been written to transform your approach to life by harnessing the power of gamification—the art of turning life's challenges into engaging, rewarding experiences. Imagine waking up every day not with a sense of dread about the tasks ahead, but with the excitement of facing new levels, unlocking achievements, and progressing toward your ultimate goals. That's the mindset we're aiming for.

We begin by exploring the essence of gamification and why it's such a powerful tool for personal and professional growth. Through real-life stories—from a factory worker who unknowingly sparked a productivity revolution with a simple chalkboard to a mother who turned her fitness journey into a thrilling battle against virtual zombies—you'll see how gamification isn't just about making life more fun. It's about making life more meaningful, more engaging, and ultimately more successful.

But before you can start playing to win, you need to understand yourself—your motivations, your desires, your purpose. This is the foundation of everything else. By digging deep and uncovering your true "why," you'll ignite a fire within that drives you to achieve things you never thought possible. It's about aligning your actions with your passions and values, so that every step you take is not just a move toward success, but a move toward fulfilment.

Once you've tapped into that inner drive, it's time to chart your course. Setting goals is crucial, but it's the planning and execution that brings those goals to life. We'll explore how to create a clear roadmap that guides you through the complexities of life, helping you see the big picture while managing the day-to-day details that will get you where you want to go.

Of course, even the best-laid plans can be overwhelming if you try to tackle everything at once. That's why breaking down your goals into manageable steps is key. Think of it as eating an elephant—one bite at a time. By focusing on small, consistent actions, you'll make steady progress, build momentum, and avoid the burnout that comes from trying to do too much, too fast. You will learn how just one strategy will help you get over 400% more done in less time, and with more joy and fulfilment.

As you move forward, you may need to refine your strategy, making decisive choices and adapting to the ever-changing landscape of life. This is where the real game begins—navigating the twists and turns, seizing opportunities, and staying focused on your ultimate objectives. It's about being both bold and flexible, knowing when to stay the course and when to change direction. Decision-making is perhaps one of the most important things you will ever learn to do efficiently.

But growth doesn't stop there. To truly excel, you need to push beyond your current limits, continually striving to improve yourself in all areas of life. Whether it's learning a new skill, advancing in your

Introduction

career, or deepening your relationships, the goal is to keep soaring higher, always reaching for new heights of achievement and personal satisfaction. If you want to soar higher, you'll need bigger wings!

However, no journey is without its storms. Life will throw challenges your way—unexpected setbacks, tough decisions, moments of doubt. But these aren't obstacles; they're opportunities for growth. By developing resilience and learning to weather the storms, you'll emerge stronger, more capable, and more determined than ever to reach your goals.

Finally, in the game of life, you must become the captain of your own ship. Leadership isn't just about guiding others; it's about leading yourself with purpose, integrity, and vision. It's about taking control of your life, inspiring those around you, and creating a legacy that extends beyond personal success. Whether you're leading a team at work, guiding your family, or making a difference in your community, true leadership is about making a positive impact that lasts.

I wrote "Winning the Game" with the intention of it being a blueprint for living a life of purpose, passion, and achievement. I hope it will encourage you to embrace the challenges, celebrate the victories, and always push forward with the mindset of a good player. Whether you're looking to excel in your career, improve your health, strengthen your relationships, or simply find more joy in everyday life, this book will show you how to turn every aspect of life into a game worth playing—and winning, and always having fun.

Are you ready to take control, rewrite the rules, and start winning the game? Let's begin.

CHAPTER 1

Game On!

Mike worked in a sprawling factory, where the chatter of workers punctuated the rhythmic sound of machinery. For several years, he was a team member on the night shift of a small production line, creating assemblies for an automotive customer. Mike enjoyed working with his colleagues, was conscientious about his paperwork, and was always on time. When his team leader was promoted to a new position, he was recommended to fill the post, and as a youthful 25-year-old with a slightly baby-face appearance, he found himself sitting at the team leader's desk next to a chalkboard. This innocuous board, dulled by time and dust, would soon become the heartbeat of a transformation.

Mike was happy to be promoted and wanted to improve himself, his team, and the company. But the skills he had as a team member were not enough to make the difference needed. As much as he was conscientious, popular and hardworking, at first, he found the promotion overwhelming. In his first production meeting, he realised it was his job to look for new ways to increase productivity. Leadership, Mike quickly realised, wasn't just about directing orders; it was about fostering teamwork, motivating members, and continually pushing the boundaries of productivity. One of the first things a friend said to him was, "Management is measurement". If you want to change something, you must first measure where you are. So that evening, driven by a desire to inspire his team, Mike decided to put that chalkboard to use, scribbling down the number of assemblies they had manufactured with the words, "Night Shift, do not remove". In doing so, without realising it, he issued an unspoken challenge. To his surprise, the following evening, he clocked in to find a fresh figure scrawled beneath his tally, accompanied by the words "Day Shift, do not remove". He shared the board's contents with his team without uttering a word about the new figure. That night, they managed to churn out 3% more than the day shift had the previous day. Thus, a friendly rivalry began. The day shift retaliated the next day, trumping the night shift's count by 2%. As the days wore on, this unspoken competition saw each shift striving to outdo the other in production numbers. To add a bit of fanfare to their game, Mike introduced a brass trophy, grandly engraved with "Team of the Month." And to add a bit of incentive, he wrote on the chalkboard: "The losing team buys the first round". By the end of the first month, the day shift narrowly claimed victory. Both teams convened at the local pub to celebrate, and the gracious night shift footed the bill for the first round. It was a fantastic opportunity for fun and camaraderie, fostering a sense of togetherness among the colleagues. The night shift, in good spirits, vowed to take the trophy the following month, a promise they kept. The brass trophy they introduced was not just an emblem of victory, but a testament to the company's evolving culture. Through this playful competition, productivity soared by over 9%, camaraderie and teamwork grew, forming bonds that transcended shift timings. Yet, what Mike and his team had serendipitously tapped into was not just the might of competition. It was the enthralling realm of gamification.

Gamification is about integrating game elements–like points, badges, and leaderboards–into traditionally non-gaming environments. It transforms mundane tasks into engaging challenges, capitalising on our innate human needs for achievement, recognition, and progression. Various sectors, from health to education, recognise its potency and integrate it for unprecedented success. Consider, for instance, the task of data entry. It is an important job within a company, but it is often dismissed as repetitive and dull. However, when sprinkled with carefully developed gamification elements, it transforms into a challenge, a race against time, accuracy, and peers. It becomes about being the best "Data Cruncher," about that rush when you earn double points and the shared joy of dominating the leaderboard. Gamification, however, is not about relentless competition. It's a tool, powerful yet subtle, which when wielded with finesse, can engender a culture of positivity, productivity, and innovation. It's about ensuring that work is not just a series of tasks but an engaging journey. The idea is to transform something mundane into something that is fun.

Circling back to Mike, his initiation into leadership might have been challenging, but his fortuitous use of a simple chalkboard encapsulates the spirit of this book. As external pressures threatened, Mike's factory wasn't just churning out car parts, but redefining its work culture and winning its unique game. Gamification, or the incorporation of game-like elements in non-game scenarios, comes with better motivation, team spirit, and results. While this is a growing trend, clear evidence of its success has been a bit hit-or-miss. Interestingly, Mike's intuitive approach is in line with what researchers have been exploring over the years. A study by Sailer, Hence, Mayr, and Mandl (2017) in Germany used an online business game, TOPSIM - easyManagement, where participants could take the reins of a virtual company. Drawing in 274 students from two leading universities, they exposed them to various combinations of game features such as personalising avatars, earning badges, competing on leaderboards and tracking progress through graphs. The researcher's key interest was understanding the human motivation behind gamification. They looked at whether these features made participants feel more skilled, in charge, or connected to their peers. They also gauged if the tasks felt valuable or were simply fun for the sake of fun. Not surprisingly, they found that badges, leaderboards, and performance graphs did ramp up feelings of skill and the sense of value in tasks. In addition, avatars and storylines boosted social connections. However, not every feature hit the mark; for instance, the sense of decision-making freedom was pretty much unchanged. An interesting takeaway was that feeling skilled and valuing the task were major drivers behind the benefits of gamification. We'll get deeper into the nuts and bolts in the chapter 'Being The Captain'.

The allure of gamification is undeniable. Transforming monotonous tasks into intriguing challenges drives motivation. As teams rally together, collaboration tightens, communication channels open up, and the collective learning curve steepens. When daily tasks morph into intriguing games, the engagement skyrockets, leading to amplified performance. Furthermore, the benefits cascade beyond task accomplishments. Yet, for gamification to cast its magic, one-size-fits-all won't work. It's pivotal to ensure that the game mechanics resonate with the players. The key questions to ponder: Is the game genuinely enjoyable? Does it make tasks more captivating? Understanding the diverse personalities and preferences of the participants is crucial. Tailoring the game elements to cater to their tastes and backgrounds can make all the difference. There is , however, a cautionary tale: Gamification, if left unchecked, can swing the pendulum from motivation to stress. An overly aggressive competitive spirit can lead to burnout and strain. Moreover, the essence of work should remain paramount. Recalibration becomes imperative if the pursuit of game rewards overshadows the intrinsic satisfaction derived from work.

Gamification stands as a formidable tool. It can revolutionise workspaces if deployed thoughtfully, boosting engagement, performance and joy. The story of Mike and his chalkboard is a testament to this transformative power, but there are many nuances in this process, as we will look in detail, as well as look into the motivational aspect of it. The big picture? It's not just about adding game elements randomly; it's about strategically choosing the right elements for each situation. Gamification, in essence, is something to be tailored, not templated.

Education: Playing the Game of Learning

Let's look at the joys of education. Do you recall a time when learning felt like an exciting journey, where the adventure of discovering new concepts was as joyous as the knowledge itself? If so, our educational experiences differ greatly. In my own school days, nestled within the soot-covered stone walls of an old Victorian comprehensive, learning often felt more akin to a tedious obligation than an exhilarating exploration. I languished in the bottom set for most subjects as I suffered with dyslexia and found both reading and writing a challenge. As much as I wanted to do well, the frequent disruptions from bored classmates only added to the challenge, turning what should have been hours of discovery into moments of trying to maintain focus amidst chaos. To be fair, one or two shining teachers could ignite some spark and turn a dreary lesson into an episode of curiosity. Yet, in this particular school, situated in a deprived corner of Northern England, such educators didn't stay there very long. The more inspiring teachers–those who could transform a classroom into a realm of endless possibility–often chose the pristine halls of newer institutions–schools set in tranquil, leafy suburbs, that offered a different world. In such schools, the sight of a raised hand meant a curious question, not the preamble to a classroom scuffle, and inspiration wasn't the exception but the rule. As I navigated my educational journey, I couldn't help but wonder what it might have been like to learn in such an environment where passion and education walked hand in hand. Instead, I was restless and bored, and each year, my school reports painted a bleak picture of my future prospects. But a pivotal revelation was waiting just around the corner, destined to reshape my self-perception and prospects.

At a crucial moment, when I was 15 years old and with final exams on the horizon, an external career advisor visited my school. His mission, guided by our test scores and teacher reports, was to nudge us toward viable career paths—an attempt to keep us off unemployment benefits. A suggested future as a fitter in a factory not only upset me, but ignited a fierce anger. I had given up every practical school subject as I successfully cut myself more often than the metal or wood I was working on. I explained that that was not the kind of work I had in mind, at which point the career advisor suggested I would spend the rest of my life unemployed. In a moment of clarity and frustration, I told him he wouldn't dictate my future. I insisted I wouldn't fall into unemployment and stormed out of his office without looking back. This encounter was followed by a reflective Christmas Eve, where my mother noticed my sombre mood. My expression of feeling stupid and constantly overshadowed by my brothers' academic success led to a surprising revelation—I had dyslexia. My mother had known since early in my childhood, but hadn't considered it necessary to share this piece of information with me. At age 12, my intelligence was gauged in a verbal reasoning test and determined to be significantly high, a stark contrast to my struggles with reading and writing.

This new information, digested over the Christmas holidays, catalysed a fervent drive within me. Returning to school, a new zest for learning and a newfound purpose propelled me forward, crafting a radically different narrative for my life. I went on to massively outperform expectations in my school exams and then to outperform expectations in college. That internal drive, born from that new perspective, has persisted in me. The transformation and the desire to play and win were internal; there were no external encouragements or competitions to compel me. It's a familiar well from which I draw strength in life and business challenges. It reminds me that potential is boundless when one's mind is determined and directed. In a beautifully full-circle manner, this relentless drive has steered me toward understanding the nuanced world of gamification, even though at that time, I had no idea that such a thing existed. I just thought about the games and sports I loved playing. I thought about how I worked so hard to improve and win more often. Sometimes I would be covered in marks and bruises, but I really didn't care. Many times, I would watch others playing and see what they did to win. This drive was a lifesaver to me and is available to all.

Developing this mindset can indeed change one's destiny. It's the same drive that comes naturally to people who love playing games.

For me, knowing I was not stupid changed my belief in what I could achieve and that created hope that I could do better. I set myself challenges that allowed me to track my progress and results. Using the same motivation for winning games with my brothers to win a new game of passing my exams.

When schools and colleges add these elements into the curriculum in a way that is fun and engaging to the students, results improve. A Fascinating study by Dichev and Dicheva from 2017 demonstrated some of the vast potential, and also pitfalls of gamifying learning. Through their lens, it is possible to see how points, badges, and leaderboards could transform the monotonous classroom environment I once knew into a dynamic, interactive playing field. I only wish the study had been done at my school.

Yet, as I delved deeper into this study, the findings revealed nuances. Not every gamified classroom guaranteed better grades. Not every leaderboard instilled motivation. The key was in the integration. It's like adding spices to a dish - the right blend can elevate it, but a mismatch can throw off the balance.

I remembered my daughter's school employing a unique blend of merit points and demerits. It wasn't just about topping the leaderboard, but about recognising consistent effort, perseverance, and improvement. This was a testament to how thoughtfully implemented gamification could cater to a spectrum of learners.

But here's the thing: gamification isn't merely about making learning fun. It's about making it impactful. It's about nurturing problem-solvers, decision-makers, and team players. It's about equipping learners with skills to win in school and the larger game of life. This is where great coaches make such a difference to teams. By creating internal belief and confidence, the players perform at a higher level, which then improves their belief and their skills.

Sir Alex Ferguson, as the architect behind Manchester United's golden era, didn't just coach a football team; he meticulously crafted a mindset that permeated every layer of the club. His approach wasn't merely about football; it was a masterclass in leveraging the power of belief, skill, and resultant success, essentially gamifying the journey to excellence.

When Ferguson took charge in 1986, Manchester United was a team in need of inspiration and direction. The club, longing for past glories, found in Ferguson a leader capable of instilling a profound belief in success. He didn't just aim to win matches; he sought to build a culture where winning became an expectation—a non-negotiable standard for every player who wore the jersey.

Ferguson's coaching went beyond the physical. He developed the mental acuity of his players, embedding a belief system that each member was part of something greater than themselves. This was the inception of a winning mindset. Ferguson knew that belief was contagious and that a strong belief in victory, even in the face of adversity, could turn the tide of games. His famous halftime talks were not just tactical discussions but sessions to recharge and reinforce this belief among his players.

Skill development under Ferguson was systematic and purposeful. He identified potential and relentlessly worked to refine it. Training sessions were rigorous, focusing not just on improving technical abilities but also on understanding the game's psychology. Ferguson's management style ensured that skill development was aligned with the team's overarching strategy, creating a squad that was versatile and adept at overcoming any challenge.

The results of this belief and skill development were evident in the team's performances. Manchester United under Ferguson was synonymous with resilience, often clinching victories from the jaws of defeat. The team's ability to perform under pressure and maintain consistency across competitions showcased the effectiveness of Ferguson's coaching philosophy.

Ferguson's tenure at Manchester United serves as an emblematic story of how belief and skill, underpinned by strategic coaching, can lead to sustained success. His approach transformed Manchester United into a footballing powerhouse, revered not just for the trophies it won but for the indomitable spirit it displayed on the pitch. The legacy of Sir Alex Ferguson is a testament to the transformative power of gamifying the process of achieving excellence—where belief, skill, and results created a virtuous cycle that propelled Manchester United to legendary status.

I was excited by the potential of gamified education. As we progress in this book, I invite you to join me on this journey of exploration as we strategize, adapt, and learn the rules of this grand game.

Healthcare: Transforming Habits, One Step at a Time

Emma, a 38-year-old mother of three, found herself in a relentless battle with weight gain that had slowly crept up on her since the birth of her third child. Life as a full-time working mom was a juggling act that left little room for personal health and fitness. As a child and young adult, Emma had always been of average weight and considered herself reasonably attractive. However, the demands of motherhood, career, and time had shifted her priorities—and her health had taken a hit.

Her struggle wasn't just physical; it was mental. The mirror reflected a version of herself she barely recognised, and the gym became a symbol of monotony and failure. Her attempts at fitness were sporadic at best, characterised by short bursts of enthusiasm followed by long periods of disinterest. The cycle of yo-yo dieting seemed endless, and the results, when there were any, were fleeting.

One evening, feeling particularly low after another failed attempt to stick to a workout regimen, Emma was idly scrolling through apps on her smartphone. That's when she stumbled upon "Zombies, Run!", an app that promised to transform her runs into a thrilling escape from hordes of zombies. Intrigued by the concept of gamifying her exercise routine, Emma downloaded the app, not fully grasping how much it would change her life.

From the first run, Emma was hooked. The app wasn't just about jogging; it was an immersive experience that cast her as the hero in a post-apocalyptic adventure. Each run became a mission where she collected supplies, dodged zombies, and built her base. The streets around her home transformed into a game map where survival depended on her feet.

The narrative-driven exercise turned what was once dull into a dynamic and exciting adventure. Her usual routes became thrilling escapades that saw her pushing herself harder than ever before. Sprinting to evade the virtual undead, Emma found herself looking forward to her runs—a stark contrast to her previous gym visits.

As weeks turned into months, the changes began to show. Not only was Emma losing weight, but her energy levels were also improving. She was sleeping better, eating healthier, and her mental health had improved significantly from the joy and accomplishment each run brought. The app's community aspect also motivated her; sharing her progress and seeing others' achievements made her feel part of something larger.

Emma's transformation was not just physical, but emotional and mental. She regained a sense of self-confidence that she hadn't felt in years. The challenge of "Zombies, Run!" reminded her that she could tackle big problems in small steps, and each step could be as enjoyable as it was effective.

The true testament to Emma's change came during a family outing at a park. As her children played, she overheard her oldest tell a friend, "My mom can outrun zombies!" It was said with such pride that Emma's heart swelled. She wasn't just getting fit; she was becoming a role model for her children.

Emma's story is a powerful reminder that turning exercise into a game can revolutionise a person's approach to fitness. "Zombies, Run!" brought fun, adventure, and a sense of accomplishment back into her life. It showed that when exercise is enjoyable, it becomes a part of your lifestyle, not just a fleeting phase. The app didn't just help her lose weight; it helped her rediscover her zest for life, proving that sometimes, to move forward, you just might have to run for your life.

Her experience demonstrates that within our daily routines lies the potential for significant change. It's not just about reaching a destination but enjoying and being motivated by the journey. Emma's transformation stands as an inspiring reminder that change, one step at a time, is not only possible but also fulfilling.

So, as we embark on our quests for better health, let's remember Emma's journey. Let's gamify our challenges, celebrate our small victories, and transform our routines into adventures of well-being.

This is backed up by research such as Sardi, Idri, and Fernández-Alemán. In 2017, they embarked on a comprehensive exploration of the burgeoning field of gamification within digital healthcare. Their research, a meticulous review of 46 separate studies spanning various sources, was a deep dive into how gamification is shaping the healthcare landscape, particularly in the digital realm. The trio of researchers focused on a wide array of digital healthcare applications, with a special emphasis on those that were gamified or designed as serious games. A significant portion of the studies they analysed centred around chronic disease rehabilitation, physical activity, and mental health. This focus highlights an emerging trend: gamification is increasingly being recognised as a potentially powerful tool in managing and improving health outcomes in these specific areas. One of the key findings of Sardi, Idri, and Fernández-Alemán's research was the positive impact of gamification on health-related behaviours and outcomes. They observed that gamification within digital health applications contributed to increased user engagement and motivation. More importantly, it appeared to boost adherence to treatment plans significantly. This is a crucial finding, as one of the perennial challenges in healthcare is ensuring that patients stick to their prescribed treatments and routines.

In addition, the study unearthed substantial evidence supporting the effectiveness of gamification in promoting physical activity, enhancing medication adherence, and improving mental health. This is particularly significant in a world where lifestyle diseases are rampant and mental health issues are increasingly coming to the fore. Gamified apps and interventions were found to catalyse behavioural changes essential for tackling such issues, suggesting a promising avenue for future healthcare strategies. The work of Sardi, Idri, and Fernández-Alemán in 2017 opened new doors in understanding the potential of gamification in healthcare. It underscored the need for further exploration in this area, potentially paving the way for innovative, engaging, and effective digital health solutions that could transform patient care and health outcomes in the years to come.

From my own experience, when I wanted to improve my fitness, I started working for "badges" on my iPhone fitness app. Although the motivation for new badges eventually declined, the habit of regular exercise had been established, and a look in the mirror contained its own motivation.

Environment: Powering Conservation Through Competition

In Jake's neighbourhood in San Diego, the spirit of friendly competition has long been a staple of community interaction, akin to the rivalries and camaraderie found at local sporting events. However, the introduction of the "San Diego's Biggest Loser Contest" brought this competitive spirit into a new arena—energy conservation. Modelled after the famous TV show that focuses on weight loss, this innovative program was designed to encourage residents to dramatically reduce their energy use, turning a serious community goal into an engaging challenge.

Each participating household in Jake's community was equipped with a smart metre, transforming every home's monthly energy usage into a score that could be tracked and compared. This wasn't just about reducing utility bills; it was about climbing to the top of the leaderboard. The rules were simple yet impactful: the more energy you saved, the higher you climbed in the rankings. What made this contest truly engaging was not just the personal savings on utility bills but also the sense of playing a vital part in a community-wide effort to save energy.

As the contest unfolded, Jake observed notable changes within his community. Neighbours began to swap tips on how to conserve energy—from upgrading to more efficient appliances to changing daily habits like reducing air conditioning use and turning off lights when not needed. The contest discussions filled the air at block parties and neighbourhood meetings, fostering a collective mission to not only win the competition but also contribute to a larger cause of environmental conservation.

This transformation was visible even in the neighbourhood's physical landscape. Solar panels appeared on rooftops, energy-efficient windows replaced old leaky ones, and gardens were redesigned to require less watering. These changes were signs of a community motivated by more than just competition—they manifested a collective commitment to sustainability.

The most profound impact, however, was seen in the monthly community gatherings where the "energy leaderboard" was updated. Cheers and applause filled the room whenever a new leader was announced, celebrating each other's achievements in reducing their carbon footprint. For Jake, who had always been environmentally conscious, seeing his own name rise in the rankings was gratifying, but the real victory was witnessing his community's enthusiasm for a sustainable lifestyle.

The success of San Diego's Biggest Loser Contest went beyond mere numbers on utility bills. It created a community ethos centred around sustainability. Residents who had once been indifferent to energy conservation were now proud advocates, showcasing that the competitive spirit could foster not only individual change but also communal transformation.

Jake's personal journey in the contest also highlighted a deeper sense of accomplishment. By participating, he didn't just reduce his energy consumption; he became a part of a larger narrative of change. Inspired by the competition, he took further steps to educate his neighbours on the importance of sustainable practices, reinforcing that individual actions, when multiplied across a community, can lead to significant environmental impacts.

This story of Jake and his community clearly illustrates pioneering research conducted by Gustafsson, Bång, and Svahn in 2009. Their study was a forerunner in demonstrating how gamified solutions could be effectively employed to motivate households to reduce their energy consumption. When a community unites for a common goal, even the smallest efforts can lead to significant environmental benefits.

Gustafsson, Bång, and Svahn's research delved into the realm of behavioural science and environmental psychology. They recognised that traditional methods of encouraging energy conservation, such as mere awareness campaigns or financial incentives, were often insufficient to instigate long-term behavioural changes. Seeking a more impactful approach, they turned their attention to gamification, exploring its potential to engage and motivate people in a more dynamic and sustained manner. Their study involved the development and deployment of a gamified system that provided households with real-time feedback on their energy consumption. This system was ingeniously designed to transform mundane daily activities, like switching off unnecessary lights or optimising heating usage, into engaging challenges. The real-time feedback acted as an immediate reward mechanism, acknowledging and celebrating every small step households took towards reducing their energy usage. But the researchers didn't stop there. They introduced an element of community competition into the mix, tapping into the natural human instinct for social comparison and competition. Households were not only able to track their own progress but also see how they fared in comparison to their neighbours. This community leaderboard added a layer of social motivation, spurring participants not just to participate, but to excel in their energy-saving efforts. The findings of Gustafsson, Bång, and Svahn were groundbreaking. They revealed that the combination of real-time feedback and community competition was significantly more effective in motivating behaviour change compared to traditional methods. Households engaged more enthusiastically in energy-saving activities, driven by the immediate rewards of the gamified system and the communal spirit of the competition.

The impact of such research extends beyond the academic sphere, offering valuable insights for policymakers, environmental advocates, and communities seeking effective strategies to promote sustainable practices. The study illustrates the power of gamification as a tool to not only motivate individual action but also to foster a sense of community around shared goals. In essence, the work of Gustafsson, Bång, and Svahn in 2009 set the stage for other innovative approaches similar to San Diego's Biggest Loser Contest. It highlighted the potential of gamified solutions to turn the serious business of energy conservation into an engaging, community-building experience, showing us that when it comes to motivating positive change, sometimes all it takes is a little bit of fun and competition.

In the ups and downs of life, I've come to understand that each success and setback is directly linked to the rules of the games we play and the strategies we use. Think about Mike, our team leader from the night shift, for instance. He worked with a company that produced car parts for a major automobile manufacturer. This is a straightforward job, devoid of any game-like intricacies to many. However, Mike saw it differently. Mike saw how gamification improved processes and productivity in the critical manufacturing sector. In this world, where precision, timeliness, and reliability matter, even a slight boost in productivity can tip the balance between profit and loss. They were in a perpetual game–striving for improvement, learning from errors, and always eyeing the prize: impeccable car parts that would be integral to someone's drive somewhere in the world.

It made me reminisce about my youthful days, competing fiercely in games with my brothers. Every match, every round, was a lesson. Some days, I emerged triumphant, relishing the sweet taste of victory. On others, defeat taught me resilience, perseverance, and the art of strategising better, much like how Mike and his colleagues operated. After my first business collapsed, in the depths of despair, I realised that the rules of the games we play, whether in business or life, aren't static. They evolve. What's essential is understanding these rules, adapting, and transforming oneself according to the changing dynamics. And that's where the essence of transformation comes into play. It's not a one-time occurrence but a continuous journey, almost like levelling up in a video game. The definitions of transformation from various dictionaries emphasise a marked, complete change in form, nature, or appearance. But isn't that akin to progressing through levels in a game, each stage demanding a new strategy and perspective? You will not find here a recipe on how to change your life or how to be successful. How can success be defined anyway? Yes, dictionaries offer definitions, and society might impose its benchmarks, but ultimately, isn't success subjective? Perhaps success is a personal metric, a feeling of contentment, an understanding that you've played your game to the best of your abilities.

I once chased the financial benchmark of success, and when I hit that coveted million pound in the bank mark, it felt like an empty victory. The win wasn't as sweet as I had anticipated. It was then I understood that my version of success wasn't just tied to wealth but to purpose, passion, and personal growth. Your perception of success might evolve, too. This book is tailored for those seeking a transformative approach to life and business. The strategies detailed were tried and tested by many accomplished business leaders. They've also been pivotal in my life, shaped by personal trials and triumphs. Insights from these influential figures, combined with my experiences, will challenge your existing notions of success. My goal is to lead you towards authentic transformation in business and personal spheres. Understanding your 'why' – your core purpose – stands paramount among the seven keys to transformational success. Understanding your 'whys' is the cornerstone of your future aspirations. Pursuing success for misguided reasons can leave you achieving goals but still feeling unfulfilled.

I've lived this framework throughout my career. I refined it, whether through successes or failures. Look at it as a holistic cycle of change, encompassing all necessary steps.

This book contains wisdom from esteemed business leaders, personal anecdotes, and gamification principles. Together, they aim to set you on a transformative voyage. The emphasis isn't solely on the destination but also on relishing the journey. See each obstacle as a level in a game, with every challenge helping you level up.

As you embark on this reading journey, I hope you'll have fun, discover the games you enjoy playing and find joy in establishing your rules, determining the results you want and celebrating getting there. Let us play our games!

CHAPTER 2

Rise Up Self

*"I believe that one of life's major lessons is learning to
understand what makes us do what we do."*
— *Anthony Robbins*

Looking back on my childhood, I fondly remember intense gaming sessions with my brothers. Whenever I played a game, my heart was set on victory. For me, playing wasn't a casual activity; it was a fervent pursuit, and I put my heart and my soul into winning. My childhood is obviously behind me now; however, my strive to 'win' is not as connected to the past, but perhaps not with the same concept that it represented for me. So what do we mean by 'winning'?

Take chess, for instance. A player aims to capture the opposing king while protecting their own. In Monopoly or football, clear-cut rules inform players about victory conditions, be it accumulating wealth or scoring goals. Thinking beyond the games for sport or entertainment, the essence of a game runs deeper than just its end goals. In childhood, the games we played served multiple purposes. Some I recognised in the heat of the moment, while others became apparent only with the wisdom of age. Winning might have been the immediate aim, but the deeper purpose? It was about forging connections and solidifying our sibling bond that remains unshaken through shared moments of joy. The purpose of games, as I've come to understand, isn't just about meeting objectives; it's the underlying force that propels us forward, both individually and collectively.

Games have an undeniable magnetic pull that draws us into their intricate webs of challenge and reward. This fascination isn't a mere relic of our youth; for many of us, it's an enduring passion that evolves with us. I find solace and stimulation in the patterns of Sudoku. Meanwhile, one of my daughters derives immense pleasure from the tactical manoeuvres of board games. Her joy can be heard in shouts of celebration when she wins a round or a game. My son's journey, in particular, stands as a testament to the profound impact games can have on our lives. His zeal for computer games was no fleeting fancy. It propelled him back into the world of academia in his late twenties. Through dedication and an insatiable curiosity, he clinched a Master's Degree in Digital Game Design. Now, he doesn't just play games; he breathes life into them, crafting digital odysseys that ensnare players in tales of adventure, strategy, and imagination. The reality is, everywhere we look, games manifest in diverse forms. Some people flex their muscles and strategy on the sports field, others test their wit against the twists of crosswords, and many more find escapism in imaginative play.

The Universal Allure of Games.

Beyond the surface, games tap into an intrinsic human essence. At our core, we're propelled by a primal quest—the pursuit of challenges and the intoxicating elation of triumphs that await. This isn't merely a chase for the finish line or the trophy at the end; in some cases, it is about survival, other times, a deeper journey of self-discovery and growth. We yearn to push our boundaries, to set personal benchmarks, and to recognise the metamorphoses, both minute and monumental, that chart our progress. Games, in all their diverse forms, offer us a mirror, reflecting our innate human desires: to challenge, to strive, to evolve, and ultimately, to celebrate the journey itself, replete with its ups and downs.

The relationship between challenge and the human species is deeply rooted in our evolutionary history and psychological makeup. Challenges, both physical and mental, have played a significant role in shaping human development and behaviours. Historically, facing and overcoming challenges has been crucial for survival. Our ancestors dealt with harsh environments, predatory threats, and the need for resource acquisition, which required constant adaptation and problem-solving. This has ingrained a natural tendency to seek out and overcome challenges as a way to ensure survival and adaptability. Challenges force individuals to push beyond their comfort zones, leading to personal growth and learning. When faced with difficult situations, people must develop new skills and strategies, leading to innovations and advancements. This is evident not just in personal development, but also in societal and technological progress. Facing challenges builds resilience by teaching individuals how to cope with stress and adversity. This resilience is crucial for dealing with the ups and downs of life and can contribute to better mental health and well-being. Challenges can provide motivation and a sense of purpose. The desire to overcome obstacles can drive individuals to remarkable achievements, providing a sense of accomplishment and satisfaction that reinforces self-efficacy and confidence. Overcoming challenges often requires cooperation and collaboration, which can strengthen social bonds and foster a sense of community and belonging. Moreover, shared struggles can form a crucial part of group identity and solidarity. On a deeper psychological level, challenges can fulfil existential needs by providing a sense of meaning and engagement in life. The psychologist Mihaly Csikszentmihalyi describes a state of "flow," which is achieved when engaging fully in challenges that are neither too difficult nor too easy. This state is associated with profound satisfaction and has been linked to happiness. The human brain rewards the overcoming of challenges with releases of neurotransmitters like dopamine, which are associated with pleasure and satisfaction. This biochemical response not only feels good but also encourages repetitive engagement with challenging tasks. In essence, challenges are a fundamental part of what makes us human. They contribute to our development, define our capabilities, and enrich our experiences, driving both individual and collective progress.

Reflect for a moment on the unyielding spirit of children. They may taste defeat time and again, yet, with a sparkle in their eyes and determination in their tiny hearts, they dive back into the game. Undeterred, undefeated. Why? Because each round, each attempt, represents more than just a game. Children are often intrinsically motivated to play games because they find them fun and challenging. The enjoyment they derive from playing motivates them to continue playing, even when they face difficulties or lose. It encapsulates hope, perseverance, and the burning aspiration to better oneself, to someday taste the sweetness of success. Children tend to be more flexible in their thinking compared to adults. They may be more willing to try different approaches or strategies to improve their gameplay, whereas adults may sometimes get stuck in patterns of thinking or behaviour. This mindset encourages them to persist even after setbacks, like losing a game.

"Rise Up Self" is about understanding your purpose, embracing challenges, and striving for continuous personal growth. It is about achieving your fullest potential and it is also about having fun. Life is more fun when you take your journey with a heart of exploration and gratitude, whatever may come.

What does it mean to "Rise Up Self"? At its core, it is the philosophy of embracing your challenges, understanding your purpose, and aligning your actions with your deeper values. It's about rising above your circumstances, learning from your experiences, and continuously striving for personal growth. Consider, for example, the journey of J. K. Rowling. As a struggling single mother, she faced numerous rejections before "Harry Potter" was accepted for publication. Her perseverance and belief in her story exemplify the "Rise Up Self" philosophy. Despite the odds, she rose above her circumstances, ultimately achieving incredible success and inspiring millions worldwide. Steve

Jobs offers another powerful example. Ousted from the very company he co-founded, he did not let this setback define him. Instead, he founded NeXT and acquired Pixar, both of which became hugely successful. His resilience and ability to innovate even in the face of failure demonstrate the power of rising up and continuing to push forward. As you navigate through this chapter, the spotlight will be on you: on understanding your aspirations, defining your version of victory, and charting a course to a fulfilling and meaningful game of life. Remember, you determine what winning looks like for you. You write the rules of the game and the outcome that you decide is 'Winning The Game'.

May 1972

As I laced up my rugby boots, I felt a sense of readiness, even though rugby wasn't my sport of choice. There was something about these boots–they fit just right, felt sturdy with their steel toecaps, that made the football fly further when I kicked it. I was excited to join my friends for a game, and my excitement was only matched by my sweet tooth. I was about to dash off to the shops for some pre-game sweets when my mother's voice stopped me in my tracks.

"Mum, I'm just off to the shops before they close," I called back, already halfway out the door.

"I need you now. The shops can wait a few minutes," she responded, her tone pulling me back with a sense of urgency I couldn't ignore.

Racing back inside, I found my entire family gathered in the living room, a palpable tension hanging in the air. As I squeezed into a spot on the floor, my mother broke the news that would pivot our lives in a new direction. "We are getting divorced", my mother said with a sad expression in her eyes. My father was to leave later that day.

Needless to say, I neither played rugby, or bought sweets on that day. This news came at a time when life seemed almost idyllic. We lived in a picturesque English village, I had a great circle of friends, and our home was always filled with the chaos and laughter that comes with having five brothers. Yet, in an instant, the foundation of my world began to crumble. In the months that followed, our family dynamics shifted dramatically. We downsized our home, my two eldest brothers moved out, and the once constant presence of my father was reduced to tension-filled weekly visits. Amidst the upheaval, my mother made the courageous decision to move us closer to her brother, seeking a fresh start and the chance to pursue her dream of becoming a midwife. This decision relocated us to a starkly different setting in the north of England, where the echoes of a once-thriving textile industry had faded into a landscape marked by cheaper properties, great poverty and high unemployment. It was a far cry from the life we knew.

So, why share this story at the outset of a chapter on purpose? It's because our formative experiences, the upheavals and traumatic events, deeply influence the purpose we carve out for ourselves, both consciously and subconsciously. My journey through significant life changes, whilst challenging, has been a testament to the idea that our early experiences don't just shape us—they can also propel us towards finding deeper meaning in our endeavours. The lives of people who faced barriers, challenges, and disheartenment and managed to continue playing their games with integrity, winning as they went, act as a source of inspiration. Our past shapes us, steering us toward our future, and even the most tumultuous events can lead us to discover a purpose that drives us forward, compelling us to rise above and find success on our terms.

As we dive into "Winning The Game," it's essential to recognise that purpose is not a static destination but a dynamic journey. It's about understanding how our purpose signposts our destination.

Let us start by looking at Nelson Mandela's amazing journey. Born in a small village in the Eastern Cape, Mandela's early years were moulded by tribal customs and British colonial law. This duality, a fusion of traditional African and Western education, laid the foundation for his unique perspective. By the 1940s, as a young lawyer in Johannesburg, Mandela became an active voice against the oppressive apartheid regime. In 1944, Mandela, along with Oliver Tambo and Walter Sisulu, founded the African National Congress Youth League (ANCYL). This organisation was pivotal in transforming the ANC from a more conservative petitioning organisation to an activist movement that sought mass involvement in the struggle against apartheid policies of the government. But his defiance wasn't a sudden spark. It was an evolving flame, fuelled by a deeper understanding of racial inequalities and a vision of a unified South Africa. Mandela played a crucial role in the 1952 Defiance Campaign, the first large-scale, multi-racial political mobilisation against apartheid laws under the ANC's banner. He travelled across the country organising resistance to discriminatory laws, advocating for nonviolent methods of disobedience and protest, which led to his first arrest for civil disobedience. In response to the Sharpeville Massacre in 1960 and the subsequent banning of anti-apartheid organisations, Mandela co-founded Umkhonto we Sizwe (Spear of the Nation), the armed wing of the ANC, in 1961. He argued that the ANC had no alternative but to turn to armed struggle, given the closing off of all channels of peaceful protest. Mandela helped organise sabotage campaigns against military and government targets, marking a significant shift in tactics in the fight against apartheid. This was not an impulsive transition, but a calculated move. He believed that for the purpose to stand robust, the approach needed to be flexible. Mandela's activities with Umkhonto we Sizwe led to his arrest in 1962 and subsequent sentencing in the Rivonia Trial to life imprisonment. During the trial, Mandela delivered his famous "I am prepared to die" speech, which eloquently laid out the justification for armed struggle and was a defiant proclamation of his commitment to the cause of ending apartheid. In 1963, this path led him to the cold confines of Robben Island. Yet, even within those prison walls,

Mandela's purpose never wavered. Instead of surrendering to despair, he became a beacon of hope, a symbol of resistance. His strategy and actions towards his purpose of the emancipation of an entire nation transformed into changing the culture of the institution he was in. In those trying times, Mandela didn't just find solace in his purpose; he found strength. Even while imprisoned, Mandela continued to be a symbol of defiance against apartheid. His continued imprisonment drew international attention and condemnation of the apartheid regime, eventually leading to increased global pressure for his release and for the abolition of apartheid. Mandela's 27 years in prison weren't just a test of his resilience; they were also a period of introspection and growth. He learned the power of dialogue, of empathy, of understanding the 'opponent'.

I wonder if, like me, you had a great shift in your life that brought you pain and sadness. Perhaps, like Mandela, you have been oppressed by a situation for a long time. Your life does not need to be defined by your circumstances. It may seem preposterous to compare myself to Mandela, but the truth is, whether we influence an entire nation or the whole world, or we change negative patterns in our thoughts and behaviours, we all have dreams and purposes. In Nelson Mandela's case, by the time he walked free in 1990, he was not just a political leader; he was a visionary, ready to shepherd his nation into a new era.

In 1994, history bore witness to the fruits of Mandela's purpose-driven life. South Africa's first democratic elections and Mandela's subsequent presidency weren't just political milestones; they were affirmations of a purpose fulfilled. I never had political aspirations, but I see my purpose as a family man, as a husband, father and as someone who has traced a journey of success, built on courage to try, to fail, to look at myself and my circumstances, learn and try again. By no means can I be seen as a success by everyone. If success is measured by power or recognition, I haven't gotten those things, and I haven't done or achieved those things. I have a beautiful family whom I love, and I know I am loved. I have the means to acquire whatever I desire, within reason. I donate a percentage of my income to charities that are close to my heart, and now I am here, with you, supporting you to craft games that you want to play in your life, according to your unique definition of success, joy and purpose. That is how I feel successful, so now let us define what makes you successful.

Purpose: The Dual Lenses

Throughout my journey, I've discerned two pivotal facets of purpose: the 'self-purpose' and the 'greater purpose'. The former delves into our personal aspirations and our roles in the intimate circles of family, work, and community. It's the internal compass directing our individual journeys and daily activities. Contrastingly, the 'greater purpose' stretches beyond the self. It encapsulates our vision for the world and our contribution to the greater good–whether its environmental conservation, societal betterment, or peace advocacy. It's when the two combine that the real power emerges.

Behind every purpose lies a vision. To realise this vision is to fulfil your purpose. For instance, if your purpose is to eradicate hunger, whether it is in your neighbourhood or community, in your city or the world, the corresponding vision would be a reality where every individual has access to nourishing food.

In our game of life, this is akin to playing not just for the immediate thrill of victory but for a legacy, for leaving the playing field (or the world) better than we found it. The game's essence isn't in the short-term wins, but in the long-term impact, the deeper connections we forge, and the larger purposes we serve.

During a balmy evening, as the sunset painted the sky in hues of oranges and purples, I sat at an old wooden cafe table across from a close friend. As is often the case on a warm summer evening, we both enjoyed a cool drink and a deeply thoughtful discussion. Our conversation naturally drifted to the age-old quest for purpose, something we had often thought about but never truly been clear about. I sipped on my drink and gazed into space, the moon now peeking out behind a soft cloud. As I watched the stars slowly appear, I realised that the search for purpose was not a unique challenge; it was a shared human experience. More often, it seems like a hunt for a hidden relic that is expected to be uncovered in profound epiphanies or divine interventions. But the reality? It's a more nuanced journey, laden with introspection and self-discovery. It's not about fleeting happiness, but about a deeper, lasting joy that comes from knowing you're on the right path.

To truly embark on this journey, your mindset is key. It's not a passive wait for purpose to magically appear; it's an active pursuit. It's about aligning your thoughts, clearing the mental fog, and pinpointing what truly resonates within you. Passion and joy often act as compasses in this exploration. Sometimes, these emotions emerge from the simplest of actions - activities we'd indulge in without any ulterior motive. For some, it might be the rush of penning down stories, while for others, it could be the joy of reading those tales to a captive audience passing on the torch of knowledge. When we confront our vulnerabilities, when we address our pain points, we often unearth the values that matter most to us. It's in these moments of introspection that our purpose begins to take shape.

I shared these reflections with my friend, and we concluded that, at its core, the journey of purpose is deeply personal. It's about understanding oneself, about listening to the silent whispers of your heart, and about having the courage to act upon them.

Nelson Mandela stepped into the battle against apartheid with a clear strategy: stir the pot, cause unrest, disrupt the norm, and make the white authorities sit up and take notice. He understood that significant change often required shaking society at its roots, and thus his early tactics embodied extremity and acute agitation. He was ready to turn the tide in South Africa, and if it took a bit of chaos to make it happen, then so be it. But all that shifted when he wound up behind bars on Robben Island. Suddenly, Mandela had to rethink his playbook. He wasn't in a position to lead marches or organise strikes anymore. He was on lockdown.

But here's where it gets interesting: Stripped of his freedom and cut off from his comrades in arms, he found himself standing at a crossroads. Mandela didn't hit pause on his life's purpose. Instead, he rewrote the rules of the game. Isolated from the world, he turned his attention to the world he was in—his fellow inmates. The conditions on Robben Island were harsh, dehumanising even. But Mandela was having none of it. What changed was not his goal but his strategy. Behind bars, he swiftly recalibrated his approach, turning what could have been a place of defeat into a starting point for a different kind of revolution. He started pushing for change from the inside, arguing for the fundamental human rights of prisoners. He advocated tirelessly for the improvement of the appalling conditions endured by his fellow inmates. His unyielding efforts and negotiations with the prison authorities gave rise to significant changes—alterations in the harsh treatment of prisoners, introduction of basic educational programs, and eventually, the provision of more humane living conditions. Each small victory was a testament to his belief in the dignity of every individual, even within the confines of a prison, meant to strip that very dignity away. He made headway—one hard-won concession at a time. His greater purpose was the freedom of all the people of South Africa, whilst his personal purpose was to create dignity and fair treatment for individuals around him.

Mandela wasn't just serving time; he was serving his cause. He realised that he couldn't overturn apartheid from his cell, but he could work on transforming the minds of those around him, including his captors. He started having hush-hush discussions with the apartheid leaders, not as enemies, but as humans capable of reason and empathy. This wasn't surrender; this was strategy. He was laying the groundwork for a future where all South Africans could coexist as equals.

Mandela's time in prison teaches us something crucial about purpose and resilience. Your circumstances don't define your end game. Sure, they might force you to take a detour, switch up your methods, or find new allies. But the goal doesn't change. You just find a new way to get there. What Mandela mastered was the art of adaptability. He held onto his core purpose like a bulldog, but stayed flexible in his tactics. His fight wasn't over when he landed in jail; it just shifted gears. And by staying nimble, staying strategic, and, above all, staying committed, he kept that fight alive. It's a reminder for all of us: stay true to your vision, but be ready to rewrite the playbook. That's how change is made.

Mandela's story underscores a profound truth: Purpose is rarely found in moments of joy or victory. Often, it's carved in adversity, sculpted in challenges. Clinical psychologist Steven Hayes said,

*"In our pain, we find our values,
and in our values, we find our pain."*

This isn't just a cute play on words; it's an insight into the very fabric of our beings.

One thing that has always captivated me is the beauty of smiles. The sheer genuineness of a heartfelt grin or the chuckles of laughter never fail to lighten my day. The very first thing that attracted me to my wife was her winning smile and cheerful disposition. Every time I witness a genuine smile, it reinforces my drive to spread happiness, armed with the knowledge and experiences I've amassed over the years. Purpose doesn't only come from the good times; it's often born out of struggle and hardship. Take my background, for example. I grew up with money being tight and opportunities scarce. Now, things are different, and I'm in a better place financially. But this change comes with its own challenges. I want to help others who are facing the struggles I faced, and sometimes, I feel pulled in a million directions trying to do just that. This urge to help everyone is a blessing, sure, but it can also be overwhelming. Still, it's clear to me that having a purpose—especially one centred on giving back—is what brings real meaning and satisfaction to my life. It's about more than just making myself happy; it's about extending that opportunity for happiness to others. That connection, that desire to uplift others, that's what really defines my sense of purpose.

To delve deeper into this intricate web of purpose, it's essential to break it down, to understand its facets, and to gain insights from diverse narratives. The basic framework for discovering and tapping into your purpose has five key steps:

1. Start with self-discovery:

Finding your purpose means starting a journey into knowing yourself better. It involves a bit of vulnerability, questioning why we do what we do, and really understanding what we're passionate about. What is it that sparks that sense of excitement in you? What activities make you lose track of time? It's all about noticing those natural tendencies we have and giving ourselves the freedom to follow those paths, with no judgement allowed.

My journey and purpose in life might not echo the grandeur or global impact of figures like Nelson Mandela, but it stems from a deeply personal place—the trials of my childhood. Growing up in hardship and poverty, I was determined that my future, and that of my family, would be different. My vision was clear: to create a life devoid of scarcity, where my children would enjoy the prosperity and experiences I never had, including holidays and the comfort of financial security. This resolve crystallised into a tangible goal: to become a millionaire, as I believed that having a million pounds in the bank was synonymous with achieving financial independence.

As an engineer with a knack for computer networking, I recognised early on the potential within this burgeoning field. In the 1980s, it was a niche area with limited expertise worldwide, yet I saw an opportunity. My ability to navigate and innovate within this technology became the cornerstone of my business venture. I aimed to offer unparalleled network solutions to companies, enhancing their efficiency while reducing costs—a valuable proposition during the digital boom. Thus, my life was guided by dual purposes: to revolutionise network solutions for businesses and secure the financial well-being of my family. The path wasn't easy. It demanded relentless effort, continuous learning, and adaptability in navigating the challenges of entrepreneurship. The sudden loss of my business partner, who was also a cherished family member, compounded these challenges, doubling my workload overnight and plunging me into a period of both professional and personal strife. Yet, it was this very adversity that honed my determination. I immersed myself in work, driven by the dual aims that had shaped my journey. This commitment bore fruit; the business flourished, transforming my financial landscape and enabling the prosperous life I had envisioned for my family.

As we journey from the phase of self-discovery towards defining our purpose, it's crucial to heed an additional step before solidifying our commitment to that purpose. My own experience revealed a profound lesson: beneath the surface of my explicitly stated purpose lay a deeper, more intrinsic purpose that I had initially overlooked. This realisation underscores the importance of delving beyond our initial perceptions and aspirations to uncover the true essence of what drives us. It's a reminder that our purpose might not always be immediately apparent, and sometimes, it requires a deeper introspection to truly understand the motivations that propel us forward. This step is essential, ensuring that the purpose we commit to genuinely reflects our core values and deepest desires, guiding us towards a path that is both fulfilling and aligned with our true selves.

2. Accept yourself:

Finding our true purpose transcends the mere act of polishing our external selves to a semblance of perfection. It involves a deep, accepting embrace of our whole selves—our flaws, failures, strengths, and triumphs. This acceptance is the key to unlocking our genuine motivations and aspirations, guiding us toward a purpose that resonates with our true selves.

I learned this lesson the hard way, after achieving my goals and realising the success I had dreamed of, only to be met with a profound sense of emptiness. I had a picturesque house with a tennis court, luxury car, and the opportunity for lavish holidays. Yet, amidst these achievements, I found myself divorced and deeply unhappy. Despite the outward signs of success, my life felt devoid of real meaning and purpose. In my single-minded pursuit of wealth, I had lost sight of what truly mattered. I hadn't grasped my core reason for being.

The root of my childhood pain wasn't just financial hardship; it was the emotional turmoil and insecurity stemming from my family's disintegration. What I truly longed for wasn't wealth but the safety and security that a close-knit family provides. This realisation highlighted a critical misalignment in my pursuit of purpose. Achieving everything I thought I wanted, only to find happiness elusive, was a sobering experience. It underscored the importance of deep self-understanding and acceptance. Crafting a purpose based on an imagined version of ourselves, rather than who we truly are, is a recipe for disillusionment. Now, my purpose is intimately tied to my family and my faith—two pillars that hold profound significance for me. By centering my life's purpose around my loved ones and spiritual beliefs, not only have I found deeper joy and happiness, but ironically, this shift has also led to greater wealth than I ever accumulated in my previous pursuits.

This journey underscores a fundamental truth: understanding and accepting your authentic self is crucial. It ensures your chosen purpose aligns with your true essence, paving the way for genuine fulfilment and meaning in your life. You may or may not have a clear picture of your purpose. It may be that you only see challenges, not a purpose. Let me tell you that your purpose may be more intertwined in your challenges than you could imagine. Let's consider the example of Sir Richard Branson, the visionary behind the Virgin Group. Branson's journey is particularly inspiring because of the challenges he faced due to dyslexia. Growing up, Branson found school to be a difficult environment, dyslexia was not well understood and he was not diagnosed, affecting his academic performance. He dropped out of school at the age of 15 with no qualifications. His head teacher told him he would either end up in jail or be a millionaire. However, his lack of formal education did not deter his ambition or entrepreneurial spirit. Branson's story is a testament to overcoming adversity and turning what some might see as a disadvantage into a unique strength. His business achievements are vast, with the Virgin Group spanning many industries. Yet, what stands out even more is how he has used his experiences to advocate for change in the educational system. Branson has been vocal about the importance of recognising and supporting different learning styles, particularly for students with dyslexia and other learning differences. His efforts extend beyond just words; through his businesses and platform, Branson has actively contributed to raising awareness and providing resources for educational initiatives. He has also set up his own university dedicated to supporting individuals with diverse learning styles. He has called it DyslexicU: the world's first 'University of Dyslexic Thinking'. His work in this area shows how understanding and accepting one's true self can lead to a purpose that extends far beyond personal success, impacting the lives of others positively. Branson's journey illustrates how our unique challenges can inspire us to enact change, emphasising that our purpose often lies in the intersection of our personal experiences and the broader impact we wish to make in the world. As you journey through this book, your purpose, your goals and how to get there will start to become clearer. Your journey is as unique as you are; as special as you are.

3. Crafting a Personal Blueprint—The Vision Statement:

Oscar Wilde once remarked, "To live is the rarest thing in the world. Most people just exist." He was astutely correct. Without purpose, life can seem dull and uneventful. As a society, we'd stagnate, unable to progress. To combat this existential ennui, we must lead lives driven by our intrinsic values.

Envision your life as a game, where every choice you make impacts your path. In this game, your main goal is to find and achieve your purpose, using your personal vision as your guide.

Think of creating this vision as plotting out the main and side objectives that will steer you through life. Start by really getting to know yourself—what are your strengths, what are you passionate about, and what do you value most? Consider what motivates you, what activities you enjoy the most, and what kind of story you want your life to tell.

Let me tell you a story of someone who found clarity around her purpose and vision. Erin Gruwell began teaching at Woodrow Wilson High School in Long Beach, California, she faced a tough environment. Many of her students, facing societal and economic difficulties, were often overlooked by the education system. But Erin aimed to do more than just teach traditional subjects. She wanted to inspire her students to overcome the challenges of violence and poverty they faced.

Despite doubts from other teachers, resistance from the administration, and the harsh realities her students dealt with at home, Erin remained committed. Many of her students came from tough backgrounds, dealing with issues like poverty and gang violence, and weren't prepared for academic success. Erin often found herself buying supplies and books with her own money to support her students.

What set Erin apart was her unwavering belief in her students' potential. Her vision was not just about improving literacy and academic outcomes; she aimed to provide a safe space for students to share their stories and learn empathy, responsibility, and the power of knowledge. Through innovative teaching methods, including encouraging her students to keep journals (later published as 'The Freedom Writers Diary'), she made education relevant and accessible.

Erin's dedication bore fruit as her once-underserved students graduated high school and many went on to pursue higher education, altering the course of their lives. The transformation was so profound that it inspired the formation of the Freedom Writers Foundation, through which Erin has continued to advocate for students and train teachers to implement her innovative educational methods.

Her story, popularised by the book and the subsequent movie "Freedom Writers", serves as a testament to the power of clear vision and perseverance in the face of systemic challenges and limited resources.

Drawing a parallel, both Musk and Erin emphasise the significance of a robust vision. While circumstances may change, technologies evolve, and challenges arise, it's this blueprint that serves as the North Star. It remains constant, guiding you towards your larger goal.

Having a clear vision is like owning a map that guides you through uncharted territories. It's about knowing not just where you want to go, but also who you want to be along the way. Crafting your personal vision involves deep introspection and imagination–it's about painting a picture of your ideal future and aligning it with your core values and strengths.

Unsure about defining your life's purpose and mission? Consider this exercise: envision the eulogy at your funeral. What do you hope people will say about you? Imagine the words of your spouse, children, friends, relatives, colleagues, and even the wider public. Picture the obituary in the press—what do you want it to highlight about your life and achievements? This exercise isn't morbid; it's a powerful tool for understanding how you want to be remembered and what legacy you wish to leave behind.

For many, including myself, this thought experiment is a potent source of inspiration. It goes beyond the mundane goal of simply paying the bills. It's about crafting a legacy that positively influences generations to come. I wanted to ensure that my influence on my children was profound and enriching, guiding them to surpass my achievements and lead a life richer than mere chance would offer.

This exercise also extends to friendships. Consider what your friends might say about you at your farewell. Will they feel grateful for having known you? Did you impact their lives positively? These thoughts can guide you in living a life that touches others meaningfully.

Furthermore, it's about considering the impact you can have on the wider world. It's about aspiring to leave something behind that inspires future generations to achieve more, to be happier and wiser. This vision for your legacy can shape your daily actions and decisions, steering you towards a life that fulfils not just your personal goals but also contributes positively to those around you and the world at large.

Nelson Mandela's state funeral on December 15, 2013, in Qunu, Eastern Cape, included a eulogy delivered by then-President Jacob Zuma. In this eulogy, President Zuma paid tribute to Mandela, characterising him as a "freedom fighter, a dedicated and humble servant of the people of South Africa, a fountain of wisdom, a pillar of strength, and a beacon of hope" for those striving for justice and equality worldwide. President Zuma also conveyed a deep sense of gratitude towards Mandela, acknowledging him as the leader South Africans deeply needed and revered during a challenging phase in their history. This eulogy encapsulated the profound impact Mandela had not only on South Africa but on the global stage, as a symbol of resilience, peace, and the enduring fight for human rights.

So, defining your vision statement, encompasses your purpose and mission in life, which can be guided by considering the legacy you want to leave. It's about envisioning the impact and memories you wish to create, influencing not just your immediate circle but potentially the world. Let this vision inspire and guide your journey, shaping a life that's meaningful and impactful.

4. Adapt and Evolve: Stay Agile

Your journey through life is dynamic, and so should be your vision. As you grow, learn, and experience new things, be prepared to adapt your vision. New opportunities will arise, and challenges will present themselves, requiring you to be flexible and responsive. Embrace these changes as part of your growth, and adjust your path accordingly. It's about creating a world of your own design. It's more than a destination; it's about crafting a life that resonates with who you are and what you value. It's a declaration of your intentions and aspirations. Take time to contemplate the world you want to create for yourself and how you fit into this larger picture. This vision is your compass, steering you towards a fulfilling, purpose-driven life, where every decision and action aligns with your ultimate goals.

In the game of life, your vision is what transforms routine tasks into steps towards something greater. It adds depth, meaning, and direction to your journey. With each mission you complete and each challenge you overcome, you're not just moving forward; you're crafting a story of personal triumph and transformation.

5. The Power of Positive Associations: Game-Changing Relationships

Jim Rohn once said, "You are the average of the five people you spend the most time with." This idea is further reinforced by Dr. David McClelland's in his seminal work, "The Achieving Society" (1961), which suggests that our associations can dramatically influence our success or failure. He recognised that our social circles can shape our motivations, behaviours, and ultimately, our outcomes. He suggested that we are more likely to adopt the attitudes, beliefs, and behaviours of those we spend the most time with. This concept highlights the critical role our social environment plays in our journey towards finding and nurturing our purpose.

Take Alex's story, for instance. When I first met him, he was battling a severe addiction, a struggle that had thrown his life into chaos. In his mid-30s, he was trapped in a self-destructive cycle, deeply entrenched in an environment that fuelled his addiction. The turning point for Alex came when he decided to join Narcotics Anonymous. This decision was more than just a step towards recovery; it was a conscious choice to surround himself with a supportive network, starkly contrasting his previous associations. The group recommended that he disassociate from active addicts and associate with people who would support his recovery. It was this shift in his social circle that played a crucial role in his transformation. Today, as a counsellor, Alex often reflects on the impact of positive, purposeful company. His experience illustrates a powerful truth: the people we choose to surround ourselves with have a significant influence on the direction our lives take.

Alex's story is a compelling reminder of the importance of carefully selecting our social circle. It's about more than just seeking companionship; it's about finding those who uplift us, challenge us, and contribute positively to our journey. The company we keep can either propel us forward or hold us back. By choosing wisely, we set the stage for personal growth, resilience, and success. Our journey, much like a well-played game, is greatly influenced by those who are part of it–every relationship shapes our story, every interaction influences our path.

6. Surrender to your purpose:

Discovering your purpose isn't a one-off event—it's a continuous commitment. It's about aligning your everyday actions with your overarching goals, revisiting and refining your purpose, and immersing yourself wholly in the journey.

Let me share the story of Jim Fruchterman, a brilliant engineer who found himself at the pinnacle of Silicon Valley innovation. Despite his success, he experienced a persistent sense that something was missing, a void technology for profit's sake couldn't fill. He craved more profound meaning in his work — he wanted his technological expertise to serve a greater purpose in society.

This realisation struck him profoundly when one of his projects, an image-recognition system designed for a missile, could also, he discovered, be used to help the visually impaired read text. The potential social impact of this technology was enormous compared to what he saw as its relatively trivial military use. However, the lack of commercial appeal meant he couldn't pursue this venture in the traditional for-profit space.

Undeterred and driven by the idea of technology as a force for good, Jim founded Benetech, a nonprofit that develops software for social good. One of their projects, Bookshare, is the world's largest accessible online library for people with print disabilities, such as the visually impaired or dyslexic. His journey didn't stop there; Benetech continues to expand its reach, addressing global problems related to human rights, education, and environmental conservation.

By aligning his daily endeavours with his inner purpose, Jim didn't just carve out a career; he blazed a trail, creating a new realm where technology serves humanity. His life became a testament to the fact that success and social impact could intersect beautifully.

As author Tony Robbins suggests, the questions we pose to ourselves often frame our outlook. Jim Fruchterman's journey is a compelling testament to that truth.

The Mosaic of Purpose

"The Mosaic of Purpose" is an ever-evolving concept shaped by the diverse experiences and interactions that mark our journey through life. Imagine this mosaic as a collection of stories, each piece representing a different chapter of our life—successes and setbacks, happiness and challenges, discoveries and lessons learned. Together, these pieces form a comprehensive picture, yet each maintains its distinct importance and contributes uniquely to our overall understanding of purpose.

This concept of purpose is dynamic, constantly influenced by our life experiences. It grows and changes as we do, reflecting the ongoing journey of learning and evolving. Each element of our lives, from our achievements to our struggles, adds depth and richness to this mosaic, creating a picture that is uniquely ours.

Consider your life as a vast, interactive game, where every interaction, every experience, is an opportunity to learn and grow. This game isn't linear; it's a complex web of paths and experiences, each adding a different layer to your understanding of your purpose. The stories of people like Scott Harrison and Blake Mycoskie are not just tales; they are integral parts of this game, offering insights and lessons that guide us in our quest to find and fulfil our purpose.

Your life's journey is like navigating an open-world game. You start with basic goals shaped by your surroundings and initial experiences. As you move forward, meeting different people and encountering various situations, you uncover new objectives. Some of these resonate deeply with your true calling. This process of discovering and pursuing your purpose can be likened to gamification–it's dynamic, filled with discovery, challenges, and moments of transformation.

Scott Harrison's life story is not just remarkable, it's transformative. Once entrenched in the glitzy lifestyle of New York City's elite nightclub scene, Scott seemed to have it all. The glittering nightlife, surrounded by celebrities and the city's high rollers, appeared to be the ultimate definition of success. Yet, beneath the surface, Scott felt a growing sense of emptiness and dissatisfaction with his path. The turning point came when Scott decided to step away from his life of luxury and volunteer in West Africa. It was there, far removed from the neon lights of New York, that Scott faced a starkly different reality. He was confronted with a severe and pervasive challenge: communities suffering from a lack of clean water. This was a basic human necessity he had always taken for granted, now glaringly absent in the lives of countless individuals. This eye-opening experience was a catalyst for a profound reevaluation of his life's purpose. Scott was moved by the struggles of those he met, people who lived every day without access to clean water, something so fundamental yet so out of reach. The stark contrast between his life in New York and the hardships faced by these communities stirred a deep desire in him to create meaningful change. Motivated by this newfound purpose, Scott returned to the United States with a clear mission. He founded Charity Water, a non-profit organisation dedicated to providing clean and safe drinking water to people in developing countries. This venture was not just a change of career; it was a complete realignment of his values and objectives. Charity Water emerged from Scott's passion to bridge the gap between the abundance he once knew and the scarcity he witnessed. His organisation has since transformed the lives of millions, bringing clean water to communities across the globe, proving that one person's change of heart can lead to global impact. Scott's journey from nightclub promoter to nonprofit founder illustrates that success isn't about personal gain; it's about making a positive impact in the world. Through his story, he inspires others to look beyond themselves and consider how they, too, can use their talents and resources to address critical global issues. Scott Harrison's transformation shows us that when we connect with a purpose greater than ourselves, we can redefine our definitions of achievement and fulfilment. Scott's story is not just about personal change; it's a revelation about the nature of purpose itself. It shows us that what we perceive as our life's mission can evolve and take on new meanings. It reminds us that sometimes, our true calling lies in unexpected places, waiting to be discovered. His journey from the nightclubs of New York to the remote villages of West Africa is a testament to the transformative power of finding and embracing a deeper purpose.

Blake Mycoskie's journey is another remarkable example of how new experiences can redefine our sense of purpose. While travelling in Argentina, Blake encountered something that profoundly affected him: children who had no shoes. This simple yet striking observation ignited a mission within him, steering him beyond the realms of mere commercial success. In response to what he saw, Blake founded TOMS Shoes, a company built on a unique business model blending commerce with philanthropy. The company's 'One for One' policy–donating a pair of shoes for every pair sold–was revolutionary. This initiative wasn't just about selling shoes; it was about creating a tangible positive impact. Blake's business model demonstrated how commerce could be leveraged for the greater good. However, Blake didn't stop there. His vision for change and impact grew, leading TOMS Shoes to expand its philanthropic efforts. The company began addressing other critical global needs, such as providing vision care and access to clean water. Blake's journey in the game of life transformed into a broader mission: fostering holistic change and making a real difference in the world. Blake Mycoskie's story is an inspiring reminder that our careers and businesses can be powerful vehicles for change. It shows that when we align our professional endeavours with a deeper purpose, the potential for positive impact is boundless. His journey from a traveller in Argentina to the founder of a socially conscious enterprise exemplifies the profound impact of embracing a mission-driven life.

The narratives of Scott Harrison and Blake Mycoskie vividly demonstrate that our life journey is dynamic and ever-changing. Their stories teach us a valuable lesson: often, our true purpose takes us away from the familiar and into uncharted territories. They remind us that we might find our most meaningful missions in paths we never anticipated when we first started our journey.

These experiences underscore the importance of continuously reassessing our goals and staying open to new possibilities that align with our deeper values and aspirations. As we navigate the various chapters of our lives, it's crucial to embrace this adaptability. Being open to new challenges and ready to align our objectives with the deeper purposes we discover can lead to profound impacts, much like what Harrison and Mycoskie achieved.

Our quests, like theirs, have the potential to extend far beyond our immediate sphere, impacting lives and creating waves of positive change. In the grand game of life, the most rewarding victories are those that contribute to the greater good, transforming our personal successes into collective achievements.

In life's intricate game, your purpose is not a fixed endpoint, but an evolving journey. It's shaped by your decisions, the routes you take, and the challenges you embrace. This journey is a mosaic of varied experiences, each adding depth and dimension to your quest. As you progress in this game, every step you take, every new discovery you make, and every transformation you undergo are significant. They are the milestones that lead you toward your true purpose. Remember, in this journey, every experience counts, and every choice matters in steering you towards a fulfilling and impactful life.

So, when you tell yourself, "I'm no Nelson Mandela," remember, you don't have to be. Your purpose, whether it's creating a positive work environment, being a dependable friend, or simply bringing joy to those around you, is equally important. It's yours. And in fulfilling it, you contribute something no one else can – a little piece of a better world, crafted by your own hands, heart, and mind.

Purpose is intertwined with our deepest desires, aspirations, and the impact we wish to make. It's about channelling our unique talents, finding our passions, and aligning them with a broader vision.

Ask yourself: If the pillars supporting your current life crumbled–your job, your business, your status–would your purpose still stand tall? Would it beckon you, guiding you towards a fresh start?

Your life's anthem, the rhythm that propels you forward, lies in the marriage of your passion and purpose. Perhaps it's in music, literature, technology, or any other field. Dedicate yourself to it. Forge a vision. Remember, to truly find your purpose: Be open to discovering yourself, accept yourself, crafting a personal blueprint–the vision statement, surround yourself with positive people, and surrender to your purpose. One's purpose isn't just a vague notion or a fleeting thought. It is the heartbeat of our existence, the rhythm to which our souls dance. When I introspect, recalling the various junctures of my life, it's clear that my most defining moments were intrinsically linked to my deeper purpose. When your purpose aligns with your actions, there's an undeniable synergy—a force that compels you to move forward, even against the strongest headwinds.

Yet, how do we navigate this intricate interplay between purpose and the objectives we set? There's a fine line between setting goals that merely look good on paper and ones that, while ambitious, are deeply anchored in our core purpose. It's the latter that holds the magic, the potential to not only transform our individual trajectories but also leave lasting imprints on our shared human journey.

Remember, our purpose isn't about mere ambition. It's a clarion call, a mission that transcends the individual, beckoning us to contribute to something greater. It's about playing our part in a much grander play, seamlessly fitting into the narrative of a collective dream. And it's this dream that forms the fabric of our society, guiding us towards a brighter, more harmonious future.

As we turn the page on this chapter, it's essential to crystallise one resounding truth: your purpose is not just a lofty ideal hovering in the background of your life; it's the very pulse of your existence, the silent drum to which your actions march. It's your 'why,' the core reason that you get up in the morning, the foundation upon which you build your decisions, and the sanctuary where you find solace when the game of life gets tough.

Every one of us is playing a unique game in life. The rules we follow, the strategies we employ, and the victories we seek are intrinsically ours. However, without understanding why we're on the field in the first place, we risk losing ourselves in the chaos of the game. Your 'why'—your purpose—is the compass that keeps you oriented, ensuring each step you take is imbued with meaning and direction.

But recognising your 'why' is only the beginning. It sets the stage, but it doesn't dictate the actions. That's where the next chapter comes in—Charting Course. Once you've unearthed your purpose, how do you translate this profound understanding into tangible milestones? How do you navigate the unpredictable seas of life with purpose as your guiding star? Goal setting is not about constraining your future into a list of checkboxes; rather, it's about giving your dreams a skeleton upon which they can stand, move, and ultimately, dance into reality.

As we dive into "Winning The Game," it's essential to recognise that purpose is not a static destination but a dynamic journey, shaped by our past and steering us toward our future. It's about understanding how even the most tumultuous events can lead us to discover a purpose that drives us forward, compelling us to rise above and find success on our terms.

In the next chapter, we'll dive deep into the art and science of goal-setting, a vital element in steering your life pursuits. But, let's be unequivocal: goals, no matter how astutely crafted, hold mere shadows of their potential if they fail to pave the way towards your ultimate purpose and vision. Such a vision must be a vibrant reflection of your intrinsic values, beliefs, and passions. It isn't merely a destination but a compass — a steadfast guide through life's meandering paths, ensuring every step, every achievement echoes the authenticity of your individual spirit and journey. Together, let's engineer a future that's unapologetically you.

Let us start reflecting about where you are in your journey. This self-assessment is designed to help you reflect on your current state of personal growth and identify areas where you can apply the concepts discussed in this chapter. Use this tool to gauge your strengths, uncover opportunities for improvement, and set a course for your transformational journey.

Part 1: Self-Reflection Questions

1. Purpose and Vision

- On a scale of 1 to 10, how clear is your sense of purpose in life?

- Can you articulate your long-term vision and goals? (Yes/No)

- What motivates you to pursue your goals?

2. Goal Setting

- Do you regularly set short-term and long-term goals? (Yes/No)

- How often do you review and adjust your goals? (Never, Rarely, Sometimes, Often, Always)

- Describe one recent goal you set and achieved. What steps did you take to accomplish it?

3. Time Management

- How effectively do you manage your time on a daily basis? (Poorly, Fairly, Adequately, Well, Exceptionally)

- Do you use any tools or methods to track and prioritise your tasks? (Yes/No)

- What is your biggest challenge when it comes to managing your time?

4. Decisiveness

- How confident are you in making decisions quickly and effectively? (Not confident, slightly confident, moderately confident, very confident, extremely confident)

- Do you tend to overthink or second-guess your decisions? (Never, Rarely, Sometimes, Often, Always)

- Provide an example of a recent decision you made and the outcome.

5. Personal Improvement

- How committed are you to continuous learning and personal growth? (Not committed, Slightly committed, Moderately committed, Very committed, Extremely committed)

- What new skill or knowledge have you acquired in the past six months?

- How do you typically seek out opportunities for self-improvement?

6. Resilience

- How do you typically respond to setbacks and obstacles? (Give up easily, struggle but persist, remain positive and adaptive, embrace as learning opportunities)

- Can you describe a recent challenge you faced and how you overcame it?

Part 2: Self-Determination Theory Components

Rate each statement below on a scale of 1 (Strongly Disagree) to 5 (Strongly Agree):

1. Autonomy

- I feel in control of my decisions and actions.

- I pursue goals that are truly meaningful to me.

- I am able to make choices that reflect my values and interests.

2. Competence

- I regularly seek out new challenges that help me grow.

- I feel capable of achieving my goals.

- I have the skills and knowledge necessary to succeed in my pursuits.

3. Relatedness

- I have supportive relationships that encourage my growth.

- I feel connected to a community that shares my interests and goals.

- I regularly collaborate and communicate with others in meaningful ways.

Part 3: Growth Mindset Evaluation

Rate each statement below on a scale of 1 (Strongly Disagree) to 5 (Strongly Agree):

- I believe that my abilities can be developed through dedication and hard work.

- I see challenges as opportunities to learn and grow.

- I am open to feedback and use it to improve my skills.

- I view failures as valuable learning experiences.

- I persist through difficulties and setbacks.

Part 4: Habit Formation and Behavior Change

Rate each statement below on a scale of 1 (Strongly Disagree) to 5 (Strongly Agree):

- I am consistent in performing daily routines that support my goals.

- I use small, manageable changes to build new habits.

- I have established cues and rewards to reinforce positive behaviours.

- I regularly reflect on my habits and make adjustments as needed.

- I find it easy to integrate new habits into my existing routines.

Summary and Action Plan

1. Reflect on Your Scores

- Which areas did you score the highest in? These are your strengths.

- Which areas did you score the lowest in? These are your opportunities for growth.

2. Set Specific Goals

- Based on your assessment, set one or two specific, actionable goals for each area of improvement. For example, if you scored low in time management, set a goal to use a planner or a task management app consistently for the next month.

By completing this self-assessment, you are taking proactive steps towards rising up and achieving your potential. Remember, transformation is a continuous process. In the next chapter, we'll dive deep into goal achievement, a vital element in steering your life pursuits. Your vision needs to be fuelled by what you really care about, what you believe in, and what you love. Life is not just about reaching goals; it's about knowing where you're headed in life. Your purpose acts like a compass, guiding you through all the ups and downs, making sure everything you do stays true to who you are and where you want to go. This book will support you as you engineer a future that's unapologetically you, based on the purpose that is shaped in you and for you, taking inspiration from others who have already crafted their dreams and purpose in life.

CHAPTER 3

Charting Course

*"Don't downgrade your dream just to fit your reality.
Upgrade your conviction to match your destiny."*
—Stuart Scott

The Marathon des Sables (MdS) stands as one of the most gruelling multi-stage races in the world, taking place annually in the vast expanses of the Sahara Desert in southern Morocco. This ultra-marathon, which spans approximately 250 kilometres—equivalent to six regular marathons over six days—presents a monumental challenge that tests every facet of a participant's endurance and resilience.

As runners traverse the harsh, sandy terrain under the relentless Saharan sun with temperatures soaring above 50 degrees Celsius, they encounter an environment that pushes them to their physical and mental limits. The race's self-sufficient format requires competitors to carry all their necessary equipment and food, with only water and a tent provided. This setup demands meticulous planning and execution, as participants must carefully manage their resources to maintain their strength and stamina throughout the race.

The MdS draws individuals from around the world, ranging from elite athletes to determined adventurers, all united by a common desire to undertake this extraordinary challenge. The motivations driving these participants are as diverse as their backgrounds, encompassing personal achievement, adventure seeking, and profound emotional journeys. Whether it's testing one's limits, escaping the routine, or honouring a personal commitment, the MdS offers a unique platform for profound self-discovery and growth.

The allure of the MdS lies not just in its physical demands but also in its mental challenges. The race embodies the quintessential test of human endurance, resilience, and spirit. It's an opportunity to confront personal fears and limitations, to push beyond perceived boundaries, and to discover the depths of one's capabilities.

Participants often describe the race as a transformative experience. The act of completing each stage, of persisting when the body screams for respite, provides a tangible sense of achievement that transcends the physical dimensions of the race. It's about mastering the art of resilience—learning to move forward even when every fibre of your being yearns to stop.

This profound journey through the Sahara also fosters a unique camaraderie among the runners. The shared hardships and triumphs forge bonds that last a lifetime, encapsulating the essence of human connection. Moreover, the race serves as a platform for various charitable causes, adding a layer of purpose to the challenge.

From a strategic perspective, the MdS requires more than physical preparation. It demands a tactical approach where planning, priority setting, and pacing are crucial. Participants must strategically manage their pace, their nutrition, and their mental focus. Every decision, from how much weight to carry to when and how quickly to move, can have significant implications for their overall experience and success in the race.

Sir Ranulph Fiennes, often called the "world's greatest living explorer," undertook the Marathon des Sables in 2015 at the remarkable age of

71. Known for his extraordinary expeditions, such as crossing both the Arctic and Antarctic by foot and climbing the highest peaks on every continent, Fiennes added the gruelling Sahara desert race to his list of accomplishments to challenge the typical perceptions of ageing and capability. Despite his age and the extreme conditions, Fiennes completed the marathon to raise funds and awareness of Marie Curie, a charity that provides care and support to people with terminal illnesses and their families.

Fiennes' participation in the race at his age was not only a testament to his personal fitness and endurance but also served as an inspiration to others. It highlighted his commitment to pushing human limits and showed that determination could defy the typical constraints of age. His endeavour also emphasised the importance of continuing to set and achieve goals, regardless of age, to maintain physical health and mental vigour.

This story is a powerful example of how challenges like the Marathon des Sables can serve as platforms for greater causes and personal testament, driving individuals to exceed boundaries and inspire others through their actions.

The lessons from the Marathon des Sables extend far beyond the race itself. They resonate deeply with the demands of daily life, emphasising the importance of setting clear goals, planning meticulously, and executing effectively. The race illustrates the power of human endurance and the profound impact of facing and overcoming extreme challenges.

By stepping into the sandy shoes of a Marathon des Sables runner, we can learn much about the resilience and tenacity inherent in all of us. It reminds us that the most daunting obstacles can be overcome with the right preparation, mindset, and spirit. The MdS is not just a race; it's a metaphor for life's challenges and what we can achieve when we commit to facing them head-on, with preparation and heart.

Our dreams need more than just wishes; they need a clear action plan. It's like playing a game of Monopoly. The goal is to be the last player left in the game, but how you get there can vary greatly. You might focus on owning specific properties such as the utilities or building houses and hotels on low-cost land. But if you lose sight of the goal to win, no strategy will work.

In life, goals give structure to our dreams and help turn them into reality. Goals set a clear endpoint to aim for. They determine how we act, keep us focused, and keep us moving forward. In the big picture of life, goals help us succeed. They're like a guide, showing us the way to our true purpose, both personally and professionally. Without goals, our efforts are like shooting arrows without aiming — they go anywhere, but rarely where we want. In the last chapter, we looked at your purpose, what it is that is important to you–your legacy–your destination! Now we need to determine how you will get there.

Goals give us a way to see and measure our progress. Instead of just wanting to 'do better,' we can set specific targets like 'increase revenue by 20% in the next quarter.' These clear goals help focus our efforts and show us how much we've grown. We can track our progress, celebrate our successes, and learn from our mistakes. Achieving these smaller goals keeps us motivated, as the satisfaction of reaching them encourages us to aim higher.

But setting goals isn't just for work. It's a guide for life. Whether you're picturing your ideal day, planning your dream home, or wanting to make a difference in the world, goals bring clarity. They encourage you to think deeply, clarify what you want, and create the legacy you want to leave.

However, it's important to remember that just setting goals isn't enough. I've learned this the hard way over the years. I've had big dreams that I've struggled to achieve, not because I lacked imagination, but because my goals weren't backed by solid planning. Traditional goal-setting can sometimes be too nebulous, without a clear strategy for achievement. Or they can be too clinical and forget that life should also be enjoyable. After all, what's a journey without a little joy?

Think of goals as a fun game, where enjoying the process is just as important as winning. Remember how, as kids, playing games would get us excited and push us to try new things? By treating goals as a game, we can make working towards them more exciting and enjoyable.

As we move forward, let's change how we think about goals. Let's see them not as boring tasks but as exciting challenges that are part of the bigger game of life.

Take John D. Rockefeller as an example. He's someone who showed how effective it can be to set strategic goals. In the mid-19th century, Rockefeller had to start working early because of his family's situation. From the beginning, he was known for being very organised and precise in his approach to work. His goal was not just about making money; it was about creating efficient systems that could make the oil business profitable and sustainable. He started with an overarching goal: to revolutionise the American oil industry. But this wasn't achieved through one large leap. Instead, Rockefeller set smaller, incremental objectives: modernising oil refining processes, forging beneficial partnerships, and even pioneering innovative railway deals to ensure the smooth transportation of his goods.

But Rockefeller's journey wasn't devoid of enjoyment. His meticulousness in business was balanced by his love for golf and art. He played the game of business with the intensity of a chess grandmaster, but he also recognised the importance of relishing life's pleasures. This holistic approach is a reminder that while our goals push us to excel, they must also allow space for joy and fulfilment.

Looking at Rockefeller's success, it's clear that big achievements don't just happen by chance. They come from setting specific goals and working towards them with determination and planning. Whether your aim is to change an industry or make your mark in a smaller way, the approach is the same: set clear goals that match your bigger vision and use them to guide you. As we talk more about this, remember that while having goals is important, the journey — with all its ups and downs, joys, and lessons — is what really shapes our experience.

Napoleon Hill famously said, "Whatever you can conceive and believe, you can achieve." This quote became a guiding principle in my life for many years. However, there's an important aspect to it that often goes unmentioned: achieving your dreams isn't just about having them and believing in them. It's about approaching them with strategy and practicality. This is where RAPID Goals come into play. This method is all about creating real change in every area of your life. It teaches you to set goals in a way that is not only ambitious but also realistic and well-planned, leading to transformative success.

Let's start with the R for Rational.

R—Rational:

"Planning is bringing the future into the present so that you can do something about it now." – Alan Lakein

I used to spend hours daydreaming about reaching the top of my field. However, I learned through experience that dreaming alone doesn't lead to success. The dreams would give me drive and ambition; they would get me out of bed early and keep me working when others would quit. But some of my goals didn't work out because they were based more on hope than on practical planning.

For a goal to move from an idea to reality, it needs to be grounded in rational thinking. Being rational doesn't mean limiting your dreams; it's about aligning them with the real world. One of the most memorable examples of this is Amy Johnson.

Amy Johnson's historic flight from London to Darwin in 1930 is a captivating story of courage, determination, and meticulous planning. Amy was a pioneering English aviator, one of the first women to gain a pilot's licence in Britain. She was not only a pilot but also a skilled engineer, which was highly unusual for a woman at the time.

Although she wasn't an experienced pilot, she was determined and had a bold dream: she aimed to become the first woman to fly solo from England to Australia. Her mission was not just to set a record, but to demonstrate that women were equally capable as men in the demanding field of aviation. She knew this was an enormous challenge. Her longest flight had only been 180 miles, but she was preparing for an 11,000-mile journey.

Johnson embarked on her journey on May 5, 1930. The era was one of significant interest in aviation records, but many such ventures ended in failure or even tragedy, which only added to the risks and challenges she faced. What made her journey remarkable wasn't just her resolve; it was her planning. She carefully planned her route, anticipating challenges and preparing for them. The flight covered approximately 11,000 miles, starting from Croydon, South London, and ending in Darwin, Australia. This route took her over numerous countries, each with its own navigational and geopolitical challenges. Amy flew a de Havilland DH.60 Gipsy Moth, a small and relatively basic aircraft for such a daunting task. The plane was named "Jason" after the trademark of her father's business, which helped sponsor the flight. Johnson's journey was fraught with difficulties: she battled severe weather conditions, navigational challenges, and mechanical failures. At one point, she crash-landed in the jungle in Burma and had to make significant repairs before she could continue. Johnson's flight was driven by a mix of personal ambition and a desire to prove her capabilities in a field dominated by men. She also hoped to inspire other women to pursue their dreams, regardless of the obstacles they might face. For me, her success showed the importance of having a plan that is ambitious but also realistic.

Reading about Amy Johnson's landing in Darwin, Australia, left me in awe. Her success story, even as told in a history book, was inspiring. What stood out to me wasn't just her achievement, but the journey itself: how she strategically and sensibly worked toward her goal with determination.

To make any real change, it's essential to have a clear vision of what success looks like. For me, this meant creating a detailed plan, anticipating potential hurdles, and figuring out how to overcome them.

Once you know where you're going, the steps to get there start to become clear. I learned to plan my goals in reverse, starting from the end and working back to where I began. This approach of planning backwards helped me set clear milestones, and achieving each small goal along the way built my confidence. It was like creating a path of stepping stones across a river, making sure each step, however bold, was on firm ground.

But dreaming big is only half the battle. You also need the right resources to turn those dreams into reality. This means recognising and using what you have, whether it's money, skills, or time. Innovation often comes not from getting new resources but from making the most of what you already have.

In short, while dreams drive us forward, it's rational planning that paves the way to success. In the upcoming chapters, we'll explore more aspects of RAPID Goals. Remember, the first step towards any significant change is to ensure it's based on sound reasoning. Rational thinking doesn't limit dreams; it's what makes them achievable.

When I first embarked on my career, my head was brimming with dreams. Like a ship setting sail toward the horizon, I was driven by a vision of reaching the pinnacle of my field. Back then, my dreams were my fuel; they got me out of bed when the sun was yet to rise, they kept me toiling when others had called it a day. Yet, in the pursuit of these dreams, I encountered a stark reality: some goals remained elusive, like stars twinkling just out of reach. They were beautiful, yes, but unattainable. The reason? They lacked a foundation in rational planning.

This realisation struck me profoundly as I delved into the life of Amy Johnson, a woman of modest background with a seemingly impossible dream, who wished to fly from England to Australia. In the world of aviation back then, this was a feat akin to reaching for the moon. Yet, what set Amy apart wasn't just her daring ambition; it was her approach. She didn't just dream; she planned.

Amy's journey was not an impulsive leap into the unknown. It was a meticulously charted voyage. She studied maps, calculated distances, and prepared for every conceivable challenge. Her preparation was thorough–from the mechanics of her aircraft to the weather patterns she might encounter. She knew her dream was colossal, but her planning was even more substantial.

Amy's story was a revelation to me. It taught me that every dream, no matter how grand, needs to be grounded in reality. I began to see my goals in a new light. It was no longer about reaching for the stars blindly; it was about building a ladder, rung by rung, to ascend to them.

This shift in perspective led me to redefine my approach to goal-setting. I started envisioning my ultimate goal and then worked backwards, dissecting it into smaller, more manageable objectives. It was like plotting a route on a map; knowing the destination was crucial, but understanding the journey to get there was vital.

Each small goal became a milestone, a checkpoint that marked my progress. This method transformed my long journey into a series of achievable steps. It was no longer a daunting marathon but a series of sprints, each bringing me closer to the finish line.

Another pivotal aspect of rational goal-achievement is the effective utilisation of resources. Often, we get caught up in what we lack, overlooking the arsenal at our disposal. I learned to take stock of my skills, my network, my knowledge–and use them to their fullest potential. Innovation wasn't about reinventing the wheel; it was about using what I had in smarter, more efficient ways.

The journey of rational goal-achievement taught me that dreams need not be wisps of imagination. They can be sculpted into tangible achievements with thoughtful planning and resourcefulness. As we delve deeper into the RAPID Goals process, remember that rationality is not the antithesis of dreaming, it is the bridge that connects the land of dreams with the realm of reality. It's about transforming the ethereal into the tangible, one well-planned step at a time. So, let's look at the process in detail.

Stephen Covey's timeless advice to "begin with the end in mind" resonates profoundly here. It's about pinpointing your destination before you set out on your journey. This approach is not just aspirational—it's strategic and sensible, especially when aligned with the 'Rational' aspect of the RAPID goal-achievement process.

Picture your dream in high resolution. If your goal is to build a thriving business, don't just visualise success in broad strokes. Instead, see the specifics–financial stability, market dominance, or a renowned brand.

This vivid mental image becomes your north star, guiding every step you take.

Embarking on the journey to your ultimate goal can be daunting when viewed as a whole. But by charting the course backwards, you transform the seemingly unattainable into a series of achievable steps. This method, akin to reverse engineering your success, begins with your end goal and works backwards to where you are now, creating a clear and actionable roadmap.

Start by asking yourself, "To reach my ultimate goal, what is the final milestone I need to achieve that makes success inevitable?" For a business, this could be reaching a specific revenue target or launching a groundbreaking product. Once this is identified, consider the preceding step that made this milestone inevitable. Maybe it was securing a partnership or developing the product prototype.

Continue this process, moving backwards through each critical phase. At every stage, ask, "What accomplishment directly led to this milestone?" This approach might reveal stages like building a robust marketing strategy, establishing a strong online presence, or acquiring key skills or team members.

As you deconstruct your journey, identify the resources and assets required at each stage. This could involve capital investment, specific skill sets, technological tools, or even building a network of industry contacts. By understanding what resources are needed for each milestone, you can prepare more effectively, avoiding last-minute scrambles or roadblocks.

Once you've mapped out the milestones in reverse, realign them chronologically from your current position forward. This realignment gives you a step-by-step action plan. Each milestone now acts as a mini-goal, leading seamlessly to the next. This method ensures that every action you take and every resource you acquire is purposefully aligned with your larger objective. And remember the importance of having fun. Celebrate every win, set rewards for achieving every goal and milestone. Add in fun things to do as you progress through your plan.

By planning in reverse, you not only outline what needs to be done but also gain insight into how each phase builds upon the previous one. This understanding is crucial for maintaining momentum and ensuring that each step you take is a building block towards your overarching goal.

Remember, while your roadmap is well-defined, it's not set in stone. Regularly review your progress against your milestones. Be prepared to adjust your plan as you gain new insights, encounter unexpected challenges, or as circumstances evolve.

Backward planning isn't just about understanding the steps to your goal; it's about creating a logical and efficient sequence of actions, each perfectly setting the stage for the next. It's a strategic approach that clarifies your path, aligns your resources, and propels you towards inevitable success. By meticulously planning your journey from the end to the present, you turn your distant dreams into an exciting, achievable reality.

By initiating your endeavour with a well-defined end in mind and pursuing your goals with rational planning, you set yourself up for a journey marked not by aimless wandering, but by purposeful strides towards tangible achievements. This methodology doesn't just transform lofty dreams into reachable goals; it charts a course for a journey that is as fulfilling as the destination. Remember, in this journey of life and success, every choice you make, every action you take, is a step closer to turning your dreams into your reality.

Amy Johnson's longest flight before flying to Australia was 180 miles, all reasonable people would have said her goal was impossible—

she had determination against the odds. Raising funds and gaining sponsors for her flight required almost as much courage and tenacity as the flight itself—she was unstoppable in her own belief. Without the sophisticated navigation tools available to modern pilots, Amy relied heavily on maps, compasses, and the landscape itself to guide her route—she worked with the ordinary tools she had. Her successful flight made headlines worldwide and significantly advanced public acceptance of women in aviation and other fields requiring courage and technical skill. Upon completing her journey, Amy was celebrated as a national hero in the UK and received various honours, including being made a Dame Commander of the Order of the British Empire. Her goal was not reasonable and went beyond extraordinary, but careful planning made it rational.

A—Assessable:

"What gets measured gets managed." – Peter Drucker

In the grand scheme of life, each of your goals is like a star in a vast universe. Your challenge? To chart a course through these celestial bodies, connecting them in a meaningful way that propels you towards your ultimate destination. This isn't about aimless meandering; it's a mission that demands precise navigation, discerning which goals to chase, their sequence, and their priority. The true measure of success in this cosmic journey hinges on your ability to define, quantify, and realistically chase these goals.

I recall an enlightening moment at a seminar. The speaker posed a seemingly simple question to the audience: "Who wants to be rich?" Almost every hand shot up. However, when he followed up with, "Who can pinpoint the exact amount that would make them feel rich?" the room was filled with hesitant glances and slowly lowering hands. This was a profound revelation: a vague aspiration, without specific targets, is a roadmap to nowhere.

Consider the universally appealing goal of financial freedom. It's a concept that varies dramatically from person to person. For some, it's about amassing enough wealth for globe-trotting adventures; for others, it's the peace of being debt-free and providing for their family. The crux of successfully navigating towards this goal is to crystallise it into tangible terms. How much money is enough? What are the concrete sources of income you need to tap into? Without these explicit markers, your journey towards financial freedom can become a disoriented drift.

Reflecting on my journey, I draw inspiration from John D. Rockefeller's methodical approach to his business. He didn't vaguely aim for 'success'; he pursued specific, quantifiable objectives. He delved into the minutiae of his business operations, from understanding the refining margins for each barrel of oil to knowing the productivity levels of his employees. This meticulous attention to measurable details was a cornerstone of his monumental success.

Applying this principle to a commonplace objective, like hitting the gym, illustrates its effectiveness. While aspiring to be more active is commendable, it's an abstract goal. Contrastingly, setting a target to jog three miles every alternate day or to bench press a particular weight within a set timeframe transforms your fitness journey. Each gym session now becomes a calculated step towards a well-defined goal, rather than a shot in the dark.

My evolution from harbouring broad ambitions to setting precise, assessable goals marked a pivotal shift in my life. It's easy to declare you want a 'successful business,' but defining what success looks like is crucial. Does it mean achieving a certain profit margin, cultivating a dedicated customer base, or having the luxury to step back while your business thrives? Ambitions without specificity can lead you on a perpetual treadmill, running tirelessly yet staying in place.

The Coffee Shop Revolution

In the bustling heart of the city, Tom's Coffee Corner was more than just another spot to get a caffeine fix. It was here that Tom poured his dreams into every cup served. Despite its popularity for cosy vibes and excellent coffee, Tom felt a deep-seated frustration that his coffee shop was just skimming the surface of its potential. He envisioned transforming it into a destination for coffee lovers city-wide—a name synonymous with innovation in the coffee scene.

This desire for transformation wasn't sparked by ambition alone. The turning point came unexpectedly one rainy Tuesday morning. Amid the clatter of cups and chatter, an elderly customer, Mrs. Henderson, who frequented the shop, commented, "Tom, I wish you'd host some book clubs or art shows here. It's so comfy, yet all I do is sip coffee and leave." Her words struck a chord. Tom realised his business could be more than a place for quick stops; it could be a vital part of people's lives, a community nucleus.

Fuelled by this epiphany, Tom set a daring goal to double his customer base within the year. He knew that reaching this would require a clear, strategic overhaul, not just passion. He began by meticulously analysing and assessing his operation—from customer demographics to daily sales. He identified that while he attracted many young professionals, there was potential to reach other community segments.

Tom structured his approach around four pivotal strategies:

1. Menu Innovation: Observing the rising trend towards health-conscious lifestyles, Tom diversified his offerings to include organic and vegan options, broadening his appeal.

2. Boosting Digital Engagement: Recognizing the power of digital influence, Tom set a target to grow his social media following by 50% in six months. He revamped his online

presence with engaging content and interactive ads tailored to his diverse audience.

3. Fostering Community Connections: Inspired by Mrs Henderson's words, Tom began hosting monthly cultural nights, from local jazz evenings to poetry slams, transforming his coffee shop into a vibrant gathering place.

4. Implementing a Feedback Loop: To fine-tune his efforts, Tom introduced a feedback system, inviting customers to share their experiences and suggestions, thus enabling him to adapt and refine his offerings continually.

As the months unfolded, the changes became palpable. The new menu options brought in health enthusiasts, while the enriched digital content attracted a younger, tech-savvy crowd. The monthly events turned the coffee shop into a cultural hotspot, drawing in a diverse group that thrived on community interaction.

By year's end, Tom hadn't just achieved his goal—he had surpassed it. Tom's Coffee Corner had evolved from a simple coffee shop into a beloved community hub, celebrated for its commitment to quality, inclusivity, and community engagement. Tom had not only reinvented his business but had also rediscovered his passion, seeing firsthand how a simple coffee shop could become a catalyst for community connection and cultural enrichment.

The story of Tom's Coffee Corner vividly underscores the impact of setting assessable goals in transforming a business vision into reality. Tom's journey from a modest local hangout to a thriving community centrepiece illustrates the compelling force of a well-defined objective, broken into clear, actionable segments.

In practice, the road to significant achievement is constructed with precise, measurable milestones. Tom began with a fundamental metric—tracking the number of daily customers and their average spend. From there, he set a concrete goal to double these figures. This methodical approach highlights the importance of not merely aiming for a distant dream but meticulously plotting the steps necessary to reach that dream. Each milestone, once reached, becomes a celebration that not only marks progress but also propels the endeavour forward with renewed vigour and clear direction.

The true strength of any venture lies not just in the breadth of the dreams it pursues but in the clarity and precision with which those dreams are segmented into achievable assessable steps. It's this strategic breakdown that transforms lofty aspirations into grounded, achievable successes, proving that with a clear plan and committed action, even the simplest business can become a cornerstone of its community.

P—Purposeful:

"The search for 'the purpose of life' has puzzled people for thousands of years. That's because we typically begin at the wrong starting point — ourselves. We ask self-centred questions like: What do I want to be? What should I do with my life? What are my goals, my ambitions, and my dreams for my future? But focusing on ourselves will never reveal our life's purpose." – Rick Warren.

The age-old quest for purpose has been the very crux of human existence. Since time immemorial, philosophers, poets, and thinkers have grappled with the essence of our existence. Yet, in our earnest pursuit, we often fumble by starting our search from the prism of self. The quintessential questions of our ambitions, dreams, and aspirations, though essential, often obscure the bigger picture — our overarching purpose.

In the annals of Hollywood, few stories resonate with the spirit of purpose and determination quite like that of Sylvester Stallone and his iconic film, "Rocky." In the early 1970s, Stallone's journey was far from the glittering success we associate with his name today. Living in a small one-room apartment and dabbling in minor roles, such as in "The Lords of Flatbush," Stallone's life was a far cry from the glitz of stardom. Stallone's journey through financial hardship was relentless, with his situation growing increasingly dire. He steadfastly refused to settle for a conventional job, believing it would trap him in mediocrity and extinguish his dreams of acting success. Despite facing rejection after rejection from movie producers and directors, Stallone's determination never wavered. This choice came at a high personal cost; as his financial crisis deepened, he faced an agonising decision. With his wife pregnant and no means of supporting them or his dog, he was compelled to sell his beloved bullmastiff, Butkus for $60. It was a decision that tore at his heart, a painful testament to the depths of his commitment to pursuing his dream against all odds.

Stallone's life took a pivotal turn one extraordinary night when he witnessed the boxing match between Muhammad Ali and Chuck Wepner. This underdog story struck a deep chord in Stallone, mirroring the struggles of his own life. It ignited a spark in him, a realisation that life, much like that boxing ring, was about standing up against the odds, enduring, and seizing opportunities.

Fuelled by this inspiration, Stallone embarked on a whirlwind of creativity, penning the script of "Rocky" in a mere three and a half days. This 90-page screenplay was not just a story; it was a piece of Stallone's soul, a metaphor for his own battles and dreams.

Fate intervened at an audition, where Stallone, realising the acting opportunity was not to be, decided to pitch his script. The producers were captivated by the narrative but reluctant to cast an unknown Stallone in the leading role of Rocky Balboa. Their eyes were set on established A-list Hollywood actors. They kept increasing the price for the script, eventually offering Stallone an eye-watering $330,000 for the script, but the deal came with a stringent condition: Stallone would not star in the film.

Faced with this offer, Stallone found himself at a crossroads. Financially, he was in dire straits, with barely $100 to his name, no car, and having recently sold his dog to make ends meet. The sum offered was a fortune in his eyes, a potential end to his financial woes. However, Stallone's vision for "Rocky" was deeply personal. He saw the character of Rocky Balboa as a reflection of his own life's struggles and aspirations. He knew in his heart that he had to play the role, believing that any success the movie had without him would be a source of lifelong regret.

Thus began a period of intense negotiation. Stallone stood firm in his conviction, insisting on not just selling his script but also portraying the central character. His persistence eventually paid off. The producers, recognising his unwavering dedication, finally agreed. They offered him $25,000 advance for the script and the role of Rocky. The budget for the film was set at a modest one million dollars - meagre even by the standards of the 1970s.

To make the most of this limited budget, the production adopted a creative and resourceful approach. The cast was filled with friends and family members, lending a personal touch to the film. Handheld cameras were used for shooting, adding a raw and authentic feel to the scenes. Most of the footage was captured in one take, necessitated by budget constraints, but also adding an element of spontaneous realism. But would such a low-budget movie be a success?

The true moment of reckoning came at The Director's Guild screening, attended by a crowd of 900 industry professionals. As the film unfolded, Stallone's heart sank. The audience's reactions were tepid; the jokes fell flat, and the fight scenes, the soul of the movie, didn't stir the expected excitement. Dejected, Stallone believed his moment had slipped through his fingers.

But as he descended the stairs into the auditorium, a tide of surprise awaited him. The audience, standing in ovation, erupted into applause and cheers. It was a genuine acknowledgement of Stallone's vision, determination, and raw portrayal of Rocky.

The journey of "Rocky" and Stallone is a testament to the unyielding human spirit. It exemplifies that true goals must transcend material aspirations, like wealth or fame. They should be deeply meaningful, driving us forward through life's challenges and doubts. Stallone's story is a beacon for anyone pursuing their dreams, a reminder that with unwavering conviction and resilience, even the most daunting of goals can be achieved.

Stallone's story is not just about achieving success in the face of adversity; it's about the power of purpose—believing in one's vision. When Stallone sold his dog, it wasn't just a financial decision; it was a sacrifice of a cherished companion, epitomising the depth of his struggle. Yet, this low point was not the end of his story, but a catalyst for his commitment to his dream.

His resolve to play Rocky was more than just an actor vying for a role; it was about a man who saw his life story reflected in the character. For Stallone, Rocky wasn't just a script; it was a personal saga of fighting against the odds, of not giving up despite the knocks and falls. His insistence on playing the role despite lucrative offers to step aside spoke volumes about his dedication to his art and his belief in the message he wanted to convey.

The success of "Rocky" is a reminder that the path to realising our dreams is often fraught with challenges and setbacks. It's a journey that requires not just talent and hard work but also an unwavering belief in our goals and the courage to pursue them despite the odds. Stallone's journey from a struggling actor to a Hollywood icon is a powerful illustration of what can be achieved when we hold steadfast to our vision and persevere through adversity.

But what about Sylvester Stallone's dog, Butkus?

Sylvester Stallone's commitment to getting his dog, Butkus, back is a touching aspect of his journey. After securing the $25,000 advance for "Rocky," Stallone immediately went to see Jimmy, the person he had previously sold Butkus to. He offered Jimmy $200 to buy back his dog. When Jimmy turned down the offer, Stallone didn't give up. He steadfastly negotiated, ultimately reaching an agreement at $3,000, plus a small role for Jimmy in the "Rocky" movie.

This story highlights Stallone's determination; it illustrates his commitment to the things that matter to him. The happy ending is twofold: Jimmy landed a part in the "Rocky" movie, and Butkus was not only back with Stallone but also featured in two films of the series.

Stallone's life underscores the essence of a purpose-driven goal. It's not merely about the accolades or the tangible achievements; it's about a deeper calling that propels you forward against all odds.

It's this unyielding spirit that encapsulates the purpose of your goals. Without a compelling purpose driving you towards your goal, any upset or roadblock has the potential to derail your progress.

We discussed creating your purpose at length in the last chapter, but there are four additional 'P's that will help you stay the course and overcome all the challenges along the way.

"The 4 Ps" of working from purpose.

- Play
- Passion
- Persistence
- Progressive

Let's look at each of these.

Play

When setting and pursuing RAPID goals, it's crucial to maintain a balance between seriousness and enjoyment. It's about making the process enjoyable, not just focusing on the outcome. Injecting creativity, humour, and joy into your daily tasks transforms the journey towards your goal into a fulfilling experience. By infusing your goal-achieving process with enjoyment, you'll find the resilience and energy needed to overcome challenges along the way. The concept of 'play' in games offers valuable insights into goal setting. In video games, the excitement of levelling up or earning a trophy creates a real sense of achievement. These moments, though virtual, provide a psychological boost and confirmation of progress. This principle of game design - celebrating small wins - is highly effective when applied to goal setting. In pursuit of life goals, acknowledging and celebrating 'mini-goals' is essential. These smaller achievements, while not the final goal, mark important progress. They generate a sense of accomplishment and motivation, much like a gamer feels driven to continue after each level is conquered. These small victories keep us motivated and on track towards our larger aspirations. These milestones are like breadcrumbs on our journey through a vast forest of dreams. They are checkpoints that confirm we are moving in the right direction. Each mini-goal we achieve stands as proof of our dedication and a guidepost for the path ahead, blending satisfaction with the excitement of what's next. While our ultimate dreams set the direction, it's the smaller achievements that pave our way, encouraging us continuously. In my own journey, I've treated each small milestone as a badge of honour, a symbol of my commitment and a guidepost leading me forward.

As we delve deeper into RAPID Goals, it's important to celebrate every minor achievement. These small victories accumulate into significant successes. Goals, akin to games, are a blend of strategy, persistence, and a succession of rewarding moments leading to the final victory. Let's embrace our journey, savouring each small triumph along the way.

Passion

In the journey of RAPID goal achievement, passion is the key ingredient that brings vitality and momentum. It's not just about applying passion to your work; it's about weaving it into the fabric of your daily life. When you cultivate passion in your everyday activities, it radiates into all facets of your life, instilling a powerful desire to persevere and excel. Passion transforms routine tasks into opportunities for joy and engagement. It's about finding excitement and purpose in the mundane, which in turn fuels your larger goals. This energy is contagious, infusing your actions with enthusiasm and attracting similar positivity from others. Your passion should align with your purpose, creating a synergy that drives you forward. This alignment results in a natural motivation that doesn't feel forced but flows effortlessly, keeping you engaged and focused. When passion underpins your goals, obstacles become challenges to overcome rather than roadblocks, and setbacks are seen as opportunities to learn and grow. Embrace passion in your life, and watch as it becomes the engine driving your journey towards achieving your goals. Let it be the constant companion that keeps you moving forward, turning every step into a stride towards success.

Persistence

In the framework of RAPID goal achievement, the power of persistence cannot be overstated. Your goal must be so compelling that it propels you through every hurdle and setback. A blend of discipline and passion fosters this persistence, equipping you with the resilience to continue despite the odds. The thin line that separates the most influential achievers from those who fall short is often just this

– persistence. It brings to mind Winston Churchill's stirring words in 1941: "Never give in, never give in, never, never, never, never – in nothing, great or small, large or petty—never give in except to convictions of honour and good sense."

Consider the world of sports, where persistence is displayed in its most raw form. As a rugby enthusiast, I recall a match that perfectly encapsulates the essence of persistence: South Africa versus England in the Rugby World Cup 2023. England was leading, seemingly on the cusp of an easy victory. But what unfolded next was not just a display of rugby skills, but a profound lesson in persistence. Faced with a daunting scoreboard and time running out, South Africa did not falter. Instead, they adapted, constantly revising their tactics—seeking vulnerabilities in their opponents. They strategically swapped out players to shift the dynamic of their team and counter the strength of the English squad. As the game progressed the tide turned, little by little the Springboks began to make headway. Their unwavering determination and refusal to give up paid off spectacularly with a narrow 16-15 victory in the closing minutes. This wasn't just a win in the game; it was a vivid illustration of the relentless spirit and the power of persistence.

This example from the rugby field mirrors our own struggles in pursuit of our goals. When faced with challenges, it's this persistent spirit that can turn the tide. It's about pushing forward, adapting, and never losing sight of the end goal, regardless of the current score in the game of life. Persistence is what bridges the gap between aspiration and achievement, driving us to turn our goals into reality.

Progressive

In RAPID goal achievement, the concept of being 'progressive' is crucial. A goal should always strive to transcend the ordinary. Merely continuing what has been done before is not goal setting; it is routine. Your goals should elevate you, your team, or your organisation to extraordinary heights, fostering growth and sparking inspiration. A truly progressive goal pushes boundaries, encouraging you to evolve as an individual and contribute positively to the world.

Life is a vast landscape filled with questions of purpose and meaning. In this journey, the most profound goals extend beyond self-interest, intertwining with a larger, shared narrative. This intersection of personal ambition and collective impact is where transformative change occurs.

John D. Rockefeller's story is a perfect illustration of progressive goals. His narrative isn't just a tale of wealth accumulation; it's a testament to visionary ambition, strategic foresight, and a steadfast commitment to a broader purpose. During the tumultuous early days of the industrial age, the oil industry was embryonic and unstable. In this chaos, Rockefeller saw not just challenges but opportunities. During an economic downturn, while others were retreating, he boldly acquired struggling competitors. This move was more than just seizing a moment; it was a deliberate stride towards a grander vision of unifying and stabilising the oil industry. Rockefeller's ingenuity didn't end with acquisitions. He relentlessly pursued efficiency and optimisation, leading to the establishment of the Standard Oil Trust. This wasn't just a business conglomerate; it was a transformative force that redefined an entire industry. The essence of Rockefeller's journey lies not just in the scale of his achievements but in the purposeful and progressive approach he adopted in each step. His vision was not confined to personal gain; it was about creating something lasting and influential, a force that would significantly shape the modern industrial world. Rockefeller's legacy is a powerful reminder—our individual goals, while seemingly small, can have a profound impact when they are progressive and aligned with a larger vision. They have the potential to not just change our lives but also contribute to the greater narrative of human progress.

I—Integrity:

"Success will come and go, but integrity is forever." – Amy Rees Anderson

In the RAPID goal achievement strategy, 'I' stands for Integrity, a fundamental aspect that gives depth and authenticity to your goals. To truly commit to a goal, it needs to be deeply embedded in your identity, echoing your core values, beliefs, and principles. When a goal is aligned with the very core of who you are, it does more than provide a roadmap; it kindles a powerful passion and relentless drive within you. Integrating a goal into your essence transforms it from a distant ambition to a personal mission, propelling you forward with a sense of purpose and commitment.

Integrity is about the entirety of your character. It's about aligning your goals with your moral compass, ensuring they not only lead you in the right direction, but also resonate with your deeper sense of purpose. This alignment is crucial; it means pursuing objectives that are not just achievements but also reflections of your personal and ethical standards. Your goals should contribute to your growth and enable you to make a positive impact on the world around you. When a goal is in harmony with your integrity, it elevates your pursuit beyond mere success. It becomes a journey of self-realisation and meaningful contribution, enhancing not just your life but also enriching the lives of others. This is the essence of integrity in goal setting: creating objectives that are true to yourself, that inspire you to be better, and that allow you to contribute positively to the world. It's about setting goals that are not just milestones to be achieved, but are expressions of your deepest convictions and aspirations.

Richard Williams, father and former coach of tennis legends Venus and Serena Williams, exemplifies the power of strategic and resilient goal setting. He made unconventional choices for his daughters' careers, emphasising their holistic development both in tennis and life. Despite scepticism, his approach proved integral to their success and well-being. One key aspect of Richard's approach was his unwavering commitment to pitching. He mastered the art of the 'elevator pitch,' succinctly presenting his daughters' potential to coaches and investors. His perseverance in the face of repeated rejections is a lesson in resilience. This tenacity is a vital trait for anyone aiming to achieve their goals, illustrating that persistence and courage in approaching others can pave the way to success. As a coach, Richard's dedication to continuous learning was a cornerstone of his strategy. Even with his success, he never ceased to seek knowledge, consistently reading interviews, analysing matches, and observing top coaches. This commitment to improvement and adaptation is critical for anyone striving to excel, showing that continuous learning is key to advancing one's skills and strategies. Richard Williams' approach to planning was meticulous and visionary. He didn't just believe in his daughter's talent; he had a detailed, 78-page plan charting their path to becoming world champions. His philosophy, "If you fail to plan, then you plan to fail," underscores the importance of a well-thought-out strategy in achieving lofty goals. Additionally, Richard instilled in Venus and Serena the principle of focusing on their own journey rather than getting distracted by others. Concentrating on immediate tasks and long-term objectives is crucial for steady progress towards goals. This approach emphasises the importance of self-focus over external comparison. Furthermore, Richard made a radical decision to pull his daughters from junior tennis, focusing instead on learning and enjoyment during their childhood. This unconventional move, though controversial, was aligned with his unique vision for their careers. It highlights the importance of sometimes defying traditional paths to create a tailored strategy that aligns with one's values and goals. Richard Williams' approach to raising and coaching Venus and Serena Williams offers powerful insights into goal achievement. His persistence, commitment to continuous learning, meticulous planning, focus on self-improvement, and willingness to defy conventions demonstrate the effectiveness of a well-rounded and strategic approach to achieving ambitious goals.

Integrating Goals with Integrity: A Practical Guide

To make your goals a tangible part of your reality, express them in the present tense. Statements like "I am" or "I have" bring the essence of your goals into your current existence, reinforcing their presence in your life.

To deeply embed a goal into your being, consider these key actions:

1. Advocate Persistently – As Richard Williams did, master the art of advocating for your goal. Be unwavering in your pursuit, consistently presenting and defending your vision.

2. Embrace Continuous Learning – Always be on the lookout for ways to improve and broaden your knowledge and skills. This commitment to growth is crucial for adapting and evolving along your journey.

3. Plan with Precision – Recognize that careful and thorough planning is vital for the success of any goal, no matter the scale.

4. Focus Intently – Keep your attention firmly on your own path, steering clear of distractions that could divert you from your objectives.

Beyond personal ambitions, integrity in your goals also means considering their broader implications:

- Environmental Responsibility: In today's world, it's essential to ensure your pursuits are environmentally sustainable. Imagine if a modern-day Rockefeller integrated ecological considerations into his business strategy.

- Societal Contribution: Reflect on how your goals can positively influence society. Philanthropy and community engagement, much like Rockefeller's, can amplify the impact of your success.

- Personal Well-being: Your goals should enhance, not compromise, your physical and mental health. Achievements should be pursued in a way that supports your overall well-being.

- Ethical Commitment: Every endeavour should be guided by ethical principles, ensuring your actions do no harm and contribute positively to the larger community.

In essence, making a goal part of your identity goes beyond mere accomplishment. It's about aligning your journey and its outcomes with your deepest values, thereby forging a legacy that extends beyond personal achievements to benefit the world at large.

D—Deadline:

"To achieve great things, two things are needed: a plan, and not quite enough time." — Leonard Bernstein.

Deadlines transform goals from abstract aspirations into concrete targets. They infuse a sense of urgency into your endeavours, turning the distant goal line into a clear target that spurs action. Deadlines serve as a crucial reminder that time is a limited resource, highlighting the ephemeral nature of opportunities.

But remember, deadlines are not a tool for creating stress. Instead, they bring clarity and foster a sense of responsibility. To appreciate the power of deadlines, consider a pivotal moment from the early 1960s.

The Moonshot: A Deadline-Driven Mission of Unprecedented Scale

When President John F. Kennedy asked Dr. Wernher von Braun what it would take to build a rocket that could carry a man to the moon and bring him back safely to Earth, von Braun answered him in five words: "The will to do it." So, on May 25, 1961, President Kennedy announced a daring and ambitious goal: to land an American astronaut on the Moon and return him safely to Earth before the end of the 1960s. This wasn't just a challenge for space exploration; it was a bold declaration of America's commitment to leadership in science and technology during the height of the Cold War.

Kennedy's announcement came at a time when the United States was trailing the Soviet Union in the space race. The Soviets had already achieved significant milestones, including launching the first artificial satellite, Sputnik, in 1957, and sending the first human, Yuri Gagarin, into space in April 1961. Kennedy's goal, therefore, was not only about exploring space but also about demonstrating American ingenuity and capability on a global stage.

The deadline was audacious and fraught with uncertainty. At the time of Kennedy's announcement, the U.S. had only accumulated a total of 15 minutes of human spaceflight experience, compared to the Soviet Union's 108 minutes. The technological challenges were immense. NASA would need to develop new types of spacecraft for travel to the Moon, landing on its surface, and returning to Earth. They also had to invent new types of space suits, life support systems, and navigation technologies.

Despite these challenges, Kennedy's deadline galvanised the nation. It mobilised resources on an unprecedented scale, with NASA's budget at one point accounting for almost 4.5% of the federal budget. The program, named Apollo, brought together over 400,000 workers and 20,000 companies and universities. It was a remarkable display of collaboration, with scientists, engineers, and technicians from diverse backgrounds uniting towards a common goal.

This collective effort led to a series of preparatory missions, each building upon the success and learning from the failures of the previous ones. Project Gemini, the intermediate step between the Mercury and Apollo programs, played a crucial role in developing the techniques needed for lunar orbit rendezvous, spacewalking, and long-duration space flights.

Finally, on July 20, 1969, shortly after my sixth birthday and eight years after JFK set the goal, my family sat around our black and white TV to watch the moment history was made and the Apollo 11 mission achieved the dream. Neil Armstrong and Buzz Aldrin became the first humans to land on the Moon, while Michael Collins orbited above. Armstrong's famous words, "That's one small step for man, one giant leap for mankind," were broadcast to millions around the world, marking the achievement not just for America but for humanity.

The Moonshot was more than a triumph of space exploration; it was a testament to what can be accomplished with clear goals, unwavering commitment, and unified effort. It showcased how a bold vision, backed by a firm deadline, can push the boundaries of human potential and achievement. The monumental success of the Apollo Moon landing powerfully illustrates the effectiveness of setting time-bound goals. Deadlines, when thoughtfully applied, fulfil several critical functions in the goal-setting and achieving process:

1. Overcome Procrastination: By replacing the indefinite 'someday' with a specific 'today', a set deadline propels you into immediate action. It transforms intention into a concrete plan of action, pushing you to start now rather than later.

2. Create Structure: Deadlines help in systematically organising tasks. They compel you to prioritise activities, allocate

resources wisely, and streamline efforts towards the goal. This structured approach ensures that every step taken is purposeful and directly contributes to the end goal.

3. Reinforce Commitment: When you set a specific timeline, your goal shifts from being an abstract idea to a tangible target. This enhances your commitment, as you can visualise the endpoint and work backwards to create a roadmap to reach it.

So, the power of setting time-bound goals goes beyond the simple act of noting dates on a calendar. Deadlines infuse your goals with urgency and direction, serving as a constant motivator and guide. They are instrumental in transforming aspirations into realities, much like they did in the successful Apollo Moon landing. By integrating deadlines into your goal-setting strategy, you harness a powerful tool that not only drives action but also aligns your efforts with a clear, achievable timeline.

Mastering the Art of RAPID Goal Achievement

Reflecting on the transformative journeys of those who have navigated the path of achievement reveals a fundamental truth: Purpose is the guiding light in our quest for fulfilment. Yet, without clearly defined goals, we are like ships adrift at sea, illuminated but aimless. Whether in business or personal life, the true essence lies not solely in attaining our dreams but in the profound personal transformation we undergo in pursuing them.

The RAPID goal-achievement framework has been my navigational tool in this journey:

- Rationality grounded my ambitions, teaching me the balance between aspiring high, and staying rooted in reality.

- Assessability brought the necessary clarity, transforming nebulous dreams into concrete, achievable objectives.

- Purposefulness steered me beyond transient motivations like wealth or fame, driving me to find deeper, more enduring reasons to persevere through challenges.

- Integrity demanded that my goals resonate with my core values, ensuring that my pursuits were not just successful but also meaningful and ethical.

- Deadlines added the crucial element of time, reminding me that goals without a timeline are dreams indefinitely deferred.

Life often resembles a complex game, filled with trials and milestones akin to the levels and bosses of video games. It's a journey where strategy and persistence turn daunting challenges into achievable victories.

Consider the story of Amy Johnson, our pioneering aviator. Her achievements unfolded like a football team winning the league, each victory a new milestone achieved, proving that focus and skill can open up new realms of possibility.

Then there's John D. Rockefeller, whose legacy transcends his business empire. In his later years, he embodied his belief that "every right implies a responsibility; every opportunity, an obligation; every possession, a duty." His philanthropy, fuelled by his wealth, was not an afterthought but a deliberate act aligned with his deepest values, leaving a lasting impact on society.

These narratives, along with the moon landing's audacious deadline and Sylvester Stallone's unwavering commitment to his vision, illustrate the multifaceted nature of goal achievement. It's a journey that respects both ambition and integrity, the grand vision and the meticulous steps towards it.

As you set out to chart your own course, remember that the journey towards achieving goals is as significant as the goals themselves. It's not just about reaching the destination, but also about growing, learning, and evolving with each step. Embrace the RAPID strategy, and you'll find that the path to your goals is not just a route to success, but a journey of personal transformation.

Final Thought: Harnessing Vision to Transform Goals into Reality

The journey towards achieving your goals doesn't end with setting them and marking a deadline. The real challenge, and perhaps the most crucial part of the process, lies in inspiring others to join you in your quest. This is the point where your personal ambition transcends into a shared venture.

To turn your goal into a collective mission:

- Develop a Clear Mission Statement: Define your goal in a way that paints a vivid picture of the desired outcome. Explain how realising this goal will impact not just you but the wider community or world at large.

- Monitor and Adjust: Keep a close eye on your progress. Celebrate the milestones you achieve along the way and be ready to adjust your strategies as necessary to stay on course.

- Communicate and Inspire: Share your vision with enthusiasm and clarity. Motivate others by showing them the value and significance of the goal, and encourage them to become active participants in this shared journey.

When goals are set with deliberate intent, backed by firm deadlines and fuelled by a compelling vision, they transform from mere aspirations into tangible realities. As you embark on this path, remember that the power to shape the future is in your hands. Plan meticulously, act purposefully, and inspire collectively. Watch as your vision unfolds into a shared success story, a testament to the power of focused ambition and collaborative effort.

Goal Setting Self-Assessment Test

Carefully read each statement and respond with either "Yes" or "No". If you answer "Yes", read the corresponding solution to help you overcome the challenge. Reflect on this and try to put the solution into practice if you find it relevant, or try to find solutions that best suit your specific situation. The following chapters will also continue to assist you on your journey. You'll get there!

1. Lack of Clear Goals

- Statement: My goals are often vague or broad, making it difficult to know where to start or how to measure progress.

- Solution:

>- SMART Goals: Ensure that your goals are Specific, Measurable, Achievable, Relevant, and Time-bound.
>- Example: Instead of saying "I want to get fit", set a goal like "I will run for 30 minutes, three times a week for the next three months".
>- Break Down Goals: Divide large goals into smaller, more manageable tasks.

2. Procrastination

- Statement: I often delay tasks and take a long time to take action.

- Solution:

    Time Management Techniques: Use methods like the Pomodoro Technique (25 minutes of focused work followed by a 5-minute break) to maintain productivity.
    - Set Deadlines: Establish firm deadlines to create a sense of urgency.
    - Accountability Partner: Share your goals with a friend or mentor who can hold you accountable.

3. Lack of Motivation

- Statement: I lose motivation halfway through pursuing my goals.

- Solution:

    - Find Your Why: Identify the deeper reason behind your goal to stay motivated.
    - Example: If your goal is to save money, your 'why' might be the financial security of your family.
    - Reward System: Create a reward system for reaching milestones.
    - Visualise Success: Regularly imagine the positive outcomes of achieving your goal.

4. Overload and Burnout

- Statement: I feel overwhelmed and exhausted when I take on too many things at once.

- Solution:

    - Prioritise Tasks: Focus on high-priority tasks and eliminate or delegate less important ones.
    - Self-Care: Make sure to take breaks and maintain a healthy work-life balance.
    - Progressive Overload: Gradually increase your workload to avoid burnout.

5. Fear of Failure

- Statement: The fear of not achieving my goal stops me from trying.

- Solution:

    - Reframe Failure: View failure as a learning opportunity rather than a setback.
    - Small Wins: Focus on achieving small victories to build confidence.
    - Growth Mindset: Adopt a mindset that embraces challenges and sees effort as a path to mastery.

6. Lack of Resources

- Statement: I don't have the necessary resources, such as time, money, or knowledge, to achieve my goals.

- Solution:

    - Resource Planning: Identify what resources are needed and plan how to acquire them.
    - Skill Development: Invest time in learning new skills that can help you achieve your goal.
    - Budgeting: Allocate funds wisely to ensure you have the necessary financial resources.

7. Inconsistent Tracking and Review

- Statement: I struggle to regularly track my progress, resulting in a loss of focus on my goals.

- Solution:

- Regular Reviews: Schedule regular check-ins to review progress and adjust plans as needed.
- Use Tools: Utilise goal-tracking apps or journals to keep a record of your progress.
- Reflect on Progress: Take time to reflect on what is working and what isn't.

8. Distractions and Lack of Focus

- Statement: I am easily distracted, which hinders my progress and reduces my productivity.

- Solution:

    - Minimise Distractions: Create a dedicated workspace, free from distractions.
    - Focus Techniques: Use techniques like mindfulness and deep work to increase focus.
    - Set Boundaries: Establish clear boundaries for work and leisure time.

9. Negative Self-Talk

- Statement: My internal dialogue is negative, which diminishes my self-esteem and hinders my progress.

- Solution:

    - Positive Affirmations: Use positive affirmations to combat negative thoughts.
    - Support System: Surround yourself with supportive and encouraging people.
    - Therapeutic Techniques: Practise techniques like cognitive-behavioural therapy (CBT) to challenge and change negative thought patterns.

10. Environmental Factors

- Statement: External factors, such as lack of support from others or an unfavourable environment, affect the pursuit of my goals.

- Solution:

- Optimise Your Environment: Modify your environment to support your goals (e.g., declutter your workspace).

- Seek Support: Find a community or group that shares your goals and can offer support.

- Communicate Your Needs: Clearly communicate your goals and needs to those around you to gain their support.

If you answered "yes" to more than one of these issues, don't be discouraged! Recognising these challenges is the first step to overcoming them. Focus on resolving one challenge at a time using the suggested solutions, and remember that each small progress is a victory. With perseverance and the right strategies, you can achieve your goals and attain personal and professional success.

CHAPTER 4

Eating the Elephant

*"There is only one way to eat an elephant:
one bite at a time."*
— *Desmond Tutu*

As we embark on the journey towards transformative success in both our personal and professional lives, we often face the challenge of initiating significant changes. This can feel akin to standing at the foot of a high mountain, gazing upwards at the path that stretches before us. The summit is in sight, yet the journey to reach it can seem daunting, a test of our resolve and capabilities.

This chapter is about embracing the art of 'eating the elephant,' a powerful approach to conquering seemingly insurmountable tasks. Imagine standing before a giant elephant tasked with the overwhelming challenge of 'eating' it. The key lies not in the enormity of the task, but in the strategy of tackling it. By breaking down this immense challenge into small, manageable bites, what once seemed impossible gradually becomes achievable.

This concept is a metaphor for time management, a crucial skill in our quest for success. It's about dissecting our grand ambitions into smaller, actionable steps, making the journey not only possible but also enjoyable. As you delve into this chapter, you'll discover how to apply this principle to your life, transforming daunting tasks into a series of manageable actions.

In 2001, as the managing director of an IT company, I was engulfed in a whirlwind of demanding work hours that extended from early mornings to well past midnight. My days began with the routine drop-off at school, followed by a relentless pace at the office until dinner. The real work, the tasks that demanded my undivided attention, started only after my children were tucked into bed. This cycle repeated daily, turning my life into a sequence of work and minimal rest, with personal time squeezed into the margins. Often when reading a bedtime story to my children, I would fall asleep from exhaustion before they did. This hectic lifestyle was far from the fulfilling life I envisioned. Weekends and breaks, which I longed for as brief escapes, were often punctuated with unfinished work tasks, making true relaxation elusive. No matter how much I enjoyed my work, the constant juggle between professional demands and personal time left me feeling perpetually overwhelmed and stressed. It was clear that a change was necessary—not just for my well-being, but for the joy and quality of my life. Determined to reclaim my time and introduce balance, I began to actively learn, apply and refine the time management strategies outlined in this chapter. These strategies weren't just methods to enhance productivity; they were lifelines that gradually restored order to my chaos. By prioritising tasks effectively, setting clear boundaries, and most importantly, learning to say no to non-essential demands, I started to experience a profound transformation. As I mastered these principles, I not only improved my efficiency during work hours but also safeguarded my evenings and weekends for what truly mattered—time with my family, hobbies, and rest. This shift did not happen overnight, but with consistent practice and dedication, I turned my overwhelming schedule into one that allowed for work, growth, and joy. This personal journey underscores the transformative power of effective time management. It is not merely about getting through the workday, but about creating a life where joy and accomplishment coexist harmoniously. As you dive into this chapter, remember that the goal is to craft a life not defined by busyness but enriched with moments of peace and fulfilment.

In 1994, Theresa Macan, a prominent psychologist, conducted a pivotal study that shed light on the profound impact of time management on stress reduction and job satisfaction in the workplace. This research, creatively titled "Time Management and Stress Reduction in the Workplace," has since become a cornerstone reference for both academic scholars and professional leaders aiming to understand and implement effective workplace strategies.

The 1990s marked a period of intense scrutiny into workplace efficiency, particularly as businesses faced increasing globalisation and technological advancements. Organisations were searching for strategies to not only boost productivity but also to enhance employee well-being. Macan responded to this need by exploring how time management could serve as a tool to manage workplace stress and improve job satisfaction.

Her study was meticulously designed to assess the relationship between time management behaviours and perceived control over time, and their subsequent effects on job-related stress and satisfaction levels. The research involved a diverse group of employees from various sectors who were surveyed about their daily routines, stress levels, job satisfaction, and time management habits.

Participants were asked to detail their typical time management practices, such as setting goals, prioritising tasks, organising activities, and handling interruptions. The study also included assessments of their perceived control over their time, a variable Macan hypothesised to be crucial in mediating stress and satisfaction.

The results of Macan's study were revealing. In the short term, participants who reported better time management behaviours experienced significantly lower levels of perceived stress and higher job satisfaction. These individuals felt more in control of their time, which contributed to a less chaotic and more rewarding work environment.

In the long term, the study suggested that consistent application of time management strategies could lead to sustained job satisfaction and reduced stress levels. This was attributed to the development of a routine that fostered a sense of predictability and efficiency, reducing the anxiety associated with unmet deadlines and cluttered workflows.

Macan identified several key time management behaviours that had a significant impact on stress reduction and increased job satisfaction:

- Goal Setting: Employees who regularly set clear, achievable goals were more likely to feel in control of their work, leading to lower stress levels.

- Prioritisation: Prioritising tasks effectively allowed employees to focus on what was most important, reducing the overwhelm from less critical tasks.

- Organising Tasks: Those who kept their workspace and digital files organised reported less time wasted on searching for materials, which directly reduced frustration and stress.

- Handling Interruptions: Employees skilled at managing interruptions maintained better focus and efficiency, contributing to higher job satisfaction.

The broader implications of Macan's findings are significant for organisational leadership. Improved job satisfaction as a result of effective time management can lead to enhanced job performance. Employees who are less stressed and more satisfied with their jobs are likely to perform better, showing increased attention to detail, higher productivity, and greater overall contribution to team and organisational goals.

Moreover, organisations with employees who manage their time effectively experience lower turnover rates. Satisfied employees are less likely to seek other employment opportunities, leading to reduced costs associated with hiring and training new staff.

It's clear that the principles outlined in Theresa Macan's study are more than just academic insights—they are practical tools that can transform our daily lives. By understanding and implementing effective time management strategies, individuals can enhance their professional performance and personal satisfaction, paving the way for a more structured and less stressful life. This study not only underscores the importance of managing one's time effectively but also highlights the direct benefits such management has on reducing stress and fostering a fulfilling and productive work environment.

Remember, time is finite, but with the right approach, its potential is limitless. Let this chapter equip you with the tools and insights to navigate the path ahead, turning each step into a victory. Reshape your approach to challenges, and embark on a journey that will lead you to the pinnacle of your aspirations, one small, manageable step at a time.

Transforming Time into Productivity

Understanding time management is akin to recognising that, while time itself is constant, our usage of it is variable and within our control. Every day, we are each allocated the same 1,440 minutes, a universal equaliser. The true measure of time management lies not in extending these minutes, but in optimising them for maximum productivity and balance.

Consider time management as a strategic endeavour. It's like a coach thoughtfully assigning players in a football match or a player in a rapid-paced board game making quick, decisive moves. Adopting a structured approach to handling tasks has been a game-changer for me. There's wisdom in the adage that a half-hour of planning can save two hours of execution. This principle holds in both our personal and professional lives. In my own experience, implementing a disciplined system in my business led to remarkable efficiency. Work that used to extend into evenings and weekends was now being completed within regular office hours.

At one time, my life was a relentless race against the clock. Balancing a demanding job, nurturing my children, and managing the daily whirlwind of home life, I often felt like a juggler, one step away from dropping all the balls. Amidst this chaos, my personal goals and well-being were sidelined, leaving me drained and unfulfilled. The breakthrough came when I started applying the time management techniques outlined in this chapter. I started with a clear vision of what I wanted to achieve in my business, family life, and personal growth. Recognising that multitasking was more of a hindrance than a help, I shifted my approach to focus on one task at a time with full attention.

I began using a structured plan to keep track of my commitments and allocated time for self-care. Gradually, my new approach began to bear fruit. At work, my productivity soared as I tackled tasks with undivided focus, leading to growth in my business. At home, my time with my children became more quality-driven, filled with undistracted interactions that deepened our bond. We would play tag, read stories, or go out for adventures. Importantly, the time set aside for myself–whether for a run, a book, or a hobby–rejuvenated my spirit and energy.

The most striking change was in myself. I transformed from a perpetually exhausted, stretched-thin single parent and overloaded business owner to a person in control of my life. My story is not just one of managing time but of having a life. I discovered that with the right strategies, finding balance and personal fulfilment is more than just a distant dream.

A strategic approach to time management can lead to personal and professional fulfilment, all while maintaining a healthy work-life balance. In essence, mastering time management is about making each minute count. It's about smart planning and focused execution. And the payoff goes beyond enhanced productivity at work; it extends to creating more time for leisure, relaxation, and play. By effectively managing your time, you open the door to a more balanced, fulfilling life.

The Seven Killers of Time Management

In the early days of my entrepreneurial journey, I frequently found myself overwhelmed by tasks that masqueraded as urgent but were merely distractions masking my true objectives. The battle to distinguish and sidestep these pitfalls became a cornerstone in lining my efforts with my goals. The 'Seven Killers of Time Management' represent the most insidious obstacles that threaten to undermine even the most disciplined approaches to managing our time. These challenges, ranging from the allure of distractions and the trap of multitasking to the creeping influence of procrastination and misaligned priorities, subtly erode our productivity under the radar.

They take shape in many ways, including through inefficient workflows, a reluctance to decline requests, excessive commitments, and ambiguous objectives. Grasping and addressing these challenges is vital for anyone aiming to seize back the reins of their time and boost their effectiveness across both personal and professional domains.

This section examines the heart of these time management foes, offering insights and tactics to neutralise them. It's a guide to navigating through the noise and clutter of daily demands, aiming to equip you with the knowledge to sidestep these common traps. By understanding how to confront these obstacles, you're taking the first step towards crafting a more structured, fruitful, and balanced existence. It's a journey many of us embark on, but with the right strategies in hand, it's one that promises to lead to a place of greater control, accomplishment, and personal satisfaction.

Reactive vs Proactive

At the heart of many productivity issues is a widespread tendency to operate reactively rather than proactively. This habitual reactivity can seriously hamper your potential and overall effectiveness, trapping you in a cycle of urgency that often prioritises less important tasks. Here, we delve into why reactivity is problematic and how it distorts your perception of what truly matters.

Reactivity in time management means being in a constant mode of response to immediate demands. These demands might come in the form of emails, phone calls, last-minute requests, or unexpected crises. While responding to these urgencies, the truly important tasks—those that significantly drive our personal and professional objectives—often fall by the wayside.

The main issue with a reactive approach is the confusion it creates between what's urgent and what's important. Urgency is characterised by tasks that demand immediate attention but don't necessarily contribute to our long-term goals. These tasks can be deceptive; they scream for attention and create a false sense of importance due to their immediacy. However, just because something needs to be addressed right away doesn't mean it's crucial to your broader success.

Moreover, some tasks may be important to someone else but not necessarily to you. This misalignment often leads to spending your time fulfilling others' priorities at the expense of your own. The pressure to react to these external expectations can distract you from focusing on tasks that genuinely advance your personal and professional aims.

Living reactively has several downsides:

- Stunted Growth: Constantly dealing with emergencies prevents you from engaging in strategic planning or long-term projects that align with your core objectives.

- Poor Work-Life Balance: Reactivity at work spills over into personal life, where it can disrupt relationships and personal time, leading to stress and burnout.

- Overwhelming Days: Days filled with reactive tasks feel longer and more exhausting, as they lack a sense of accomplishment and control.

For many, including myself, the realisation that a reactive lifestyle is unsustainable comes from personal experience. In my case, long work hours dominated by immediate tasks left little room for family, self-care, or relaxation. This relentless schedule not only affected my health but also strained my relationships and overall satisfaction with life. Real change began when I critically assessed my priorities and aligned my daily activities with my long-term goals instead of external demands.

By understanding the importance of proactive management, you can start implementing strategies to manage your time more effectively. This includes setting boundaries, using tools like structured daily planners, and focusing on tasks that advance your overarching objectives.

While the full exploration of solutions will be detailed later in this chapter, it's crucial to recognise that the shift from reactivity to proactivity involves:

- Setting Clear, Strategic Goals: Define what you truly need to achieve and differentiate these from distractions.

- **Establishing Boundaries:** Learn to say no or delegate tasks that do not align with your primary objectives.

- **Prioritising Tasks:** Use methods like the Eisenhower Matrix to sort tasks by urgency and importance, focusing first on those that are both important and urgent.

This approach not only improves productivity and job satisfaction but also restores a sense of control and purpose to your professional and personal life. As we move forward, we'll explore specific strategies that can help solidify this transformation, turning proactive time management into a powerful tool for achieving a balanced and fulfilling life.

Again and Again

In the exploration of effective time management, one prevalent challenge that often emerges is the repetitive revisiting of tasks without achieving resolution—what I term the "Again and Again" syndrome. This behaviour is characterised by actions such as marking emails as unread to address them later, putting documents back into an in-tray rather than processing them immediately, and re-listening to voicemails without responding. While these actions might seem minor individually, collectively, they contribute to a significant pattern of redundancy that saps productivity and mental energy.

The primary issue with revisiting tasks repeatedly is the inefficiencies it creates. Each return to a task forces you to spend additional time reacquainting ourselves with the material, which could have been directed toward more productive efforts. This not only clutters your physical and mental workspaces but also promotes a feeling of being constantly overwhelmed. Perhaps most critically, it represents a substantial loss of time—research indicates that people may spend up to 170 hours each year reprocessing information that could have been efficiently handled on first contact. This is not merely about losing hours; it is about missing opportunities for personal growth, professional advancement, and relaxation.

Several factors contribute to this counterproductive cycle:

- Decision Uncertainty: Often, tasks are postponed because we are unsure how to respond or need more clarity. This indecision leads to repeated postponements.

- Perceived Time Shortage: At times, we feel there isn't enough time to fully deal with a task on first encounter, thinking it will be handled later, which often leads to it never being fully addressed.

- Procrastination: Avoiding tasks due to their perceived difficulty or our own reluctance can lead to multiple revisits without resolution.

For years, I was caught in a relentless cycle of re-reading emails, re-listening to voicemails, and shuffling the same papers daily. I would often open an email, read it, decide I couldn't deal with it now, and simply re-mark it as unread. The same applies to letters: I would open an envelope and read it, and if I wasn't able to spend time on it now, I would simply put it back in my in-tray to be read again at a later date. Each revisit consumed my time and energy.

When I realised how much time I lost to this repetitive loop, it struck me deeply. I discovered I was losing weeks of my time, every year to tasks that added no real value to my life. I was already trying to spend more time with my family, so this realisation that time re-reading information could be spent with my family created a new drive in me. Determined to break free from this cycle, I adopted a new approach: treating each piece of information as a unique challenge requiring immediate action.

When an email arrived, I would read it and immediately decide whether to respond, delegate, or file it away. The same went for physical mail and voicemails. This simple yet profound shift in approach transformed my days. No longer was I revisiting and reprocessing the same information. Each decision to act immediately was a step forward in my daily productivity.

This change was more than just a timesaving tactic; it was a mental shift that brought me a sense of accomplishment and control. Each task I completed efficiently was a small victory, contributing to a larger sense of progress and achievement. This new method streamlined my workflow and infused a sense of purpose and momentum into my work.

There is power in changing our approach to the mundane tasks that fill our days. By embracing the principle of immediate action, you will transform a source of frustration into an opportunity for efficiency and growth.

The journey from being overwhelmed by incessant tasks to mastering them with confidence and clarity not only transforms your professional life but also enriches your personal experiences, making each day more manageable and fulfilling. Later in this chapter, we will explore detailed strategies that build on this foundation, guiding you toward a more organised and effective way to manage your time.

The 'Open-Door' Policy

The 'Open-Door' policy, often hailed as a symbol of approachability and transparency in leadership, has its own set of intricate challenges, especially when it comes to effective time management. Misunderstood and misapplied, this policy can often lead to a significant drain on productivity due to constant interruptions and unscheduled interactions.

At its core, the problem with an overly liberal open-door policy is the disruption it invites. Each interruption, while seemingly brief, can significantly disrupt the flow of work, requiring additional time to regain focus and momentum. This issue is compounded in environments where the nature of work demands deep concentration or creative thinking.

Interruptions can vary widely but typically fall into several categories:

- Immediate Queries: Quick questions or requests for decisions that, while minor, demand immediate attention and pull you away from focused work.

- Unscheduled Meetings: Drop-ins by colleagues or team members who see the open door as an invitation to discuss issues without prior arrangement, leading to prolonged and often unproductive conversations.

- External Distractions: Calls or visits from outside the immediate work environment which may not always be urgent but are treated as such due to the accessibility the open-door policy provides.

These interruptions are not only disruptive but are often not as important as they seem. Many could be deferred or handled through more structured communication channels. Moreover, what is urgent for one person may not be a priority for another, leading to a misalignment of immediate tasks versus long-term goals.

A significant challenge arises when tasks that appear urgent are not actually important—at least not to the person being interrupted. This misconception can lead to a skewed priority list where strategic, impactful work is continually sidelined for tasks that cater more to the urges of others than to one's own professional objectives or the organisation's goals.

While the full range of strategies to combat the inefficiencies of an open-door policy will be explored later, it's crucial to start by recognising the need for boundaries. Effective time management under such a policy begins with defining when and how you are available for interruptions.

Redefining the open-door policy to better fit the demands of modern work environments involves finding a balance between being approachable and maintaining productivity. It's about creating a culture where communication is encouraged but also structured in a way that respects everyone's time and productivity. By understanding the challenges and rethinking your approach to open-door policies, you can pave the way for more effective time management that enhances not just your productivity but also the overall health of the organisation.

My transformation in mastering time management was a journey marked by subtle yet significant changes, both in my professional and family life. At work, my 'open-door' policy was redefined. I was known for my approachability, a trait my colleagues valued greatly. However, I realised that being constantly available was eating into my productive hours, so I began setting specific time slots for meetings and discussions, communicating these changes to the team. My colleagues initially took time to adjust, but soon, they noticed that our interactions became more focused and productive. I was no longer juggling tasks mid-conversation, but was fully present and attentive. This shift enhanced my productivity and improved the quality of our collaborations.

At home, the dynamics were different, but the challenge of interruptions was just as real. My two young children, who naturally sought my attention, had to adapt to the new structure. I set up a workspace in a quiet corner of the house and had a heartfelt conversation with them. I explained that when I was in my workspace, I needed uninterrupted time to focus on my work. The children, though young, gradually understood that my work time was important. They learned to wait for my 'office hours' to end before sharing their day's stories or seeking help with a puzzle.

This change wasn't instantaneous. There were days of slip-ups and gentle reminders. But over time, a new rhythm emerged in our household. The children adapted, learning a bit about patience and respect for others' commitments.

This is a common struggle - balancing professional aspirations with the richness of family life. By managing your time and interruptions thoughtfully, you can reclaim control over your workday and foster a deeper understanding and cooperation within your family. The improved productivity will also result in more time to spend with your family as fewer tasks spread out beyond your working hours. You will experience the positive ripple effect that thoughtful time management can have, extending beyond personal productivity to enrich the lives of those around you.

The Perils of a Very Long 'To-Do' List

Addressing an overly long to-do list is like solving a complex puzzle, requiring both strategic planning and precise execution. Reflecting on my past experiences, I recall how my to-do lists used to be intimidatingly extensive, often containing upwards of 70 items. This enormity not only brought a sense of being overwhelmed, but also posed the challenge of determining where to start and how to prioritise tasks effectively. The sheer length of the list made it difficult to discern which tasks were crucial and which could wait, turning what should have been a helpful tool into a source of daily anxiety and inefficiency.

A lengthy to-do list, while appearing thorough, often falls into the trap of counterproductivity. One significant pitfall of such lists is the psychological urge to tackle simpler, less time-consuming tasks first, driven by the desire for quick completion and the reduction of an overwhelming list. This approach, though seemingly efficient, can lead to spending disproportionate amounts of time on tasks with minimal impact. It's similar to a player in a game who focuses on minor side quests, overlooking the main objectives that offer substantial progress and rewards.

In my own experience, I frequently found myself at the end of the day having checked off numerous small tasks, yet having left untouched the four or five critical items that required more attention but promised greater results. This skewed focus echoes the Pareto Principle, where a majority of our efforts often contribute minimally to our overall productivity.

Another pitfall of an excessively long to-do list is the paralysis it can create. Faced with too many choices, it's easy to become overwhelmed and unsure where to begin. This can lead to procrastination or a scattered approach to work, where tasks are started but not completed due to a lack of clear prioritisation.

Additionally, long to-do lists can obscure your view of what's truly important. With so many items vying for attention, it becomes challenging to identify and focus on the tasks that align with your long-term goals and objectives. This misalignment can lead you down a path of busywork, where you are constantly engaged but not necessarily in activities that propel you towards our desired outcomes.

The key to avoiding these pitfalls lies in curating a to-do list that is not only manageable but also strategically aligned with our priorities. By doing so, you ensure that your efforts are concentrated on activities that yield the highest returns, both in your professional and personal life.

To combat this, I began approaching my to-do list as if it were a game, applying strategies to optimise effectiveness and efficiency. This involved breaking down the list into priority and potential impact categories. Each task was evaluated not just on its urgency but also on its importance and contribution to my overall goals.

By reorganising and gamifying my to-do list, I found that the quality and quantity of my work improved significantly. I was able to focus on tasks that had the most substantial impact on my goals, rather than getting bogged down by numerous smaller, less significant tasks.

Mastering the art of managing a to-do list is essential for anyone aiming to be highly effective and efficient in achieving their goals. It's about prioritising strategically, allocating time wisely, and approaching tasks with a game-like mindset that values both the journey and the outcome. This approach transforms an overwhelming list into a structured game plan, turning the daunting task of managing a long to-do list into an engaging and productive experience.

We'll delve deeper into this topic later in the chapter. For the moment, take a closer look at your current to-do list. Assess its efficiency and consider whether it truly aligns with your priorities and productivity goals.

Not Having a Daily Schedule

In the realm of time management, failing to establish a comprehensive daily schedule is a significant misstep commonly overlooked by professionals at all levels. The allure of spontaneity or the fear of stifling creativity often deters people from rigorously planning their day. However, this lack of structure can spiral into a series of productivity pitfalls, ranging from missed deadlines to overlooked opportunities.

For many, the resistance to strict scheduling stems from a misconception that it limits flexibility. They fear that a rigid timetable may constrict their ability to adapt to the day's evolving demands. Others feel daunted by the task of plotting out each day's activities, worried they might not strictly adhere to the plan, which can lead to feelings of failure or frustration.

The absence of a daily schedule typically manifests in several detrimental ways:

1. Missed Opportunities and Deadlines: Without a schedule to guide their day, individuals often find themselves reacting to tasks as they come up rather than proactively addressing them. This reactive approach makes it easy to miss critical deadlines or forget important tasks until it's too late.

2. Increased Stress and Overwhelm: Without clear boundaries and priorities set for the day, everything feels urgent. This can lead to increased stress as the individual struggles to decide what to tackle next, often leading to decision fatigue and reduced cognitive resources.

3. Inefficient Task Management: Unscheduled days tend to breed task inefficiency. People find themselves repeatedly checking their to-do lists, trying to determine what to do next, which splits their focus and disrupts their productivity. Critical tasks get the same weight as trivial ones, leading to poor allocation of time and energy.

4. Extended Work Hours: A common consequence of not having a scheduled plan is the extension of work hours into personal time. When tasks are not confined to specific times, work can bleed into evenings and weekends, eroding work-life balance and leading to burnout.

In my earlier professional years, before embracing the principles laid out in this chapter, I fell victim to many of the pitfalls associated with not having a well-defined daily schedule. My calendar was a jumble of meetings, often booked back-to-back, because there was nothing else scheduled that could conflict. This seemingly minor oversight in planning led to significant disruptions in both my professional productivity and personal life. Each day, my schedule was dictated not by a strategic plan, but by the demands of others. Without designated times for focused work tasks, any new meeting request seemed reasonable to accept. This constant availability made me a prime candidate for endless meetings, leaving no room to breathe or to engage deeply with any one project during regular work hours. This approach to scheduling—or rather, the lack of it—meant that I was always reacting, never proactive. My workday was a series of interruptions, and without blocks of time earmarked for specific tasks, I found myself juggling priorities with no clear direction. The consequence was that I spent the majority of my day in meetings, discussing work rather than doing it.

The lack of structured task time didn't just affect my workday; it split over into my home life as well. Evenings, which should have been dedicated to unwinding with my family and recharging for the next day, were instead consumed by the tasks I couldn't complete during office hours. Bedtime stories for my children were often rushed through, so I could get back to my computer. This routine took a toll not just on my health and well-being, but on my relationships as well. My wife and children bore the brunt of my divided attention, and I missed countless small but precious moments with them. It became painfully clear that not scheduling my tasks was not only inefficient but also harmful to the very fabric of my family life.

Realising the unsustainable nature of my work habits was a wake-up call. I began to see the importance of a scheduled, well-organised day not just for professional success but for personal happiness and family well-being. Integrating specific times for tasks into my daily schedule became a priority. This shift allowed me to manage my time more effectively, drastically reducing the need to extend my workday into the evening.

While the full range of strategies to combat these issues will be explored in subsequent sections, it is crucial to acknowledge the foundational solution: the integration of a structured daily planner. By embracing a daily schedule that includes not only appointments and meetings but also dedicated times for specific tasks, you can regain control over your workday.

The transition to a structured daily schedule was not instantaneous, nor was it without challenges. However, the clarity it brought to my workday was transformative. By discussing the practical application of these scheduling principles later in this chapter, I hope to provide guidance that can prevent others from falling into the same traps that once ensnared me. Through careful planning and prioritisation, we can all reclaim our time and restore balance to our lives.

No system for managing projects and documents

In the early stages of my career, I faced the daunting challenge of managing projects and documents, reminiscent of navigating an intricate labyrinth in a strategy game. My initial approach was rudimentary—a desk drawer that quickly spilt over into a tray on my desk. This haphazard method led to inefficiencies and frustrations, as I often found myself wasting precious time searching for information or revisiting projects due to misplaced details.

A lack of a structured system for storing and managing information can create chaos, affecting not just the physical workspace but also one's mental clarity. This disorganisation can take various forms: a jumbled computer filing system, a cluttered desk brimming with lost papers, and an overall ineffective work environment. Just as a gamer struggles without a clear strategy, this disorganisation leads to difficulties in tracking progress and managing tasks efficiently.

I remember a meeting with a business manager whose office was the epitome of this chaos. His desk was buried under a mountain of files and papers. He claimed to have a system and knew the location of every item, but the reality was a far cry from efficiency. On one occasion, he spent over three hours searching for a critical letter misplaced among other files. This incident highlighted a crucial point—relying solely on memory in a disorganised system inevitably leads to lost or misplaced information.

For this manager, his chaotic system was a misguided attempt at making himself indispensable. He believed that by being the only one who could navigate through his disorganised system, he was securing his position. However, this approach backfired. It hindered his ability to delegate tasks and ultimately led to a reduction in his responsibilities to aid the company's growth.

This also meant that he could not go away on holiday. He was rarely able to take more than a single day off at a time, which resulted in a deterioration of his health over time. Eventually, he had a heart attack and was off work for several months. The company was forced to organise his files, and a system was put in place while he was away that allowed other staff members to take up the slack. So much so that his job became redundant. So instead of securing his position within the company, he had inadvertently become a roadblock to progress. When he returned to work, the company was able to redeploy him in a role with less stress and one that allowed him to use his knowledge and talents to help the company grow rather than acting as a roadblock to growth.

Confronted with similar challenges, I adopted a gamified approach to organisation and delegation. I developed a system where each document and project had a specific place, both in the physical and digital realms. This systematisation was akin to mapping out a game world, where every item had its designated 'territory' or 'level.'

Additionally, the importance of effective delegation became clear to me. In gaming terms, this is like building a team where each member has a distinct role and can step in when needed. By ensuring others could easily understand and navigate my system, I not only enhanced efficiency but also fostered collaboration and team empowerment.

Transforming from a disorganised to a meticulously organised system was a pivotal moment in my journey towards effective project and document management. It taught me that success in business and work, much like in a strategic game, requires a well-planned system that supports personal efficiency and team collaboration. Embracing organisation and delegation, we can sidestep the pitfalls that ensnare many capable individuals and instead clear a path for greater success and growth.

My struggle with organisation in my work and home life was a significant hurdle that echoed the challenges faced by many trying to juggle multiple responsibilities. At work, my desk was a constant battleground of clutter–stacks of papers, unsorted documents, and a digital desktop littered with unorganised files. This chaos was not confined to my office space. My home life mirrored this disarray, with important household documents mixed up with children's school papers, and personal projects left unfinished amidst the daily whirlwind of family life. Many DIY projects would be left at the barely functional stage because I didn't have the time to complete them.

In my business, my disorganisation manifested in late nights, overlooked emails, and a constant feeling of being behind on my projects. The clutter on my desk was more than just a physical barrier; it represented a mental block, hindering my ability to think clearly and prioritise tasks effectively. Important documents would often get buried under piles of papers, leading to frantic searches and wasted time. This lack of organisation in my workspace spilt over into meetings and collaborations, where I sometimes appeared unprepared or scatterbrained.

At home, the effects of this disorganised approach were equally palpable. Vital bills would get lost in the shuffle, appointments were often forgotten, and the overall environment felt chaotic. This disarray added to my stress, making it difficult for me to relax and enjoy my time with my family. The clutter wasn't just physical; it was an ever-present reminder of tasks undone and a schedule unmanaged.

The constant back-and-forth between my disorganised work and home environments left me feeling drained and often defeated. I realised that my inability to manage my documents and projects effectively was not just a matter of misplaced papers or cluttered spaces; it was a significant impediment to my productivity and peace of mind.

Organisation is not just about neatness or cleanliness. It is about creating an environment, both physically and mentally, that fosters efficiency, clarity, and tranquillity. The journey towards overcoming this challenge involves not only decluttering your physical spaces but also adopting systematic approaches to managing projects and documents, both at work and home. This transformation is essential in helping you regain control of your time, reduce stress, and create a more harmonious balance between your professional and personal life.

The Burden of Clutter

As I delved deeper into the principles of effective time management and productivity, I recognised that one of the more insidious obstacles was the accumulation of unnecessary information and the broader issue of clutter in all its forms. This clutter wasn't confined to the digital realm of old emails and promotional materials; it extended into the physical world, encompassing everything from old letters, emails, promotional materials, and obsolete stock items to bits of wood, old magazines, and even toys my children had outgrown. The principle was the same: holding onto items "just in case" I might need them someday, which resulted in both a physical and a mental overload.

The presence of clutter—whether it's piles of unread documents, overflowing storage of unused stock, or shelves laden with knick-knacks—can dramatically impede efficiency and effectiveness. In the workplace, I observed environments where every piece of paper was filed and every promotional item was stashed away, creating a labyrinth that made it challenging to locate anything promptly. This physical manifestation of clutter was paralleled in the digital space by inboxes filled with thousands of unread or undealt emails, each one a tiny weight adding to a sense of overwhelming burden.

In my personal experience and visits to various businesses, the accumulation of physical items often mirrored the hoarding of digital information. Workspaces were cluttered with both the tangible and intangible, leading to environments that were as mentally taxing as they were physically crowded. It was not uncommon to see offices where desks were buried under piles of paper and storage rooms filled to the brim with items that had long lost their relevance or utility.

The consequences of such hoarding were multifaceted. Physically, it created spaces that were hard to navigate and maintain, requiring extra time and effort to clean and organise. Mentally, it fostered a workspace that was visually and cognitively overwhelming, making it difficult to focus and process information efficiently. Just as a cluttered desk can stop you from finding your notes for an important meeting, a cluttered inbox can hide urgent tasks among less critical communications.

In certain industries, like insurance and banking, regulatory requirements necessitate the retention of specific documents for a defined period. However, the challenge lies not in the mandated keeping of essential records but in the indiscriminate accumulation of documents and items beyond their useful or required period. This "just in case" mentality can turn manageable collections into unmanageable hoards, turning the task of locating essential information or items into a search for a needle in a haystack.

In my office, my desk and computer were swamped with piles of outdated documents, old letters, and promotional materials that had lost their relevance. This accumulation was not just physical; it created a mental clutter that made it challenging for me to focus and find important information quickly. Each file and email I held onto added to a growing sense of disorder, believing they might be needed someday.

This hoarding stemmed partly from a desire to maintain control over my work. I believed that keeping all this information at hand would prepare me for any situation, thinking they might contain useful information in the future. However, this misguided attempt at control led to the opposite effect. The clutter made it harder for me to navigate my tasks efficiently, leading to wasted time and increased stress.

The parallel to hoarding in my personal life was striking. Just as someone might struggle to throw away old belongings, needing a sense of control that ultimately eludes them, I found it difficult to let go of items that no longer served a purpose. This reluctance to discard unnecessary things stemmed from a fear of losing something important, a sentiment echoed in both my business and personal life. The impact on me of this hoarding behaviour was multifaceted. It not only hampered my productivity and effectiveness at work but also spilt over into my personal life, where I found myself mentally exhausted and unable to unwind and relax. The constant feeling of being surrounded by unsorted, unorganised information was like living in a house cluttered with unused items, each vying for attention and space. My journey to overcome this challenge involved not just physical decluttering but also a mental shift in how I viewed the information I kept. By learning to let go of redundant data, I began to clear the mental and physical space needed for a more focused, efficient, and stress-free work environment. This transformation was a crucial step in regaining control over my work life and finding a sense of peace and clarity that had been missing.

The Transformative Power of Urban Cleanliness

Urban decay is a significant challenge in cities across the globe, manifesting in neglected infrastructure, unkempt public spaces, and the visible decline of neighbourhood aesthetics. This often leads to increased crime rates and a diminished quality of life for residents. However, an emerging body of research and several practical initiatives highlight a transformative solution: revitalising these areas can lead to substantial societal benefits, including reduced crime rates and enhanced community pride. One of the most compelling illustrations of this principle is the application of the "Broken Windows Theory" in New York City during the 1990s.

The "Broken Windows Theory," proposed by social scientists James Q. Wilson and George L. Kelling in 1982, posits that maintaining and monitoring urban environments to prevent small crimes such as vandalism helps to create an atmosphere of order and lawfulness, thereby preventing more serious crimes. The theory suggests that visible signs of disorder and misbehaviour, such as broken windows, abandoned buildings, and unkempt public spaces, encourage further crime and anti-social behaviour.

In the early 1990s, New York City was struggling with high crime rates and widespread urban decay. The city's subway system was particularly notorious, covered in graffiti and perceived as unsafe by many of its users. The Metropolitan Transportation Authority (MTA), led by then-Chairman Richard Ravitch and later by David Gunn, embarked on a comprehensive cleanup program to tackle the graffiti problem head-on.

The strategy involved removing subway cars from service the moment graffiti was spotted, ensuring that they were clean before being returned to the tracks. This approach sent a clear message that vandalism would not be tolerated. The cleanup campaign extended beyond the subway cars to the stations themselves, which were regularly cleaned and maintained to project a sense of order and respect for the law.

The results were dramatic. As the subway system transformed from a graffiti-covered to a clean and orderly service, public confidence grew. There was a significant drop in subway crimes, from muggings to fare evasion, which further extended to the streets of the city. During the tenure of Mayor Rudy Giuliani, who took office in 1994, these principles were applied more broadly as part of the city's quality-of-life campaign, which targeted minor crimes to prevent larger ones.

Researchers later analysed crime data from this period and found a significant correlation between the cleanup efforts and a reduction in crime rates, supporting the theory that enhancing the physical environment could lead to broader social benefits.

The New York City cleanup of the 1990s serves as a compelling case study of how environmental cues influence human behaviour. The city's experience highlights several critical lessons:

1. Preventative Measures: Addressing small problems like graffiti can prevent larger issues, like serious crimes, from flourishing.

2. Community Engagement: Clean environments improve citizens' morale and encourage them to maintain public order.

3. Economic Benefits: As the perception of safety in the city improved, so did tourism and investment, contributing to economic revitalisation.

The principles demonstrated by New York's experience remain relevant today. Cities around the world continue to implement similar strategies to improve urban spaces and reduce crime. These efforts underscore the importance of the environment in shaping human behaviour and the role of meticulous urban management in fostering safer, more vibrant communities.

The cleanup of New York City's subway system and the broader application of the "Broken Windows Theory" not only transformed the city's public spaces but also fundamentally altered its approach to urban governance and crime prevention. This case study powerfully demonstrates that the state of our surroundings can directly influence the quality of our social and civic life, making a strong case for the importance of cleanliness and order in urban planning and management. In a city, this is a massive undertaking that can take years to implement, but in our own lives, we can start with something as simple as cleaning up the space around us.

Addressing this issue requires a shift in how we perceive the value of what we keep. It's essential to assess not just the immediate utility of an item or piece of information but also its long-term relevance to our personal and professional goals. In the subsequent sections, we will explore strategies to combat clutter, focusing on principles like the 'Touch it once!' rule for handling items and information—deal with it once, decisively, whether that means replying, filing, delegating, or discarding. As we prepare to explore these solutions, it's crucial to understand that decluttering is not just about physical and digital cleanliness. It's about creating an environment that enhances focus, efficiency, and, ultimately, personal and professional fulfilment. The journey from cluttered chaos to streamlined simplicity is not just about cleaning up; it's about setting up a foundation for continued productivity and success.

In addressing the seven killers of time management, I was able to navigate through these common pitfalls that hinder productivity and efficiency. From reactive habits to hoarding useless information, these challenges are surmountable with the right strategies and mindset. So, let's explore the seven steps to perfect time management, giving practical solutions to transform these obstacles into stepping stones for success.

The 7 Steps to Perfecting Time Management

Embarking on the path to perfecting time management is a transformative process that requires focus, prioritisation, and astute discernment. In my own journey through the complexities of business and life, mastering this art has been a cornerstone of my success. Through trial and error, I have refined my approach, turning time management into a structured, methodical process. In the following pages, I'll share the seven key steps that reshaped my approach, offering practical strategies to elevate your time management skills and enhance your productivity.

The Six Most Important Things

Warren Buffett is one of the world's most successful investors and a renowned business magnate. Buffett's approach to managing his priorities is a lesson in simplicity, effectiveness, and strategic foresight.

Buffett's method involves a simple yet profound practice. He advises writing down the top 25 career goals and then circling the five most crucial ones. This exercise forces a hard distinction between what is essential and what is merely desirable. For Buffett, the focus then shifts entirely to the top five, while the remaining 20 become an 'avoid-at-all-cost' list. This principle is at the heart of "The Six Most Important Things," where the emphasis is on a laser-focused approach to tasks and goals.

In his daily routine, Buffett prioritises tasks that align with his top goals, often relegating or delegating the rest. This methodology allows him to channel his energies and resources into areas where they will have the most significant impact. Buffett's day is not cluttered with an endless series of tasks; instead, he concentrates on key decisions and actions that align with his primary objectives.

What makes Buffett's approach inspiring is not just his incredible success, but also his commitment to this principle of prioritisation. He avoids the temptation to overextend himself across too many projects or commitments. This discipline has allowed him to build and maintain a level of productivity and effectiveness that few can match.

Buffett's example shows how adopting "The Six Most Important Things" strategy can lead to profound success and influence. His approach demonstrates that by focusing intently on a few critical areas, one can achieve more than by spreading oneself thin over many. Buffett's career stands as a testament to the power of strategic focus, offering valuable insights for anyone looking to make significant strides in their professional journey.

As previously mentioned, long to-do lists can feel overwhelming, much like piecing together different parts of a complex problem, where each task requires deliberate attention to move forward. To bring clarity and order to this chaos, I honed in on identifying the six most important tasks for each day. This approach wasn't about neglecting the smaller tasks but rather about prioritising those that demanded immediate and significant attention.

Drawing on the principles of Dwight Eisenhower's time management approach, the Eisenhower Box method helps you navigate your daily tasks with clarity and priority. This structured method sorts tasks into four specific categories, enabling you to tackle your days with strategic precision and effectiveness. Here's how it works:

1. **Important & Urgent (Box 1)**: These tasks are the day's top priorities. Due to their urgency and significance, they demand immediate action. Addressing these first ensures that critical deadlines are met and pivotal issues are managed promptly. These are the tasks that drive forward your personal and professional goals, and that have a deadline they necessitate urgent action.

2. **Urgent but Not Important (Box 2)**: These tasks require quick attention but have little long-term impact. They should be handled swiftly and efficiently to avoid becoming distractions. However, they should never overshadow the tasks in Box 1. It is important to recognise that these tasks should be delegated to another team member or even ignored if they are not important to your aims and objectives.

3. **Important but Not Urgent (Box 3)**: These are essential for long-term success and require deliberate planning and thoughtful execution. By scheduling dedicated time for these tasks, you ensure continuous progress on strategic goals without the pressure of an immediate deadline.

4. **Neither Important Not Urgent (Box 4)**: The lowest priority tasks, these are not crucial to your daily productivity or long-term goals. They should be tackled only if time permits and often, they can be set aside or even removed from your list altogether to streamline your focus. These tasks can be wasteful distractions and should be ditched whenever possible.

The Eisenhower Box

IMPORTANT

U R G E N T	1—Urgent and important	2—Urgent but not important
	3—Important but not urgent	4—Neither important nor urgent

By categorising tasks this way, prioritisation becomes straightforward. This method not only aids in recognising what needs your immediate attention but also in identifying what can wait or be delegated. This clear segmentation helps you maintain focus on tasks that propel you towards your goals, minimising wasted time and effort on low-impact activities.

Before adopting the Eisenhower Box method, my days were a mosaic of disorganisation, characterised by an erratic and exhausting schedule. Each morning, I plunged into a sea of meetings, often scheduled back-to-back without any strategic consideration for my time or energy levels. This relentless pace left little room for focused, task-oriented work, pushing me to extend my professional responsibilities into the evenings. Such an approach not only diminished my productivity during regular work hours but also encroached severely on my personal life. Nights that should have been reserved for rest and family time were instead consumed by attempts to catch up on unfinished tasks, leaving me feeling perpetually behind and disconnected from those I cared about.

The change began with a simple yet profound adjustment to my daily planning. I started each day by reviewing my Eisenhower Box, focusing on tasks categorised as 'Important & Urgent'. This methodical approach allowed me to tackle the most critical tasks during my peak productive hours, significantly reducing the need for late evening work. By prioritising these tasks, I ensured that my energy was directed towards activities with the highest impact, enhancing overall productivity and reducing overtime.

Creating a daily schedule became about more than just slotting in meetings; it was about the intentional design of my day. I began to incorporate dedicated blocks of time for specific tasks, aligned not only with my professional objectives but also with my personal energy rhythms. This structured flexibility included strategic breaks to recharge and periods for low-intensity tasks to ensure sustained productivity throughout the day. By respecting my natural workflow and allowing for downtime, I could maintain a high level of efficiency without the burnout that once seemed inevitable.

This newfound approach had a transformative effect on both my work output and my personal satisfaction. Work became a space of achievement rather than a source of stress. I managed to complete my tasks within designated hours, which brought a profound sense of accomplishment and control. At home, the extra hours gained from efficient time management were invested back into my family and personal hobbies, which greatly enhanced our relationships and my overall well-being. This balance between professional obligations and personal life created a more harmonious daily existence, leading to greater happiness and reduced stress.

Adopting structured time management strategies, such as the Eisenhower Box, revolutionised how I approached each day. This strategy not only improved my professional life by maximising productivity and efficiency but also enriched my personal life by restoring time for what truly matters. By prioritising effectively and respecting my need for balance, I was able to transform overwhelming chaos into a fulfilling and manageable routine. This method proves that, with the right tools and mindset, it is possible to master the art of time management, leading to a more productive and enjoyable life.

Mastering Time Allocation

Eliud Kipchoge, the Kenyan long-distance runner, who broke the two-hour barrier for the marathon, an achievement once considered beyond human reach, attributes much of his success to meticulous planning and disciplined time management.

Kipchoge's daily routine is a study in precision. Every aspect of his training, from the intensity and duration of his runs to his rest periods and recovery sessions, is carefully planned and executed. He understands that each element of his preparation, no matter how small, plays a critical role in his performance. This approach to time allocation extends beyond his physical training to include mental preparation, nutrition, and even time spent with family, ensuring a balanced life that supports his athletic goals.

Kipchoge's strategy mirrors the 'first eat the frog' principle, often tackling his most challenging training sessions early in the day when his physical and mental energy is at its peak. This disciplined approach ensures that he can face the rest of his day with a sense of accomplishment, knowing that he has already conquered the hardest part of his training.

The result of Kipchoge's meticulous time allocation and prioritisation is not just evident in his record-breaking run, but in the consistency of his performances over the years. He has remained at the pinnacle of long-distance running, a feat that requires not just talent and hard work but the strategic allocation of time and resources.

Kipchoge's journey is a compelling example for anyone striving to achieve their best, whether in sports, business, or personal endeavours. It demonstrates that success is not just about the quantity of time spent but the quality of its use. His story inspires us to view our own routines through a lens of strategic planning and disciplined execution, reminding us that mastering time allocation is key to unlocking our full potential.

In my pursuit of transformational success, mastering the art of time allocation has been pivotal. When multiple tasks are critical and each minute counts, time allocation ensures continuous and consistent progress. My approach starts after identifying the six most important tasks of the day. I then allocate a specific amount of time to each task, involving a careful assessment of each task's importance and urgency, bearing in mind the principle of 'first eat the frog'.

For larger tasks that couldn't be completed in a single day, I adopted a multi-day strategy. This involves breaking down the task into manageable daily segments. The amount of time dedicated to each task was a reflection of its importance and urgency, with the most critical tasks receiving the largest time blocks.

Flexibility was a key component of this strategy. I made sure that the time dedicated to priority tasks didn't exceed 75% of my available workday. This buffer was crucial for accommodating unexpected challenges and interruptions, similar to how a military strategist reserves resources for unforeseen events in a war. If a task took longer than anticipated, this buffer allowed me to adjust my schedule accordingly without disrupting the entire day's plan. And, I didn't hesitate to ask for assistance with tasks that proved too daunting to handle alone.

My schedule became a strategic map, with each task a critical mission. Prioritising the most important and challenging tasks first was important because it ensured I tackled them when my mental and physical resources were at their highest. Incorporating breaks between tasks, typically 15 to 30 minutes, served two purposes: they provided time for rest and strategic reassessment and acted as buffers for unexpected interruptions or adjustments.

Minimising distractions during focused work time was essential, just as undivided attention is necessary for success in any game. I also allocated specific times in my day for brief questions and impromptu meetings, understanding the importance of team dynamics and quick consultations. Regular, well-structured team meetings functioned as strategic alignment sessions, keeping us focused and efficient.

Unexpected interruptions were handled promptly, and the built-in buffer times were instrumental in getting back on track without derailing the entire day's plan. By treating my schedule as a strategic map where each task was a mission with its own time slot and priority, I transformed what was once a source of stress into a manageable and even enjoyable process. This approach not only enhanced my productivity but also instilled a sense of control and accomplishment in my daily work.

In my quest for transformational success, mastering the art of time allocation has been a crucial strategy. Each task is a critical move in the direction of my most important goals, and every minute is valuable. Here's how I tackled the challenge of time allocation:

- **Allocating Time to Top Priorities.** As discussed before, identifying the top six tasks of my day was just the beginning. The next crucial step was allocating a specific amount of time to each task. This required a thoughtful assessment of each task's importance and urgency, ensuring the most critical tasks received the attention they deserved.

- **Strategising Large Tasks.** For larger tasks, employ a multi-day strategy. I estimated the total time needed and then broke it down into daily, manageable segments.

- **Building Flexibility and Contingency Plans.** Flexibility is key in time management. Ensure that the time dedicated to priority tasks doesn't exceed 75% of your available workday. Leave a buffer for unexpected challenges and interruptions.

- **Adapting and Collaborating.** When tasks take longer than expected, the buffer time allows for adjustments without disrupting the entire day's plan. Don't hesitate to ask for help when needed.

- **Strategic Scheduling.** Treat your schedule as a strategic plan, where each task is a key operation in a strategic mission. Assess time-bound tasks first, altering the sequence of operations as needed.

- **Incorporating Breaks and Flexibility.** Scheduled breaks between tasks provide much-needed rest and space for strategic reassessment. These pauses also act as buffers for unplanned interruptions or adjustments.

- **Minimise Distractions.** Ensuring focused work time with minimal interruptions is crucial. Even small interruptions break the flow of focused work and take valuable time away from being productive.

- **Time for Team Dynamics.** Allocating specific times for brief interactions and impromptu meetings maintains team dynamics without derailing your main tasks.

- **Effective Team Meetings.** Regular, well-structured team meetings functioned as strategic alignment sessions, keeping you focused and efficient. But, every meeting must have a start time, end time, agenda and clear objectives that are known to all before they start.

- **Dealing with Unplanned Interruptions.** Unexpected interruptions will always happen from time to time and must be handled promptly, with buffer times helping to return to the planned schedule swiftly.

By treating your schedule as a strategic map, each task becomes a mission with its own priority and time slot. This approach not only boosts your productivity but also brings a sense of control and accomplishment to your work, transforming a potential source of stress into an efficient and enjoyable process.

By adopting a focused and strategic approach to my tasks, I experienced transformative changes that reshaped my daily life, both at work and at home. Initially overwhelmed by endless tasks, I found that prioritising my work and adopting a flexible schedule led to a remarkable boost in my productivity during office hours. This efficiency meant I no longer needed to extend my working day late into the evenings, freeing up precious time previously lost.

With this newfound time, I was able to dedicate more quality moments to my family. I became more present and engaged during these times because I applied the same structured approach to my personal life as I did at work. Planning family activities with the same importance as work tasks ensured they received the attention and time they deserved, making these moments richer and more fulfilling.

Moreover, I noticed a significant decrease in my stress levels. The clarity and organisation provided by my daily planning, reduced the anxiety of juggling multiple tasks, giving me a sense of control over my schedule. This not only made my day-to-day life more manageable but also improved my decision-making abilities. With the most challenging tasks tackled early, when my mental energy was at its peak, I experienced less decision fatigue, leading to better choices and outcomes in all facets of my life.

Strategic time allocation also brought me a greater sense of accomplishment. Completing tasks efficiently and seeing tangible progress at the end of each day boosted my confidence and motivation. This sense of achievement didn't just stay confined to my work life; it spilt over into my personal endeavours, encouraging me to explore new hobbies and learning opportunities that enriched my life further.

A structured and prioritised approach to time management can profoundly impact your quality of life and results. It enhances your work productivity and focus and significantly improves your personal life, allowing you to enjoy a more balanced, fulfilling, and stress-free lifestyle. Transform your overwhelming schedule into a harmonious blend of productivity and personal satisfaction.

First, Eat the Frog

The principle of "First, Eat the Frog" has been a game-changer in my productivity toolkit. This powerful concept, inspired by Mark Twain and popularised by productivity guru Brian Tracy, suggests that you tackle your most daunting or unpleasant task—the 'frog'—right at the start of your day. These are the tasks that would normally cause you to procrastinate. Get them out of the way first and fast. Imagine clearing the tallest hurdle first thing in the morning; what follows seems much less daunting. This isn't just about conquering challenges;

it's about setting a tone of achievement and momentum from the moment your day begins.

I, too, struggled with procrastination, especially when facing tasks that I found daunting or unappealing. These 'frogs' often caused unnecessary stress and a looming sense of dread over my day. By scheduling these challenging tasks first, I transformed my mornings. Tackling the toughest parts of my to-do list early meant that nothing else could hold me back. The result? My days ended on a victorious note, filled with a profound sense of accomplishment.

This methodology does more than streamline your day—it enhances your decision-making capabilities. Research suggests that our willpower depletes as the day progresses, so handling the most demanding tasks while our cognitive resources are fresh makes us vastly more effective. This strategic use of energy maximises both productivity and satisfaction.

But it's not all about hard tasks. Balancing the frogs with tasks that bring joy ensures that work remains enjoyable and sustainable. This balanced approach has helped me forge a daily rhythm that nurtures both my productivity and personal happiness. By embedding enjoyment into the structure of my day, I stave off burnout and remain consistently motivated.

Adopting the "First, Eat the Frog" principle is more than a mere time management tactic—it is a profound shift in mindset. It compels us to face our biggest challenges head-on and harness our peak morning energy, paving the way for not only a productive day but also a fulfilling one. This approach doesn't just move tasks from 'pending' to 'done'—it transforms them into stepping stones towards greater personal and professional fulfilment.

By integrating this practice into your life, you embrace a proactive stance against procrastination. It's about making a conscious decision every day, not just to manage but master your time. This mindset doesn't just prepare you for the day; it sets you up for success in life. It's a commitment to facing obstacles bravely and improving continuously, ensuring that each morning contributes to a richer, more productive life.

So, why not start tomorrow? Identify your frog for the day and do it first. It could be anything from a difficult email, a complex report, or even a tough conversation. Whatever it is, tackle it head-on. You'll find that with the frog out of the way, the rest of your day unfolds with more ease and possibility.

Remember, the goal isn't just to complete tasks, but to create a life that feels as rewarding as it is productive. By mastering this principle, you not only enhance your daily output but also enrich your overall life experience, proving that how you start your day can indeed transform how you view and live your life.

First Things First

Following on from First, Eat the Frog, there is another factor that must govern the order of your to-do list. This ensures you are building a foundation of success in your day–Putting First Things First.

The world-renowned New Zealand national rugby team, the All Blacks, is known for its dominance on the rugby field. Their success is not just a product of physical prowess, but a testament to their strategic prioritisation and mental preparation.

The All Blacks stand as a towering figure in the realm of international rugby. Their name is synonymous with excellence, discipline, and an unparalleled winning legacy. Their impressive statistics and achievements paint a picture of a team that not just competes but dominates on the world stage. With a winning percentage of 77.12% across 612 Tests since 1903, they hold the highest success rate of any men's rugby team. Their prowess is further highlighted by their three Rugby World Cup victories in 1987, 2011, and 2015—a record no other men's team has matched. Beyond the World Cup, their dominance extends to regional competitions, with 10 Tri-Nations trophies and seven Rugby Championships under their belt, along with a 20-year reign holding the Bledisloe Cup from 2003 to 2023. Since the introduction of the World Rugby rankings in October 2003, the All Blacks have maintained the number one position for over 80% of the time, further cementing their legacy with seven consecutive World Rugby Team of the Year titles from 2010 to 2016. With a total of 2,552 points scored in Rugby World Cup history, the All Blacks' record is not just impressive; it's unparalleled.

In the context of such staggering achievements, the All Blacks' approach to time management and prioritisation—especially their principle of "First Things First"—offers invaluable insights. This principle, integral to their strategy on and off the field, has been a cornerstone of their consistent success and can serve as a powerful lesson for anyone aiming to excel in their endeavours.

At the core of the All Blacks' philosophy is a principle they call "sweeping the sheds." Despite their global fame and numerous victories, every player is responsible for cleaning their locker room after games. This task, seemingly menial for elite athletes, is a profound exercise in humility and prioritisation. It instils a culture where no task is beneath anyone, and the focus on the team's welfare is paramount. This approach ensures that every action, no matter how small, is aligned with the team's broader goals of unity, discipline, and excellence.

Furthermore, the All Blacks' preparation for matches showcases their mastery of prioritisation. They focus intensely on the most crucial aspects of their game plan, dedicating significant time to studying their opponents, identifying key areas where they can exploit weaknesses, and sharpening their skills in those specific domains. This targeted approach means that when game day arrives, the team has honed its efforts on what will truly make a difference on the scoreboard.

The All Blacks also prioritise mental toughness and resilience, conducting meetings where players share personal stories, vulnerabilities, and goals. This practice strengthens their bond and collective focus, ensuring that when they face challenges on the field, they are mentally prepared to overcome them together.

The results of this "First Things First" strategy speak for themselves. The All Blacks are not just a team with an impressive win record; they are a symbol of excellence, discipline, and strategic mastery in sports. Their approach demonstrates how focusing on the right priorities, both on and off the field, can lead to unparalleled success.

The All Blacks' story is a powerful reminder that success in any field, be it sports, business, or personal development, begins with mastering the art of prioritisation. By focusing on what truly matters and maintaining discipline in every action, achieving greatness is not just possible but inevitable.

The principle of "First Things First" transcends being merely a statement; it has become a cornerstone of my daily routine, a reminder that true efficiency springs from tackling the most critical tasks at the outset. This guiding philosophy, while simple in theory, presents its real challenge in application. Our minds, naturally gravitating towards comfort, often tempt us to address less demanding tasks first, pushing the vital ones down the list. However, I've discovered that succumbing to this inclination leads down a path of inefficiency and missed opportunities.

Consider the task of cold calling in sales, a task that many dread due to its challenging nature. Recognising its importance in driving business growth, I committed to facing this task head-on each morning. Instead of focusing on the volume of calls, I set specific, outcome-oriented goals for each session, such as pinpointing a certain number of potential prospects or securing meetings. This strategy didn't just make the process more manageable; it infused it with a sense of purpose and achievement.

At the heart of this approach lies the 80/20 rule, or the Pareto Principle, which posits that 80% of our outcomes are derived from 20% of our efforts. Embracing this principle meant rigorously analysing my tasks to identify the crucial 20% that would yield the most significant results. It involved differentiating between what is merely 'urgent' and what is genuinely 'important,' ensuring that my efforts were consistently focused on activities with the highest impact.

I started to view my task list as a strategic game, where each decision was carefully weighed for its potential to drive substantial outcomes. This gamification of my workflow introduced an element of challenge and engagement, transforming the mundane task completion into a quest for maximising impact.

The benefits of adopting this prioritisation strategy were manifold. Not only did it elevate my productivity, but it also brought an increased sense of fulfilment and accomplishment. Tasks that once seemed daunting became attainable, instilling a profound sense of control and purpose in my professional life.

Embracing the "First Things First" mantra is transformative in mastering time management and productivity. It aligns our daily endeavours with our overarching goals, ensuring that every step taken is a deliberate move towards achieving our aspirations. As we delve further into the strategies outlined in this book, let's remember that the journey to success starts with prioritising the right tasks at the right time, ensuring that our efforts are not just busy work but steps towards meaningful achievements.

The principle of "First Things First" will have a profound impact on your life. Once I was overwhelmed by the ceaseless demands of my business and personal life, I was constantly playing catch-up, my days were a blur of unsorted tasks and dwindling deadlines. Embracing the "First Things First" principle, was a move that reshaped my daily existence from the ground up.

By identifying the most critical tasks each day and addressing these first, I began to experience immediate changes. This wasn't merely about sorting my to-do list; it was a strategic approach to my entire day, focusing my energies where they could make the most significant impact. The daunting tasks that once loomed large became manageable, tackled with fresh morning resolve before they could become monsters in my mind.

This shift in strategy brought clarity and a sense of accomplishment that fuelled the rest of my day. Tasks that I had dreaded, like the sales cold calls, transformed from insurmountable barriers to stepping stones towards my goals. By applying the 80/20 rule, I honed in on activities that delivered the most value, ensuring my efforts were not just busy work but genuinely productive endeavours.

The ripple effects of this newfound focus were profound. In my professional life, my productivity soared, I accomplished more with less, my workdays no longer stretching into the night. This efficiency bled into my personal life as well, where I found myself with more time for family, hobbies, and relaxation. The evenings once lost to work were now opportunities for rejuvenation and connection.

Moreover, this approach to prioritisation brought a newfound sense of control over my life. The stress and anxiety that had once clouded my days began to dissipate, replaced by a confident calm. I no longer felt at the mercy of my schedule but rather in command, guiding my days with purpose and intention.

The "First Things First" principle goes beyond choosing the tasks to complete, it is also reflected in the importance you place on things, not on your to-do list. With the All Blacks, they placed importance on emotions and cleaning their locker room at the end of the game. These do not seem as though they will impact their performance on the pitch, but they do. Likewise, in your own life, how important is your family, your colleagues' well-being, your health and your fitness? All these elements have an impact on your success. This book is about building your life, not just about goals.

Prioritisation underscores that, with the right focus, anyone can turn the tide and overwhelm and reclaim their time, energy, and life. By mastering the art of "First Things First," you will not only enhance your productivity but also enrich your life, embodying the change that is possible when you align your daily actions with your most vital goals.

Touch It Once

Elon Musk, the CEO of SpaceX and Tesla, is known for his groundbreaking work in electric cars, space exploration, and renewable energy. His ability to manage multiple, high-stakes projects simultaneously is legendary. Central to his efficiency is a rigorous application of the "Touch It Once" principle, which he integrates seamlessly into his workday to ensure maximum productivity and focus.

Musk's approach to emails—an often overwhelming source of distraction for many leaders—is illustrative of this principle. He is known for his quick, decisive action on each message he receives, making immediate decisions on what needs his attention, what can be delegated, and what can be dismissed. This method allows him to avoid the common trap of re-reading and postponing, which can significantly eat into valuable time and mental bandwidth.

Moreover, Musk's scheduling strategy reflects the "Touch It Once" ethos. He breaks his day into a series of five-minute slots, each meticulously planned to ensure that every task, meeting, or piece of information is addressed once and with full attention. This disciplined approach to time management ensures that he can navigate the immense complexity of his responsibilities without falling into the inefficiency of handling tasks multiple times.

His success is not just a result of his visionary ideas but also his mastery of effective work habits. By applying the "Touch It Once" principle, he demonstrates how maintaining focus and taking decisive action can lead to unparalleled achievements. His example serves as a powerful inspiration for anyone looking to enhance their productivity and impact, showing that with the right strategies, even the busiest individuals can manage their time effectively and pursue their goals with unrelenting focus.

Adopting the 'Touch It Once' principle marked a pivotal shift in how I approached my daily tasks and managed information, sparking a revolution in my workflow and productivity. This method, centred around the philosophy of making each interaction with a task or piece of information count, reshaped my entire routine. The awakening came upon realising that the average business person squanders a significant amount of time, over a month each year, just by revisiting and re-reading information. This cycle of inefficiency, characterised by briefly scanning emails or documents and deferring them for future action, not only drains time but also mental energy.

The breakthrough was found in decisive, immediate action. Be it jotting down a note, responding succinctly, or beginning a draft, the objective was clear: eliminate the need to circle back to the same task or information. This approach didn't just cut down on time wastage; it also decluttered my mind, paving the way for heightened focus and efficiency.

My path to cultivating more productive habits was built on several foundational strategies. First, immediately organising all files—digital and physical—with precise, clear labelling made retrieving information seamless and intuitive. I tackled the constant barrage of email notifications by dedicating specific times for email review, thus safeguarding my concentration on more pressing tasks. The critical choice between acting immediately or delegating tasks streamlined my workflow. Tasks that can be dealt with swiftly and immediately and completed there and then, while those necessitating more time or better suited to others' expertise were assigned out. This strategy not only optimised task management but also encouraged a spirit of teamwork and collaboration.

The transformation brought about by the 'Touch It Once' principle extended far beyond mere productivity enhancements; it fundamentally altered my work and life approach. It served as a potent reminder that even minor, consistent shifts in our habits could drive remarkable change. Embracing the 'Touch It Once' philosophy is about more than reaching our goals—it's about exceeding our own expectations with unparalleled efficiency and clarity. Before this change, I found myself constantly swamped by a never-ending stream of tasks, my days a repetitive cycle of opening emails, skimming documents, and then setting them aside for later—a later that seemed to never come. This routine not only ate into my productivity but also left me feeling perpetually behind, trapped in a cycle of inefficiency and mental clutter. As I started by tackling emails with decisive action—replying, delegating, or deleting on the spot. Documents were read and processed immediately, decisions were made without unnecessary delay, and each piece of information was handled just once. This approach dramatically cut down on the time spent re-reading or reconsidering tasks and significantly reduced my mental load, clearing the way for a more focused and efficient workflow. The impact of this change was immediate and far-reaching. My workdays became more productive, allowing me to accomplish my tasks within normal working hours and freeing my evenings from the grip of extended work. This newfound efficiency opened up space for what truly mattered to me—spending quality time with my children, pursuing hobbies, and caring for my well-being. By applying the "Touch It Once" principle, I not only transformed my professional life but also achieved a more fulfilling and balanced personal life.

There is a ripple effect of adopting the "Touch It Once" principle. My colleagues noticed the change in my productivity and overall demeanour. They too began to adopt this approach, leading to a more efficient, collaborative, and motivated work environment. The transformation from being overwhelmed by tasks to mastering them with confidence and clarity became a source of inspiration, demonstrating the power of immediate action in creating meaningful change.

The "Touch It Once" principle illustrates that significant improvements in our lives often start with small, consistent actions. By choosing to tackle tasks immediately, we can break free from the cycle of procrastination and inefficiency, paving the way for greater achievements, satisfaction, and balance.

Organise It!

The "Organise It!" principle can be found in the work habits of Marie Kondo, the world-renowned organising consultant and author. Kondo's method, known as the KonMari method, has not only transformed homes around the globe but also offers profound lessons in efficiency and focus that apply beyond personal spaces to the business world.

Marie Kondo's philosophy centres on keeping only those items that "spark joy," a principle that also extends into her professional life. For Kondo, organisation is not just about tidiness but about intentional living and working. She applies this ethos to her business by meticulously organising her tasks, commitments, and digital spaces to ensure that every aspect of her work aligns with her core values and goals.

For instance, Kondo's approach to emails and documents mirrors her method for decluttering physical spaces. She keeps her digital files meticulously categorised and purges anything that is no longer relevant or necessary, ensuring that her work environment—both physical and digital—is conducive to productivity and devoid of unnecessary distractions. This disciplined approach to organisation allows her to focus her energy on activities that are meaningful and aligned with her objectives, such as writing, speaking engagements, and developing her brand.

Moreover, Kondo's success in building a global brand is a testament to the power of the "Organise It!" principle. By delegating tasks that do not require her direct involvement and building a team that shares her vision and commitment to organisation, Kondo has been able to expand her influence far beyond individual consulting, reaching millions through her books, Netflix series, and online content.

Marie Kondo's application of her organising principles to her professional life illustrates how effective organisation can lead to significant achievements. Her ability to distil her goals into actionable, joy-sparking activities and eliminate the superfluous has not only made her a global icon in personal organisation but also a highly successful businesswoman. Kondo's story is a powerful reminder that organising our tasks, our time, and our priorities is a critical step toward realising our ambitions, inspiring anyone looking to bring more order and focus into their professional endeavours.

Embracing organisation transformed my approach to both life and work, underscoring its role not just as a skill but as a fundamental pillar of achievement. Disorganisation, I learned through personal and second-hand experiences, is far more than an inconvenience—it's a barrier to success, capable of causing significant setbacks. Stories of missed vacations due to an expired passport or frantic searches for essential items leading to missed flights highlighted the steep cost of disorganisation, showing that the stakes could be much higher than mere frustration.

The journey to becoming organised began with establishing systems, the backbone of effective organisation. At home, a simple yet transformative strategy for bill management involved noting due dates and sorting bills into 'unpaid' and 'paid' files, ensuring timely payments and avoiding the consequences of oversight. Similarly, assigning a designated spot for crucial items like passports and car keys eradicated the anxiety and disruption of losing them, a lesson learned after a couple of lockouts.

In the workplace, the organisation extended to both digital and physical files, requiring the development of an intuitive system accessible to everyone in the company. Tailoring this system to fit the unique needs of the business was essential, proving that effective organisation respects the individual structure and requirements of each context.

Facing incomplete tasks and the overwhelm of large projects necessitated a shift in strategy. Understanding that not completing a task is merely a step in the process, I learned to adapt by adjusting schedules, seeking help, or starting earlier. Breaking down large projects into manageable steps and scheduling time for each transformed overwhelming tasks into a series of achievable actions, making progress less daunting and more tangible.

Incorporating gamification into my organisational strategy introduced a layer of engagement and fun, turning tasks and projects into levels in a game where each completion felt like a victory. This not only made the organisation process enjoyable but also fostered a sense of momentum and accomplishment.

I realised that organisation is more than a method—it's a mindset that, when embraced, can significantly optimise our efficiency and effectiveness. It's about converting chaos into order, complexity into simplicity, and unlocking our full potential. As we advance in our quest of "Winning the Game," it's clear that organisation is not just a tool but a secret weapon in achieving our goals, propelling us toward success with clarity and purpose.

Dump It!

Michael Jordan is arguably the greatest basketball player of all time. His illustrious journey is peppered with strategic choices that echo the essence of focusing on what truly matters and shedding the unnecessary, both on and off the court. Known for his unparalleled work ethic and focus, Jordan applied a version of the "Dump It!" philosophy by concentrating intensely on aspects of his game and professional life that would elevate his performance to legendary status. He famously cut out distractions that could impede his training or game-day preparation, dedicating his time and energy exclusively to activities that enhanced his skills, physical condition, and mental toughness.

One notable aspect of Jordan's career was the "Dump It!" The principle was vividly illustrated in his approach to criticism and failure. Rather than dwelling on negative feedback or past setbacks, Jordan chose to "dump" these as counterproductive, focusing instead on learning from these experiences to improve. This mindset allowed him to bounce back from challenges with even greater determination, a testament to his psychological resilience and focus.

Moreover, Jordan's commitment to prioritising was evident in his training regimen. He identified areas of his game that needed improvement and dedicated himself to refining those skills, effectively "dumping" any complacency towards his natural talents. This relentless pursuit of excellence, prioritising the development of a well-rounded skill set, was fundamental to his success and his six NBA championships with the Chicago Bulls.

The "Dump It!" principle also manifested in how Jordan managed his commitments outside of basketball. He was selective in his endorsements and business ventures, ensuring that each aligned with his values and long-term goals. This selectiveness allowed him to build a brand that was authentic and aligned with his identity as an athlete and a person, maximising his impact both on and off the court.

Michael Jordan's application of the "Dump It!" principle—his ability to focus relentlessly on what mattered most and let go of the rest—offers an inspiring blueprint for success. It shows how anyone, in sports, business, or any area of life, can achieve greatness by concentrating their efforts on what truly drives progress, learning to let go of what doesn't serve their ultimate objectives.

Embracing the principle of "Dump It!" revolutionised my approach to managing information and tasks, teaching me the invaluable skill of discerning what truly matters and eliminating everything else. In today's world, where information overload is a constant challenge, understanding how to navigate through the noise to focus on what's essential has become crucial. Decades of research into "data hoarding" has shown that both businesses and individuals tend to hold on to far more information than they actually use. A study conducted by the IT research firm Gartner estimated that 80% of the data stored by businesses is never used again after its initial capture. This includes emails, documents, and other forms of information that, once filed away, is never retrieved. This accumulation not only hinders access to important information but also squanders time in maintenance and retrieval.

The transformative question I began to ask myself was simple: "Will it kill me to dump this?" Surprisingly, the answer was almost always no. Whether dealing with physical clutter or digital excess, purging unnecessary items created a streamlined, efficient system that significantly improved my workflow.

Email management became a prime example of this efficiency in action. By archiving emails older than six months and regularly clearing out the outdated archives, my inbox transformed into a space for current relevance, not a repository of the past. This method kept me focused on the present, ensuring that I wasn't bogged down by information no longer pertinent to my needs.

This philosophy echoes the wisdom of Steve Jobs, who famously emphasised the importance of innovation through refusal, teaching that true innovation involves saying 'no' to a thousand things. This principle became a guiding light for me, reinforcing that focus isn't just about pursuing your primary goal, but also about the resolve to turn away from distractions. Managing multiple ventures taught me that effectiveness doesn't come from juggling numerous projects but from prioritising, delegating, and empowering a capable team to excel in their domains, allowing me to direct my energies toward what demands my direct input.

The art of saying 'no' emerged as a vital skill, safeguarding my time and, by extension, respecting the time of others. Being selective with commitments meant that my time was seen as valuable, with people approaching me only with issues of real significance.

One of the most significant lessons I've learned is the power of concentrating on one major goal at a time. In an ambitious flurry, I once tried to learn a new language, master piano, and kick-start a side hustle all at once, only to find myself too scattered to excel in any. By choosing to focus on one objective, I was able to achieve mastery and effectiveness, proving that sometimes, letting go is the path to genuinely grasping what we seek. This journey of simplification and focus has been about achieving goals and cultivating a life of purpose and clarity.

For me, embracing the "Dump It!" principle was nothing short of transformative. Before this pivotal change, my life was a maze of clutter—mental, digital and physical—that constantly dragged my focus away from my true goals. Emails piled up, unread documents cluttered my workspace, and my commitments stretched me thin, leaving me feeling perpetually overwhelmed and unfocused.

The "Dump It!" principle taught me the value of simplicity and focus, leading to a more organised, efficient, and fulfilling life. It illustrates that courageously letting go of what doesn't serve us makes room for growth, success, and a greater sense of fulfilment.

Fun, Play, and Joy

Google, known for its innovative approach to technology and workplace culture, has consistently been ranked among the top places to work. This is largely due to its commitment to integrating fun and well-being into the very fabric of its operations.

At the heart of Google's campus are spaces dedicated to play and relaxation: from volleyball courts and bowling alleys to nap pods and on-site gardens. These facilities aren't mere perks; they are a testament to Google's belief in the power of joy, relaxation, and play as catalysts for creativity and productivity. Google understands that breakthrough ideas don't always come from staring at a computer screen but often emerge from moments of leisure and play. This philosophy is woven into their workday, where employees are encouraged to take breaks, engage in activities that bring them joy, and collaborate with colleagues in light-hearted, creative settings.

The impact of this approach is evident not just in the high morale and job satisfaction reported by Google employees but also in the groundbreaking products and services the company continues to produce. Google's success story underscores the principle that fun, play, and joy are not antithetical to hard work and achievement but are, in fact, essential components of sustained innovation and excellence.

This ethos, championed by one of the most successful companies in the world, serves as a potent reminder that creating a joyful work environment is not just possible; it's profitable. It illustrates that when companies invest in the happiness and well-being of their employees, they are not just improving lives but are also building a more dynamic, creative, and resilient organisation. Google's commitment to fostering an environment where fun and work are not mutually exclusive but mutually reinforcing offers an inspiring model for businesses everywhere, proving that joy and play can be serious business.

Finding the delicate balance between work and joy is not just beneficial; it's fundamentally necessary. Throughout my journey, I've come to understand that the true essence of life doesn't solely reside in relentless productivity or the achievement of milestones. It's equally about the moments of laughter that punctuate a team meeting, the unplanned coffee breaks that bring us together, and the celebration of small victories that often go unnoticed. Incorporating fun and joy into our daily lives, both professionally and personally, fosters an atmosphere ripe for both productivity and well-being.

In my quest to create a more harmonious work environment, I realised the importance of allowing for breaks and rewards amidst the hustle. This philosophy doesn't just benefit the atmosphere; it transforms it, breeding a culture of camaraderie and motivation. There's something magical about a workplace where team members genuinely enjoy their tasks—productivity doesn't just increase; it flourishes. It's about striking a balance where light-heartedness and laughter find their place alongside the seriousness of deadlines and strategies.

But life extends far beyond the confines of business. It's a rich tapestry of experiences, where joy can be found in the smallest of moments. I've learned to cherish the impromptu conversations, the shared laughter, and the collaborative brainstorming that often sparks the most innovative ideas. These moments of joy enrich our work life, making the path we tread as rewarding as the achievements that mark our progress.

As you venture into setting goals, it's crucial to recognise that these aren't just targets on a checklist. They represent waypoints on your larger journey, imbuing the process of striving and achieving with joy and passion, making every step towards them not just necessary but enjoyable. Even as you make challenging decisions and navigate the complexities of your aspirations, this ethos of joy and balance should remain your constant companion.

And when it comes to sustaining motivation, especially through tasks that might seem daunting or mundane, remember that you're not alone. It's a universal challenge, but one that can be overcome by celebrating your wins, no matter how small. This act of acknowledgement not only fuels your drive but also reminds you of the progress you're making, keeping the flame of motivation alive even in the face of adversity.

Imagine a football player scoring a goal. The stadium erupts in cheers, the player runs off in jubilation, arms aloft, maybe sliding on their knees across the grass. For a moment, their celebration is as exuberant as if they've just clinched the FA Cup. Yet, in reality, it's just one goal, one small win in the long journey of an entire season. But that celebration, that moment of unbridled joy for a single achievement, is crucial. It's a physical manifestation of recognising success, no matter how small, in the larger journey.

In our pursuit of larger goals, the significance of small victories can easily be overshadowed. However, acknowledging and celebrating these moments is a powerful source of motivation and joy. Each small win, be it completing a mundane task, making a sale, or simply ticking off a to-do item, is a step in the right direction and deserves to be recognised.

In a fast-paced world that constantly pushes us to achieve more, taking time to appreciate our own progress is vital. This practice grounds us in the present, enhances our sense of gratitude, and keeps our motivation burning bright. These small victories are the building blocks of success. They are tangible evidence of progress, commitment, and our ability to overcome the challenges of each day.

So, why not take a page from the football player's playbook? Celebrating doesn't have to be elaborate; it can be as simple as acknowledging your effort and success, taking a moment to do something you enjoy, or treating yourself to a small reward.

To help foster this positive mindset, here are 50 simple yet delightful ways to celebrate your daily successes and keep the flame of motivation alight. Each suggestion is crafted to bring a moment of joy, a sense of accomplishment, and a renewed drive to continue on your path toward achieving your larger dreams.

1. Take a Five-Minute Dance Break: Put on your favourite song and dance like nobody's watching.

2. Indulge in a Favourite Treat: Have a piece of chocolate or your favourite snack.

3. Take a Relaxing Bath: Add some bubbles or bath salts for extra luxury.

4. Savour a Cup of Speciality Coffee: Treat yourself to a gourmet coffee blend.

5. Write in Your Gratitude Journal: Jot down what you accomplished and how it made you feel.

6. Post Your Achievement on Social Media: Share your success with friends and family.

7. Take a Short, Relaxing Walk: Breathe in the fresh air and clear your mind.

8. Read a Chapter of a Book: Indulge in some literary escapism.

9. Watch a Funny Video: A good laugh is a perfect celebration.

10. Call a Friend or Family Member: Share your joy with someone you love.

11. Draw or Doodle: Unleash your creativity on paper.

12. Listen to a Motivational Podcast: Get inspired by others' success stories.

13. Play with a Pet: Spend some quality time with your furry friend.

14. Light a Scented Candle: Create a serene atmosphere.

15. Enjoy a Favourite Snack: Satisfy your taste buds.

16. Do a Quick Meditation Session: Re-centre and refocus your energy.

17. Take a Power Nap: Recharge with a short, refreshing nap.

18. Stretch or Do Yoga: Rejuvenate your body with some gentle exercise.

19. Plan a Fun Weekend Activity: Give yourself something to look forward to.

20. Phone a friend or family member: Spread the Joy.

21. Play a Quick Game: Engage in a short round of your favourite game.

22. Watch the Sunset or Sunrise: Connect with the beauty of nature.

23. Try a New Recipe: Experiment with cooking or baking something new.

24. Plant a Flower or Herb: Nurture life as a symbol of your growth.

25. Donate to a Favourite Charity: Make a difference as a form of celebration.

26. Take Some Creative Photos: Capture the world around you.

27. Listen to Your Favourite Song: Turn it up and enjoy.

28. Paint Your Nails: Add some colour to your day.

29. Visit a Local Park: Spend time in a green space.

30. Start a New TV Series Episode: Indulge in some screen time.

31. Write a Poem or Short Story: Channel your feelings into words.

32. Create a Vision Board: Visualise your future successes.

33. Practise a New Hobby: Spend time doing something you love.

34. Have a Picnic, Even Indoors: Change your dining routine.

35. Do a Random Act of Kindness: Spread the joy to others.

36. Rearrange Your Workspace: Refresh your environment.

37. Buy Yourself Flowers: Brighten up your space.

38. Do a Puzzle: Challenge your brain in a fun way.

39. Plan a Future Trip: Dream about your next adventure.

40. Learn Something New Online: Expand your knowledge.

41. Take Some Deep Breaths: Centre yourself with mindful breathing.

42. Write a Letter to Your Future Self: Reflect on your current achievements.

43. Organise a Small Space: Declutter for mental clarity.

44. Have a Mini Spa Moment: Pamper yourself with a face mask or foot soak.

45. Make a New Playlist: Compile songs that lift your spirits.

46. Watch a Documentary: Educate yourself on a topic of interest.

47. Craft Something: Engage in a hands-on creative project.

48. Watch a Sunrise or Sunset: Connect with the beauty of nature.

49. Try a New Exercise: Boost your endorphins with physical activity.

50. Simply Sit in Silence: Embrace the peace of doing nothing for a moment.

Remember, the path to big wins is paved with these smaller moments of triumph. By celebrating them, you not only acknowledge your progress but also boost your motivation to tackle the next challenge. So, go ahead, pick one (or a few) from this list and celebrate your daily victories in style!

After years of exhausting hard work and long hours that sapped me of energy and passion, I jumped at the opportunity to weave the threads of fun, play, and joy into the fabric of my everyday life, marking a departure from a life characterised by relentless pursuit and the heavy burden of unyielding productivity. This pivot towards incorporating elements of joy into my daily routine wasn't just a change of activity; it was a profound shift in mindset that touched every aspect of my life, both personal and professional.

Before this shift, I was trapped in a cycle of constant work, where the lines between professional obligations and personal time blurred, leaving little room for the spontaneous moments of joy that light up life. The realisation dawned on me that achieving milestones and accumulating successes were endeavours of diminishing returns if they didn't allow for the laughter shared among teammates, the impromptu breaks that refresh the spirit, and the celebration of both the monumental and the mundane victories along the way.

Embracing the principle of "Fun, play, and joy," I began to integrate moments of leisure and enjoyment into my workday strategically. I initiated team meetings with ice-breaker games to foster a sense of camaraderie, introduced "joke breaks" where team members could engage in an activity that made them and others laugh. These changes transformed the work environment from one of stress and deadlines to a space where creativity and productivity flourished amidst a culture of positivity and support.

The changes extended beyond the confines of the office. I rediscovered hobbies that I had long set aside in the name of work. I learned that moments spent reading for pleasure, exploring nature, or simply engaging in playful activities with my children were not wasted but were, in fact, investments in my well-being and happiness. This balanced approach to life and work brought a newfound vitality and enthusiasm that was contagious, inspiring those around me to also find joy in their endeavours.

True success is not measured solely by the achievements listed on our LinkedIn profile but by the joy we experience and share along the journey. By allowing ourselves to embrace joy, we not only enrich our own lives but also elevate those around us, creating a ripple effect of positivity and fulfilment.

These time management principles serve as quiet invitations to realign our daily practices with what genuinely matters to us. The path now leads us to the realm of decision-making, a landscape often met with apprehension. It's common to find the act of making decisions daunting, something many of us might shy away from or delay. Yet, mastering this subtle art is crucial for navigating life's complexities and carving out a path to success. Armed with the nuanced understanding of time we've cultivated, we're better positioned to face decision-making not as a source of fear but as an opportunity for growth. This next chapter doesn't just aim to explore decision-making in the abstract, but to offer a gentle guide through the process, recognising the challenges and embracing the potential it holds for transforming our lives.

CHAPTER 5

Setting the Sails

*"When someone makes a decision, he is really diving
into a strong current that will carry him to places he had
never dreamed of when he first made the decision."*
— Paulo Coelho

There is a modern-day phenomenon that tests our resolve at every turn: the paradox of choice. In an era marked by an unprecedented abundance of choices in every facet of life—from the careers we aspire to, to the myriad of products vying for our attention—this abundance, rather than liberating us, often ushers in feelings of overwhelm and anxiety. This paradox, a concept that Søren Kierkegaard, a pioneer in existential thought, wrestled with nearly two centuries ago, challenges us to navigate a sea of endless possibilities without losing sight of our true course.

Kierkegaard observed that stress emerges not from scarcity but from the overwhelming nature of our freedom to choose. With each choice carrying the weight of our hopes and the dread of missed opportunities, it's no wonder that many of us find ourselves adrift, paralysed by indecision. This dilemma, amplified in our contemporary world, turns even the simplest decisions into sources of anxiety and discontent.

However, Kierkegaard also provided a beacon of hope through this fog of choice: the realisation that our distress can be a catalyst for authentic living. By facing our angst head-on, we can learn to make decisions that resonate with our deepest values, rather than being swayed by the currents of societal expectations or the fear of missing out. This approach demands that we engage in a profound exploration of our desires, fears, and values, understanding that not all decisions hold the same weight and that liberation can be found in accepting our limitations.

To truly set our sails and navigate the paradox of choice, we must become adept at decision-making. It's an act of defiance against the paralysis that threatens to engulf us, a declaration of our agency in a world brimming with possibilities. Each decision we make is a testament to our existence, a step forward on the unique path we carve for ourselves. It's not about making the perfect choice from an endless array of options but about making choices that are unequivocally ours, each one a deliberate stroke in the painting of our lives.

The quote from Paulo Coelho illustrates the power of decisions as currents that carry us to unforeseen destinations, a testament to the transformative potential that lies in our choices. From the simplicity of selecting daily necessities to the complexity of life-altering financial choices, the decisions we face sculpt the chapters of our personal journey. Yet, the shadow of hesitation, the fear of erring in our choices, often paralyses us, coaxing us into a state of inaction. Echoing Tony Robbins' insight, it becomes clear: "It's in our moments of decision that our destiny is formed". Indecision, then, is not merely a stumble; it is a barrier to the evolution and transformation we seek.

As we delve into this chapter, let us embrace the complexity of our era's choices with both caution and courage. The simple strategies in this chapter offer a pragmatic exploration of decision-making to understand that the essence of our journey lies not in the multitude of paths that lay before us but in our capacity to choose with intention and purpose. By mastering the art of decision-making, we can transform the overwhelming ocean of choices into a navigable waterway, steering ourselves toward a life of meaning and fulfilment.

We will dissect the mechanisms of decision-making, understanding its pivotal role in the shaping of our destiny and learning how to harness it as a catalyst for growth. Transforming decision-making from a source of apprehension to a conduit of empowerment, we aim to demystify the process, making it a deliberate act of steering one's life towards desired outcomes. Each decision presents an opportunity to mould our journey, to consciously choose the paths that align with our deepest aspirations.

Approach these strategies with an open mind and a readiness to confront the decisions that await. This journey promises to refine our ability to navigate life's myriad choices, equipping us with the foresight to choose wisely and the courage to embrace the possibilities that our decisions unlock.

Embarking on my first business venture thrust me into the realm of decision-making much sooner and more forcefully than I had anticipated. As the founder and driving force behind my company, the buck stopped with me. In those early days, my team looked to me for direction—not because I was infallible, but because I was the one with the vision and the technical know-how that our young business depended on. The absence of seasoned experts in our ranks meant that deliberation was a luxury we couldn't afford; decisions had to be made, swiftly and decisively.

I vividly recall my first business partner's words, a mix of encouragement and stark reality: I was the sole navigator of our enterprise. His assertion that growth hinged on our willingness to make tough calls resonated deeply with me. It became clear that stagnation was the real enemy, and indecision was its closest ally. With this understanding,

I began to embrace my role not just as a decision-maker, but as the architect of our company's future.

This necessity to act, to choose a path at each crossroads, propelled me into a crash course in decision-making. It was on-the-job training in its purest form, learning by doing, with the stakes as high as the potential rewards. Through trial and error, successes and setbacks, I honed my ability to assess situations, weigh options, and commit to a course of action.

The strategies and principles outlined in this chapter are not abstract theories; they are the distilled essence of those formative experiences, coupled with the wisdom gained from books, mentors and courses. They represent the lessons learned in the crucible of entrepreneurship, where every decision carries the weight of potential outcomes. By applying these strategies, I was able to guide my business through turbulent waters to growth and prosperity.

This journey of learning to make decisions—boldly, wisely, and with an eye on the horizon—has been transformative. It taught me that decision-making is less about avoiding mistakes and more about seizing opportunities. Each choice, each commitment to a path forward, was a step toward realising the vision that drove me to start my business in the first place.

The art of decision-making is a skill to be developed, a muscle to be strengthened. These tools will empower you and help you navigate the challenges and opportunities of your endeavours. Whether you're leading a startup, steering a project, or simply looking to take more control of your personal journey, mastering the art of making decisions is foundational to achieving success and fulfilment.

Decision-making is at the heart of our daily lives, shaping our path in profound ways. Antonio Damasio's groundbreaking work has highlighted the essential role emotions play in this process, challenging the traditional view that decisions are made purely through logic. His insights, detailed in "Descartes' Error," reveal that our feelings significantly influence both our choices and their outcomes.

Building on this foundation, research by Daniel Kahneman, a Nobel Prize winner in Economic Sciences, introduced the concept of two systems of thought. In his book "Thinking, Fast and Slow," he describes System 1 as fast, instinctual, and emotional, and System 2 as slower, more deliberate, and logical. This dual-process theory helps us understand the complex interplay between instinct and reason in our decision-making.

The field of positive psychology, led by Martin Seligman, explores how decision-making ties into our well-being. Seligman's research suggests that the freedom to make our own choices is key to happiness and fulfilment. Being able to decide based on our values and goals gives us a sense of control and contributes to our overall well-being.

Neuroscience has also shed light on how our brains navigate decisions. Functional magnetic resonance imaging (fMRI) studies show that regions like the prefrontal cortex, responsible for planning and impulse control, and the amygdala, linked to emotions, are critical in the decision-making process. These findings provide a neural basis for the interconnection of emotion and reason in our choices.

Taken together, these studies offer a comprehensive view of decision-making. They uncover a process influenced by cognitive biases, emotional intelligence, well-being, and brain function. This knowledge doesn't just deepen our understanding of how we make choices; it equips us with the tools to make better decisions. By appreciating the intricate dance between our emotions and logic, we can navigate our lives with more awareness and purpose, leading to a more fulfilling and successful existence.

Winning the Game

At 13, huddled with my brothers around the Risk game board on a spring day that belied the approach of summer with its wintry chill, we unknowingly embarked on a masterclass in decision-making. Risk, with its grand strategy and battles for global supremacy, became more than a mere pastime. It evolved into a crucible where the skills of strategy, foresight, and diplomacy were not just honed but intertwined with the fabric of our growth, teaching us lessons that far transcended the confines of the game.

In this arena, alliances were forged and dissolved with the same ease as they might in the corridors of power, each moving a delicate balance between bold ambition and cautious diplomacy. A particularly memorable game unfolded, a microcosm of the broader lessons that Risk sought to impart. In the midst of battle, I allied with one brother against another, a tactical decision aimed at mutual benefit. Yet, the real lesson came not from the alliance but from its dissolution - a premature betrayal that exposed not just a vulnerability in my defences but a deeper insight into the nature of decision-making itself.

This unexpected defeat laid bare the intricate dance between logic and emotion that underpins every decision. My downfall was not merely a tactical error but a lesson in the sway that emotions hold over our choices. In the heat of competition, excitement clouded judgement, a misstep that my brother exploited with a keen understanding of timing and opportunity.

Reflecting on those afternoons spent in strategic combat, I recognise how Risk mirrored the complexities of real-life decisions. It was a sandbox for the mind, allowing us to experiment with strategies and confront the outcomes of our choices without real-world stakes. This safe space for decision-making, for testing the waters of strategy and consequence, imbued us with a deep appreciation for the nuanced interplay of thought and feeling in every choice we make.

Setting the Sails

These games taught us the value of perspective, of considering the long game over immediate gratification, and the importance of adapting to the evolving dynamics of any situation. The lessons learned at that game board, of strategy tempered with patience and the critical role of adaptability, have been a guiding light in navigating the complexities of life beyond the play.

Risk, in essence, was more than a game; it was a preparatory course for life's myriad challenges. It instilled in us the understanding that decision-making is as much about intuition as it is about logic. That success often lies in our ability to anticipate and adapt to the unforeseen. These lessons in strategy, risk management, and the importance of emotional intelligence have informed my approach to both personal and professional challenges, serving as a constant reminder that every decision, like every move on the Risk board, is a step towards shaping our destiny.

As I look back, I see the board game as a foundational experience, a formative journey through the art of decision-making. It was there, amid the clash for territories and the strategic tussle for supremacy, that we learned not just to play but to think, plan, and dream. Those afternoons of Risk became lessons in life, teaching us that every choice, no matter how small, influences the course of our journey, offering new paths to victory and success in the vast, unpredictable game of life.

In the realm of decision-making, the gathering and synthesis of information stand as the bedrock upon which sound decisions are built. It's about grasping the full spectrum of implications, understanding who will be affected, and contemplating the potential ripple effects of our choices. Too often, decisions are made within a narrow frame, resulting in outcomes that fall short of our intentions or potential. Broadening our lens, as advocated by Harvard Business School Professor Francesca Gino, is not merely a suggestion; it's a strategic imperative to counteract the biases that can cloud your judgement.

The distinction between what demands our immediate attention and what is genuinely important is another cornerstone of effective decision-making. Here, the Eisenhower Matrix shines as a beacon, guiding us to categorise tasks by their urgency and importance. This framework isn't just about managing time; it's a philosophical approach to life that empowers us to focus on what truly matters, ensuring our decisions lead us closer to our goals and values.

Moreover, the decision-making journey should seldom be walked alone. The richness of diverse perspectives cannot be overstated, as research on collective intelligence from MIT and Carnegie Mellon suggests. The synthesis of varied viewpoints often paves the way for more creative and robust solutions than those we might arrive at in isolation. This collaborative approach to decision-making harnesses the collective wisdom and experience of a group, leading to outcomes that are not only more informed but often more innovative.

Reflecting on my own journey, I've found that the decisions that later seemed misguided were often those made with incomplete information. There were times when, had I sought out more data or consulted more widely, the road taken might have led to a different destination. The advent of Google and, more recently, AI technologies, has transformed the landscape of decision-making, providing access to a vast expanse of knowledge and insights at our fingertips. This wealth of information, when approached with a discerning eye, enhances our ability to make informed decisions.

Incorporating these insights into my decision-making process has been transformative. It has taught me the value of pausing to gather information, consulting with others to gain different perspectives, and utilising tools like the Eisenhower Matrix to differentiate between the urgent and the essential. This approach has not only improved the quality of my decisions but has also made the process more rewarding.

As we navigate through the complexities of life, let us remember that each decision we make is a step on the path to our desired destination. By broadening our perspectives, prioritising effectively, and embracing the power of collective wisdom, we equip ourselves to make decisions that are not only informed but also inspired, guiding us toward a future that resonates with our deepest aspirations and values.

Once a decision is made, it requires unwavering commitment and the initiation of steps toward realising the chosen direction. The field of psychology offers profound insights into the aftermath of decision-making, particularly emphasising the crucial phase of implementation. This stage is pivotal not only for the fruition of decisions but also for safeguarding against the all-too-human tendency to falter in the face of uncertainty.

Psychologist and acclaimed author Susan Jeffers, in her influential book "Feel the Fear and Do It Anyway," delves into the interplay between decision-making, action, and the cultivation of personal confidence and clarity. Jeffers' work is a testament to the power of decisiveness, illustrating how the act of firmly committing to a decision—and subsequently acting upon it—can significantly bolster one's sense of self-assurance and purpose. Her insights suggest that the moment of decision is just the beginning; it's the steadfast pursuit of that decision that carves the path to true empowerment.

The inertia of the status quo, a comfortable yet stagnating force, often looms as a formidable barrier to action. This inertia is not merely a passive state but an active deterrent to growth and achievement. It's the gravitational pull that tempts us to remain in familiar territory, even when such territory no longer serves our aspirations or potential. Jeffers' teachings urge us to confront this inertia head-on, advocating for a proactive stance where immediate action following a decision is non-negotiable.

The significance of this approach cannot be overstated. In a world where opportunities and challenges coexist, the propensity to linger in the realm of 'what ifs' and 'maybe laters' can derail even the most well-intentioned plans. The act of decisively moving forward, therefore, is not just a step toward achieving specific goals; it's a declaration of one's commitment to personal growth and the relentless pursuit of fulfilment.

Susan Jeffers' message is a clarion call to break free from the shackles of hesitation and the seductive lure of the status quo. It's an invitation to embrace the dynamism of life by actively implementing the decisions we make, thereby transforming the abstract into the concrete. This philosophy champions the idea that decisiveness, coupled with action, is a formidable force—one that propels us toward clarity, confidence, and the realisation of our fullest potential.

As we navigate the complexities of life's myriad decisions, let us carry with us the wisdom of Susan Jeffers. Let her insights inspire us to not only make decisions with conviction but to act on them with determination, ever mindful of the transformative power of stepping boldly in the direction of our chosen paths. In doing so, we not only transcend the inertia of the status quo but also forge a legacy of purposeful action and unwavering resolve.

Jim Collins, a luminary in the field of business research and leadership, provides invaluable insights into decision-making and leadership within organisations. His groundbreaking work, notably in "Good to Great" and "Built to Last," offers a profound understanding of how leadership and strategic decisions can catapult organisations from mediocrity to unparalleled success. Collins delves into the essence of what propels companies to sustain excellence over time, emphasising that leadership transcends personal charisma or visionary prowess. It's about adopting disciplined principles that elevate decision-making to an art form.

A pivotal concept introduced by Collins is Level 5 leadership, which redefines leadership effectiveness. These leaders combine personal humility with indomitable professional will, focusing not on personal accolades but on the enduring success of their organisation. Their decision-making is rooted in this blend of humility and resolve, aiming not for short-term gains but for long-term sustainability and legacy.

Through the "Hedgehog Concept," Collins further illuminates the significance of simplicity in focus and decision-making. He posits that successful leaders, much like hedgehogs, concentrate on one overarching goal or principle, simplifying complex decisions and aligning them with the organisation's core purpose. This focused approach ensures that decisions are not mere reactions to fleeting trends but are deeply integrated with the organisational mission.

Collins's research underscores that exceptional leaders don't just respond to their environments; they actively shape them. Their decisions, grounded in disciplined thought and action, foster a culture of continuous improvement and innovation. These leaders are adept at confronting harsh realities while maintaining an unwavering belief in their eventual success, a balance that guides them in navigating through challenges.

In illustrating these principles, Collins showcases companies that have achieved greatness through strategic leadership and decision-making. These organisations exemplify how effective leadership, characterised by deliberate, value-aligned decisions and a steadfast commitment to growth, can forge a path to lasting excellence.

Jim Collins's contributions to understanding leadership and decision-making in business are both inspiring and practical. He offers a blueprint for leaders aspiring to make impactful decisions that not only drive immediate results but also secure a legacy of success. His work is a compelling call to action for leaders to cultivate a deep sense of purpose, embrace disciplined decision-making, and lead their organisations to greatness with humility and strategic foresight.

However, even the best decision-making processes are not without their challenges. In a world that evolves at an unprecedented pace, flexibility becomes key. Peter Drucker, a renowned expert in the management field, emphasised the importance of leaders being able to pivot and adapt their strategies in response to new insights and shifts in the environment.

At the heart of impactful decision-making is the alignment with one's vision and core purpose. It's this alignment that ensures our choices not only make sense in the moment but also contribute to our long-term objectives, steering us closer to where we want to be.

Becoming proficient in decision-making requires a commitment to ongoing learning. By continually refining our decision-making skills and sharing this knowledge within our circles, we cultivate a community adept at making wise choices, thereby elevating our collective capacity for success.

Navigating the journey of life, and especially leadership, involves much more than just deciding when to act. It also involves understanding when it's wise to hold back, to wait for the right moment, or to gather more information. This discernment between action and inaction is a subtle art that can mean the difference between success and failure. It's about setting our sails just right, so we can catch the winds of opportunity and sail through the uncertainties that life inevitably throws our way, with confidence and precision.

The Difference Between a Decision and a Choice

Understanding the nuances between making a decision and making a choice illuminates the path to effective decision-making. The distinction, though subtle, highlights the depth of commitment and the implications of our actions. The term "choice" finds its roots in the flexibility of selecting among alternatives without a deep dive into evaluation or accountability. It's the simpler, often less consequential act of picking an option when faced with multiple possibilities.

Conversely, the term "decision" carries a weight that extends beyond mere selection. Originating from the Latin *decidere*, the word comes from a combination of two words: *de,* meaning 'OFF' and *caedere,* meaning 'CUT', which signifies a definitive action. Similar to how an incision involves cutting into something with precision, and an excision means removing something entirely, making a decision implies a deliberate choice to eliminate other alternatives. It's a commitment to a selected path, forsaking other avenues and embracing the consequences of this choice.

This etymological exploration sheds light on the gravitas of decision-making. It's not merely about choosing; it's about committing to a course of action with an understanding that this choice has eliminated other possibilities. The act of deciding is a pledge to pursue a specific direction, understanding that it comes with the responsibility of its outcomes.

Grasping this difference empowers us to approach decision-making with the seriousness it deserves. It encourages us to weigh our options not just with a preference for one over another, but with a recognition of the commitment each decision entails. When we decide, we're not just selecting an option; we're charting a course forward and closing the door on alternatives. This realisation enhances our responsibility to our choices, encouraging a deeper level of thought, consideration, and dedication to the paths we choose to follow.

My mother's story is one of courage, determination, and the profound understanding of commitment inherent in true decision-making. Growing up, our family life took a dramatic turn when my parents separated, leaving my mother to shoulder the responsibility of providing for us. This pivotal moment required her to make decisions that would chart the course of our lives. With no prior work experience, having dedicated her life to raising us, she faced a daunting task. Yet, she embraced it with a resilience and clarity that has inspired me throughout my life.

Her first decision was to move closer to her family in the north of England, seeking both emotional support and a fresh start. This move was coupled with her decision to pursue a career that would not only fulfil her but also ensure our financial security. The choice? Midwifery. It was a profession she had long admired, drawn to it by her natural compassion and nurtured by her experience as a mother of six. The path seemed clear; a two-year course would lead to a stable job, a reliable income, and a pension. Yet, life is seldom so straightforward.

To support us through these years, she turned to her passion for painting. What began as a means to an end soon blossomed into a profound source of joy. Nights spent painting became her solace and strength, even as the demands of her midwifery course weighed heavily upon her. As she neared the completion of her studies, a realisation dawned on her. Her love for painting eclipsed her pursuit of midwifery.

With just two months to go, she made a decision that stunned everyone, myself included. She withdrew from her course, sold our family home, and bought a small shop with a living space above it. Her plan was audacious yet simple: to make a living through her art.

I remember questioning her, perplexed and concerned. Why abandon a nearly completed path for the uncertainty of an artist's life? Her response illuminated the essence of true decision-making. She explained that by finishing her midwifery course, she'd leave a door open, a fallback that, in moments of hardship, might tempt her away from her true passion. To fully commit to her art, she needed to eliminate that option entirely. She had to "burn her boats."

Years later, a conversation between her and my grandfather further revealed the depth of her conviction. He questioned her relentless work ethic, the long hours for seemingly little reward. Her answer was a testament to the fulfilment she found in her decision: "I haven't worked a single day since I bought this shop. Every day, I do what I love. My life is wonderful."

Her decision, a true "cutting off" of alternatives, had allowed her to embrace her passion wholly, without reservation or retreat. It was a bold move that not only secured our survival but also taught me the power of decisive commitment. In making a decision, we close the door on other paths not out of fear or shortsightedness but to dedicate ourselves to the journey we have chosen wholly. My mother's story is a reminder that the most impactful decisions in our lives are those that come from a deep understanding of ourselves, our passions, and our capacities to overcome. Through her, I learned that a decision, in its truest form, is an act of courage, a pledge to pursue our chosen path, no matter the challenges that lie ahead.

The Art of Knowing When to Decide

The art of decision-making isn't just about what choices you make but also when you choose to make them. Jeff Bezos, the visionary behind Amazon, distinguished between two types of decisions to guide this timing: 'Type 1' and 'Type 2'. Type 1 decisions are significant, often irreversible, and require a deep level of thought and consideration. These are the decisions that, once made, set you on a path that's hard to leave. Type 2 decisions, in contrast, are more flexible and allow for experimentation—they can be made quickly and, if necessary, undone with relative ease.

Understanding whether you're facing a Type 1 or Type 2 decision is crucial for determining how to approach it. For Type 2 decisions, where the stakes are lower, and reversibility is possible, it's beneficial to move swiftly. This approach encourages innovation and learning, allowing you to adapt and respond to feedback without being hindered by the fear of permanent consequences.

When confronted with a Type 1 decision, it's essential to broaden your perspective and gather as much information as possible. These decisions demand more caution, as they often represent one-way doors that, once passed through, mark a commitment from which there's no easy return. In these cases, fostering a culture of healthy debate and consulting various viewpoints can illuminate the best path forward. Yet, it's equally important to recognise that consensus may not always be possible. Bezos advises approaching such disagreements with humility, acknowledging that committing to a decision, even one that's not universally agreed upon, can sometimes lead to unexpected and valuable discoveries.

Allowing individuals the autonomy to explore and implement their ideas, particularly for Type 2 decisions, cultivates an environment of trust and creativity. This empowerment, coupled with the understanding that decisions can often be modified or reversed, helps to demystify the decision-making process. It encourages a proactive stance towards making choices, emphasising the importance of discerning when to make a decision based on its potential impact and irreversibility.

The crossroads of change demand decisive action. This truth is starkly illustrated in the contrasting destinies of Blockbuster and Netflix. Blockbuster, once a titan of entertainment, faced a pivotal moment with the rise of digital streaming. Their hesitation, a reluctance to depart from the familiarity of DVD rentals, marked the beginning of their decline. On the other side of the coin, Netflix recognised the wind of change. They made a bold decision to pivot from their

DVD rental model to embrace online streaming. This choice wasn't just about adapting; it was about foreseeing and aligning with the future of entertainment.

Netflix's leap into the unknown set them on a path to global dominance in the streaming industry, illustrating the power of strategic decision-making in the face of change. This narrative serves as both inspiration and a cautionary tale. It underscores the critical importance of recognising when stagnation signals the need for action. Decisions, especially those made at the brink of significant change, can be the difference between irrelevance and innovation.

Embrace the prompt of change as a catalyst for decision-making. Whether in your personal endeavours or business strategies, staying attuned to the signs of stagnation and being ready to make bold, informed decisions can set the stage for unprecedented success. Let the story of Blockbuster and Netflix be a reminder: the future belongs to those who decide to meet change head-on, transforming challenges into stepping stones towards achievement.

How to Make Critical Decisions

Elon Musk, the visionary behind five multi-billion-dollar enterprises, including Tesla, SpaceX, and X (formerly Twitter), is celebrated for his exceptional decision-making skills that have catapulted his companies to the forefront of innovation. Musk's approach to navigating the complex challenges of launching and sustaining groundbreaking businesses can be distilled into six pragmatic steps, providing a blueprint for making informed, critical decisions.

1. **Initiate with a Question**: Every decision starts with the fundamental step of asking the right question. This frames the problem or challenge you're facing and sets the direction for finding a solution.

2. **Gather Evidence**: The next step involves an exhaustive collection of data and information relevant to the question at hand. This includes understanding the issue deeply and exploring all possible angles and answers.

3. **Weigh the Options**: With evidence in hand, Musk devises multiple potential solutions, assessing each for its likelihood of success. This step is about broadening your perspective to consider various outcomes and their feasibilities.

4. **Logical Evaluation**: Musk then evaluates these options through a logical lens, questioning their practicality, relevance, potential to achieve the desired outcome, and success probability. This critical examination helps refine the choices to those most viable.

5. **Challenge Your Conclusion**: Perhaps the most crucial step is actively seeking to disprove the chosen course of action. This involves inviting critique and counter arguments to test the decision's strength and uncover any overlooked insights.

6. **Final Review**: If the conclusion withstands this scrutiny without being effectively challenged, it's likely a solid decision. However, Musk remains open to reevaluation and is ready to pivot if a better solution emerges.

Musk's method emphasises the distinction between making decisions grounded in evidence versus those swayed by emotion. By meticulously following these steps, you can enhance your decision-making process, ensuring it's driven by logic and information rather than bias or haste.

This disciplined approach to decision-making doesn't just apply to billionaire entrepreneurs; it's accessible to anyone willing to apply these principles. By adopting Musk's strategy, you can make more informed choices, whether you're running a business, tackling personal goals, or facing daily dilemmas. It's about empowering yourself with a clear, methodical process that guides you to thoughtful, effective decisions.

When Not to Decide

In the realm of decision-making, understanding when to act and when to hold back is a delicate balance. The contrasting tales of Kodak and Apple offer profound lessons in the timing of strategic decisions.

Kodak's leadership, amid the digital photography revolution, faced a pivotal decision that would dictate the company's future trajectory. Despite pioneering the digital camera in 1975, Kodak opted to prioritise its lucrative film business, underestimating the digital technology's potential impact and market demand. This strategic choice, influenced by the desire to protect its existing film market dominance and a conservative approach to innovation, led to Kodak's gradual market share decline. As digital photography gained popularity, Kodak struggled to adapt and compete, ultimately filing for bankruptcy in 2012. This turn of events underscored Kodak's failure to anticipate the rapid adoption of digital technology and to innovate accordingly, marking a significant fall for a company once emblematic of photographic excellence.

This cautionary example highlights the peril of rushing into decisions without fully embracing the potential of emerging trends. Kodak's failure to adapt and explore the digital frontier illustrates how precipitous choices can have lasting consequences.

On the flip side, Apple's approach to entering the smartphone market exemplifies the strategic advantage of patience. By delaying its entry, Apple was not first to the smartphone scene but instead observed the landscape, learned from the early missteps of competitors, and meticulously planned its foray. The result was the iPhone, a device that not only catapulted Apple to the forefront of technology but also redefined the smartphone industry. Apple's willingness to wait allowed them to innovate and perfect, ultimately unveiling a product that set new standards for mobile computing.

These stories together underscore the wisdom of measured decision-making. While Kodak's swift choice led to a missed opportunity and decline, Apple's calculated patience paved the way for groundbreaking success. The lesson here is clear: not all decisions should be rushed. Taking the time to gather information, understand the market, and anticipate future trends can be the difference between failure and transformative success.

In navigating the complex waters of decision-making, let the tales of Kodak and Apple serve as guiding lights. They teach us that sometimes, the most powerful decision is to wait, watch, and learn. By adopting a strategic approach to timing, we can make choices that are not just reactive but visionary, steering our paths toward innovation and long-term achievement.

In the world of strategic games and high-stakes adventures, the timing of decisions can often spell the difference between triumph and defeat. The deliberations of a chess grandmaster and the critical choices made by mountaineers offer valuable insights into the art of strategic delay in decision-making.

A chess grandmaster views the board with a blend of keen insight and patient strategy. Every move is pregnant with potential, each decision carrying weighty implications for the outcome of the game. Grandmasters excel not just because they can predict their opponent's moves, but because they know when to act and when to wait. In moments when the board presents a complex puzzle, their choice to pause, to deliberate further, or even to wait for their opponent to reveal more, becomes a tactical advantage. This principle of strategic patience is a powerful tool, applicable beyond the chessboard and into the realms of life and business, teaching us the value of measured action and the foresight to hold back when clarity is needed.

Similarly, the decisions of a mountaineer encapsulate the critical balance between ambition and restraint. For climbers, the journey to the summit is fraught with choices that hold real consequences. The decision to press on or to retreat in the face of adverse conditions tests not only their physical endurance but also their judgement. A seasoned mountaineer knows that the mountain will remain, and the decision to turn back today does not spell failure but preserves the chance for future success. It's a reminder that strategic delay, the choice not to decide hastily, can be an act of wisdom that safeguards well-being and ensures longevity in pursuit of our goals.

These examples teach us that strategic patience is not a sign of indecision or weakness but a deliberate choice that prioritises long-term success over immediate gratification. Whether it's the calculated pause of a chess grandmaster assessing the board or the mountaineer choosing safety over summit glory, these scenarios underscore the importance of knowing when to move forward and when to wait.

In our fast-paced world, where the pressure to act is constant, these lessons remind us that sometimes, the most strategic decision is to allow ourselves the time to gather more information, to see further than the immediate horizon, and to choose our moments of action with care. By embracing the wisdom of strategic delay, we learn to navigate the complexities of life and business with a deeper sense of purpose and effectiveness.

The Pitfalls of Optimism and Pessimism

In decision-making, balancing optimism and pessimism is critical to evaluating the full spectrum of potential outcomes. Both extremes—unwavering optimism and relentless pessimism—can cloud judgement and lead to poorly considered decisions. This section explores the pitfalls associated with each mindset and underscores the importance of a balanced evaluation of upsides and downsides to make informed, strategic choices.

A Battle Lost

Maeve Boothby O'Neill was a vibrant, intelligent young woman with a zest for life. Her diary entries capture the essence of her youthful spirit and optimism, especially as she celebrated her 13th birthday. However, as the years passed, she began experiencing unexplained fatigue that progressively worsened, ultimately leading to a debilitating condition that left her unable to perform basic functions. By 27, Maeve's life was tragically cut short, with her final months dominated by her battle with myalgic encephalomyelitis (ME), also known as chronic fatigue syndrome (CFS).

Maeve's life offers a poignant illustration of the dangers of lopsided decision-making, especially in medical contexts. Maeve's struggle with ME, underscores the crucial need for balanced decision-making that weighs all potential outcomes, not just the most immediate risks.

When Maeve was first admitted to the hospital, she was already struggling to eat and maintain her weight. Her mother, Sarah Boothby, advocated for a nasogastric (NG) feeding tube to ensure Maeve received the necessary nutrients. Despite Maeve's dire condition and weight loss, the hospital staff were hesitant, citing concerns over aspiration and infection. This hesitation exemplifies a critical imbalance in the decision-making process.

Throughout her treatment, medical professionals at the hospital often focused narrowly on the risks associated with artificial feeding methods, such as potential infections and complications. However, they did not give equal weight to the consequences of not providing adequate nutritional support, which led to Maeve's severe malnutrition and eventual starvation.

The consequences of these decisions were devastating. By not addressing the immediate need for nutrition, Maeve's health continued to deteriorate. In her final months, she was unable to sit up or swallow, conditions that could have been mitigated with earlier, proactive nutritional interventions.

Dr. William Weir, a leading voice on ME, together with Maeve's GP, expressed grave concerns that she would starve to death without proper nutritional support. Despite these warnings, the hospital's reluctance to use NG or intravenous (IV) feeding resulted in a tragic outcome. Maeve's parents and supporters argued that a more balanced consideration of the risks and benefits of artificial feeding could have saved her life.

Maeve's story does not end with her passing. It became a powerful catalyst for change, highlighting the need for improved medical education and policy reform regarding severe ME. The hospital where Maeve was treated has since revised its policies, and another severely ill ME patient is now receiving artificial feeding at home.

Maeve's father, Sean O'Neill, has been vocal about the need for a better understanding of ME within the medical community. He underscores that Maeve's experience reflects a broader issue of disbelief and mismanagement in treating ME patients. Maeve's inquest resulted in a Prevention of Future Deaths report, advocating for increased funding, research, and specialist care for ME.

Maeve Boothby O'Neill's journey is a heartbreaking reminder of the importance of balanced decision-making. Her story illustrates the critical need to consider all potential outcomes in medical decisions, weighing the risks of action against the risks of inaction.

Her case teaches us that effective decision-making requires a comprehensive evaluation of all factors involved, ensuring that the immediate and long-term needs of patients are met. Maeve's legacy calls for a more empathetic and informed approach to treating complex conditions like ME, emphasising that the cost of inaction can be just as significant as the risks associated with proactive treatment.

In the broader context of decision-making, Maeve's story serves as a powerful example for all of us to strive for balanced, well-informed choices. Whether in healthcare, business, or personal life, the lessons from Maeve's experience remind us to weigh all possibilities and outcomes, ensuring that our decisions are both compassionate and comprehensive.

The Dangers of Over-Optimism

Optimism has been both a curse and a blessing for me. Without an optimistic outlook on life, I definitely would not have enjoyed the successes I have, but sometimes, I have been overly optimistic, and that has cost me dearly. Fortunately, the benefits of optimism have outweighed the downsides or overoptimism, but I would have liked to have avoided the costs.

Optimism is a powerful driver of innovation and resilience, fostering a forward-looking and hopeful perspective. However, an overly optimistic mindset can blind decision-makers to potential risks and challenges, leading to several pitfalls:

1. Underestimating Risks:

    Optimists tend to focus on potential rewards and may downplay or ignore the risks involved in a decision. This can result in a lack of preparedness for adverse outcomes, potentially jeopardising the success of the venture.

2. Overcommitment to a Single Path:

   With a focus solely on positive outcomes, optimists might commit too heavily to a particular course of action without considering alternative strategies or contingency plans. This tunnel vision can lead to significant setbacks if the chosen path proves unviable.

3. Ignoring Warning Signs:

   Critical feedback and early warning signs of failure might be dismissed or underestimated by those with an overly optimistic outlook. This can prevent timely corrective actions that could mitigate losses or pivot strategies towards more successful outcomes.

The Dangers of Excessive Pessimism

Conversely, a predominantly pessimistic outlook can also hinder effective decision-making. While it is essential to consider potential downsides, excessive focus on risks can stifle innovation and lead to missed opportunities:

1. Paralysis by Analysis:

   Pessimists may become bogged down in the potential negatives of every decision, leading to indecision or excessively delayed action. This hesitation can result in missed opportunities and an inability to capitalise on favourable conditions.

2. Inhibited Risk-Taking:

   A focus on avoiding risks can prevent the pursuit of innovative or ambitious projects that, while carrying inherent risks, also offer significant rewards. This conservative approach can lead to stagnation and a failure to achieve breakthrough success.

3. Disregarding Potential Upsides:

    By fixating on potential pitfalls, pessimists might overlook or undervalue the positive aspects of a decision. This can lead to a negative bias that skews the evaluation process, resulting in overly cautious and suboptimal choices.

Balanced Decision Making: Evaluating All Outcomes

To navigate the complexities of decision-making effectively, it is crucial to adopt a balanced approach that thoroughly evaluates both the upsides and downsides of all potential options:

1. Comprehensive Risk Assessment:

    Identify and analyse all potential risks associated with each decision. Understand the likelihood and impact of these risks to develop strategies for mitigation and contingency planning.

2. Exploring Opportunities:

    Equally important is the identification and evaluation of potential benefits. Understand how each decision could lead to positive outcomes and the conditions necessary for these benefits to materialise.

3. Comparative Analysis:

    Weigh the pros and cons of each option against one another. Consider scenarios where both upsides and downsides could occur and how they balance out. This helps in choosing the option with the highest likelihood of a positive outcome, taking into account both risks and rewards.

4. Scenario Planning:

   Develop multiple scenarios for each decision, including best-case, worst-case, and most likely outcomes. This comprehensive view helps you understand the full spectrum of potential results and prepare for various eventualities.

For example, the NASA Apollo programme's mission to land a man on the moon is a quintessential example of balanced decision-making. This historic achievement exemplifies how optimism, rigorous planning, and risk management can harmonise to achieve extraordinary goals.

President John F. Kennedy's bold declaration in 1961 to land a man on the moon by the end of the decade set a high-stakes, ambitious goal. This vision was underpinned by a profound sense of optimism about human potential and technological capability. However, turning this vision into reality required more than just optimism; it demanded meticulous planning and an acute awareness of the risks involved.

NASA's engineers and scientists undertook an immense task, breaking down the mission into manageable stages: launching the spacecraft, landing on the moon, and ensuring the astronauts' safe return. Each stage was meticulously planned, with a focus on every conceivable detail. This was not just an exercise in logistics, but a demonstration of foresight and strategic planning.

Risk assessment was integral to the Apollo program. The space environment is inherently hazardous, with the vacuum of space, extreme temperatures, and potential technical failures posing significant threats. NASA's approach involved identifying potential risks at every stage and developing contingencies to address them.

For instance, the decision to include the Lunar Module (LM) as a separate vehicle for landing on the moon was a result of extensive debate and risk evaluation. This decision allowed the Command Module to remain in lunar orbit, reducing the complexity and risks associated with a single, all-purpose spacecraft.

NASA's path to the moon was not without setbacks. The tragic Apollo 1 fire in 1967, which resulted in the loss of three astronauts, was a sobering reminder of the program's inherent dangers. The incident prompted a thorough investigation and significant redesigns of the Apollo spacecraft to improve safety and reliability.

These changes were not mere reactions, but strategic adjustments that reflected NASA's commitment to learning from failures. The organisation's ability to adapt and improve was crucial in ensuring the success of subsequent missions.

On July 20, 1969, Apollo 11's Lunar Module, Eagle, landed on the moon, and Neil Armstrong took his historic first step, uttering the iconic words, "That's one small step for man, one giant leap for mankind." This achievement was the culmination of years of balanced decision-making, where optimism and ambition were tempered by realistic planning and risk management.

The success of the Apollo missions hinged on meticulously planning for potential failures and having robust backup plans. This balanced approach demonstrates how evaluating both upsides and downsides can lead to historic achievements.

The story of NASA's Apollo program offers profound lessons for decision-making in any context. Here are key takeaways:

1. Set Ambitious Goals: Like NASA's moon landing, aim high. Ambitious goals inspire and drive progress.

2. Plan Meticulously: Break down goals into manageable steps and plan each phase carefully.

3. Assess Risks: Identify potential risks and develop contingencies. Learn from setbacks and adapt accordingly.

4. Balance Optimism with Realism: Maintain a positive vision but ground it in practical, realistic planning.

5. Commit to Learning: Embrace failures as opportunities to learn and improve.

These principles are not just applicable to space exploration but to any endeavour. By adopting a balanced approach to decision-making, combining ambition with meticulous planning and risk assessment, we can achieve extraordinary outcomes and turn visionary goals into reality.

In the journey of self-improvement and achievement, the principles of balanced decision-making are essential. The NASA Apollo program's legacy reminds us that with the right combination of ambition, planning, and risk management, we can soar to new heights. Let us embrace these lessons, continually strive for excellence, and commit to becoming the best versions of ourselves.

The Illusion of the 'Wrong' Decision

In the intricate game of life, where every move and turn is dictated by the decisions we make, understanding the nature of decision-making becomes not just an art but a necessity. Far too often, the fear of making the "wrong" decision paralyses us, holding us back from taking the steps that could lead to our most significant achievements and deepest fulfilments. Yet, what if we reframe our perspective on decision-making? What if we see each decision not as a potential misstep but as a step forward, regardless of the outcome?

Consider for a moment the essence of decision-making. At its core, every decision we make is a reflection of the best information available to us at the time. It's akin to a captain navigating a ship through foggy waters, relying on their current visibility, knowing well that it's limited. This analogy brings us to the heartening journey of Howard Schultz, the visionary who transformed Starbucks from a simple coffee bean seller into a global coffeehouse chain. Schultz's initial decision was based on his understanding of the market at the time. It was his openness to new insights and his willingness to adapt that led to Starbucks' monumental success.

This story underscores a fundamental truth about decision-making: it is, at its heart, a pursuit of knowledge. As we gather more information, our understanding evolves, and so do our decisions. The evolution of Google from a mere search engine to a tech giant sprawling across various domains exemplifies this. Larry Page and Sergey Brin, Google's founders, didn't just stick to their initial focus; they adapted their strategy as they learned more about technological advancements and market needs, continually refining their decisions based on new knowledge.

In a world that moves at breakneck speed, decision-making often requires us to act swiftly, sometimes with limited information. Anna, a small bakery owner, found herself in such a predicament during the COVID-19 pandemic. Faced with the prospect of shutting down, she pivoted to online orders and local deliveries—a decision made under duress, but one that ultimately saved her business and sparked new growth avenues. Her story teaches us about the balance between making quick decisions and the importance of basing those decisions on the best available information.

Adaptability is crucial in the face of evolving information. The tech industry, known for its rapid pace of innovation, often releases products in beta versions, using user feedback and data to refine and improve. This approach to decision-making—iterative, flexible, and responsive—highlights the importance of being willing to revise decisions as new information emerges.

Yet, in today's world, the abundance of choices available in every aspect of life presents a unique challenge—the paradox of choice. While having options is liberating, it can also lead to feeling overwhelmed and indecisive. Søren Kierkegaard, the Danish philosopher, insightfully addressed this, suggesting that true despair arises not from a lack of choices but from the burden of too many, coupled with the responsibility to choose. He proposed that overcoming despair involves making decisions that imbue our lives with personal meaning, rather than succumbing to societal expectations or the fear of missing out.

To navigate the paradox of choice and make meaningful decisions, we must first reflect on what truly matters to us. This process involves a deep examination of our desires, fears, and values, recognising that not every choice needs to be monumental and that there's freedom in embracing our limitations. Moreover, committing to a decision—any decision—can be an act of defiance against the despair of indecision, asserting our existence and carving out our unique path in the world.

The journey of Howard Schultz and the evolution of Google, among others, teach us that decisions evolve with our growing understanding. In certain situations, like that faced by Anna or in the adaptive strategies of the tech industry, swift decisions are necessary. Yet, these decisions are always based on the best information available at the time, underscoring the dynamic nature of decision-making.

Embracing this perspective on decision-making liberates us from the fear of making the "wrong" choice. It encourages us to see each decision as an opportunity for growth and learning, to embrace the uncertainties of life with conviction, and to view every choice as a step forward on our journey. Whether in business or personal life, this mindset not only enhances our ability to navigate challenges but also empowers us to transform perceived mistakes into opportunities for development.

In essence, decision-making is about embracing the unknown with the knowledge that our choices are stepping stones on the path of life. It's about recognising the power of adaptability, the value of continuous learning, and the importance of aligning our decisions with our deepest values and aspirations. With this perspective, we can set sail into the vast seas of possibility, confident in our ability to chart a course toward a fulfilling and purpose-driven life.

Understanding that there is rarely a singular "wrong" decision fosters a more forgiving and adaptive approach to decision-making. This mindset not only enhances our ability to navigate life's challenges but also empowers us to transform perceived mistakes into opportunities for personal and professional development. It's in the art of choosing that we assert our existence and carve out our unique path in the world. Each choice becomes a brushstroke in the masterpiece of our lives, meaningful not because it was the best possible decision among countless others, but because it was ours.

In today's world, where choices seem endless and often overwhelming, the insights from historical figures like Kierkegaard are more relevant than ever. They remind us that living authentically is not about having all the options, but about making meaningful choices that reflect our true selves. By confronting and embracing the paradox of choice, we can find a path to existential fulfilment and ward off the despair that threatens to consume us in our quest for meaning in an overly abundant world.

Let this chapter serve not just as a guide through the nuances of decision-making, but as an invitation to embrace each decision as an opportunity to steer your life in the direction of your dreams. With each choice, we have the power to shape our destiny, to turn aspirations into achievements, and to navigate the complex tapestry of life with purpose and conviction.

As we turn the page from mastering the art of decision-making, we embark on an even more profound journey in the next chapter: Soar Higher. To conquer the peaks beyond our past accomplishments and realise our dreams, we must evolve into the very person capable of such feats.

The upcoming chapter invites us into the realm of self-development, a critical aspect often overlooked in the pursuit of success. Much like a golfer who must continuously hone their skills to achieve greater and greater success, we too must commit to refining our most precious resource: ourselves. Our ability to reach new heights in both our professional and personal lives is intrinsically linked to how diligently we cultivate our minds and emotional resilience.

This next chapter is not just a continuation of our journey but a call to action—a challenge to invest in our growth with the same vigour we apply to achieving our goals. As we explore the landscapes of intellect and emotional intelligence, remember that every step forward in self-development is a step closer to becoming the architect of our dreams. Let's dive into this transformative process together, ready to learn, adapt, and grow, so we can not only envision a future of unparalleled wins but also become the person who can truly achieve it.

Decision-Making Framework

One powerful tool to guide the process of decision-making is the *Decision Matrix*—a structured, logical framework that helps you evaluate options based on criteria that matter most to you. The Decision Matrix doesn't just help you choose an option; it allows you to identify the most fitting choice based on a methodical analysis, ensuring that your decision is grounded in both rationality and personal values. Let's explore this process step-by-step so you can feel empowered to approach complex decisions with clarity and confidence.

Step 1: Identify the Decision to Make

The first step in the decision-making process is identifying the decision that needs to be made. It could be anything from a career decision, such as whether to accept a new job offer, to a personal decision, like choosing between moving to a new city or staying where you are.

Imagine you're at a career crossroads:

"Should I accept a new job offer, continue at my current job, or start my own business?"

Each option has its own set of pros and cons, and the weight of this decision is significant. This is where the Decision Matrix shines—by helping you systematically evaluate these options against what matters most to you.

Step 2: List Your Options

Now, identify the different options you're considering. In our career decision example, your options might be:

1. Accept the new job offer
2. Stay at your current job
3. Start your own business

Step 3: Define Your Criteria

Next, list the criteria that are most important to you in making this decision. These are the factors that will influence how satisfied you'll be with the outcome. For example, in a career decision, criteria could include financial stability, job satisfaction, work-life balance, growth opportunities, and location.

It's also important to assign a *weight* to each criterion based on how crucial it is to you. This ensures that the most important factors carry more influence in your final decision. For instance, if financial stability is your top priority, it might receive a weight of 5, whereas location might only get a weight of 2.

Example criteria and weights:

- Financial Stability (5)
- Job Satisfaction (4)
- Work-Life Balance (3)
- Growth Opportunities (4)
- Location (2)

Step 4: Evaluate Each Option

Once you have your options and criteria, the next step is to rate how well each option meets each criterion on a scale of 1 to 5, with 1 being "not at all" and 5 being "extremely well." This evaluation forces you to consider each option in relation to your priorities and values.

Here's an example of how the evaluation might look:

Criteria	Weight	Option 1 New Job	Option 2 Current Job	Option 3 Start Business
Financial Stability	5	4	3	2
Job Satisfaction	4	3	4	5
Work-Life Balance	3	2	4	3
Growth Opportunities	4	5	3	5
Location	2	3	5	4

Step 5: Calculate Weighted Scores

To make an informed decision, you'll need to calculate the weighted score for each option. Multiply the rating of each criterion by its assigned weight, and then sum the results to get the total score for each option.

For example, the weighted score for the new job offer (Option 1) would look like this:

- Financial Stability: 4 x 5 = 20
- Job Satisfaction: 3 x 4 = 12
- Work-Life Balance: 2 x 3 = 6
- Growth Opportunities: 5 x 4 = 20
- Location: 3 x 2 = 6
- **Total Score: 20 + 12 + 6 + 20 + 6 = 64**

Repeat this calculation for each option to compare their total scores. In this scenario:

- Option 1: New Job = 64
- Option 2: Current Job = 65

- Option 3: Start Business = 67

Step 6: Analyse the Results

Once you've calculated the scores, you'll have a clearer picture of which option aligns best with your priorities. In this example, "starting your own business" has the highest score (67), suggesting it might be the best option based on your criteria.

However, it's important to remember that while the Decision Matrix provides a structured, objective analysis, it shouldn't be the only factor in your decision. Reflect on the results and consider how they align with your long-term goals, values, and emotions.

Step 7: Reflect and Decide

Before making a final decision, take time to reflect on the results. Does the highest-scoring option resonate with you emotionally? Does it align with your long-term vision for your life or career? It's essential to balance logical analysis with your intuition and gut feelings. In the example of a career choice, starting your own business may have additional factors to consider that the other options didn't have. These could be the need for investment or staff that you cannot meet.

Ask yourself:

- Does the highest-scoring option support my long-term goals?
- How do I feel about each option emotionally?
- Are there any risks or uncertainties I haven't considered?

This reflection ensures that your decision is not just based on numbers, but also aligned with your deeper values and desires.

Step 8: Take Action and Evaluate

Once you've made your decision, it's time to take action. Implement your choice with confidence, knowing that you've thoughtfully considered all angles. After some time, evaluate the outcome. Did the decision meet your expectations? What lessons did you learn from the process?

This reflection will improve your decision-making skills for the future. The more you engage with this structured process, the better you'll become at navigating complex choices with clarity and ease.

The Decision Matrix is more than just a tool—it's a framework that empowers you to make informed, thoughtful decisions. It encourages you to step back, identify what matters most, and evaluate your options in a clear, structured way. By using this framework, you take control of your decision-making process, balancing logic with intuition, and ensuring that your choices are aligned with your goals and values.

Next time you face a tough decision, give yourself the gift of clarity. Use the Decision Matrix to navigate your options, and trust that the path you choose will lead you toward the success and fulfilment you're striving for.

Practical Exercise: Decision-Making Framework

Do you have a decision to make? Is there a decision you made in the past that you would like to reconsider? In this exercise, use the Decision-Making Framework to look at the options and analyse which one is likely to be the best for you.

Step 1: Identify a Decision to Make

Choose a decision that you need to make soon. It could be personal, professional, or related to a project or goal you are working towards.

This decision should ideally involve multiple options and require careful consideration.

Step 2: List Your Options

Identify the different options available to you. These should be the potential choices you are considering.

Step 3: Define Your Criteria

List the criteria that are important to you in making this decision. Consider any and all factors that are important to you. Assign a weight (1-5) to each criterion based on its importance, with 5 being the most important.

Step 4: Evaluate Each Option

For each option, rate how well it meets each criterion on a scale of 1 to 5, with 1 being "not at all" and 5 being "extremely well."

Example Evaluation Table:

Criteria	Weight	Option 1	Option 2	Option 3
Factor 1				
Factor 2				
Factor 3				
Factor 4				
Factor 5				

Step 5: Calculate Weighted Scores

For each option, multiply the score by the weight for each criterion and sum the results to get the total weighted score.

Step 6: Analyse the Results

Review the total weighted scores for each option. The option with the highest score indicates the best overall fit based on your criteria and their respective importance.

Step 7: Reflect and Decide

Consider the results and reflect on any emotional responses or additional factors that may influence your decision. Remember that the Decision Matrix provides a structured way to analyse options but should not be the sole determinant. Your intuition and additional considerations are also important.

Step 8: Take Action and Evaluate

Once you make your decision, take the necessary steps to implement it. After some time, reflect on the outcome and what you learned from the process. This reflection will improve your future decision-making skills.

This exercise aims to help you approach decisions with a clear and structured mindset, balancing both rational analysis and personal values. Now it is your time to apply these steps. I hope it will help you to make more informed and confident choices in important aspects of your life.

CHAPTER 6

Soar Higher!

"The only way that we can live is if we grow. The only way that we can grow is if we change. The only way that we can change is if we learn."
— C. Joybell. C

When I embarked on the journey of founding my first business, I quickly encountered a stark realisation: possessing expertise in building computer networks was vastly different from knowing how to run a computer networking business. My business partner, seasoned with years of experience in managing ventures, was an invaluable resource. Yet, his guidance served merely as a bridge, granting me the time to acquire the knowledge I critically needed for our business to thrive.

This early phase of my entrepreneurial journey underscored a fundamental truth about business and personal growth: the necessity of continuous learning. To carve a path toward success, I found myself diving into realms far beyond my initial expertise. Sales, marketing, accounting, and administration became the new territories I needed to conquer, alongside deepening my understanding of computing and support.

This relentless pursuit of knowledge wasn't just a requirement; it became the fuel that propelled our business forward. With each new skill acquired and concept mastered, I noticed a direct impact on our business's growth. It was evident that the expansion of my knowledge base was inextricably linked to the expansion of our business. This relationship between learning and growth wasn't coincidental; it was foundational.

Looking back, it's clear that if my commitment to learning had wavered, our business's trajectory would have mirrored that stagnation. The relentless pace at which technology and market demands evolve meant that standing still was synonymous with falling behind. The journey from a fledgling startup to a thriving enterprise was paved with lessons learned, challenges overcome, and an unyielding commitment to personal development.

As we delve into this chapter, "Soar Higher," I invite you to explore the transformative power of continuous learning and self-improvement. The story of my first business is not unique; it's a universal narrative shared by those who dare to dream big and understand that becoming the person who achieves those dreams requires an insatiable appetite for growth. Let this chapter serve as both a guide and an inspiration for your journey towards mastering the art of personal development, and watch as new horizons unfold before you.

In the world of sports, Michael Jordan's journey with the Chicago Bulls stands as a beacon of relentless improvement, a testament to the enduring power of continuous growth and learning. Jordan, renowned as one of basketball's all-time greats, embodied more than just innate talent; he exemplified an insatiable drive to evolve, a commitment to being coached, and a steadfast pursuit of excellence that transcended the physical confines of the game.

Jordan's early career showcased his raw talent, yet it was his dedication to refining his skills that distinguished him. His practice regimen was rigorous, extending beyond physical training to include a deep dive into the strategic elements of basketball. He engaged with the game on a level that combined physical prowess with an intellectual understanding of play, demonstrating an openness to feedback that was instrumental in his growth.

This ethos of continuous improvement was epitomised when Coach Phil Jackson introduced the triangle offence—a strategic approach that demanded a departure from Jordan being the sole focal point to a more team-centric play. It was a pivotal shift, requiring Jordan to trust in a collective effort and to learn a new system that emphasised spacing, movement, and the shared responsibility of the ball. This adaptation wasn't immediate; it required patience, a willingness to learn, and an unwavering trust in the process.

Jordan's journey wasn't confined to on-court activities. His off-court efforts were equally relentless. He analysed game films, seeking insights into his performance and identifying strategies to counter opponents. His physical training was legendary, aiming to achieve unmatched strength, speed, and endurance.

This philosophy of never-ending improvement, strategic adaptation, and the quest for mastery led the Bulls to secure six NBA championships. Jordan's legacy is a powerful reminder that success is not solely the fruit of natural talent but the result of a persistent commitment to growth, the courage to embrace change, and the pursuit of excellence in all facets of one's craft.

The Bulls' mastery of the triangle offence serves as a vivid example of this philosophy in action. Initially met with scepticism, particularly by Jordan, the offence required a collective effort to understand and execute a strategy that was at odds with conventional wisdom. The learning curve was steep, challenging the team to reassess and realign their approach to the game. The 1990-1991 season marked a turning point as the Bulls, under Jackson's guidance, began to realise the offence's potential, ultimately leading to their first NBA championship.

The effectiveness of the triangle offence was showcased dramatically in Game 5 of the 1991 NBA Finals against the Los Angeles Lakers. On June 12, 1991, the Bulls demonstrated the offence's dynamic versatility, with Jordan leading the charge not just as a scorer but as a pivotal part of a cohesive unit. This game was not just a win but a testament to the power of adaptation, teamwork, and strategic execution.

The Bulls' transformation into a team that could outmanoeuvre opponents with intelligence and teamwork had a profound impact. Offence became a core component of their identity, underpinning their dominance in the 1990s. This evolution from reliance on individual brilliance to strategic team play highlights the significance of continuous development, the value of coaching, and the relentless pursuit of excellence.

Jordan's embrace of the triangle offence, his acceptance of a strategy that prioritised the team, and the Bulls' dedication to perfecting this approach underscore the importance of adaptability and continuous learning. Their journey from scepticism to triumph inspires and reminds us of the transformative power of dedication, strategic thinking, and the unyielding pursuit of growth.

As we reflect on Michael Jordan and the Chicago Bulls' legacy, their story transcends sports, offering profound lessons on the power of persistence, the importance of embracing change, and the endless pursuit of excellence. It's a narrative that inspires us to remain lifelong students of our pursuits, to face each challenge as an opportunity for growth, and to understand that in the quest for success, our greatest adversary is complacency.

A Relentless Journey Within and Without

Ascending to greater heights in both personal and professional realms isn't just about reaching upward; it's fundamentally about delving inward and expanding outward. It's a journey of relentless self-improvement, where the mind, your most potent tool, requires constant refinement and nourishment to unlock its full potential. Just as elite athletes dedicate countless hours to practise, honing their physical abilities for moments of competition, so too must we commit to the rigorous cultivation of our intellectual and emotional faculties.

The pathway to exceptional achievement is paved with the continuous expansion of knowledge and skills. The essence of self-development lies in the understanding that our capacity to influence, lead, and innovate is directly tied to the breadth and depth of our insights and abilities. Success, in any endeavour, mirrors the extent of our commitment to self-evolution. The pursuit of self-development, therefore, is not merely a component of achieving excellence; it is its very foundation.

Moreover, this pursuit is integral not only to our personal fulfilment but also to our ability to contribute meaningfully to the world around us. Enriching our understanding, expanding our perspectives, and refining our competencies is how we enhance not only our lives but also those of the people we touch.

So, let's embark on a detailed exploration of the imperative of self-development. Let's delve into strategies for fostering a mindset geared towards continuous growth, highlighting the importance of cultivating curiosity, embracing challenges, and learning from every experience. It's about recognising that development is a perpetual process, an endless ascent where each step forward elevates not just ourselves but also our collective potential.

As we navigate through these concepts, it's crucial to remember that the journey of self-improvement is as rewarding as the destinations it leads us to. Injecting elements of fun, joy, and creativity into our growth process not only makes the journey more enjoyable but also enriches our experiences, making each moment of learning and each milestone of development deeply fulfilling.

Let this chapter serve as your guide to refining and expanding your mental faculties, pushing the boundaries of what you believe is possible, and embracing the lifelong quest for knowledge and growth. Here, we lay the groundwork for soaring to new heights, driven by the relentless pursuit of excellence and the unwavering commitment to become the best versions of ourselves.

Expanding Beyond

Understanding self-development is pivotal because it embodies a journey of continual improvement in all facets of life. It's a deliberate endeavour to enhance one's knowledge, skills, and overall well-being, thereby fostering both personal and professional growth. This journey is marked by setting measurable goals and actively working towards achieving them, ensuring that with every step, you are refining and evolving yourself.

The advantages of investing in self-development are profound and far-reaching. It enables you to break free from stagnant thinking and outdated methods, sparking innovation and creativity. Engaging in self-improvement activities not only enriches your life but also propels you toward realising your fullest potential. Whether it's picking up a new hobby, acquiring a new skill, dedicating time to physical fitness, or applying insights gained from books, the essence of personal growth lies in intentionality. With a focused approach, you'll witness a transformative impact on both your personal life and career.

However, stepping into the workforce armed merely with academic qualifications is often insufficient for navigating the complexities of today's professional landscape. Achieving excellence demands a continuous commitment to personal and professional development. Leadership, for instance, isn't an innate trait but a skill cultivated through learning and experience. To excel as a leader and business professional, developing certain characteristics and skills is indispensable.

Life invariably presents a myriad of challenges, and navigating these obstacles with grace often requires a well-honed emotional intelligence. Facing new and unforeseen challenges can be daunting without the foundation of emotional intelligence. Hence, the importance of persistent self-development cannot be overstated—it's the bedrock of sustained growth and success.

As we travel through life, the need for expansion and personal evolution becomes increasingly clear. While life experiences contribute to our growth incrementally, actively pursuing self-development accelerates this process, enabling us to achieve greater outcomes. It's about more than just moving forward; it's about expanding our horizons and continually evolving to meet the demands of our personal and professional lives. Through committed and intentional self-improvement, we unlock the door to a richer, more fulfilling life, setting the stage for unlimited success.

Personal growth transcends the mere enhancement of your physical and mental capabilities. It involves a continuous process of expanding your understanding of the world and adapting your perspectives accordingly. This journey of self-discovery and improvement varies from one individual to another, encompassing a wide array of activities like immersing yourself in literature, mastering a new language, or exploring different cultures through travel. Understanding the significance of embarking on this path is the first step. Now, let's delve into how to initiate this transformative journey.

There are a plethora of self-development methods available, each offering a unique pathway to unlocking your full potential. The key is to remain open to experimentation, vary your approach, and incorporate multiple strategies to foster comprehensive growth.

Enrolling in training sessions presents a fantastic opportunity to acquire new skills. While self-learning is a viable option, participating in organised classes offers additional benefits, such as collaboration, community building, and networking. Thanks to advancements in technology and the proliferation of online courses, accessing educational resources from anywhere in the world has become remarkably convenient. Whether you're interested in enhancing your digital proficiency, personal development, or physical well-being, an abundance of options is at your fingertips. Start by identifying a course that aligns with your aspirations, and commit to actively engaging in the learning process.

Diving into books across various genres, from fiction and philosophy to self-help, is another powerful tool for self-improvement. Each book offers insights applicable to different facets of your life, enriching your understanding and broadening your horizon. To truly harness the power of reading, it's crucial to maintain a diverse reading list. This not only builds your knowledge base but also sharpens your critical thinking skills, allowing you to navigate complex ideas with ease.

When I launched my first business, my expertise was in computer systems engineering and networking. I knew the tech inside out but realised quickly that knowing the tech wasn't the same as knowing how to sell it, especially in the business-to-business realm, where I had little experience. Back then, without the internet or online training courses, options for quick upskilling were limited.

Determined to overcome this gap, I followed a recommendation to pick up a sales book. This wasn't just any book—it was a practical guide that laid out a clear path from generating leads to closing deals, even when facing stiff competition. Each night, after a day's work, I'd dive into this book, soaking up its strategies and applying them the next day.

What set me apart wasn't just the adoption of new strategies but a relentless drive to refine and adapt them based on real-world feedback. In an industry where closing 30% of sales was the norm, the strategies led me to an 85% success rate. The few times I didn't win were less about losing to the competition and more about projects being cancelled.

This experience taught me a valuable lesson early on: mastery and success come from a commitment to continuous learning and adaptation. It's not just about working harder but about working smarter, applying new knowledge directly, and iteratively improving upon it. This mindset of growth and adaptation powered my journey from a technical expert to a successful business owner. It proved that with dedication to learning and applying knowledge, you can surpass even your own expectations.

True transformation lies in applying acquired knowledge. As you journey through this book, I invite you to jot down key takeaways and actionable steps. Planning and executing these strategies catalyse real change, impacting your personal growth, professional development, and overall worldview.

Embarking on the path of self-development is a journey towards becoming a more informed, skilled, and well-rounded individual. By embracing a variety of learning experiences and applying the insights gained, you equip yourself with the tools necessary to achieve your highest potential. Let this journey be a source of inspiration, continuously driving you to evolve and enrich your life in meaningful ways.

"The saddest aspect of life right now is that science gathers knowledge faster than society gathers wisdom."

— Isaac Asimov

The Power of Linguistic Diversity

Learning a new language opens up a world of possibilities. It's not merely about acquiring the ability to communicate in different tongues but about the personal transformation that accompanies this journey. Engaging with a new language allows you to embrace new cultures, expand your perspectives, and connect with people on a deeper level. Whether it's navigating the vibrant streets of a foreign land or forming stronger bonds in a diverse community back home, the benefits of this endeavour extend far beyond simple communication.

However, mastering a new language is a formidable challenge, one that calls upon your deepest reserves of dedication and discipline. This journey demands consistent effort, patience, and an unwavering commitment, making the eventual mastery of the language all the more rewarding. It's a testament to your mental fortitude and a powerful reminder of your capacity to grow and adapt.

Moreover, the discipline and cognitive flexibility honed through learning a new language lay the foundation for acquiring other essential life skills. It's an exercise in expanding your mental capabilities, pushing the boundaries of your comfort zone, and cultivating a lifelong habit of learning. As you navigate the complexities of a new language, you're not just learning to communicate; you're reshaping your brain, enhancing your problem-solving skills, and opening yourself up to a wealth of new experiences and viewpoints.

Embrace the challenge of learning a new language as an integral component of your self-development journey. Let it be a source of inspiration, driving you to continually seek growth, understanding, and connection in an increasingly interconnected world.

Getting a Bigger Box

Embarking on self-development often starts with a specific goal in mind, perhaps improving physical health or acquiring a new skill. Yet, the journey of self-improvement often leads to unexpected benefits that transcend the initial area of focus. Take, for instance, the commitment to a healthier lifestyle through better nutrition and consistent exercise. This endeavour does more than enhance physical well-being; it becomes a profound lesson in discipline and self-regulation. The dedication required to maintain these habits strengthens your willpower, a quality that spills over into every aspect of your life, fueling personal and professional growth.

Similarly, expanding your knowledge in seemingly unrelated areas such as history, geography, or science enriches your perspective far beyond academic interest. Understanding historical contexts can provide invaluable insights into current market trends or cultural sensitivities, which are crucial for navigating the global business landscape. Likewise, a grasp of scientific principles can inform decision-making in health-related matters or innovation processes, underscoring the interconnectedness of knowledge across domains.

This holistic approach to learning and development underscores a fundamental truth: growth in one area invariably contributes to our capability in others. Cultivating a habit of continuous learning not only equips us with specific skills or knowledge but also enhances our overall cognitive abilities, emotional intelligence, and social skills. It prepares us to approach challenges with a more informed and versatile mindset, enabling us to make connections that others might miss and to innovate in ways that break new ground.

Therefore, the pursuit of knowledge should not be confined to our immediate needs or interests. Embracing a wide range of learning experiences enriches our understanding of the world and our place within it. It fosters empathy, broadens our cultural awareness, and equips us to engage more effectively with the diverse challenges and opportunities we encounter in life and work.

In essence, the act of learning itself, irrespective of the subject matter, is transformative. It's an investment in ourselves that pays dividends in unexpected ways, fueling our growth, enhancing our adaptability, and enriching our interactions with the world around us. So, as you chart your course in personal development, remember that every new skill, every bit of knowledge acquired, contributes to a broader, more nuanced understanding of life, opening doors to opportunities you might never have anticipated.

Let this realisation inspire you to seek knowledge both within and beyond your immediate field of interest. In doing so, you not only become more proficient in specific areas but also cultivate a richer, more versatile intellect capable of navigating the complexities of our ever-changing world. This journey of continuous learning and adaptation is not just about personal or professional success; it's about leading a more fulfilled and impactful life.

Expanding Your Worldview

Understanding and transforming your worldview is pivotal to personal and professional growth. Every action, decision, and goal stems from the lens through which you see the world. This perspective is shaped by a myriad of factors—your environment, experiences, and interactions. To truly excel in any aspect of life, it's essential to broaden this lens, to see beyond the familiar and embrace a more expansive view of the world.

Your worldview influences your reactions to life's events and challenges. A narrow perspective can limit your effectiveness, hindering your ability to connect with others, innovate in your business, or even empathise with those around you. For instance, to design services that genuinely meet the needs of the underprivileged, you must first understand their daily realities. This level of insight requires looking beyond your immediate experiences and actively seeking to understand lives differently from your own.

The journey to broadening your worldview starts with an inward examination, challenging the notion that your current perspective is the only or the 'right' way to view the world. Recognising this is the first step towards profound personal transformation. It involves questioning the foundations of your beliefs and asking yourself critical questions about your assumptions and values. What underpins your view of the world? Do you see it as a place of opportunity or hostility? What do you hold most dear, and why?

Expanding your worldview doesn't just mean adopting new views wholesale, but involves a deep, introspective analysis of your beliefs and attitudes. It's about stepping back to gain a broader perspective, one that allows you to see beyond your immediate context and understand the vast tapestry of human experience. This process is not about discarding your values but enriching them with a more nuanced understanding of the world.

As you embark on this journey of expanding your worldview, you'll find it not only enriches your personal life but also enhances your professional endeavours. With a broader perspective, you can better understand your customers, develop more inclusive and innovative solutions, and build more meaningful connections. This shift in perspective enables you to navigate the complexities of life and business with greater empathy and effectiveness.

Ultimately, expanding your worldview is about embracing growth and understanding. It's a commitment to continuous learning, to seeing the world in its complexity, and recognising the value in diverse perspectives. It's about stepping out of your comfort zone, challenging your preconceptions, and, in doing so, unlocking a richer, more fulfilling path to success.

Expanding your worldview is a journey of self-discovery and growth, essential for personal and professional development. It begins with introspection and an honest assessment of your perceptions and biases. By asking yourself a series of reflective questions, you can uncover the foundations of your worldview and identify areas for expansion.

Consider how you react upon meeting someone from a different cultural, racial, or ethnic background. What are your first impressions, and how do they shape your interactions? Explore your feelings towards working under someone of a different gender. These questions prompt you to confront and understand your inherent biases, setting the stage for transformative growth.

Embarking on new experiences, like trying unfamiliar cuisines or visiting new places, can also reveal much about your openness to change and adaptation. Recognising what irritates or unsettles you, and understanding your personal stumbling blocks, are crucial steps in identifying barriers to your growth.

Evaluating your criteria for success—both your own and others'—can illuminate your values and priorities. After this self-assessment, articulating your worldview becomes a crucial step towards understanding and eventually expanding it.

However, recognising the need to broaden your perspective is just the beginning. You must set clear goals for this transformation and approach it with the same discipline and dedication you would apply to any other area of personal development.

Identifying areas in your life where you feel stuck or limited can highlight beliefs that constrain you. Whether it's your career trajectory, business growth, or personal relationships, understanding these blockages is vital for initiating change.

Travel, for those who can, offers a profound way to broaden your perspective. Experiencing new cultures firsthand, understanding diverse lifestyles, and seeing the world through different lenses can significantly shift your understanding and appreciation of global diversity.

Cultivating relationships with people from varied backgrounds is another powerful method of expanding your worldview. Engaging with individuals who differ from you in culture, career, and life experiences exposes you to new ideas, perspectives, and ways of living.

Transforming your worldview is not an overnight task. It requires continuous effort, an open mind, and a willingness to challenge and change long-held beliefs. By embracing this journey of growth, you not only enrich your own life but also contribute to a more understanding, diverse, and interconnected world. This process of expansion is a pathway to unlocking your full potential, driving success in every aspect of your life, and fostering a deep, empathetic connection with the world around you.

Embarking on a journey of personal transformation requires more than just a willingness to learn; it demands the courage to challenge deeply ingrained beliefs and the openness to embrace change. My journey of self-discovery and change began when I dared to question the atheist worldview I was raised in, a foundation that had shaped my identity for decades. This process was neither easy nor straightforward. It involved delving into realms of thought and spirituality that I had previously dismissed or outright rejected, driven by a quest for meaning that transcended my existing paradigms.

As I explored various spiritual paths, each exploration, each conversation, each book peeled away layers of my long-held convictions, exposing me to a diversity of perspectives that I had never considered. This journey was not about disproving my atheism as much as it was about understanding the vast landscape of human belief and experience. Yet, despite my research, I found myself confronted with events in my life that defied rational explanation, pushing me further into the realms of faith and spirituality.

Meeting my future wife was a pivotal moment. Her faith, something I might have once viewed as a barrier, became a bridge to deeper inquiry. Her beliefs, and the community she was part of, challenged me to re-examine my own with a level of honesty and humility I had never before applied. It was in seeking to understand her worldview that I began to genuinely question my own, not with the intent to change it, but to understand it genuinely.

The transformation that followed was not sudden but gradual, marked by moments of doubt, resistance, and profound realisation. It was a conversation that suggested I direct my questions not at people but at God, and the understanding that belief might never come without the willingness to believe, that catalysed a significant shift in my perspective. This advice struck a chord deep within me, highlighting the limitations of my approach and the biases that had coloured my search for truth.

Embracing the possibility of change, allowing myself to consider perspectives I had previously dismissed, and ultimately, opening my heart to faith were steps that transformed not just my spiritual beliefs but my entire approach to life. It was a stark reminder that true growth requires us to step beyond the comfort zones of our convictions, to ask difficult questions, and to be prepared for answers that might fundamentally alter our course.

This experience taught me that the essence of personal development lies not in the accumulation of knowledge or the rigid adherence to a set of beliefs, but in the willingness to remain open to new possibilities. It underscored the importance of engaging with the world around us with curiosity and humility, recognising that our worldview is but a single perspective in a rich tapestry of human experience.

To truly soar higher, to achieve the fullest expression of ourselves, we must be willing to embark on this journey of continuous learning and self-reflection. It's about being open to change, willing to confront uncomfortable truths, and taking the steps, however daunting, towards the life and person we aspire to be. It's a journey that demands not just intellectual engagement but emotional courage, a willingness to face the unknown, and the resilience to forge a path aligned with our deepest values and aspirations.

Self-care

In the journey toward self-improvement and actualising your fullest potential, the cornerstone of all progress is a steadfast commitment to self-care. This concept extends far beyond mere physical wellness—it encompasses a comprehensive approach that nurtures your mental, emotional, and spiritual well-being. Our discussions have highlighted the significant impact of physical health on mental clarity and resilience, yet true self-care is a more encompassing endeavour. It's about cultivating a state of holistic health that empowers you to thrive in every facet of life.

On their website, Daily Ten Minutes shared an insightful story that accurately expresses this sentiment:

"A cobbler lived in a large village. He was the only cobbler in town, so he was responsible for repairing the boots of everybody else. However, he didn't have time to repair his shoes. At first, this wasn't a problem, but his shoes began to deteriorate and fall apart over time. While he worked feverishly on everyone else's boots, his feet got blisters, and he started to limp. His customers started to worry about him, but he reassured them that everything was OK. However, after a few years, the cobbler's feet were so injured that he could no longer work, and no one's boots got repaired. Consequently, soon the entire town started to limp in pain, all because the cobbler never took the time to repair his own boots."

— Daily Ten Minutes, 2016

Embracing self-care is the acknowledgement that to inspire change, to foster growth, and to navigate the complexities of life and business, you must first ensure that you are operating from a place of strength and balance. Without a foundation of self-care, efforts to transform your life and reach your goals can become unsustainable, leaving you depleted rather than enriched.

Real, lasting self-development demands that you prioritise your well-being, recognising that each aspect of self-care—physical, mental, and spiritual—is interlinked, contributing to your overall ability to face challenges and seize opportunities. When you nurture your body with exercise and nutrition, your mind with learning and reflection, and your spirit with practices that connect you to a deeper sense of purpose, you create a powerful synergy. This synergy fuels not only your capacity for achievement but also your resilience in the face of adversity.

The essence of self-care is understanding that you are your most valuable asset. To neglect this vital aspect of your being is to undermine your potential for success and fulfilment. By committing to a holistic self-care routine, you lay the groundwork for transformative change, not just in your personal life but also in your professional endeavours. It is only from a place of holistic wellness that you can fully engage with the world, bringing your best self to every endeavour and touching the lives of others in meaningful ways.

Therefore, let us delve into the nuances of self-care, exploring how a comprehensive approach to well-being can become the foundation upon which you build a life of purpose, joy, and unparalleled success. This section aims to equip you with the knowledge and tools to embrace self-care not as a luxury, but as a fundamental aspect of your journey toward achieving your dreams and becoming the person you aspire to be.

In the pursuit of excellence, whether as an entrepreneur, a leader, or in the personal realm as a friend or family member, the act of self-care emerges not as an optional indulgence but as a critical responsibility. To extend your best to others—be it wisdom, support, or service—you must first ensure that your reservoir of well-being is amply filled. This principle holds true across all spectrums of life; you cannot pour from an empty cup. Your ability to positively impact those around you—your team, clients, and loved ones—is directly proportional to how well you care for yourself.

Acknowledging the necessity of self-care is the first step towards embracing a life where your well-being is given precedence. In the dynamic landscape of business and personal challenges, neglecting self-care is a disservice not only to yourself but also to those who depend on you. Without it, the quality of your output, the richness of your interactions, and the vibrancy of your presence diminish, leaving both you and your circle the poorer for it.

Reflecting on your self-care practices can be revealing. Consider the last time you truly took a moment for yourself, not as a luxury, but as a vital aspect of your daily routine. When was the last time you expanded your knowledge not out of necessity, but from a genuine desire for personal growth? How often do you indulge in activities that sharpen your skills or invite new ones into your life? The answers to these questions are indicators of how much you value and practice self-care.

Self-improvement and learning should be ongoing processes, adding to your professional expertise and enriching your personal life as well. Regular physical activity, for instance, isn't just about maintaining health; it's about respecting your body's need for movement and the mental clarity that comes with it. Similarly, delving into books on topics new or familiar expands your horizons, broadening your understanding and appreciation of the world.

Self-care isn't always about grand gestures. Sometimes, it's the small pauses—the deep breaths, the quiet moments of reflection, the short breaks that rejuvenate your spirit—that make all the difference. These acts of self-preservation are not selfish but essential, laying the groundwork for sustained effort and enduring success.

Therefore, as you move forward in your endeavours to impact the lives of others positively, remember that the foundation of all you wish to achieve lies in how well you take care of yourself. Embrace self-care as the cornerstone of your journey towards fulfilling your potential. Let it be the force that empowers you to offer the world the best of who you are, knowing that by caring for yourself, you are, in turn, enhancing your capacity to care for others. In this way, self-care becomes not just an act of personal well-being but an integral part of your legacy, influencing your business, your relationships, and the broader community in profoundly positive ways.

Embracing Struggle

The concept of embracing struggle is a profound one, deeply rooted in the journey of transformation, both personal and professional. The paradox that during our toughest times, self-care seems the most distant is a reflection of our natural inclination to focus outwardly, neglecting the inner work necessary to forge through adversity. It is through the fires of hardship that we learn the most about endurance, perseverance, and the transformative power of resilience. Struggles do not merely challenge us; they are the crucibles in which our strongest selves are formed, honing our minds into tools of unparalleled strength and versatility.

Reflect for a moment on the times you've faced your greatest challenges. More often than not, these periods of struggle catalyse significant internal growth, reshaping our perspectives, values, and priorities in ways that comfort and ease never could.

The narrative "The Butterfly Struggles" by Dan Western poignantly illustrates this principle.

"A man found a cocoon of a butterfly. One day, a small opening appeared. He sat and watched the butterfly for several hours as it struggled to force its body through that little hole. Until it suddenly stopped making any progress and looked like it was stuck. So the man decided to help the butterfly. He took a pair of scissors and snipped off the remaining bit of the cocoon. Although it had a swollen body and tiny, shrivelled wings, the butterfly emerged quickly. The man didn't think anything of it and sat there waiting for the wings to enlarge to support the butterfly. But that didn't happen. The butterfly spent the rest of its life unable to fly, crawling around with tiny wings and a swollen body. Despite the man's kind heart, he didn't understand that the restricting cocoon and the struggle needed by the butterfly to get through the small opening were God's way of forcing fluid from the butterfly's body into its wings. To prepare itself for flying once it was out of the cocoon."

— Western, 2022

The well-intentioned act of cutting the butterfly free from its cocoon, though born from a desire to help, ultimately deprives the butterfly of its necessary struggle. This struggle, as nature ingeniously designed, is essential for pushing fluid into the butterfly's wings, preparing it for flight. Without it, the butterfly is rendered incapable of doing what it was born to do—fly.

This allegory powerfully reminds us of the necessity of struggle in our lives. Our trials, like the butterfly's effort to escape its cocoon, are not merely obstacles but essential processes that prepare us for greater things. They push us beyond our perceived limits, fostering growth and resilience that is impossible in the absence of challenge. Struggles break us down, but only to build us up stronger and more capable than before.

In the realm of business, embracing struggle is equally crucial. Every entrepreneur and business leader has faced their share of difficulties. Consider Steve Jobs, whose ousting from Apple, the very company he co-founded, could have been seen as the ultimate defeat. Yet, it was this setback that propelled him into new ventures, acquiring new skills and insights that would, upon his return, elevate Apple to unprecedented success. Jobs' journey underscores the transformative power of adversity, turning potential defeat into the foundation for triumph.

The way we respond to and grow from our struggles is unique to each individual's journey. There is no universal blueprint for overcoming adversity. However, by applying the principles discussed in this chapter—self-care, continuous learning, courage to change, and the expansion of our worldview—we equip ourselves with the resilience needed to navigate life's inevitable challenges. It's through these practices that we ensure not just our survival but our ability to thrive and transform in the face of adversity.

In summary, the struggles we encounter are not just obstacles to be avoided, but valuable opportunities for growth and transformation. Like the butterfly, we must endure the struggles of our cocoons to emerge stronger, ready to soar to new heights. By embracing our struggles and committing to continuous self-development, we prepare ourselves for whatever challenges lie ahead, ensuring that when we do take flight, we do so with wings robust enough to carry us to our dreams.

As we close this chapter on personal development, it's clear that maintaining a mindset geared towards success is pivotal. The journey of self-improvement is continuous, demanding not just a transformation of skills but a profound reshaping of how we view the world and ourselves within it. This readiness to evolve is what arms us against the myriad challenges life throws our way, providing the resilience needed not just to face but overcome these hurdles. Such a mindset isn't just about achieving professional success; it enriches every facet of life, paving the way for a fulfilling and meaningful existence.

In his book The Alchemist, Paulo Coelho encapsulates this journey with a simple yet powerful message: "The secret of life, though, is to fall seven times and to get up eight times." It's a reminder that perseverance, the steadfast determination to rise after every fall, is at the heart of personal development and success.

As you stand on the threshold of applying these strategies to your life, take a moment to reflect deeply on the following questions. Don't rush through them; instead, allow yourself the space to contemplate your answers truly.

- What do I hope to achieve with this strategy? Why am I embarking on this journey?

- What is the ultimate goal of this process? Where do I see it leading me?

- How will this enhance my life or business? What tangible benefits do I anticipate?

Answering these questions with sincerity and thoughtfulness will guide you in choosing the strategy that aligns most closely with your goals and aspirations. It's not merely about selecting a path but understanding why you're stepping onto it and where you hope it will lead.

The journey of personal development is as much about the questions we ask ourselves as the answers we find along the way. By embracing this journey with an open heart and a willing mind, you set the stage for a life of continuous growth, resilience, and, ultimately, success.

CHAPTER 7

Weathering the Storms

> *"Storms don't come to teach us painful lessons, rather they are meant to wash us clean."*
> — Shannon L. Alder

In our journey toward transcending the ordinary and achieving the extraordinary, we are bound to encounter storms. These challenges are not detours or setbacks, but essential parts of the path forward. As Shannon L. Alder beautifully articulated, "Storms don't come to teach us painful lessons, rather they were meant to wash us clean." This perspective is vital as we navigate through the trials and tribulations on our journey to success.

Facing obstacles is an inevitable aspect of pursuing significant goals. Breakdowns and challenges are not signs of failure, but indicators of the ambitious path you've chosen. Recognising this can transform your approach to facing difficulties, turning daunting obstacles into springboards for growth.

The journey to greatness is paved with moments of struggle. It's during these times that your resilience is tested, and your capacity for innovation is challenged. The difference between those who achieve their dreams and those who fall short is often their response to adversity. Viewing challenges not as barriers but as opportunities to jump higher and learn more about yourself is the key to turning breakdowns into breakthroughs.

Embracing the struggle requires a shift in mindset. It's about seeing every problem not as a dead-end but as a detour on the road to success—a chance to strengthen your resolve, refine your strategies, and deepen your understanding. This chapter is dedicated to equipping you with the mindset and tools needed to navigate through storms, leap over hurdles with grace, and emerge stronger on the other side.

The narratives of the most successful individuals are replete with stories of perseverance through hard times. This universal truth reminds us that adversity is not unique to us; it's a shared human experience, a common thread in the tapestry of achievement. The readiness to face and overcome challenges is a prerequisite for success. It is in the heart of the storm that true strength is found, not in avoiding the storm but in pushing through it with determination and grace.

This chapter will guide you through strategies that reframe difficulties into opportunities for growth. You'll learn how to navigate the inevitable challenges that arise when striving for significant goals, turning what may seem like insurmountable obstacles into stepping stones for success. Remember, it's not the presence of challenges that defines us, but how we choose to respond to them.

As we embark on this journey through the storms, let's do so knowing that every challenge faced is an opportunity to demonstrate our resilience, test our strategies, and affirm our commitment to our goals. Let this chapter be your guide in transforming breakdowns into breakthroughs, ensuring that every storm you weather brings you closer to the extraordinary life you are meant to lead.

Yelena Isinbayeva's journey from a gymnastics enthusiast to becoming the greatest female pole-vaulter of all time is a remarkable testament to resilience and adaptability. Her early years were dedicated to gymnastics, where she dreamt of achieving world champion status. Training rigorously from the tender age of 5, gymnastics wasn't just a sport to Yelena; it was her life's ambition. However, nature had a different plan. Growing too tall for gymnastics, standing at 1.74 metres (5 ft 8.5 in), she found herself at a crossroads at the age of 15. The dream that had fuelled a decade of her life suddenly seemed out of reach.

In this moment of potential despair, Isinbayeva's story could have taken a turn towards defeat. She could have walked away from sports entirely, letting her training and her dreams fade into memory. Instead, she saw an opportunity. Drawing on the strength, balance, and flexibility honed through years of gymnastic training, she redirected her focus towards pole vaulting. In this field, her attributes were not a disadvantage but a significant asset.

This pivot was not a fallback but a leap into a realm where her unique skills set her apart. Her gymnastic training, which included rigorous discipline, balance, and core strength, translated seamlessly into pole vaulting. It wasn't long before she was breaking records, soaring over heights that no other woman had reached before. She cleared the five-metre barrier, set world records (28 times, no less), and won two Olympic gold medals along with three World Championships. Her world record of 5.06 metres, set in Zürich in August 2009, remains unbeaten, cementing her legacy in the annals of athletic history.

Isinbayeva's story is more than just a tale of athletic prowess; it's a powerful illustration of how setbacks can be reframed into stepping stones for greater achievements. When faced with the breakdown of her gymnastic dreams, she didn't let despair dictate her future. Instead, she adapted, pivoted, and found a new path to success. Her journey underscores a vital lesson: breakdowns, no matter how devastating, can become breakthroughs if approached with the right mindset.

Yelena Isinbayeva's experience teaches us that life's storms can indeed wash us clean, preparing us for achievements beyond our initial aspirations. Her ability to transform a personal disaster into an asset that propelled her to unprecedented heights in a completely different sport is a profound reminder that embracing change and being willing to shift our goals can lead to extraordinary, life-altering success.

Frame of mind

Christmas of 1981 remains one of my most memorable holidays, largely thanks to a game of Twister that turned our family gathering into an unforgettable comedy show. After indulging in a lavish lunch and participating in our traditional toast during the Queen's speech, we embarked on an afternoon of games. Charades and Twister were the main events, leading to much laughter and a healthy dose of competitive spirit among my five brothers, two cousins, and me.

However, this particular game escalated from our usual competitive fun to an episode of pure hilarity, thanks to my great aunt's spontaneous decision to join. Her spirits were high from the sherry trifle and a couple of glasses of sherry; she was determined to outmanoeuvre us all. We watched in amazement as she twisted and turned with surprising agility, dodging under arms and stepping over intertwined legs. Her commitment to winning was both admirable and, given her state of joyful inebriation, a recipe for comedy.

The inevitable happened as she stretched too far, perhaps tempted by fate or another glass of sherry. Her balance wavered, and with a dramatic twist, she lost her fight against gravity. The domino effect ensued; she tumbled onto one brother, who then collided with another, resulting in a heap of laughing relatives. My great aunt, now on her back with a view of the ceiling and her dignity in an uproar, became the star of the show. The room erupted in laughter, not at her expense, but in shared joy at the absurdity of the moment.

She returned to her sofa and her sherry, the applause of her audience ringing in her ears. This moment encapsulated the essence of our family gatherings: laughter, resilience, and an unspoken agreement that no setback was too serious to overcome or too sacred to laugh about.

This is the mindset that transforms ordinary challenges into opportunities for growth, laughter, and bonding. In the realm of games, setbacks are merely part of the fun, moments to be cherished rather than feared. They remind us not to take life too seriously and that, often, our most challenging moments can lead to our greatest joys. Just as in the game of Twister, life requires flexibility, a sense of humour, and the understanding that sometimes, a fall is just an invitation to get back up and try again, perhaps with a different strategy or, in my great aunt's case, a little less sherry.

Embracing challenges and transforming breakdowns into breakthroughs begins with cultivating a mindset that thrives on solving problems. This mindset, much like the strategies employed in gameplay, hinges on the ability to view issues from a fresh perspective, focusing on solutions rather than dwelling on obstacles. It's about shifting from a mindset that magnifies problems to one that eagerly seeks out solutions, thereby unleashing your potential to achieve greater outcomes.

The initial step is to embrace the challenges you encounter as mere hurdles in your journey, not insurmountable barriers halting your progress. Often, the term 'problem' triggers a negative response, catapulting our minds into a state of stress, preoccupied with what's amiss rather than how to rectify it. However, when you start to see challenges as integral parts of life's race—obstacles to overcome rather than dead ends—you begin to navigate through them with ease and agility.

Focus intently on finding solutions. Shift away from ruminating over the mishaps and direct your energy toward identifying viable solutions. Begin by outlining every conceivable solution, jotting them down on paper, a digital note, or even discussing them with a team or a group of trusted individuals. This brainstorming process not only cultivates a solution-oriented mindset but also broadens your perspective, enabling you to view the problem from various angles and thereby formulating a well-rounded approach to addressing it.

Once you've compiled a list of potential solutions, delve into the root cause of the problem. Understanding the origin of the challenge, combined with your arsenal of potential solutions, positions you to make informed and balanced decisions. Investigate the circumstances that led to the current situation, question why it unfolded as it did, and consider how it might have been averted. This analytical approach not only aids in solving the present issue but also fortifies your ability to preempt future challenges.

Adopting this new perspective on problem-solving marks a significant transformation in how you perceive and tackle challenges. View each obstacle as an opportunity for personal and professional growth—a chance to expand your knowledge, refine your skills, and enhance your resilience. Embracing this mindset not only improves your capacity to resolve current dilemmas but also equips you with the foresight and adaptability to efficiently navigate future challenges.

By redefining how you perceive and approach problems, you unlock the door to continuous improvement and innovation. This shift in perspective is a testament to the power of a solution-focused mindset, turning every challenge into a stepping stone towards achieving your highest potential and rendering you unstoppable in the pursuit of your goals.

Transforming breakdowns into breakthroughs

In the chilling January air of 2018, Cecilie Fjellhøy stepped into a private plane, bound from London to Bulgaria, a journey that promised the adventure of a lifetime. Her companion, Simon Leviev, a man she had met on Tinder, epitomised the charm and mystery one might expect from the son of the "king of diamonds," Lev Leviev, a famed Russian-Israeli diamond oligarch. This date was not just dinner and drinks; it was a flight across continents, a bold leap into a whirlwind relationship that was too good to be true. This is the story of the Tinder Swindler, a narrative that weaves through the delicate fabric of trust and betrayal, leading to a remarkable transformation from despair to empowerment.

Simon's Tinder profile was a gallery of luxury, a life punctuated by jets, yachts, and the sparkling allure of expensive wines. He styled himself as the Prince of Diamonds, a moniker that promised more than just wealth—it hinted at a fairy tale waiting to unfold with just one swipe right. The reality, however, was far from a fairy tale. Simon Leviev's scheme was cunning in its simplicity: he presented himself as a wealthy heir embroiled in the perilous diamond trade, starting long-distance relationships while ostensibly travelling for work. The luxury and opulence his dates witnessed were funded by a chain of deception, with each woman unknowingly financing the lifestyle of her successor.

Cecilie, like others before her, was drawn into Simon's orbit under the pretence of romance and wealth. Their relationship, while promising on the surface, unfolded mostly across the distance, punctuated by elaborate tales of danger and pleas for financial help. Simon claimed that his life was threatened by enemies in the diamond business, necessitating the use of others' credit cards to avoid detection. The requests for financial assistance spiralled into a vortex of loans, maxed-out credit cards, and promises of repayment that never materialised, leaving Cecilie and others like her in crippling debt.

The unravelling of Simon Leviev's web of lies was a turning point, not just for Cecilie, but for a network of women ensnared in his deceit. After the cheque he gave her bounced, Cecilie's visit to the bank unveiled the grim reality: she had been victim to a professional scammer, a man whose crimes spanned continents and whose victims were left shattered in his wake. Leviev's eventual capture in Greece and extradition to Israel marked the end of his spree but not the end of the story for his victims.

Faced with the daunting task of rebuilding their lives, Cecilie and others refused to remain silent. Their collective effort to expose the dangers of online dating culminated in a documentary, a testament to their resilience and a warning to others. This story is not just about the deception practised by the Tinder Swindler; it's about the indomitable spirit of those who, having been pushed to the brink, chose to fight back.

Transforming from victims to champions, these women did not simply recover from their ordeal; they transcended it. The documentary was more than a cautionary tale; it was a cathartic journey that allowed them to reclaim their agency and use their harrowing experiences to educate and protect others. The proceeds from their story helped mitigate the financial ruins left by Simon Leviev, but more importantly, they fostered a sense of community and strength among those who had suffered at his hands.

The narrative of the Tinder Swindler serves as a potent reminder of the vulnerabilities inherent in our search for connection. It highlights the darker facets of online dating, where the anonymity of the digital world can mask deceit and ulterior motives. Yet, amidst the shadows of betrayal, the story of Cecilie Fjellhøy and her counterparts shines brightly as a beacon of resilience, empowerment, and hope. They transformed their breakdowns into breakthroughs, emerging not as victims but as victors, heroes who turned disaster and betrayal into triumph and growth.

This chapter is a tribute to their journey, a narrative that moves from the depths of deception to the peaks of perseverance. It's a testament to the human spirit's capacity for recovery and transformation, an inspiring reminder that even in our darkest moments, we possess the strength to write new chapters of courage, wisdom, and redemption.

The journey from breakdown to breakthrough begins with a profound shift in perspective, a change in the narrative that frames our lives. It's about stepping back, evaluating the pieces of our personal or professional crises, and daring to see them not as endpoints but as catalysts for growth and transformation. This process, while daunting, holds the promise of remarkable change, turning our greatest challenges into our most significant achievements.

Take the game of Twister, as played by my great aunt, as a metaphor for life's unpredictable challenges. Just as the game demands flexibility, balance, and the resilience to stand up after a fall, so too does life compel us to navigate its twists and turns with grace and determination. It's in the moments of imbalance, when we find ourselves sprawled on the floor, that we face a choice: to remain down or to rise, learn, and adapt.

Acknowledging the reality of our struggles is the first critical step towards transformation. It's about facing the discomfort head-on, recognising the fear, the loss, and the uncertainty without diminishing or exaggerating its impact. This honest assessment lays the groundwork for genuine change, providing a clear starting point from which to chart a new course.

Embracing our breakdowns with openness and honesty allows us to begin reconstructing our narrative, to see beyond the immediate pain towards the potential for renewal and growth. This is not about broadcasting our troubles to the world but about owning them privately, understanding their scope, and preparing ourselves for the journey ahead.

This initial stage of acknowledgement is more than just an exercise in self-awareness; it's a pivotal moment of empowerment. It marks the transition from being passive recipients of our circumstances to active architects of our future. By clearly identifying where we stand, we can start to map out a path forward, one that leads not just back to where we were, but to new heights we never imagined possible.

The transformation from breakdown to breakthrough is not a journey you embark on lightly. It requires courage, resilience, and the willingness to embrace change. But for those who dare to take the first step, the rewards are immeasurable. Not only does it offer the chance to overcome our immediate challenges, but it also equips us with the strength, wisdom, and perspective to navigate future storms.

In the end, the story of our lives is not defined by the obstacles we encounter, but by how we choose to respond to them. By acknowledging our struggles, learning from our falls, and courageously stepping into the unknown, we can turn our most significant challenges into our most transformative victories. This is the essence of turning breakdowns into breakthroughs—a journey that begins with a single, brave step forward.

As we embark on the journey of transforming breakdowns into breakthroughs, the importance of clarity cannot be overstated. The first crucial step is to evaluate the reality of the situation—stripped of narrative and emotion—to grasp the unvarnished truth of our predicament. It's about discerning the simple, unembellished facts: what has happened, what is currently happening, and what the immediate consequences are.

This unflinching honesty with oneself is foundational. Avoid the trap of dramatising the situation, which only serves to amplify fear and uncertainty. Similarly, resist the urge to downplay or sugarcoat the challenges you face. Neither extreme is helpful. Instead, strive for a clear, objective understanding of where you stand. It's about facing the raw truth of your breakdown, whether it's a personal loss, a professional setback, or a combination of challenges that threaten your sense of stability and progress.

Knowing the real truth about your breakdown—seeing it neither worse than it is nor disguising its severity—is the only way to accurately map out a path to where you want to be. This clear-eyed assessment provides a solid foundation from which to start crafting your breakthrough. It's the groundwork that enables you to plan effectively, identify the resources you'll need, and begin the process of rebuilding stronger and more resilient than before.

This initial step of acknowledging the reality of your situation is more than just an act of acceptance; it's an act of empowerment. It signifies your readiness to take control of your narrative, to move beyond victimhood and towards victory. By being clear and straight with yourself about where you currently are, you unlock the potential to navigate towards where you aspire to be.

Embracing this clarity is the key to transforming your breakdowns into breakthroughs. It equips you with the knowledge and perspective needed to face your challenges head-on and to start the process of turning obstacles into opportunities. Remember, the path to overcoming and growing from your struggles begins with a clear understanding of the terrain you must traverse. Only from this standpoint can you chart a course towards recovery, growth, and ultimately, triumph.

The journey from breakdown to breakthrough necessitates a profound act of self-forgiveness. It's all too common, in the throes of difficulty, to fall prey to negative self-talk, anger, and even self-repudiation. We become our own harshest critics, magnifying our missteps and miring ourselves in a quagmire of self-blame. This merciless self-judgement not only exacerbates our suffering but also impedes our capacity to navigate through tough times with resilience and grace.

The act of forgiving yourself, however, can serve as a powerful catalyst for transformation. It's about acknowledging that, like anyone else, you are susceptible to errors and misjudgments. More importantly, it's about understanding that these do not define your worth or your potential. Self-forgiveness liberates you from the chains of past mistakes, enabling you to approach your situation with a clearer mind and a lighter heart.

Forgiving yourself is not an exercise in absolution for the sake of avoidance, but a crucial step towards reclaiming your self-esteem and momentum. It paves the way for a more compassionate and constructive dialogue with yourself, one that recognises your humanity and fosters growth. By lifting the weight of self-condemnation, you open up space for healing and allow yourself the freedom to move forward with confidence.

This newfound self-compassion is instrumental in regaining momentum towards both personal and professional success. It shifts your focus from dwelling on what has been to what can be, instilling in you the belief that recovery and progress are within reach. Embracing self-forgiveness is thus not merely about overcoming a moment of failure; it's about equipping yourself with the resilience and self-assurance needed to navigate future challenges more effectively.

In essence, the path to breakthroughs is paved with forgiveness—forgiveness that starts with yourself. It's a pivotal step in transforming your breakdowns into opportunities for profound personal transformation and a testament to your strength and capacity for renewal.

Now that you've acknowledged the reality of your situation and offered yourself forgiveness, it's time to re-engage with your goals. This step is crucial, not merely as a form of rededication, but as an act of self-assertion in the face of adversity. Depending on the extent of the disruption caused by your setback, this could mean revisiting and refining your immediate objectives or perhaps reassessing your journey toward your ultimate goal. It's a moment to recalibrate, to ensure that your aspirations remain aligned with your current reality and capacities.

Actively recommitting to your goals involves concrete actions: jot them down in your journal, pin them to your fridge, or mark them on your calendar. Such visible reminders serve as daily cues of what you're striving towards, reinforcing your commitment and keeping your focus sharp. The motivation behind pursuing these goals is as critical as the goals themselves, injecting purpose and direction into your efforts.

Furthermore, it's essential to adapt your timelines and deadlines in light of the setbacks you've encountered. Life rarely follows a linear path, and flexibility in the face of changing circumstances is a hallmark of resilience. Adjusting your plans is not a sign of concession but a strategic response to the challenges you've faced.

Staying focused on your desired outcome amidst turmoil is undoubtedly challenging, yet it's not insurmountable. The key lies in transforming obstacles into opportunities, and roadblocks into routes for progression. This approach doesn't just pave the way for a smoother journey and greater success; it fundamentally changes you. Each hurdle overcome enriches your experience, equipping you with the wisdom and strength to not just survive but thrive. The transformation wrought by navigating through breakdowns to breakthroughs is profound, reshaping your understanding of what it means to pursue and achieve your goals. It's a testament to the power of resilience and the unyielding human spirit to rise above and beyond, charting a course through stormy seas to brighter horizons.

To craft a compelling and inspiring narrative about Abraham Lincoln's battle with melancholy and his rise to becoming a revered president, we'll first create a detailed outline. This narrative will blend your notes with researched information, ensuring accuracy and depth.

Abraham Lincoln is often celebrated as a paragon of leadership, wisdom, and integrity, universally acknowledged as one of the greatest presidents in American history. His monumental achievements, including the preservation of the Union and the emancipation of slaves, have etched his legacy into the very fabric of the nation. However, beneath the surface of this revered figure lay a tumultuous inner world dominated by a profound sense of melancholy. Those closest to him observed a man often shrouded in gloom, describing him as "the image of gloom," his demeanour reflecting a deep-seated despair that seemed almost palpable. Lincoln's struggle was not merely a temporary affliction but a persistent shadow that followed him throughout his life, a melancholy he believed was "set there by God." Despite this, Lincoln's story is not one of succumbing to despair but rather of an extraordinary journey of resilience, a testament to his strength and his ability to lead a nation through its darkest hours.

Abraham Lincoln's path was fraught with adversity from the outset. Born into the modest surroundings of a log cabin in Kentucky in 1809, Lincoln faced hardship and loss early in life. His mother's death when he was just nine years old and the challenging frontier conditions of his upbringing could have easily set the stage for a life constrained by circumstance. Yet, it was these early experiences that forged Lincoln's resilience and determination. His quest for knowledge was unquenchable; self-educated, Lincoln devoured books, teaching himself law and eventually entering the political arena. These early years were marked not only by intellectual growth but also by Lincoln's first encounters with what he and those around him termed "melancholy," a condition that would shape his character and outlook on the world.

Lincoln's journey was punctuated by professional failures and personal tragedies that tested his fortitude. His early endeavours into business were unsuccessful, leaving him with debt that took years to pay off. His political career, too, was initially marked by defeats, with multiple unsuccessful bids for political office. Perhaps the most poignant of his personal losses was the death of Ann Rutledge, a close friend, and possibly his first love, whose death in 1835 plunged Lincoln into profound grief. Yet, these setbacks did not deter him. Instead, they deepened his compassion and understanding of human suffering, qualities that would become hallmarks of his leadership.

Lincoln's melancholy, as those around him noted, was not merely a transient sadness but a profound and pervasive sense of despair. In today's terms, Lincoln might well have been diagnosed with chronic depression. His contemporaries described him as a man who carried with him an air of sadness, a profound gloom that seemed almost to emanate from his being. Lincoln himself was acutely aware of his condition, referring to his "hypochondriasis" or "the hypo," as he called it, acknowledging the deep impact it had on his psyche and worldview. Despite this, Lincoln did not view his melancholy as a flaw, but rather as a condition that allowed him a greater depth of empathy and understanding.

Remarkably, Lincoln found ways to channel his melancholic disposition into a source of strength and reflection. He was drawn to poetry and literature that echoed his own experiences of sorrow and loss, finding solace and understanding within their verses. Humour, too, became a vital coping mechanism, with Lincoln known for his keen wit and ability to lighten the mood even in the darkest times. His marriage to Mary Todd, though tumultuous, provided him with a family life that offered moments of joy and respite from the weight of his responsibilities and internal struggles.

Lincoln's presidency, defined by the Civil War, was perhaps the ultimate test of his resilience and leadership. Faced with a nation torn apart by conflict and the immense burden of decisions that would shape the course of history, Lincoln's melancholy provided him with a profound sense of moral clarity and purpose. His leadership during these years was marked by a deep empathy for the human condition, a trait that guided his decisions and helped to heal a divided nation. The Emancipation Proclamation and the Gettysburg Address stand as enduring symbols of his vision, his commitment to equality, and his belief in the American ideal.

Abraham Lincoln's life is a powerful narrative of triumph over adversity, a testament to the strength of the human spirit in the face of overwhelming odds. His journey from the depths of melancholy to the heights of presidential greatness serves as an enduring inspiration, reminding us that it is often through our struggles that we find our greatest strength. Lincoln's legacy is not just one of political achievement but a deeply personal story of resilience, empathy, and the unyielding belief in the possibility of change. In his life, we find a message of hope and perseverance that resonates as strongly today as it did over a century ago.

Lincoln was not just a figure of historical importance but a person whose inner battles shaped him into the leader he became, offering lessons of resilience and determination that remain relevant to all who face their own struggles. Recognise that there is more to the world than just you, and you can reclaim your direction by taking a step forward.

Nine Steps to Resolving a Breakdown

In the journey of life and work, we all face moments that test our resolve, challenge our capabilities, and sometimes lead to breakdowns. These moments, as daunting as they may seem, hold the seeds of transformation and breakthrough. It is not the absence of challenges, but our response to them that defines our path forward. This guide aims to provide you with practical, actionable steps to turn any breakdown into a breakthrough.

Understanding Breakdowns

Breakdowns are part and parcel of our lives. They can range from minor hiccups in our day-to-day routines to significant obstacles that seem to derail our plans completely. At their core, breakdowns are disruptions — moments when things do not go according to plan. This can be as simple as missing a deadline, facing a challenging situation at work, or encountering personal setbacks. The common thread in all these scenarios is the sense of being stuck or blocked from achieving our intended goals.

Breakdowns often result from a combination of factors, including unforeseen circumstances, internal misalignments, or external pressures. They can stem from overambition, lack of resources, or unexpected changes in our environment. Sometimes, they are the result of our own actions or inactions, while at other times, they are entirely out of our control.

The impact of a breakdown is not just physical or external; it carries significant psychological and emotional weight. It can lead to feelings of frustration, disappointment, stress, and even self-doubt. These emotions, if not managed properly, can cloud your judgement and hinder our ability to find effective solutions.

However, it's crucial to recognise that within every breakdown lies the potential for significant growth and learning. By facing these challenges head-on, we can gain insights into our resilience, adaptability, and true potential. Breakdowns force us to pause, reassess our paths, and perhaps even rediscover our passions and goals. They can serve as catalysts for change, pushing us to explore new avenues and solutions we might not have considered otherwise.

To transform a breakdown into a breakthrough, the first step is to shift our perspective. Instead of viewing obstacles as insurmountable problems, we can see them as opportunities to reassess our strategies, learn from our mistakes, and emerge stronger.

As we move forward, remember that understanding the nature of breakdowns is the foundation upon which we can start building our pathway to breakthroughs. The next section will guide you through reconnecting with your goals, a critical step in navigating through breakdowns with purpose and clarity.

As we embark on the nine steps to transforming breakdowns into breakthroughs, let's consider a real-life scenario that perfectly illustrates this process. Picture a journey, not unlike one I undertook for work a few years back. The destination was Congleton in Cheshire, a solid three to four-hour drive from where I live. I meticulously mapped out my day, aligning everything from dropping my daughters off at school to ensure I'd return home well before 7pm, to greet friends who were coming for dinner. My plan accounted for potential delays, including a thirty-minute stop to charge my car on the way there and another on the return leg. Everything was neatly scheduled, with each segment of the journey placed in my diary.

However, life has a knack for demonstrating that even the best-laid plans can veer off course.

Step 1: What's the Breakdown?

As we delve into the first critical step of transforming breakdowns into breakthroughs, it's crucial to isolate and identify the breakdown in its most unembellished form. In this process, the distinction between the superficial obstacles we face and the actual jeopardy to our goals becomes clear. It's not the external barriers themselves that define our breakdowns; it's how these barriers threaten our objectives.

Take, for instance, the scenario of my journey back from Congleton. The smooth start and meticulous planning suggested a seamless return home, aligning perfectly with the evening's plans. However, the real test emerged not from the predictable twists and turns of travel but from an unforeseen roadblock throwing my schedule into disarray. At this juncture, it was evident: the breakdown wasn't the traffic jam or the road closure but the jeopardised goal of returning home by 7pm. This simple yet significant realisation is what we're aiming to achieve in this first step.

Understanding that the breakdown is specifically "the impossibility of arriving home by 7pm as planned" strips the situation of its complexity and emotion. It transforms a potentially overwhelming scenario into a clear, manageable issue. By focusing on this direct impact on our goal, we avoid being ensnared in the details of the road closure or the frustration it might cause. Instead, we can direct our energy towards navigating around this specific challenge.

This refined understanding encourages us to look beyond the immediate obstructions and evaluate how our path to achieving our goals is obstructed. It compels us to acknowledge the situation in unemotional terms: the target time for arriving home will not be met under the current plan. Recognising this allows us to move forward with clarity and purpose, laying the groundwork for the subsequent steps in turning our breakdowns into avenues for breakthroughs.

In essence, this initial step isn't about spotting the hurdle; it's about precisely pinpointing how our current trajectory falls short of our goal. By doing so, we set the stage for a deliberate and effective response to any setbacks, armed with the insight and focus needed to steer our journey back on course.

As we wrap up this crucial first step of identifying our breakdown, let's underscore the empowering aspect of this process. Declaring a breakdown is not a sign of defeat, but a proactive acknowledgement that propels us towards resolution and growth. It's a declaration that you're ready to tackle challenges head-on, transforming obstacles into opportunities.

Now, it's your turn to take this empowering step. Reflect on your current goals, mini-goals, or milestones. Is there one that you're at risk of not achieving? Perhaps you've already missed a target and have been pressing forward, hoping to correct course along the way without formally acknowledging the setback. This moment is your opportunity to bring clarity and intention back into your journey.

Declare your breakdown with clarity and confidence. Whether it's a project falling behind schedule, a personal goal that's veered off track, or a team target that's not progressing as planned, naming it strips away the power of ambiguity and puts you back in control. Remember, acknowledging a breakdown is a positive, forward-moving action, not an admission of failure or weakness.

So, what is your breakdown? Be specific about what goal or milestone is in jeopardy. This step isn't about dwelling on the problem but about identifying it clearly so you can address it effectively. Embrace this moment to be honest with yourself. Pretending everything is fine when it's not only delays the solution and hampers progress.

State your breakdown boldly and move forward. By doing so, you're taking the first, crucial step toward navigating your way out of this challenge and toward your goals. This is the first step in turning your breakdown into your breakthrough. Once you've declared your breakdown, you're ready to proceed to step 2, armed with the knowledge and clarity to overcome obstacles and continue your path to success.

Step 2: Assess the Current Situation Factually

In the whirlwind of a breakdown, our first instinct might lean towards letting our emotions steer the ship—leading to an overwhelming sense of frustration, anxiety, or disappointment. Yet, the true course of navigating through these turbulent waters requires a moment of pause, a step back to assess the situation from a standpoint of pure fact, devoid of the haze of emotional bias.

The Imperative of Detaching Emotion

Emotions, inherently tied to our human nature, have the power to warp our perception, amplifying obstacles or conjuring issues from thin air. By anchoring your assessment in facts, you cut through the fog, allowing the reality of the situation to crystallise. This clear-eyed view is your cornerstone in crafting a viable plan of action.

Strategies for Objective Evaluation

1. Lay Out the Facts: Start with laying down the concrete details. What is the situation? What are the immediate consequences? Keep it succinct and focused.

2. Sidestep the Blame Game: Assigning blame, be it towards yourself, others, or the circumstances, only muddles your understanding and stalls your progress.

3. Distinguish Between Reality and Reaction: Separate the actual events from your emotional response to them. Recognise how you feel, but temporarily shelf these emotions for this particular analysis.

Consider the scenario where you're stuck in traffic, risking a missed appointment. The factual breakdown might go, "I am presently in traffic, which will delay my arrival at my lunch meeting." This straightforward acknowledgement paves the way for a solution-oriented approach, unburdened by emotional turmoil.

On my return trip from Congleton, recognising that an on-time arrival home was slipping through my fingers could easily have spiralled into a whirlwind of frustration. I could have cursed the immovable traffic, lamented over the congested roads, or vented my irritation at the endless sea of vehicles blocking my path—none of which would propel me any closer to my destination.

Succumbing to annoyance clouds judgement, impairing our capability to dissect the predicament and devise logical solutions. In the heat of frustration or sorrow, our analytical abilities are significantly hampered.

The decision to pull over before diving into the gridlock was pivotal. Though it seemed counterintuitive, like an unnecessary delay, it was a calculated pause for clarity. It afforded me the space to cool down and recalibrate. In those moments, I reassessed not just the blockade ahead but realigned with my ultimate objective, thus priming my mind for strategic thinking.

This step, stripping down to the bare facts, is an exercise in regaining control. By disentangling our emotions from the equation, we equip ourselves to face the challenge head-on, with a level head and a clearer perspective. It's about transforming the reactive into the proactive. As you face your own junctions and roadblocks, remember this crucial step: assess the current situation factually. It lays the groundwork for the strategic manoeuvres you'll employ to navigate through to your desired outcome.

Step 3: Identify What Worked

Step 3 in our journey to transform breakdowns into breakthroughs calls for a moment of introspection, a pause to identify what has propelled us forward thus far. It's easy, especially in times of difficulty, to be enveloped by what seems to be going wrong, to let setbacks overshadow our achievements. However, it's crucial to remember that no matter how entrenched in a challenge we feel, we've made strides from where we started. Acknowledging the strategies and actions that have borne fruit up until now is not just an exercise in positive thinking but a strategic move to uncover potential solutions for the hurdles at hand.

Highlighting Effective Measures

This step encourages you to cast a reflective glance over the journey you've embarked on towards your goals. What milestones have you passed? What strategies have contributed, even in the smallest measure, to the progress you've charted? Identifying these successful elements offers a beacon, guiding you through the fog of current challenges.

Capitalising on What Works

1. Catalogue Successes: Begin by cataloguing the actions or strategies that have shown results in the past or are yielding benefits in the present, related to this goal.

2. Decipher the Success Code: Delve into the reasons behind these successes. Was it the timing, the allocation of resources, or perhaps a specific method that tipped the scales in your favour? Grasping the underlying reasons for success is as crucial as the successes themselves.

3. Strategic Application: With these insights in hand, ponder how you can adapt and apply these proven strategies to the current scenario you're navigating. Often, the key to unlocking the solution lies in amplifying what has been working and minimising the ineffective.

Imagine, for instance, that in past challenges, passing responsibilities to others more qualified to handle them effectively paved the way for overcoming obstacles. This reflection may reveal that incorporating allocation of tasks into your strategy could once again serve as a valuable tactic in addressing the current issue at hand.

In the midst of navigating the unexpected twists and turns of my journey back from Congleton, I took a moment to pause and reflect on the first leg of the trip that had unfolded exactly as I had envisioned. This reflection wasn't just a brief interlude; it was a deliberate effort to recognise the aspects of my planning that had worked in my favour.

I had meticulously crafted my day with buffers for unforeseen events, a strategy that paid off when I found myself with enough spare time to enjoy a cup of coffee and a snack. This wasn't merely a break; it was a mini-reward, a testament to the effectiveness of my planning. Moreover, the adaptive navigation system I relied on played a crucial role, intelligently recalibrating the route to account for traffic conditions.

This moment of introspection highlighted my ability to plan with precision and foresight. I had not cornered myself with back-to-back commitments that left no room for the smallest of delays. Instead, I had woven flexibility into my schedule, acknowledging that the unpredictable nature of travel demanded such an approach.

This reflection was a powerful reminder of the strengths in my planning and execution up to that point. It served as a beacon, illuminating the skills and strategies that had served me well and could be leaned on as I navigated the challenges ahead. Recognising these victories, no matter how small, reinforced my confidence in my ability to adapt and overcome. It was a testament to the importance of not just planning for the journey but also recognising the value of the journey itself.

This third step is more than just a pat on the back for what you've achieved; it's a strategic pivot that leverages your past successes to illuminate the path forward. By recognising what has worked, you're not only affirming your progress but also equipping yourself with a toolkit of proven strategies ready to be deployed against the present breakdown. It's a reminder that within the narrative of your journey, the solutions to today's challenges may already lie in the chapters of your past successes. Let this step guide you in harnessing the power of reflection to transform today's obstacles into tomorrow's triumphs.

Step 4: Analyse Ineffective Actions

The journey to transforming breakdowns into breakthroughs is as much about discerning what hasn't worked as it is about recognising what has. In the pursuit of our goals, it's inevitable that some strategies fall short. Understanding these missteps is not an exercise in self-flagellation, but a critical step towards improvement.

Identifying the Causes of Ineffectiveness

When examining the aspects of our efforts that haven't yielded the expected results, the aim is to approach this analysis with objectivity and a spirit of learning. What strategies fell flat? Which actions, thought to be catalysts for progress, turned into stumbling blocks?

Approach for a Constructive Analysis

- List Ineffective Actions: Clearly identify the actions or decisions that did not contribute to progress. This could range from specific tasks to broader strategies.

- Unearth Root Causes: Delving deeper into why these actions were ineffective is crucial. Was the timing off? Did a lack of resources play a role, or was there a misalignment in team efforts?

- Incorporate Lessons Learned: Armed with this insight, the next step is to adapt. By learning from these missteps, future strategies can be fine-tuned to avoid similar pitfalls.

For instance, if reflecting on a project delay, it's possible to uncover that the root cause was an overly ambitious timeline. This realisation isn't about placing blame but about refining future planning processes.

Reflecting on my journey home from Congleton, I had to concede that my reliance on the GPS system's predictions was, in this instance, misplaced. While not always foreseeable, traffic incidents like the one I encountered can significantly derail plans. This realisation prompted me to consider the value of having alternative plans and allowing for more generous time buffers, especially when timing is critical.

Learning from the Journey

This step of pinpointing what hasn't worked is integral to crafting a more resilient and adaptable approach to goal achievement. By acknowledging these lessons, we can forge a path that is not only more resistant to unforeseen challenges but also enriched by the wisdom of past experiences.

As we move forward, the journey involves a deeper reflection on not just the external actions, but also the internal states that may have contributed to the situation. This holistic view is the cornerstone of transforming potential setbacks into opportunities for growth and development.

Step 5: Reflect on Ineffective States of Being

On the path to transforming breakdowns into breakthroughs, understanding our emotional and psychological states is as crucial as the actions we take. It's not merely the obstacles we face that define our journey, but also the mindset with which we approach them. This realisation underpins this step.

Unpacking Emotional Reactions

Every challenge we encounter can stir a whirlpool of emotions—frustration, demotivation, anxiety, and fear are common guests in these moments of turmoil. Recognising these feelings and their profound influence on our decision-making and actions is critical. It's the first step toward a meaningful change in how we navigate through difficulties.

Strategies for Emotional and Psychological Shifts

- Acknowledge Your Current State: Honesty with oneself is the foundation of transformation. Identifying and accepting your feelings paves the way for genuine progress. Denial, on the other hand, is a roadblock to your growth.

- Understand the Source: Delve into the reasons behind your emotional state. Is it a fear of failure, or perhaps a lack of self-confidence that's holding you back? Pinpointing the root cause is essential for addressing it effectively.

- Choose to Shift: Conscious decision-making is powerful. Opt to transition into a more beneficial state of mind. This could mean cultivating curiosity over fear, determination over frustration, or calmness in place of anxiety.

Take, for example, the common hurdle of procrastination, often rooted in a fear of failure. Recognising this fear, exploring its origins, and reframing the task as a chance for personal growth can transform procrastination into productivity.

Reflecting on my return journey from Congleton, I identified a complacency in relying on the GPS's estimated travel times and a similar laxity in my approach to charging my car. In retrospect, a dose of vigilance and proactive planning could have mitigated the setbacks I faced. This acknowledgement is not about dwelling on what went wrong, but about leveraging these insights for future planning and execution. As a result, I took a few moments to reflect on my state and determined to shift to a state of empowerment and purpose. To clear my thinking and focus on the outcome of being at home in time for my guests' arrival.

By taking the time to examine and shift our emotional and psychological states, we arm ourselves with a more nuanced and empowered approach to overcoming challenges. This step is about building resilience not just on the surface level of our actions, but at the core of our being. Moving forward, this deeper understanding of ourselves becomes a cornerstone in our ability to turn potential breakdowns into significant breakthroughs.

Step 6: Gauge the Impact of the Breakdown

This step in transforming a breakdown into a breakthrough revolves around evaluating the ramifications of the current issue. It's about assessing the scope and depth of how this challenge affects you, those around you, and the broader objectives at hand. By understanding the true weight of the breakdown, you position yourself to tackle it with precision, ensuring that your responses are proportionate to the actual problem and not clouded by misplaced anxiety or undue stress.

Understanding the Impact

Begin by stripping the situation down to its core, identifying the direct consequences it bears on your project, timelines, relationships, and overall goals. What shifts will this breakdown necessitate in your plans? How does it ripple through your team or affect the people connected to your goal? This step requires a balanced mix of objectivity and foresight, looking at immediate setbacks while considering long-term effects.

Strategies for Insightful Impact Assessment

- Quantify Where Possible: Assign numerical values to the impact. This could be in terms of time delays, financial costs, or resource allocations. Quantification offers a concrete perspective that can guide your decision-making process.

- Prioritise by Severity: Not every consequence of a breakdown holds the same weight. Some impacts might be superficial, while others can have profound implications. Distinguish between these varying degrees of severity to focus your efforts where they're most needed.

- Seek Out the Hidden Opportunities: In every challenge lies the seed of opportunity. A setback could unveil areas for innovation, efficiency improvements, or even personal growth. By adopting a mindset that looks for these hidden gems, you can turn a seemingly negative situation into a catalyst for positive change.

Reflecting on my own predicament of being delayed and potentially missing an evening with guests, it's clear that while the situation is less than ideal, its true impact is manageable. The immediate inconvenience to my family and friends, though regrettable, is not insurmountable. Communication and a bit of flexibility can mitigate the negative effects, turning an uncomfortable situation into a minor hiccup.

It's essential to approach this step with a level head. While the emotional and logistical fallout of a breakdown can seem daunting at first glance, a detailed and rational assessment often reveals that the sky isn't falling. In fact, it's through navigating these very obstacles that we often find new paths to our goals, learn valuable lessons, and forge stronger connections with those around us.

As you consider the impact of your own breakdown, challenge yourself to view it through a lens of opportunity and learning. What can this situation teach you? How can it refine your strategies or strengthen your resolve? By understanding the true extent of a breakdown's impact, you equip yourself with the knowledge to turn adversity into advantage, setting the stage for a powerful comeback.

Step 7: Letting Go of Negative Beliefs and Emotions

Step 7 in our journey to transform breakdowns into breakthroughs is about shedding the weight of negative emotions and limiting beliefs. It's about understanding that while our feelings towards setbacks are valid, they don't have to define our next steps or cloud our judgement. This stage is crucial for clearing the path towards resolution and progress.

Embracing Emotional Agility

The task now is to navigate away from the storm of negative thoughts and emotions that might be swirling around. These feelings, while a natural response to challenging situations, can cloud our vision and impede our capacity to find effective solutions.

Strategies for Emotional Release

- Identify and Confront: Begin by pinpointing the exact emotions and beliefs that are acting as obstacles. Is it fear of judgement? Is it disappointment in not meeting your own standards? Naming these feelings gives you power over them.

- Challenge the Validity: Once identified, question the accuracy of these negative beliefs. Are they based on facts, or are they assumptions coloured by emotional bias? This reflection can diminish their hold on you.

- Direct Your Focus: Concentrate on elements within your influence. While you may not be able to change the past or certain external circumstances, you can control your response and the steps you take moving forward.

Consider the transformative potential of adopting a more positive outlook. For instance, missing a deadline doesn't have to signify failure; it can be an opportunity for enhancement or refinement. This shift in perspective can dramatically change the course of action and open up new avenues for problem-solving.

In the context of my delayed journey home, the realisation of being late stirred a mix of emotions. Initially, anger at the unforeseen traffic, frustration over my planning, and sadness over disappointing my guests dominated my thoughts. However, I recognised that dwelling on these feelings would only hinder my ability to think clearly and find a viable solution. By consciously choosing to let go of these negative emotions, I opened myself up to constructive thinking and creative problem-solving.

The Liberating Effect of Letting Go

Letting go isn't about ignoring your feelings or pretending they don't exist. It's about acknowledging them, understanding their root causes, and then making a deliberate choice not to let them dictate your actions. This liberating step is about empowering yourself to approach the situation with clarity, creativity, and a renewed sense of purpose.

As you confront your own breakdown, remember that the power to move forward lies in your ability to release unhelpful emotions and beliefs. By doing so, you not only navigate the current challenge more effectively but also enhance your resilience and capability to handle future obstacles. This step is a testament to your strength and a vital component of your journey toward breakthroughs and success.

Step 8: Recreating Your Outcomes and Goals

Step 8 brings us to a pivotal moment in our journey of transformation: the decision to either recommit to our original goal or forge a new path forward. This decision isn't about giving up; it's about adapting to the realities we've uncovered through this process and moving forward with purpose and clarity.

Adapting Goals to Reality

Our journey thus far has equipped us with a deeper understanding of the situation and ourselves. Now, with a more rational and less emotionally charged perspective, it's time to evaluate our goals in the light of recent insights.

- Assessing Feasibility: Look objectively at what is now achievable within the current constraints. It's crucial at this juncture to maintain a clear head, steering clear of emotional biases that might skew your assessment.

- Embracing Adaptability: The ability to pivot and explore alternative pathways is a hallmark of resilient leadership. Openness to new methods and strategies can unveil opportunities previously overlooked.

- Leveraging Insights: The wisdom garnered from identifying what worked and what didn't is invaluable. It guides the realignment of your goals, ensuring they're both ambitious and grounded in reality.

For example, revising a project timeline might initially seem like a setback. Yet, this recalibration could provide an unforeseen opportunity to enhance the project's outcome, benefiting from additional research or resources that weren't initially available.

My Personal Pivot

Reflecting on my journey back from Congleton, faced with the prospect of disappointing my guests and my wife, I found myself at a crossroads. The easy choice would have been to resign myself to lateness and its consequences. Instead, I chose to reassess my situation with fresh eyes. I was determined to find a way to meet my original goal: arriving home in time for dinner. At that moment, the specifics of my new plan were unclear, but my commitment to my goal was unwavering. My resolve to adapt and explore new strategies kept the possibility of success alive.

Moving Forward with Determination

This step isn't just about making pragmatic adjustments to our goals; it's about reaffirming our commitment to the outcomes we cherish. It's a testament to our growth, resilience, and unwavering dedication to achieving success, no matter the hurdles.

As you stand at this juncture, ask yourself: How can I adapt my goals to better fit the current reality? In what ways can I leverage my newfound insights to forge a path to success? The answers to these questions will guide you towards a more informed, flexible, and achievable set of objectives.

Remember, the essence of leadership and personal growth lies in our ability to navigate uncertainties with grace, adaptability, and foresight. Recommitting to your goals or charting a new course is not just a step in the process; it's a bold declaration of your resilience and capacity to thrive in the face of adversity.

Step 9: Formulating Actions for Moving Forward

As we approach the culmination of transforming breakdowns into breakthroughs, Step 9 beckons us to the vital task of crafting a concrete action plan. This step is about bridging the gap between where we are and where we aim to be, propelled by the refined goals and insights we've garnered along the way.

Crafting Your Blueprint for Success

- Detailing the Path Forward: Begin by dissecting your adjusted goal into tangible steps. Employ the RAPID goal achievement framework to ensure your plan is both robust and believable. Each action should be a deliberate stride towards your reimagined objectives.

- Strategic Resource Allocation: Clearly define the roles and responsibilities within your team. Understand the resources at your disposal and align them effectively with the tasks at hand. This step is about orchestrating your assets and talents for maximum impact.

- Milestones as Your Guideposts: Establishing deadlines for each segment of your plan introduces structure and urgency. These time-bound milestones serve not only as checkpoints but also as motivators, keeping you and your team focused and driven.

Applying Lessons to Overcome Obstacles

Let's revisit the scenario of my delayed return journey from Congleton. Recognising that my initial route was compromised, I pivoted, identifying alternative strategies to mitigate the delay. My decision to search for alternative charging stations opened up a new pathway home, sidestepping the gridlock and dramatically reducing my expected lateness.

This adaptability in the face of unforeseen challenges exemplifies the essence of Step 9. It wasn't merely about finding another charging station; it was about reimagining the journey within the constraints I faced. By assessing the traffic flow and adjusting my route accordingly, I crafted a plan that, while not perfect, significantly improved my situation.

Finally, as I set off on my new planned route, I took one additional action, I phone my wife to let her know of the challenge. I also informed her that I was taking an alternative route and that I expected to be a few minutes late, but that I would adjust my route whenever it might save time with the aim of shaving a few minutes here and there to be on time.

This step acknowledges the commitment I made to my wife to be there when our guest arrived and that I am committed to overcoming the breakdown and being on time. It also gives her the opportunity to prepare for my late arrival should that be the case.

Your Blueprint for Moving Forward

Now, it's your turn. With your goals recalibrated and a clear understanding of what's at stake, outline the steps needed to navigate out of your current predicament. This plan should be your roadmap, detailing the who, what, when, and how of your strategy to achieve your goals.

Remember, the strength of your action plan lies in its specificity and realism. It's a document that breathes life into your aspirations, transforming them from abstract ideas into achievable realities. As you chart this course, remain flexible, open to adjustments, and, above all, committed to the journey ahead.

In every challenge lies the seed of opportunity. By formulating a detailed action plan, you're not just plotting a course out of a breakdown; you're setting the stage for a breakthrough. This is your moment to turn obstacles into stepping stones, channelling your renewed focus, determination, and resources towards not just recovering, but thriving.

Transforming breakdowns into breakthroughs is not just about managing crises—it's about growing from them. By following these nine steps, you cultivate resilience, adaptability, and a deeper understanding of both your challenges and your strengths. This process doesn't just apply to individual setbacks, but can also guide teams and organisations through difficult times.

Remember, every breakdown presents an opportunity for growth and learning. With the right mindset and approach, what initially seems like a setback can become a powerful catalyst for positive change.

The story of Oprah Winfrey is not just a tale of success; it's a testament to the human spirit's resilience, the power of determination, and the courage to defy the odds stacked against us from birth. Born into poverty in rural Mississippi, to a single teenage mother, Oprah's early life was marred by challenges that would have subdued many. Living with her grandmother in a state of financial hardship so severe that she wore dresses made from potato sacks, Oprah's beginnings were humble, to say the least.

The adversities didn't end with financial hardship. Moving to inner-city Milwaukee exposed Oprah to a darker side of life, where she faced molestation, rape, and abuse during her childhood and teenage years.

These experiences could have broken her spirit, yet they became part of the crucible that forged her resilience. At the tender age of 14, Oprah's trials intensified when she became pregnant, only to face the heartbreak of losing her baby boy shortly after his premature birth. This period of her life could have been a point of no return. However, Oprah's story was far from over.

The pivotal turn in Oprah's life came when she was sent to live with Vernon Winfrey in Nashville, Tennessee. Vernon, the man she regards as her father, provided a stable and supportive environment, enabling Oprah to tap into her latent potential. It was here, amidst new beginnings, that Oprah's fortunes began to change. While still in high school, she secured a job at a local radio station, a move that marked the dawn of her journey into the media world. By 19, Oprah was co-hosting the evening news, captivating audiences with her natural charisma and genuine empathy—an empathy born from her own experiences of suffering and resilience.

Oprah's success on the evening news was not just a stepping stone, but a launchpad. Recognising her unique ability to connect with people, she was promoted to host a daytime talk show. This platform allowed Oprah to harness her storytelling prowess, engaging presence, and, most importantly, her unwavering belief in the power of human connection to inspire change. Oprah's approach to talk show hosting was revolutionary. She didn't just speak to her guests; she connected with them, sharing in their joys, sorrows, and triumphs, thereby fostering a deep sense of community among her viewers.

The Oprah Winfrey Show, which began in Chicago, was more than a television program; it was a cultural phenomenon. Under Oprah's stewardship, the show explored topics that other programs shied away from, breaking taboos and bringing societal issues to the forefront of public consciousness. Oprah's empathetic interviewing style and her commitment to using her platform for positive change resonated with millions, propelling her to unprecedented levels of fame and influence.

Oprah Winfrey's journey from a poverty-stricken childhood to becoming a media mogul and a beacon of hope and inspiration for millions around the globe is a powerful illustration of her own philosophy: that our past does not define us, but how we rise from it does. Oprah's life is a clear message that it is not the circumstances of our birth that determine our destiny, but our actions, our decisions, and our determination to overcome the hardships we encounter.

Oprah's success story is not merely about achieving financial wealth or celebrity status. It's about breaking cycles of abuse and poverty, challenging societal norms, and opening doors for others to follow. It's about the transformative power of education, self-belief, and the relentless pursuit of one's dreams. Through her philanthropic efforts, Oprah has extended her impact far beyond the realms of entertainment, contributing significantly to education, women's rights, and children's welfare.

Oprah Winfrey's narrative teaches us that roadblocks and hindrances are inevitable components of the human experience. Yet, it's our response to these challenges that defines us. She exemplifies that with hard work, resilience, and a heart open to giving and receiving love, it is possible to turn the most painful experiences into our greatest achievements. Oprah's story is not just inspiring; it's a compelling call to action—a reminder that no matter where we come from, we have the power to shape our destiny, influence the world, and create breakthroughs from the difficulties in life.

In Oprah's own words and life, we find a guide to transcending our limitations and reaching for the stars, not just for personal gain but for the betterment of humanity. Her legacy is a beacon of hope, showing us that with empathy, integrity, and determination, every individual has the potential to make a significant impact on the world. Oprah Winfrey's life story is a testament to the fact that with perseverance, a positive outlook, and an unyielding spirit, every obstacle can be turned into a stepping stone towards achieving our most audacious dreams.

You have all the tools to transform your personal and business lives, but now it's time to become a leader. Followers rarely do anything more than the ordinary, so breaking the mould and stepping forward with confidence is vital.

In reflecting on the journey of navigating through unexpected setbacks to breakthroughs, my own trip back from Congleton stands as an example of resilience and adaptability fostered by the nine-step process. Despite the unforeseen obstacles that threatened to derail my plans, the strategic application of each step empowered me to recalibrate and press forward with determination.

By meticulously assessing the situation, adjusting my goals, and formulating a dynamic action plan, I was able to reclaim control over my circumstances. This journey wasn't merely about combating traffic or recalculating routes; it was an exercise in perseverance, strategic thinking, and emotional intelligence.

The culmination of this experience was arriving home just three minutes shy of 7pm, a moment that underscored the essence of this entire process. It wasn't just about adhering to a schedule; it was about fulfilling a commitment to my wife and to myself. The ability to navigate through adversity, making judicious adjustments along the way, didn't merely bring me to my physical destination—it also reinforced the invaluable lesson that, with the right mindset and strategies, breakdowns can indeed be transformed into breakthroughs.

This narrative serves as a simple reminder that, regardless of the challenges we face, the capacity for overcoming them lies within our grasp. Through the intentional application of these nine steps, we equip ourselves not only to meet our immediate challenges but to cultivate a resilience and resourcefulness that will serve us across all facets of our lives.

If this is an area you'd like to explore further, here are some videos and TED Talks easily accessible online that I would recommend:

- **"The Power of Vulnerability" by Brené Brown (TED Talk)**
  An inspiring TED Talk about the strength we can find in vulnerability and authenticity.

- **"How to Make Stress Your Friend" by Kelly McGonigal (TED Talk)**
  Kelly McGonigal discusses how changing our mindset about stress can help us better cope with challenges and adversities.

- **"Grit: The Power of Passion and Perseverance" by Angela Duckworth (TED Talk)**
  In this TED Talk, Duckworth explores the idea that determination and passion are essential for long-term success.

- **"The Puzzle of Motivation" by Dan Pink (TED Talk)**
  Although focused on motivation, this TED Talk offers valuable insights into finding internal motivation to overcome adversities.

CHAPTER 8

Being the Captain

"Leadership is not about being in charge. It is about taking care of those in your charge."
- Simon Sinek

Leadership is not a title bestowed upon someone, but a mantle earned through experience, perseverance, and the ability to inspire those around you. Few people embody the essence of true leadership better than Sir Clive Woodward, the mastermind behind England's 2003 Rugby World Cup victory. His journey from a young rugby player to one of the most revered coaches in sporting history is a testament to the power of vision, adaptability, and the relentless pursuit of excellence.

Born in 1956, Woodward's early career as a rugby player was marked by promise, but it was his transition into coaching that truly showcased his leadership potential. After retiring from playing professionally, he ventured into the world of business, applying what he had learned on the field to the corporate world. His time in business taught him valuable lessons about communication, team dynamics, and the importance of creating an environment where people could thrive.

When Woodward took over as head coach of the England rugby team in 1997, the team was far from being world champions. Yet, Woodward had a clear vision for what he wanted to achieve, and more importantly, he had a roadmap for how to get there. He believed in innovation, challenging the status quo, and using data and technology to drive performance. His approach to leadership was unconventional, blending the worlds of business and sport in a way that had rarely been done before.

Woodward's leadership style was built on several key principles: empowering individuals to take ownership of their roles, fostering a positive and engaging team culture, and using communication as a tool to unify and inspire. He introduced the concept of "Teamship," where every player had a voice and responsibility, creating an environment where leaders could emerge at every level of the team. His emphasis on learning, growth, and resilience became the foundation of his success.

The culmination of Woodward's leadership journey came in 2003, when England won the Rugby World Cup for the first time in history. It was not just a victory for the team but a triumph for the leadership methods that Woodward had instilled over years of hard work and commitment. His ability to blend fun and intensity in training, his use of technology to analyse performance, and his knack for fostering a sense of unity and trust within the squad became hallmarks of his legacy.

In this chapter, we explore the qualities that made Woodward not just a great coach but an exemplary leader. His story provides a powerful illustration of how anyone can rise to the challenge of leadership by cultivating the right mindset, embracing innovation, and focusing on the growth and well-being of their team.

The importance of being a stellar leader cannot be overstated, for leadership is the foundation of any successful venture, be it steering a corporation, spearheading a community initiative, leading your family, or simply being a leader to yourself. Exceptional leaders inspire, energise, and empower those around them to realise their fullest potential. They cultivate environments ripe for creativity, where every voice finds an audience, and collective ambitions are pursued with fervour and commitment.

At the heart of leadership lies communication. This crucial aspect goes beyond mere information exchange; it's about forging connections, grasping people's aspirations, apprehensions, and dreams, and uniting them towards a shared goal. Outstanding leaders are communication virtuosos, skilled in narrowing divides and nurturing relationships that endure.

The question then arises: Can anyone become a leader? Is leadership an inherent gift, or can it be developed? This chapter takes you on a voyage from an ordinary individual to an impactful leader. It explores the attributes that characterise a leader, the shifts in mindset required, and the actions that can amplify your leadership presence.

Through discussions aimed at achieving results, we investigate how effective communication can transform aspirations into tangible outcomes. We offer a blueprint for communication that catalyses action, propelling progress and creating a climate where everyone feels acknowledged and understood.

A pivotal aspect of leadership is the ability to motivate others. It's about kindling an inner spark in people, urging them to surpass their boundaries and attain excellence. This segment sheds light on techniques to inspire and motivate, fostering a culture of achievement and resilience.

Enhancing communication in your daily life is imperative—not only in your professional sphere, but in every interaction. It's about becoming a source of positivity, clarity, and inspiration, irrespective of your setting or activity.

As you venture into this concluding chapter, bear in mind that leadership is an ongoing journey of personal evolution, learning, and adaptation. "Being The Captain" serves as your compass through the intricate dynamics of leadership, arming you with the necessary tools, strategies, and insights to lead with assurance, empathy, and valour. Get ready to transform both yourself and those around you, embracing the mantle of a leader who doesn't just envision a brighter future but actively brings it to fruition.

Why is leadership so important?

The significance of exceptional leadership cannot be overstated. It's the backbone of progress, the catalyst for change, and the beacon that guides us towards collective achievements. Great leaders are the architects of dreams, the orchestrators of teamwork, and the visionaries who inspire us to transcend our limitations.

Nowhere is this more evident than in the story of Sir Clive Woodward and the England rugby team. England had participated in every Rugby World Cup since the tournament's inception in 1987, yet despite their talent, the ultimate prize had always eluded them. Under several different coaches, the team had come close but lacked that extra edge needed to reach the pinnacle of world rugby.

That all changed when Clive Woodward took the reins as head coach in 1997. Inheriting a team that had the potential but not the consistency, Woodward set out to do more than just tweak tactics. He sought to revolutionise the way England approached the game, not only on the pitch but in their mindset, preparation, and teamwork. It wasn't just about playing better rugby—it was about transforming the culture of the team and instilling the belief that they could, and should, be world champions.

Woodward's leadership went beyond mere strategy. He created an environment of relentless learning and innovation, challenging the team to embrace new ideas and improve continuously. His use of technology and data, combined with his emphasis on mental and emotional resilience, pushed the players to operate at a higher level, both individually and as a unit. Under his guidance, the England team grew from a squad of talented individuals into a unified force capable of achieving greatness.

In 2003, Woodward's leadership culminated in England winning the Rugby World Cup for the first time in history. It was a moment that demonstrated just how crucial leadership can be in turning potential into reality. Since Woodward's departure, England has yet to replicate that success, despite having strong teams and world-class players. This further highlights the importance of the right leadership, as it wasn't just talent that made the difference, but the ability to harness that talent in the right way.

Woodward's leadership style—one that fostered responsibility, innovation, and a winning mindset—was the missing ingredient that took England from contenders to champions. His tenure serves as a reminder that leadership is not simply about managing; it's about inspiring, guiding, and unlocking the full potential of a team. Without the right leadership, even the most talented group may never realise their ultimate goal.

Consider the leaders who have left a mark on your life—the mentors, innovators, and pioneers whose influence spurred you to reach further and aim higher. These individuals underscore a fundamental truth: leadership is not about commanding; it's about inspiring. Great leaders ignite a passion within us, pushing us to explore the realms of what's possible, both individually and collectively.

In the grand tapestry of human achievement, teamwork emerges as the golden thread. The remarkable feats of civilisation were not accomplished by solitary individuals but by groups of people united under a common purpose. This synergy of effort, directed and nurtured by effective leadership, is what propels society forward. Your breakfast scenario serves as a perfect metaphor for the complexity and interconnectedness of teamwork. It's a vivid illustration of how, under the guidance of adept leadership, disparate efforts can coalesce into something as simple and essential as the start of your day.

The importance of being a great leader, then, transcends mere organisational success. It's about fostering an environment where teamwork can flourish, where each individual's contribution is valued and where collective goals are pursued with unwavering commitment. Great leadership is the alchemy that transforms individual potential into collective achievement.

Moreover, great leaders understand that their role is not to be the sole source of ideas or solutions. Instead, their greatness lies in their ability to harness the diverse talents, perspectives, and energies of their team, channelling them towards a shared vision. They create spaces where creativity is encouraged, where failures are seen as stepping stones, and where every team member feels empowered to contribute their best.

In essence, the journey toward significant accomplishments—whether personal, corporate, or societal—begins with great leadership. It's about setting the course, lighting the path, and walking alongside your team as you navigate the challenges and celebrate the victories. The call to be a great leader is a call to action, an invitation to step up and make a difference not just in your own life but in the lives of those around you and, ultimately, in the fabric of the world itself.

As we delve deeper into this subject, remember: to be a great leader is to be a steward of potential, a champion of progress, and a custodian of the human spirit. Your leadership can be the difference between what is and what could be. Embrace the responsibility, rise to the challenge, and lead with courage, compassion, and conviction.

Jacinda Ardern's ascent to becoming New Zealand's Prime Minister is a remarkable tale of empathy, resilience, and visionary leadership.

Born in Hamilton, New Zealand, on July 26, 1980, Ardern's early life in a small rural town instilled in her a profound sense of community and social justice. Her initial foray into leadership began with her active involvement in the Labour Party at a young age, fuelled by a passion to make a tangible difference in people's lives.

Ardern's political journey is marked by her rapid rise through the ranks, characterised by her ability to connect with people on a deeply personal level. Her academic background in communications studies provided her with a robust foundation for effective public engagement, which became a hallmark of her leadership style.

Assuming office in October 2017, Ardern became the world's youngest female head of government at the time. Her leadership was soon tested by unprecedented challenges, notably the Christchurch mosque shootings in March 2019 and the global COVID-19 pandemic. In the face of these crises, Ardern's response was exemplary, demonstrating a leadership style deeply rooted in empathy, transparency, and decisive action.

Following the Christchurch tragedy, Ardern's immediate and compassionate response resonated globally. She unequivocally condemned the attack, while her genuine empathy for the victims and their families showcased her deep humanity. Ardern's leadership extended beyond emotional support; she swiftly enacted significant gun reform laws, proving her ability to translate empathy into decisive policy action.

The COVID-19 pandemic further tested Ardern's leadership mettle. New Zealand's response under her guidance was swift and science-led, resulting in one of the world's most effective strategies in combating the virus. Ardern's clear and consistent communication, alongside her willingness to take early and tough measures, saved countless lives. Her "team of 5 million" approach fostered a collective spirit among New Zealanders, uniting the country under a common cause.

Ardern's leadership style is a beacon of how empathy and decisiveness can coexist. Her ability to communicate effectively, coupled with her unwavering commitment to her values, has not only guided New Zealand through crises but has also inspired a new generation of leaders around the globe. She embodies the belief that to lead is to serve, and her legacy is a testament to the transformative power of compassionate leadership.

The challenges Ardern faced, from national tragedies to a global pandemic, have only strengthened her resolve and leadership. Her journey from a small-town girl with a big heart to a global leader admired for her empathy and strength underscores that leadership is not just about making tough decisions; it's about making those decisions with a profound sense of humanity and a vision for a better future.

Jacinda Ardern's story is a clarion call to aspiring leaders everywhere: leadership is about lifting others, facing challenges with courage, and above all, leading with heart. Her journey illustrates that with empathy, resilience, and a commitment to action, it's possible to navigate the storms of our times and emerge stronger, together.

Communication is key

At the heart of every successful team lies clear, consistent, and meaningful communication. For Sir Clive Woodward, communication was more than just passing information; it was a powerful tool to inspire, guide, and unite the England rugby team on their journey to World Cup glory. Woodward recognised early in his coaching career that if communication was effective, it could not only sharpen players' skills but also forge a shared vision of success.

One of Woodward's innovations was his use of data-driven performance analysis, which revolutionised the way his team understood and improved their game. He didn't just tell his players where they needed to improve; he showed them through clear, visual feedback, empowering them with the knowledge of exactly what they needed to work on. This transparency ensured that each player was engaged in their own development, taking ownership of their progress and striving to meet the high standards he set.

Woodward also used communication to keep his team aligned with a greater goal. His visionary conversations were not limited to technical improvements but also focused on the bigger picture—winning the World Cup. He constantly reinforced the team's purpose and the steps they needed to take to reach their objectives, creating a sense of clarity and shared responsibility that kept everyone focused and driven. For Woodward, communication was the glue that held the team together, turning individual excellence into collective achievement.

Effective communication, as Woodward demonstrated, is not just about talking; it's about creating understanding, providing feedback that motivates, and ensuring every member of the team knows their role in achieving the shared vision.

Without the ability to communicate effectively, even the most profound dreams and ambitious goals can wither, unseen and unheard. Leaders who master the art of communication don't just share their vision; they make it resonate, inspiring others to join their cause and contribute to a shared future.

The essence of leadership communication lies in its capacity to motivate and unify. A compelling vision articulated well can galvanise individuals, drawing them together under a common purpose. It's about painting a picture so vivid and appealing that others see their role in it, becoming eager participants rather than passive observers. This dynamic interaction doesn't just gather followers; it cultivates future leaders, empowered by the clarity and conviction of your message.

Effective communication goes beyond rallying a team around a vision; it's also about nurturing that team through the highs and lows of the journey. Consider the analogy of a carnival — a spectacle of coordination, skill, and entertainment, where every performer plays a pivotal role. In this lively environment, clear communication acts as the conductor's baton, orchestrating movements and ensuring that each contribution aligns with the overall performance. It's a delicate balance of guidance, encouragement, and collaboration, where every member's success elevates the whole.

Moreover, leadership communication is about infusing everyday tasks with a sense of joy and creativity. By fostering an atmosphere of fun and playfulness, you not only enhance team cohesion but also bolster resilience against challenges. Enthusiasm is contagious; a leader who approaches obstacles with a positive and inventive spirit inspires their team to do the same, transforming setbacks into opportunities for growth and innovation.

As we delve deeper into the power of communication, it's clear that it's not just about transmitting information; it's about creating connections, building trust, and fostering an environment where ideas flourish. Great leaders understand that communication is a two-way street, where listening is as important as speaking. They engage in conversations that encourage feedback, value diverse perspectives, and stimulate collective problem-solving.

In mastering the art of communication, leaders amplify their influence, fostering a culture where mutual respect and understanding drive progress. Mastering the tools to leverage conversations will help you achieve team goals, enhance your confidence, command respect, and make you more approachable. By integrating effective communication strategies into your leadership approach, you set the stage for a journey marked by shared success and enduring impact. This is the beginning of a transformative journey in leadership, where your words inspire action and your vision becomes a shared reality.

In leading my businesses, I prioritise clear and meaningful communication. Recognising the crucial factors that boost team effectiveness, I consistently focus on key aspects of our work culture. It's important to me that each team member feels genuinely valued, not just for their skills, but as individuals with lives and families outside the office. Demonstrating this care and interest fosters a supportive environment where everyone feels seen and appreciated.

Moreover, I make it a point to highlight the significance of each person's work. Understanding how their efforts contribute to the company's success and the well-being of their colleagues instils a sense of purpose and belonging. This connection to the company's broader goals ensures that everyone knows their work matters, enhancing motivation and dedication.

Visualising and sharing the company's vision is another critical component of my approach to leadership. I want every team member to see themselves within this vision and recognise how their contributions help us move closer to our shared objectives. By integrating their roles into the company's future, team members become more than just employees; they become integral parts of a collective journey towards a vision.

This focus on communication is more than a strategy; it's a commitment to building a workplace where every individual is empowered, engaged, and aligned with our common goals. By nurturing these connections and emphasising the value of each contribution, we create a stronger, more cohesive team poised for long-term success.

Can anyone be a leader?

Leadership is often seen as an inherent quality possessed by only a few, but Sir Clive Woodward's approach to coaching the England rugby team challenges this notion. Woodward believed that leadership was not reserved for a chosen few but could be nurtured in every individual willing to step up and take responsibility. His philosophy, known as "Teamship," embraced the idea that everyone in the team could—and should—develop leadership qualities, regardless of their official title or position.

Under Woodward's guidance, leadership roles were distributed across the team. Each player had a voice and the autonomy to make decisions in their area of expertise, whether that was leading a section of the training session or making critical calls on the field. This empowerment created a culture where leadership was a shared responsibility, fostering a sense of ownership and accountability throughout the squad.

Woodward's "Teamship" concept highlights a vital truth: leadership is not about having formal authority; it is about influence, initiative, and the ability to inspire others. By fostering leadership at every level, Woodward created an environment where players developed the confidence to lead in their own right, both on and off the field. His approach shows that leadership can be developed in ordinary people, transforming them into key contributors to a team's success.

This philosophy not only helped England secure their World Cup victory in 2003 but also offers a powerful lesson for leaders in any context—great leadership is not born, it is built.

At the heart of every compelling story of leadership, whether in the boardrooms of Fortune 500 companies or the gritty arenas of sports, lies the fundamental belief that leadership is more than just a role; it's a transformative force that compels individuals to transcend their limitations and unite towards a common goal. Consider the tale of the 2016 Leicester City Football Club in the English Premier League. Before the season started, Leicester City was considered one of the ultimate underdogs, with pre-season odds of winning the league at 5000-1. They had narrowly avoided relegation in the previous season and were not seen as contenders for the title by any stretch of the imagination.

However, under the leadership of Claudio Ranieri, a manager who had been previously dismissed as past his prime, Leicester City began to defy expectations. Ranieri's leadership was not about radical tactical innovations or demanding huge sums for star players; instead, it was rooted in creating a profound sense of belief within the team, fostering a strong, united spirit, and focusing on the strengths of his squad.

Ranieri's approach was characterised by his calm demeanour, encouragement, and belief in his players' abilities, many of whom were not widely recognised as top-tier talent before the season. He was adept at managing personalities, creating a cohesive unit that played for each other and the team's cause, rather than individual glory.

The team, led by the likes of Jamie Vardy, Riyad Mahrez, and N'Golo Kanté, played with heart, determination, and a tactical discipline that was finely tuned by Ranieri's strategic insights. Their story was not just about a tactical victory on the pitch; it was about the power of leadership to transform underdogs into champions, uniting a group of relatively unknown players into a formidable force that clinched the Premier League title.

Leicester City's triumph is a testament to the fact that leadership is about much more than strategy and skills; it's about inspiring belief, fostering unity, and leading with integrity and purpose. Ranieri emerged as a leader who, from the shadows of doubt and underestimation, guided his team to achieve what was deemed impossible, cementing their story in football folklore as one of the greatest sporting underdog stories of all time.

The heart of leadership is about caring deeply for something and igniting that same passion in others. It's about creating a synergy of shared desires, goals, and visions, rallied under the banner of someone who inspires—not by command, but by conviction. This collective caring pulls people into groups, tribes bound not just by shared passions but by a collective mission to change something they hold dear.

The concept of leadership and belief extends far beyond the domain of sports, weaving its potent magic in the intricate world of business as well. My own entrepreneurial voyage offers a vivid illustration of this dynamic at work. As I ventured into the establishment of my first enterprise, I was fortunate to forge a partnership with someone who was not just a business partner but a visionary leader in his own right. With an extensive background of over twenty years in business management, he brought a wealth of experience and a deep understanding of the transformative power of belief in achieving success. His role was pivotal, focusing on the administrative backbone of the business, thereby allowing me to dedicate myself entirely to our clients through sales and service. Despite my technical know-how and industry experience, I struggled with self-confidence. His steadfast confidence in me, however, was the wind beneath my wings, pushing me towards achievements that seemed beyond my reach.

Our partnership was more than a division of labour; it was a shared journey of growth and learning. His belief in me did more than just fuel my success; it catalysed a profound transformation within me. As he envisioned my future leadership of the business, he meticulously trained me in all facets of operations—from managing finances and processing payroll to negotiating with suppliers. However, the most invaluable lesson he imparted was the art of envisioning and nurturing a unified vision for our company—a vision that was destined to be the beacon for our entire team.

This vision was not a nebulous dream, but a carefully crafted picture of what we aspired to achieve, with each team member holding a crucial piece of this grand puzzle. Like a masterfully constructed jigsaw, every role within our team was designed to fit seamlessly into the larger image of our business goals. This approach ensured that each individual not only understood their unique contribution but also saw how their efforts were integral to the collective achievement of our vision. It was a process of alignment that transformed individual accomplishments into a cohesive, dynamic force propelling our business forward.

This unity of purpose, underpinned by a shared belief in the vision and in each other, created a powerful synergy. It was a testament to the fact that when a singular, compelling vision guides a team, and when every member's role is recognised as essential to the whole, the potential for success is boundless. This journey from a fledgling startup to a thriving business was not just a testament to the power of effective leadership, but also a profound personal journey of becoming the leader my partner saw in me. Through this process, I learned that true leadership is about more than just guiding a team—it's about inspiring a collective belief in a shared vision, where every individual plays a critical role in painting the broader picture of success.

Yet, the path to leadership is not trodden by many. The few who do embark on this journey often ponder the question: Is leadership the exclusive domain of those touched by the grace of inherent traits, or can it be a mantle assumed by anyone who dares to lead?

Conventional wisdom suggests that a leader is defined by a set of core competencies and practices: intelligence spanning logical, practical, and creative realms; unwavering determination; unshakeable self-confidence; remarkable sociability; and uncompromising integrity. While these qualities may seem straightforward on the surface, their depths are profound, each a universe of meaning waiting to be explored.

- Intelligence is not merely about academic brilliance, but encompasses a broader spectrum that includes logical reasoning, practical wisdom—often dubbed 'street smarts'—and the creative genius to innovate and solve problems.

A leader doesn't need to be a polymath, but possessing a balanced mix of these intellectual faculties is necessary.

- Determination then becomes the fuel that drives a leader to persist, to push boundaries not only for themselves but to inspire those they lead to reach for their own stars.

- Self-confidence is the bedrock of a leader's resolve: a steadfast belief in one's abilities to make a difference, chart a course, and navigate through storms with assurance.

- Sociability underscores the essence of leadership as a relational endeavour, emphasising the importance of building connections, understanding and empathising with others, and fostering a culture of mutual respect and support.

- Finally, integrity stands as the beacon of trust, the principle that guides every decision, action, and interaction. It's the quality that binds leaders to their followers, establishing a foundation of trust that is both earned and honoured.

As we journey through the story of our underdog sports team, their rise from obscurity to prominence vividly illustrates these principles in action. Leaders emerge not because they are predestined to lead but because they embody these traits, cultivated through challenges, failures, and successes.

So, can anyone be a leader? The journey of our sports team and the exploration of the key qualities of leadership suggest an affirmative answer. Leadership is not a gift bestowed upon a chosen few, but a mantle that can be claimed by anyone willing to nurture these core competencies and step into the role of inspiring others towards a common goal.

Returning to the pivotal question— can anyone be a leader?

Absolutely, yes. Leadership qualities can be nurtured and developed. While some individuals might naturally gravitate towards leadership roles with ease, truly anyone can embark on the journey to become a leader. For many, it's not about inherent traits but rather a burning passion that propels them forward. This passion becomes the catalyst for their leadership journey, proving that with determination and learning, leading is within reach for all. Whether you're born with a knack for guiding others or you find your path through the force of your passion, leadership is a skill that can be cultivated and mastered over time.

In the landscape of modern entrepreneurship, technology has indeed democratised the ability to lead, giving rise to global businesses spearheaded by individuals whose passion outshone their initial lack of traditional leadership attributes. A compelling example of this phenomenon is the story of Airbnb, founded by Brian Chesky and Joe Gebbia.

Initially, Chesky and Gebbia were not the archetypical leaders etched in the annals of traditional business lore. They were simply passionate designers in San Francisco, struggling to pay their rent. However, they saw an opportunity when a major design conference came to town, and all hotels were booked. They decided to rent out air mattresses in their living room and offer breakfast to their guests. This simple act of ingenuity sparked the idea for what would become Airbnb.

The rise of Airbnb from a makeshift bed-and-breakfast in a San Francisco apartment to a global powerhouse in the hospitality industry is a testament to the power of passion driving leadership. Chesky and Gebbia, together with their later addition, Nathan Blecharczyk, leveraged technology to share their vision with the world, disrupting traditional models of accommodation.

Their journey underscores the essence of modern leadership—it's not solely about possessing inherent qualities or being placed in a position of power. Instead, it's about having a vision fuelled by passion, the determination to bring that vision to life, and the ability to inspire others to join you on that journey. The founders of Airbnb learned to lead by navigating through challenges, iterating their business model, and continuously engaging with both hosts and travellers to refine their service.

Airbnb's story is a powerful reminder that leadership can emerge from the most ordinary circumstances. It illustrates that with passion, resilience, and a clear vision, even those who never considered themselves potential leaders can transform industries and impact the world. This narrative not only inspires but also invites individuals from all walks of life to recognise their potential to lead, innovate, and shape the future.

So, how can an ordinary person become a leader?

Embarking on the journey to leadership is not reserved for the chosen few born with innate talents; it's an attainable goal for anyone willing to learn, grow, and embrace the challenge. The essence of true leadership lies in a set of core qualities, including a spectrum of intelligence, determination, self-confidence, sociability, and integrity. But beyond these, certain universal attributes stand as the bedrock of successful leadership, accessible to all who aspire to lead.

- Positive Outlook. Leadership begins with mindset. A positive outlook is not just a nice-to-have; it's an essential tool for inspiring those around you. Leaders who maintain a hopeful and optimistic view of the future can inspire their team to overcome obstacles and aim higher. This positivity becomes infectious, setting the tone for an environment where challenges are viewed as opportunities for growth rather than insurmountable problems.

- Igniting Passion. Passion is the fuel of leadership. It transcends mere enthusiasm, embodying a deep, enduring commitment to a cause or purpose. Passionate leaders are magnetic; they draw people towards them, lighting a fire in others to pursue collective goals with zeal. This energy sustains both the leader and their followers through thick and thin, making every effort more meaningful and every success sweeter.

- Vision. Leadership demands vision. It's about seeing beyond the immediate, charting a course towards a brighter future. Great leaders are visionaries who can articulate a compelling picture of what lies ahead, engaging their team's imagination and commitment. This forward-looking perspective ensures that every action taken today aligns with where the team aims to be tomorrow, fostering a sense of purpose and direction.

- Accountability. A hallmark of effective leadership is accountability. True leaders stand by their words and actions, accepting responsibility for their outcomes. They create a culture where promises are kept, and commitments are met with action. This sense of duty not only encourages personal excellence but also instils a collective responsibility within the team, ensuring that everyone is aligned and motivated to achieve shared objectives.

For those wondering if they can step into a leadership role, know this: leadership is not about perfection or possessing an extraordinary set of skills from the outset. It's about growth, learning, and the willingness to step out of your comfort zone. By fostering a positive attitude, nurturing your passion, developing a clear vision, and upholding accountability, you can transform not only your own trajectory but also that of those around you.

Mike's story is a powerful example of how anyone, regardless of their background or natural inclinations, can step into a role of leadership and make a profound difference. He didn't have the charisma typically associated with leaders, nor did he have formal training in leadership techniques. Yet, Mike understood something fundamental about the people he worked with: the human desire to be part of something greater, to compete, and to share in the camaraderie of a team striving towards a common goal.

By connecting the company's objectives with what his team valued—competition, recognition, and social connection—Mike transformed the nightly routine into a mission. The competition wasn't just about outperforming the day shift; it was about coming together as a unit, pushing each other to excel, and ultimately, enjoying the fruits of their labour together. The trophy symbolised their collective effort and achievement, while the promise of a night out served as a tangible reward for their hard work and dedication.

Mike's initiative shows that leadership is not about having all the answers or dictating from on high. It's about understanding what motivates people, harnessing those drives for the collective good, and fostering an environment where everyone feels valued and engaged. His approach to leadership wasn't founded on authority but on the principle of inclusion and motivation. He saw his team not as subordinates but as collaborators in a shared journey towards success.

This narrative serves as an inspiration to anyone doubting their ability to lead. It underscores the idea that leadership isn't reserved for the chosen few with innate abilities or extensive training. Leadership is accessible to anyone willing to connect with others, recognise their needs and aspirations, and creatively align them with a broader purpose.

Mike's story is a testament to the impact that can be achieved when ordinary individuals embrace the opportunity to lead. It illustrates that the essence of leadership lies not in titles or accolades but in the ability to bring people together for a common cause, inspiring them to achieve more than they thought possible. Through his simple yet effective competition, Mike not only boosted productivity but also built a team united by a sense of purpose and belonging. His journey from a regular night shift worker to a leader who unlocked the potential of his team exemplifies the transformative power of leadership—a power that resides within each of us, waiting to be unleashed.

Remember, every great leader once started as an ordinary person with a desire to make a difference. It's the journey of continuous improvement and the commitment to lead with purpose that sets them apart. So, dare to believe in your potential to lead. Embrace the qualities that make an effective leader, and step forward with confidence. The path to leadership is open to you, ready to be navigated with determination, insight, and a heart committed to positive change.

Leadership Beyond the Boardroom, Embracing Play

Leadership transcends traditional exercises, reaching into life's essence to shape one's ability to lead by example. Beyond formal training lies a world rich with opportunities for personal development—through the joy and challenges of play.

Games and activities, from chess and football to rock climbing and jogging, do more than entertain; they teach strategy, teamwork, perseverance, and adaptability. These pursuits, often undertaken for pleasure, subtly hone the skills necessary for effective leadership.

The concept of 'play' in our daily lives, whether through sports, intellectual games, or solitary challenges, serves as an unconventional yet effective classroom for leadership qualities. It's in these moments of engagement and challenge that we learn the most about leading ourselves and others.

True leadership development extends into all facets of life. Whether it's through sports, adventures, or hobbies, activities outside the workplace can significantly enhance your leadership qualities. For instance, rock climbing can teach resilience and confidence, while playing tennis can sharpen focus and competitive spirit. Each activity adds a piece to the puzzle of your leadership identity, similar to how each team member's role contributes to the overall vision of a business.

By welcoming diverse experiences that push our limits and encourage growth, we invite the essence of leadership into every aspect of our lives. This approach—finding leadership lessons in play—prepares us to inspire and guide with confidence and integrity. Let's look beyond the boardroom and embrace the vast playground of life as the foundation for developing the heart of a leader.

Character: The Foundation of Leadership

At the core of any successful leader lies a strong character, built on principles of integrity, generosity, and responsibility. Sir Clive Woodward understood this better than most, recognising that character is the bedrock of effective leadership. For Woodward, leadership was not just about skills or strategy; it was about who you are when no one is watching and how you conduct yourself in the face of challenges.

During his tenure as head coach of the England rugby team, Woodward placed immense importance on fostering a positive and resilient team culture. He encouraged his players to embody the values of hard work, respect, and accountability, knowing that these traits would not only strengthen the individual but also bind the team together. For him, character was the key to long-term success, creating leaders who could inspire others through their actions, not just their words.

Woodward's focus on character was evident in how he led by example, instilling discipline and a sense of responsibility throughout the squad. He believed that great leadership came from consistency—maintaining high standards in everything from preparation to execution. This emphasis on integrity and self-discipline allowed the team to develop a culture where each player was accountable not only to themselves but also to their teammates.

By building a team culture grounded in strong character, Woodward laid the foundation for leadership that could endure under pressure, leading England to their historic World Cup victory in 2003. His approach illustrates that while tactics and talent may win games, it is character that sustains leadership and drives lasting success.

Character shapes the essence of effective leadership. It's not merely about the roles we assume but about who we are at our core—our values, ethics, and principles. This fundamental attribute dictates how we interact with others, face challenges, and navigate the complex landscape of leadership.

Character in leadership is what keeps a team grounded when facing adversity. Woodward understood that talent alone is not enough to overcome challenges. When the stakes are high and the pressure is immense, it is the leader's character that will shine through. The ability to stay calm under pressure, to make decisions rooted in principle rather than panic, and to inspire others through personal conduct, is what distinguishes great leaders from the rest.

Moreover, Woodward's emphasis on character helped his players develop a sense of ownership over their roles. When individuals operate with integrity and responsibility, they naturally take on leadership roles within the team. This, in turn, fostered the "Teamship" mentality that Woodward was so famous for—a culture where every player felt accountable not only to their own performance but also to the success of their teammates.

In the business world, just as in sport, character is the foundation on which trust is built. Leaders with strong character inspire loyalty, foster a sense of fairness, and cultivate an environment where people feel valued and motivated to contribute their best. When leaders demonstrate integrity, they not only set the tone for their teams but also create a ripple effect of positive behaviour that strengthens the entire organisation.

In conclusion, Clive Woodward's leadership of the England rugby team highlights the importance of character as the foundation of leadership. His ability to foster a culture of accountability, resilience, and mutual respect was crucial in transforming a talented group of individuals into world champions. Whether in sports, business, or life, leadership rooted in strong character has the power to unite teams, overcome challenges, and achieve extraordinary success.

Confidence: The Visible Backbone of Leadership

Confidence is often seen as the most outward expression of leadership. It is the visible force that allows a leader to make decisions with clarity, inspire trust in others, and remain steady under pressure. Yet, as Sir Clive Woodward demonstrated throughout his tenure as head coach of the England rugby team, confidence is not simply an innate quality. It is something that can be developed, honed, and reinforced through preparation and mental conditioning.

Woodward understood that confidence doesn't just come from talent or experience. It comes from a deep sense of preparedness and the ability to stay composed in high-stress situations. To instil this in his players, he placed a strong emphasis on mental conditioning, working with sports psychologists to help the team develop psychological resilience. He knew that, in the heat of a World Cup final, the team's physical ability would only carry them so far. It was their mental strength—their confidence in their own and each other's ability to perform—that would make the difference.

One of Woodward's key strategies was the creation of high-pressure scenarios during training. These were designed to simulate the intense, often chaotic nature of real matches, pushing players to the edge of their mental and physical limits. By repeatedly exposing the team to stressful situations, Woodward helped them build the mental fortitude to stay calm and focused when it mattered most. This approach allowed the players to develop a belief in their ability to handle whatever challenges came their way.

For Woodward, confidence wasn't just about how his players felt; it was about how they performed under pressure. He recognised that confidence is contagious within a team—when players see their leader and teammates responding to difficult situations with poise and self-assurance, it fuels their own confidence. This was especially true in high-stakes moments, like the 2003 Rugby World Cup final, where England's ability to maintain their composure and execute their game plan under immense pressure was a direct result of the mental conditioning they had undergone.

In addition to mental conditioning, Woodward fostered confidence by empowering his players to take ownership of their development. Each player was given clear goals and the tools to track their progress, creating a sense of personal responsibility and achievement. This structured approach to improvement helped players feel in control of their performance, further boosting their confidence.

The lesson from Woodward's leadership is clear: confidence is not a fixed trait but a muscle that can be strengthened through preparation, resilience, and a clear sense of purpose. By creating a culture where his players felt empowered and prepared for any situation, Woodward ensured that confidence became a cornerstone of their success.

In leadership, the same principles apply. Confidence comes from knowing you've done the work, prepared for the challenges, and built the resilience needed to face adversity. Leaders who cultivate this in themselves and their teams foster an environment where people feel capable, supported, and ready to perform at their best. Confidence, when nurtured through preparation and mental strength, becomes the backbone that supports all other aspects of leadership.

Embracing Challenges: The Crucible of Leadership

Leadership isn't just about steering the ship in calm waters; it's about being at the helm when the storm hits, turning challenges into opportunities for growth. It demands stepping out of your comfort zone and confronting difficulties directly. This principle applies equally in personal and professional realms, from undertaking physical endeavours like rock climbing to enhance confidence, to tackling complex projects at work.

I've always been fuelled by challenges, a trait my wife playfully exploits by hinting at tasks being beyond my reach due to age or suggesting they're better suited to someone younger. This usually spurs me into action, provided it's an endeavour I genuinely care about. Of course, there are exceptions, like gardening or DIY, where I'll happily concede to her suggestions.

Penning this book presented one of my greatest challenges. As someone with dyslexia, translating thoughts to paper has always been a daunting task. This manuscript marks my fifth attempt, a testament to my commitment to overcoming personal obstacles and sharing my journey.

A pivotal moment in my life was deciding to participate in Tough Mudder at the age of 50. This wasn't just any challenge; it was a gruelling test of physical and mental endurance. With a reputation as the premier obstacle course worldwide, it asks each participant, "Do you have what it takes?" Accepting this challenge required a leap of faith, especially since I had just finished a beginner's running program.

After being persuaded by a friend, I embarked on an 18-month training regimen that transformed my physical capabilities.

The day of the event tested every fibre of my being. From braving icy waters to conquering high walls, each obstacle pushed me to my limits. Despite the pain and fatigue, completing the course was incredibly empowering. It underscored a powerful lesson: with determination and the right preparation, I could surpass even my own expectations.

This experience mirrored the essence of leadership—facing challenges head-on and emerging stronger. It showed me that embracing difficulties isn't just about personal achievement; it's about setting an example and inspiring those around you. Whether leading a team, a community, or simply guiding your own life, the ability to tackle and overcome challenges is what transforms an ordinary person into an extraordinary leader.

Risk-Taking: The Courage to Lead

Leadership and risk-taking go hand in hand. True leadership requires the audacity to take steps others might shy away from, demonstrating faith in the collective vision, even when the path is fraught with uncertainty. It's about calculated risks, where the potential for reward justifies the leap into the unknown. Sir Clive Woodward's tenure as the head coach of the England rugby team is a prime example of how bold, innovative leadership can drive a team to extraordinary success. Woodward's willingness to embrace new ideas and challenge conventional wisdom demonstrated the courage it takes to lead from the front, even when the path forward is uncharted.

In the traditionally conservative world of rugby, Woodward stood out by taking risks that others might have shied away from. One of his most significant and controversial decisions was his embrace of cutting-edge technology and data analysis as integral parts of the team's preparation. At a time when most rugby coaches relied on instinct and experience, Woodward introduced detailed performance metrics and video analysis to track player progress and identify areas for improvement. This data-driven approach allowed the team to gain deeper insights into their strengths and weaknesses, but it was a radical departure from the norm, and not everyone was convinced at first.

Yet Woodward's willingness to risk criticism and push forward with this innovation proved to be a game-changer. By using technology to provide his players with precise feedback and measurable goals, he enhanced their performance in ways that traditional methods could not. This decision to go against the grain, to invest in new tools and approaches, ultimately paid off when England secured their historic Rugby World Cup victory in 2003. It was a clear demonstration that leaders must sometimes be willing to step outside their comfort zones and take risks in order to achieve extraordinary outcomes.

Woodward's risk-taking didn't stop at technology. He also redefined how the team trained and prepared for matches, implementing strategies that had not been seen before in rugby. From mental conditioning programs to high-pressure scenario training, he constantly sought new ways to push his team's limits and give them an edge over their competitors. His bold decisions were not without resistance from both within the rugby establishment and from his own players, but his unwavering belief in the long-term benefits of these innovations kept him moving forward.

Taking risks as a leader requires courage—the courage to challenge tradition, to try new things, and to face the potential for failure. But it is often these very risks that create breakthroughs and drive progress. Woodward's leadership exemplifies this principle. By embracing innovation and being willing to risk short-term comfort for long-term success, he transformed his team and led them to a world title.

In leadership, as in rugby, those who take risks are often the ones who change the game. Woodward's example teaches us that being a leader means having the courage to pursue new paths, even when they are fraught with uncertainty. The willingness to innovate, adapt, and take calculated risks is what separates great leaders from the rest. It's not enough to maintain the status quo—true leadership lies in the courage to push boundaries and explore new possibilities.

Decisiveness: The Will to Act

Understanding the path forward is only the beginning. True leadership shines in the ability to take decisive action, transforming vision into results. This vital quality goes beyond mere decision-making; it's about igniting change through determined action.

Chess serves as a powerful metaphor for decisiveness. Each move demands not only strategic foresight but also the courage to proceed with conviction. In this game of infinite possibilities, players evaluate their positions, choose a direction, and boldly move forward, always ready to adjust as the game unfolds. Chess teaches the balance between calculated risk and decisive action, echoing the leadership journey of navigating complex situations with confidence and adaptability.

Basketball offers another dynamic arena for cultivating decisiveness. On the court, players make instant decisions that can alter the game's momentum. The choice to shoot, pass, or drive is made in moments, requiring clarity and resolve. It's a relentless exercise in assessing quickly and acting with purpose, mirroring the swift decision-making needed in leadership. The game instils a sense of urgency and precision, essential for leading teams through challenges with poise and decisiveness.

These examples, from the strategic depth of chess to the fast-paced decisions of basketball, illustrate the essence of decisiveness. They remind us that leadership is not just about knowing what to do but having the will to make it happen. As we explore the journey of leadership, remember: that embracing decisiveness in all aspects of life enriches your capacity to lead effectively, turning challenges into opportunities for growth and success.

Adaptability: Mastering the Art of Change

In the ever-changing landscape of leadership, the ability to adapt is crucial to sustained success. Sir Clive Woodward's leadership of the England rugby team offers a powerful example of how adaptability—the willingness to evolve and respond to new challenges—can make the difference between good and great. Woodward's success wasn't just the result of innovative strategies; it was his ability to continuously adapt those strategies to the needs of his team and the demands of the game that set him apart as a leader.

Woodward understood that what worked yesterday wouldn't necessarily work tomorrow. His leadership was characterised by a constant search for improvement and a readiness to embrace change. This adaptability was most evident in his training routines, which were frequently modified to keep the players engaged and challenged. He refused to settle into a rigid pattern, knowing that stagnation could lead to complacency. Instead, he created an environment of continuous evolution, where each training session presented new opportunities for growth and learning.

Central to Woodward's adaptability was his embrace of new technologies. As the game of rugby evolved, so too did the tools available for enhancing performance. Woodward was quick to incorporate video analysis, data tracking, and performance metrics into his coaching, using these innovations to gain deeper insights into both individual and team dynamics. This willingness to leverage new technologies allowed him to make informed decisions and adjust tactics based on real-time feedback—a significant advantage over competitors who relied solely on traditional methods.

But Woodward's adaptability didn't stop at technology. He also listened closely to his players, valuing their feedback and incorporating it into his evolving strategies. By fostering an open line of communication, Woodward ensured that his players felt heard, and he could adjust his leadership approach to meet their changing needs. This flexibility made the players feel more invested in the team's success, knowing that their input had a tangible impact on the direction of the group. It also created a culture of mutual respect, where adaptability became a shared value between leader and team.

Perhaps the greatest example of Woodward's adaptability came in the form of tactical adjustments during high-pressure situations. Throughout England's 2003 Rugby World Cup campaign, Woodward demonstrated a keen ability to read the flow of a match and make critical adjustments on the fly. His leadership in adapting game plans when situations changed allowed England to outmanoeuvre opponents and stay ahead in tightly contested games.

In leadership, adaptability is more than just a skill—it's an essential mindset. The ability to embrace change, adjust tactics, and evolve with new insights is what keeps a team or organisation moving forward. Leaders who remain rigid in their approach risk becoming obsolete in a rapidly shifting world. Woodward's example teaches us that true leadership requires constant learning and flexibility, a willingness to try new things and shift course when necessary.

Adaptability, as Woodward proved, is the art of staying one step ahead. It's about responding to challenges not with resistance but with creativity, and seeing every change as an opportunity to grow. As a leader, mastering the art of change is what allows you to navigate uncertainty and lead your team toward success.

Engagement: Fostering a Deep Connection with Your Team

One of the hallmarks of exceptional leadership is the ability to foster a deep sense of engagement within the team. For Sir Clive Woodward, engagement wasn't just about showing up to train—it was about creating an environment where players were fully invested, motivated, and excited to be part of the team's journey. Woodward's leadership of the England rugby team offers a powerful example of how to cultivate that connection, blending hard work with enjoyment to ensure that his players were both challenged and energised.

Woodward knew that to get the best out of his players, they needed to love being there. He created a positive, stimulating training environment where the players were constantly pushed to their limits but never felt burnt out or disengaged. His sessions were designed to be tough, but he also made them fun and varied, incorporating game-like drills, friendly competition, and innovative exercises that kept the players engaged mentally and physically. By making training enjoyable, Woodward was able to keep the team motivated even when the demands were high.

Engagement, for Woodward, went beyond just making training fun. He built a team culture where each player felt valued, listened to, and part of something bigger than themselves. His "Teamship" approach gave players ownership over their roles and responsibilities, fostering a sense of personal connection to the team's success. This empowerment made players more than just participants—they became active contributors, fully engaged in both their own development and the collective mission of winning the World Cup.

Woodward also understood the emotional aspect of engagement. He knew that for players to give their best, they needed to feel connected not only to the team's goals but also to each other and their leader. He cultivated strong relationships with his players, showing genuine interest in their well-being and ensuring that they felt supported both on and off the field. This emotional connection built trust and loyalty, allowing the team to function as a cohesive unit.

Furthermore, Woodward paid close attention to the balance between work and play. He recognised that while pushing his players hard was essential, so too was giving them moments to relax, bond, and recharge. This balance was key to maintaining long-term engagement, preventing burnout, and keeping morale high even during the most intense phases of preparation. By fostering a sense of camaraderie and fun alongside the hard work, Woodward created an atmosphere where players wanted to be, where they were willing to push themselves not just for personal success but for the team.

In leadership, engagement is the fuel that drives performance. It's not enough for leaders to simply give instructions—they need to connect with their teams on a deeper level, inspiring a shared sense of purpose and enjoyment. By making the team's journey rewarding, both emotionally and professionally, Woodward ensured that his players were committed not just to the outcome but to the process itself.

As leaders, we must understand that fostering engagement means more than creating a productive environment—it means building an emotional connection where people feel valued, motivated, and inspired. Woodward's success with the England rugby team shows us that when people love being part of the team, they are willing to go the extra mile, stay resilient in the face of challenges, and ultimately, achieve extraordinary things.

Inspiration: Fuelling the Fire Within

Beyond rallying people around a cause, extraordinary leaders ignite a passion in their team members, encouraging them to exceed their own expectations. By understanding and addressing their needs, you can inspire them to achieve greatness.

Steve Jobs' journey with Apple is a compelling testament to the power of vision and resilience in leadership. His story isn't just about technological innovation; it's about inspiring a team to reimagine the future and relentlessly pursue excellence.

In 1985, Jobs faced a significant setback when he was ousted from Apple, the very company he co-founded. Yet, this setback didn't deter him. Instead, it fuelled his determination to continue innovating, leading to the creation of NeXT and Pixar. His ventures during this period were critical in shaping the leader he would become, emphasising the importance of persistence, innovation, and vision.

Jobs' return to Apple in 1997 marked the beginning of a new era for the company. At the time, Apple was on the brink of bankruptcy, but Jobs' unwavering belief in his vision for the company quickly began to turn its fortunes around. He initiated a product revolution, starting with the launch of the iMac, which not only saved Apple from financial ruin but also set the stage for a series of groundbreaking products like the iPod, iPhone, and iPad.

What set Jobs apart was his ability to inspire his team to push the boundaries of what was possible. He fostered an environment where creativity and innovation flourished, challenging his team to "think different" and work on projects that they were passionate about. Jobs' leadership style was not without its critics, but his ability to connect with his team on a shared vision and drive them towards achieving it was unparalleled.

Under Jobs' leadership, Apple didn't just create products; they crafted experiences that fundamentally changed the way people interact with technology. His legacy is a reminder that extraordinary leaders ignite a passion in their team members, encouraging them to exceed their own expectations. Through understanding and addressing their needs, Jobs inspired his team to achieve greatness, turning Apple into one of the most valuable companies in the world.

Steve Jobs' story is a powerful illustration of how an extraordinary leader can fuel the fire within their team, inspiring them to achieve beyond what they thought was possible. His journey underscores the essence of inspirational leadership—transforming challenges into triumphs and rallying a team around a vision that changes the world.

Trust: The Glue of Leadership

Trust is the foundation of any strong relationship, including those between a leader and their team. By trusting your team and earning their trust in return, you create a culture of loyalty, commitment, and open communication. Trust is the invisible force that holds a team together, allowing it to function smoothly, even under pressure. For Sir Clive Woodward, trust was not just a passive element of leadership—it was something to be actively cultivated and reinforced within the England rugby team. Through his innovative "Teamship" concept, Woodward demonstrated that trust is built by empowering others, giving them responsibility, and ensuring that every individual plays a vital role in the team's success.

Woodward believed that trust was not a one-way street between coach and player; it needed to flow in all directions. To foster this, he delegated significant responsibility to his players, encouraging them to take ownership of their roles both on and off the pitch. He trusted his players to lead, to make decisions, and to hold each other accountable, knowing that by doing so, they would develop mutual respect and confidence in each other's abilities. This sense of shared leadership created a strong foundation of trust across the entire team.

One of the most powerful ways Woodward built trust was by empowering his players to have a voice. He encouraged open communication and ensured that each player's perspective was valued, no matter their position or experience level. This inclusive approach reinforced the idea that every team member had something important to contribute, and in turn, fostered a deep sense of trust between the players and their coach. They knew that their opinions mattered, and that they were trusted to help shape the direction of the team.

Woodward's trust in his players was most visible in how he approached decision-making during crucial moments. Rather than micromanaging every aspect of the game, he allowed his players the freedom to adapt and make key decisions on the field. This trust empowered the team to think critically and act decisively under pressure, knowing that their coach believed in their ability to handle tough situations. It also encouraged players to trust each other's judgement, strengthening their bonds and fostering a cohesive unit that could adapt to the challenges they faced.

The concept of "Teamship" exemplified how trust, when built intentionally, becomes the glue that binds a team together. By giving each player a stake in the team's success, Woodward created an environment where trust was earned through responsibility and accountability. Players knew they could rely on one another to deliver because they were all invested in the same goal. This shared sense of trust was key to England's World Cup triumph in 2003, enabling the team to perform at its highest level when it mattered most.

In leadership, trust is the foundation upon which everything else is built. Without it, even the most talented teams can falter. Woodward's example reminds us that trust is not simply given; it must be earned through consistent action, delegation, and open communication. Leaders who foster trust create teams that are not only more resilient but also more empowered, collaborative, and capable of achieving extraordinary success.

Ernest Shackleton's Endurance expedition to the Antarctic is a timeless narrative of survival, leadership, and trust under the most extreme conditions imaginable. In 1914, Shackleton set sail with his crew, aiming to cross the Antarctic continent. However, their ship, the

Endurance, became trapped in ice and was eventually crushed, leaving the crew stranded on the ice floes.

The remarkable aspect of this story is not just their incredible struggle for survival, but how Shackleton's leadership forged an unbreakable trust among his men. Shackleton's ability to maintain morale, instil hope, and keep his crew unified in the face of seemingly insurmountable odds is a testament to his extraordinary leadership.

From the moment the Endurance was trapped, Shackleton's focus shifted from exploration to the survival and safe return of his crew. His decisions, often made under extreme pressure, were grounded in the well-being of his men. He rationed food and supplies meticulously, ensured equitable treatment for all, and, when necessary, made the harrowing decision to lead a small party across the treacherous seas in a lifeboat to seek rescue.

What stands out most in this saga is Shackleton's unwavering trust in his crew and his ability to inspire trust in return. He delegated responsibilities that played to each member's strengths, listened to their concerns, and led by example, sharing in every hardship. This mutual trust became the cornerstone of their survival strategy.

Despite the unimaginable challenges they faced, not a single life was lost—a testament to Shackleton's leadership and the trust he fostered within his team. The Endurance expedition remains a powerful example of how trust, coupled with resilient leadership, can overcome the most daunting obstacles. Shackleton's story teaches us that trust is not merely a component of leadership; it is the glue that binds a leader to their team, enabling them to weather the storms together.

Embracing Play

In leadership, one of the most overlooked but essential aspects of success is ensuring that your team genuinely enjoys the process of achieving their goals. When work feels rewarding, people become more invested, motivated, and resilient, even in the face of tough challenges. Enjoyment doesn't come from doing less or working less hard—it comes from building a culture that integrates community, challenge, play, and purpose into the fabric of everyday work. This approach doesn't just make the process enjoyable; it drives performance to new levels.

Sir Clive Woodward understood this profoundly during his tenure as head coach of the England rugby team. His revolutionary approach to training showed that even the most gruelling preparation could be made enjoyable, motivating his players to engage deeply and push themselves to new heights. Woodward fostered a culture of enjoyment through a mix of community, challenge, and play.

Community: Building a Positive Team Culture

Woodward was highly intentional about creating a positive, supportive team culture where players felt connected not only to their goals but to each other. He nurtured an environment where players celebrated successes together and learned from their mistakes without fear of harsh criticism. By empowering his players to take ownership of their roles and giving them a voice in their preparation, Woodward increased their investment in the team's progress. This sense of belonging and mutual support turned the team into a close-knit community, where players genuinely enjoyed being part of something greater than themselves.

When team members feel a sense of community, the workplace becomes a space of shared purpose rather than a transactional environment. Leaders can build this by encouraging open communication, recognising individual contributions, and creating opportunities for collaboration and collective growth. In Woodward's case, fostering this community spirit kept his players engaged even when training reached peak intensity.

Challenge: Creating Personal and Team-Wide Goals

For enjoyment to flourish, people must feel challenged in a way that pushes them to grow. Woodward knew that providing his players with a steady stream of personal and team challenges would foster engagement. He often set specific, measurable goals for players during training sessions, turning each drill into a "mission" that offered a sense of achievement when completed. On a team level, he created collective challenges that motivated players to work together, building camaraderie and pushing the limits of what they could achieve.

This principle can easily apply to business. Leaders who introduce challenges that align with personal and team growth foster a culture of healthy competition and continuous improvement. It's this constant striving for mastery, rather than simply ticking boxes, that makes the process of work enjoyable and rewarding.

Play: Mixing Fun with Hard Work

Woodward incorporated play into his training sessions to make even the toughest drills feel enjoyable. He would mix serious, game-like scenarios with lighter, playful moments—turning fitness sessions into competitions or small-sided rugby games with custom rule variations. These elements of play helped his players work just as hard physically, but they enjoyed the process because it felt more like playing a game than enduring a monotonous routine.

In any high-performing environment, injecting elements of fun can transform the way people approach hard work. Leaders can incorporate this by introducing friendly competitions, gamified learning experiences, or team-building activities that add a playful spirit to serious tasks. By embedding play into the process, work becomes an experience people look forward to rather than something they endure.

Creativity: Variety and Innovation in Daily Routines

One of the ways Woodward kept his players engaged was by ensuring that training never felt repetitive. He continuously adapted drills and routines, using a wide variety of exercises that worked different aspects of the game. This approach kept players mentally and physically stimulated, preventing the boredom and mental fatigue that often come with repetitive training.

For leaders in any field, encouraging creativity within the work process can re-energise a team. By introducing variety—whether in meeting formats, problem-solving approaches, or development opportunities—leaders ensure that work remains dynamic and engaging.

Recognition: Rewarding Hard Work and Success

Woodward understood the power of recognition in building enjoyment and motivation. He created a reward system where both big and small achievements were publicly acknowledged, whether through light-hearted awards like 'player of the session' or symbolic gestures of recognition. This constant reinforcement made players feel valued and appreciated, giving them extra motivation to continue working hard.

In a business context, recognising individual and team accomplishments can have a profound impact on morale. Leaders who make an effort to highlight success, no matter how small, build a culture of recognition that enhances engagement and enjoyment.

Mental Conditioning: Ownership and Resilience

Woodward was a pioneer in using mental conditioning as a tool to foster enjoyment and ownership. By working closely with sports psychologists, he equipped his players with techniques to manage pressure, focus their minds, and build resilience. He also gave them ownership of their training, empowering them to engage more deeply with their progress and development. This personal investment in the process turned hard work into something more meaningful and rewarding.

Leaders in any industry can adopt this approach by promoting mental well-being and giving team members autonomy over their tasks. When people feel ownership over their work and are mentally prepared to handle challenges, the process becomes both fulfilling and enjoyable.

Enjoying the Journey

Clive Woodward's leadership showed that enjoyment isn't about reducing effort—it's about creating a culture where the hard work itself is rewarding. Whether through building community, setting challenges, incorporating play, or recognising achievements, leaders can foster an environment where the process of working towards a goal becomes a positive, engaging experience. When people enjoy the journey, they are not only more productive but also more resilient and committed, making extraordinary success far more likely.

Communication is the Medium of Leadership

Communication is key to great leadership. You must let people know what you are doing, what you expect them to be doing, and how you can all work together to accomplish your goals. There are several conversations you will need to facilitate as a leader. Each of these conversations has a specific function.

1. The Foundational Conversation: Cementing the Core of Team Dynamics

At the core of transformative leadership lies the 'Foundational Conversation,' a critical dialogue that not only sets the framework for team interactions but also cements the roles, relationships, and responsibilities that underpin team success. This conversation is not a preliminary check-in, but a continuous dialogue that evolves and reinforces team dynamics over time. It is the backbone of team coherence, ensuring every member clearly understands their role and how it contributes to the larger mission of the team.

The power of the Foundational Conversation lies in its ability to clearly define how each individual relates to the team, the leader, and each other. This ongoing discussion fosters a sense of belonging and purpose, integrating personal ambitions with the collective goals of the team. It's not merely about roles; it's about crafting a shared vision that elevates individual contributions while driving the team forward.

Leaders who master this conversation can cultivate a culture where mutual respect and support are the norms, not the exceptions. It's an opportunity to acknowledge the unique strengths of each team member, aligning them with the team's objectives to maximise impact. This dialogue is crucial for building a cohesive and motivated team that is equipped to handle the complexities of their tasks with confidence and clarity.

Moreover, the Foundational Conversation is iterative—its relevance echoes throughout the project's lifespan. It's essential to revisit this dialogue periodically to reaffirm roles and expectations as projects evolve and team dynamics shift. Even when team members retain their roles without change, refreshing their understanding of how they contribute to the team's success is vital. This not only enhances clarity but also invigorates the team's commitment and energy.

By continuously engaging in the Foundational Conversation, leaders lay the groundwork for a high-performing team that is not only aware of its objectives, but is also deeply invested in achieving them. It is through this foundational dialogue that a team can truly unite, drawing strength from its clarity and purpose to achieve exceptional results. This is where the magic of connectivity flourishes, turning individual efforts into collective achievements.

2. The Visionary Conversation: Setting the Course for Team Success

In the realm of leadership, setting a goal goes beyond the mere achievement of tangible outcomes. The Visionary Conversation also encompasses the evolution of 'becoming' and the essence of 'being' that underpins the journey towards these goals. This broader perspective enriches the vision, transforming it from a destination to a journey of growth and character development for the entire team.

The 'becoming' aspect of your vision involves the transformation your team members will undergo as they work towards the goal. It's about the skills they'll develop, the resilience they'll build, and the deeper understanding of their own potential they'll gain. This transformative journey is as crucial as the goal itself because it shapes individuals into more capable, confident, and cohesive team members.

Similarly, the 'being' component is about the character and culture of the team. It's about fostering a collective identity that resonates with the core values and ethics you envision for your group. This shared ethos is what will guide your team's actions, decisions, and interactions, ensuring that the journey towards the goal is marked by integrity, excellence, and mutual respect.

Incorporating 'becoming' and 'being' into the Visionary Conversation means:

1. Highlighting Growth: Articulate how the journey towards the goal will contribute to each member's personal and professional growth. Emphasise the development opportunities that lie ahead.

2. Defining Character: Clearly define the values and principles that will guide the team's behaviour and decisions. Make sure these are not just words, but lived experiences that define the team's identity.

3. Creating a Culture: Foster an environment where the 'being' aspect is nurtured through rituals, shared stories, and practices that reflect the team's core values.

4. Modelling the Way: As a leader, embody the characteristics and behaviours you wish to see in your team. Lead by example in both your actions and your approach to challenges.

By weaving the concepts of 'becoming' and 'being' into your vision, you transform the Visionary Conversation into a powerful tool for not just achieving goals but for crafting a journey that enriches your team's experience. This approach ensures that the path to success is not just about what you achieve but about who you become and the values you espouse along the way.

3. Opportunity Cultivation Conversation: Maximising Potential

The "Opportunity Cultivation Conversation" goes beyond traditional brainstorming; it is a pivotal dialogue within the leadership toolkit, designed to maximise the team's potential by strategically identifying and harnessing both existing and potential opportunities. This conversation is twofold: it not only highlights the immediate chances available to the team but also focuses on the development, creation, or acquisition of new opportunities necessary for achieving the collective goal or vision.

In this dialogue, a leader maps out the landscape of possibilities, from roles and resources to time and finances, creating a clear path toward the team's objective. It's about looking beyond the present, understanding what's missing, and how to bridge that gap. Whether it's integrating new talents into the team, securing additional funding, or reallocating time to crucial tasks, this conversation ensures that every aspect of the team's potential is explored and utilised.

By engaging in the Opportunity Cultivation Conversation, leaders empower their teams to not just react to their current environment but to proactively shape it. It's a strategic session that invites creativity, encourages initiative, and fosters a proactive approach to problem-solving and goal achievement.

This type of dialogue instils a sense of ownership and responsibility in team members, as they are actively involved in identifying opportunities for growth and improvement. It transforms the team into a dynamic unit that's not just working within a set framework but actively expanding it to accommodate new possibilities.

Ultimately, the Opportunity Cultivation Conversation is about building a fertile ground for the team's success, ensuring that every potential avenue for progress is considered and acted upon. It's a testament to the belief that the best teams are those who can see beyond the horizon, continuously adapting and evolving to meet their goals.

4. Action Initiation Conversation: Cultivating Commitment and Clarity

Without action, nothing happens. The "Action Initiation Conversation" stands at the heart of leadership, transforming vision into momentum. This dialogue isn't just about delegating tasks; it's about fostering commitments and shaping the pathway to collective achievement. True leadership transcends the mere management of people; it involves guiding the commitments and promises they willingly undertake.

This conversation is where vision aligns with action, where the goals of the team intertwine with the individual capabilities and dedication of its members. It's about clarifying, not commanding, engaging, not ordering. Leaders and team members come together to define the commitments necessary to advance towards their shared vision, creating a mutual agreement that lays the foundation for progress.

Here, clarity and commitment are paramount. This dialogue ensures that every team member understands their role, the expectations set upon them, and the significance of their contributions towards the greater goal. It's an opportunity to align individual aspirations with team objectives, ensuring everyone is invested in the outcome.

Leadership through "Action Initiation Conversations" is about empowering team members to own their part of the journey. It's a recognition that while you can't manage people directly, you can inspire them to commit to actions that lead to success. This conversation is the catalyst for action, turning potential into reality by making clear the promises and commitments that pave the way forward. Through this dialogue, leaders and teams co-create the roadmap to achievement, embodying a partnership where every commitment is a step towards realising their shared vision.

An important difference to note is that activity is not action. Activity can be seen and reported but does not necessarily lead to the desired outcome—it isn't opportunity and vision-based. Taking action is outcome-orientated, it moves the project towards the vision, creating a resource, or completing a mini-goal.

Blueprint for the Action Initiation Conversation

Leadership thrives on clear communication, and the Action Initiation Conversation is a pivotal strategy for transforming vision into action. This conversation framework is not just about assigning tasks; it's about forging a partnership between leaders and team members, ensuring everyone is aligned, committed, and clear on the path forward. Here's a deeper dive into each conversation type with examples to guide you:

1. Request: A request is much more than a simple ask; it's a pivotal moment of engagement between a leader and their team member. When you articulate a request with clarity and specificity, like "I request that you compile the monthly performance report in Word format and email it to me by next Wednesday at 3 PM," you do more than delegate a task. You lay down a clear path, inviting your team members to embark on a meaningful journey towards a shared goal. This moment is not just about the task at hand, but about aligning individual efforts with the larger mission of the team or organisation.

This level of detail in a request does several things simultaneously. First, it conveys respect for the recipient's time and abilities, showing that you've considered what's needed and trust them to deliver. It also demystifies expectations, leaving no room for misinterpretation about what constitutes success for the task. By specifying the format ("in Word format"), the method of delivery ("email it to me"), and a precise deadline ("by next Wednesday at 3 PM"), you empower the team member with all the information they need to prioritise effectively and manage their workload accordingly.

Moreover, framing a request in this manner underscores the importance of the task within the broader objectives the team is striving to achieve. It communicates to the team member that their contribution is vital, fostering a sense of ownership and responsibility towards collective success. This clarity and specificity boost motivation, as individuals understand exactly how their efforts fit into the larger picture and the impact they have.

In essence, making a clear and specific request is an act of leadership that extends beyond mere task delegation. It embodies the principles of effective communication, mutual respect, and shared purpose. It sets the stage for action, not as a solitary endeavour but as a collaborative effort towards achieving something greater. By mastering the art of the request, leaders can inspire their team members to engage fully with their work, contribute their best, and move confidently towards the team's goals, knowing precisely what is expected of them and why it matters.

2. Promise: This response, "I promise to complete [task] by [deadline]," signifies commitment. When a team member responds with a promise, such as "I promise to compile the monthly performance report in Word format and email it to you by next Wednesday at 3 PM," they're doing more than just agreeing to a task. This promise is a declaration of their commitment, a signal that they have not only understood the request but are also prepared to take ownership of it. It's a pivotal moment where responsibility is acknowledged, and a personal assurance is made to see the task through to completion.

In this specific example, the promise carries weight because it involves detailed parameters—the format of the report, the mode of delivery, and a precise deadline. Such clarity in the promise ensures that both the requester and the promiser are aligned in their expectations. This alignment is crucial for maintaining trust within the team and for the smooth progression of projects.

Promising to complete a task by a certain deadline also implies that the team member will prioritise this task accordingly, managing their time and resources to honour their commitment. It reflects an understanding of the task's importance within the larger project context and a willingness to be held accountable for its completion.

Moreover, the act of making a promise in a professional setting fosters a culture of reliability and trustworthiness. It reassures the team leader and other team members that everyone is working towards common goals with a shared sense of purpose and urgency.

However, a promise is not just about the commitment to a task; it's also about open communication. If unforeseen challenges arise that may affect the promised deadline or deliverables, it's expected that the individual will communicate these changes promptly. This ensures that any necessary adjustments can be made to the plan, maintaining the fluidity and adaptability essential for navigating complex projects.

By making and keeping promises, team members reinforce their reliability and contribute to a positive, collaborative work environment. It sets a standard of accountability and professionalism, encouraging everyone to match that level of dedication. When promises are consistently honoured, it builds a foundation of trust that is crucial for any team's success. This trust, in turn, enhances collaboration, facilitates open communication, and strengthens the team's cohesion, making it more resilient in the face of challenges.

Thus, the promise is more than just a response; it's a cornerstone of effective teamwork and leadership, embodying the values of commitment, responsibility, and mutual respect. It's a reminder that, in the realm of leadership and collaboration, actions speak louder than words. Each fulfilled promise is a step towards achieving the team's collective goals, and every task completed as promised is a victory in building a strong, reliable team.

3. Decline: Declining a request is not about refusal but about fostering a culture of transparency and trust within a team. When you say, "I cannot complete [task] by [deadline]," it's an act of integrity, acknowledging your current limitations while prioritising the quality of work and well-being. For instance, openly stating, "I cannot compile the report by 3 PM next Wednesday due to prior commitments," is an exercise in honesty that benefits everyone involved.

This approach does several important things. Firstly, it maintains the trust between you and your leader or team members by setting realistic expectations. It prevents scenarios where promises are made but cannot be kept, which can lead to disappointment and a breakdown in team cohesion. By being upfront about your capacity, you allow the team to plan more effectively, perhaps reallocating tasks or adjusting deadlines to accommodate the true bandwidth of its members.

Moreover, a respectful decline encourages a dialogue about priorities and workload management. It opens the door for discussions on what can be reshuffled or re-prioritised, not just for the immediate task, but in the broader context of team goals and individual well-being. This kind of dialogue is crucial for building a supportive work environment where team members feel valued and understood, not just as workers, but as individuals with their own set of challenges and commitments.

Declining also teaches a valuable lesson in self-awareness and boundary setting. It demonstrates that knowing your limits and communicating them effectively is a strength, not a weakness. This realisation empowers individuals to manage their responsibilities more proactively, leading to better work-life balance and overall job satisfaction.

Ultimately, the ability to decline respectfully is an essential component of a healthy, dynamic team. It signifies a mature understanding of one's capabilities and a commitment to the collective success of the team over individual accomplishment. By valuing honesty and respect in communications, leaders can cultivate an environment where team members feel safe to express their true capacity, leading to more realistic planning, stronger commitments, and a culture where everyone strives to bring their best to the table.

4. Counter-Offer: A counter-offer is more than just an alternative; it's a testament to a team member's commitment to finding solutions. It's saying, "I am dedicated to contributing to our shared goals, and here's how I can do it within my current constraints." For example, stating, "I can compile the report for you, but by Friday at 10 AM instead of Wednesday," isn't just about adjusting a deadline; it's about showcasing adaptability and a collaborative spirit in the face of challenges.

This practice encourages a culture where flexibility and problem-solving are valued as much as following the original plan. It recognises that while circumstances may change, the commitment to the team's objectives remains steadfast. By proposing an alternative, you demonstrate an active role in the project's success, offering creative solutions that maintain progress while accommodating unforeseen hurdles.

Counter-offering serves a dual purpose. It keeps projects moving forward by adapting to the realities of the team's situation and reinforces the importance of open dialogue in project management. It acknowledges that, while initial plans are valuable, the ability to adapt and collaborate in response to new information is equally crucial. This flexibility can lead to discovering more efficient ways to achieve goals or even enhance the quality of the outcome, as additional time or resources might provide unexpected insights or opportunities for improvement.

Moreover, engaging in counter-offers builds a sense of shared responsibility and mutual respect among team members. It sends a message that everyone's time, workload, and challenges are recognised and that the team values constructive contributions from all its members. This not only enhances the team's ability to navigate obstacles but also strengthens the bonds between team members, fostering a more cohesive and supportive work environment.

In essence, the act of making a counter-offer embodies the essence of teamwork and leadership — it's about working together to find the best path forward, even when the original plan needs adjustment. It's a reminder that leadership and collaboration are about more than just following orders; they're about working together to find the best solutions for the team and the project. Through this process, teams can become more resilient, adaptable, and ultimately, more successful in achieving their goals.

5. Revoke: Revoking a commitment, such as saying, "I can no longer complete the report by next Wednesday as promised," is not a sign of failure but a demonstration of integrity and respect for the team's objectives. It acknowledges that the landscape of work is ever-changing, and being upfront about these changes is crucial for collective adaptability and progress.

This conversation is pivotal in maintaining trust within the team. By openly communicating changes in your ability to meet a commitment, you're showing that you value the project's success and the team's time. It allows for the reassignment of tasks or the adjustment of timelines in a way that minimises disruption to the overall project. This openness encourages a work culture where honesty is valued over unrealistic promises.

The act of revoking a commitment also highlights the importance of flexibility in project management. It recognises that despite our best intentions, external factors or unforeseen challenges can impact our plans. The key is not to cling stubbornly to a commitment when circumstances have changed, but to communicate these changes promptly, allowing the team to respond effectively.

Moreover, revoking a commitment responsibly demonstrates a high level of professional maturity. It involves evaluating the situation, acknowledging the impact of the change, and communicating it in a way that focuses on solutions rather than problems. This might mean proposing a new deadline, reallocating resources, or identifying another team member who can take on the task.

Ultimately, revoking a commitment should be seen as an opportunity for growth and learning. It offers a chance to review and improve planning and execution processes, making them more resilient to changes. It also reinforces the value of teamwork, as it shows that navigating challenges is a collective effort, with each member playing a vital role in adapting to new circumstances.

In essence, the *revoke* conversation is about acknowledging the dynamic nature of work and handling changes with grace and responsibility. It's a testament to the understanding that in the journey towards achieving goals, how we manage change is as important as how we plan for success. By embracing change with honesty and openness, leaders and teams can build a stronger foundation for navigating the complexities of their projects and achieving their objectives together.

6. Cancel: Cancelling a request isn't a step back; it's a strategic pivot that ensures resources are directed where they're most needed. Saying, "Given the project's new direction, I no longer need the report by next Wednesday," is about recognising that the landscape of work is ever-evolving, and so must our priorities. This kind of conversation highlights a leader's ability to adapt to new information and redirect efforts to align with the most current objectives.

This approach not only optimises resource allocation but also signals to the team that flexibility and responsiveness to change are valued traits. It shows that leadership is always attuned to the broader vision and ready to make adjustments to ensure that the team's work remains relevant and impactful. Moreover, it respects the time and effort of team members by freeing them from tasks that no longer serve the team's goals, allowing them to concentrate on initiatives that do.

When a leader cancels a request due to shifting priorities, it demonstrates a commitment to effective and efficient work rather than just busy work. It's an acknowledgement that every task should contribute meaningfully towards the team's objectives and that when those objectives change, so too should the tasks. This kind of adaptability in the face of change is crucial for maintaining momentum and morale in dynamic environments.

Furthermore, this conversation fosters an atmosphere of open communication and trust. It reassures team members that decisions are made with thoughtful consideration of the project's needs and their contributions. This level of transparency encourages a culture where team members feel valued and informed, strengthening the collective drive towards achieving the team's redefined goals.

In summary, cancelling a request in response to new priorities or insights isn't a sign of indecision or wasted effort; it's a strategic move that underscores the importance of adaptability, efficient resource use, and clear, purpose-driven action. It's a reminder that in the fast-paced world of work, being agile and responsive is key to navigating changes successfully and keeping the team's efforts aligned with the most current and compelling objectives.

7. Declaring Completion: Declaring the completion of a task isn't just ticking off a checkbox; it's the culmination of dedication, effort, and a promise kept. Saying, "I've finished the monthly performance report and emailed it to you," is a testament to reliability and the successful fulfilment of a commitment made. It signifies not only the end of a task but also the effectiveness and integrity of the person who completed it.

This final step in the conversation sequence is crucial for several reasons. Firstly, it provides closure to the assigned task, allowing both the leader and the team member to acknowledge the completion of a job well done. It's a moment of recognition for the effort put in, reinforcing the value of hard work and commitment within the team.

Secondly, declaring completion facilitates the timely progress of projects. It ensures that tasks don't just disappear into the void but are recognised as completed, allowing the team to move forward to the next steps or projects. This kind of punctuality and clarity in communication helps maintain momentum and keeps the entire team aligned and focused on their collective goals.

Moreover, it opens the door for feedback and learning opportunities. By clearly stating that a task has been completed, team members invite feedback on their work, fostering a culture of continuous improvement and skill development. This conversation is an integral part of the learning process, allowing both the leader and the team member to reflect on what was done well and what could be improved in the future.

Finally, declaring completion reinforces the trust between a leader and their team. It shows that team members are accountable and dependable, strengthening the bonds of mutual respect and confidence within the team. This trust is the foundation of a strong, cohesive team that can tackle any challenge with assurance and unity.

In essence, declaring completion is more than just an administrative note; it's a critical communication that celebrates achievement, fosters learning, and strengthens team dynamics. It's a vital part of the conversation that underscores the importance of follow-through, accountability, and the celebration of small victories on the journey to achieving bigger goals.

Crafting the Path to Achievement: Deadlines and Conditions of Satisfaction

In the realm of leadership and teamwork, setting a deadline isn't merely about marking a date on the calendar; it's about creating a shared sense of purpose and urgency. By stating, "Please ensure the report is ready by next Wednesday at 3 PM," you're not just asking for a task to be completed; you're inviting your team to join you in a focused journey towards a clear target. Deadlines serve as the heartbeat of project management, pulsing with the rhythm of progress and anticipation, ensuring that every team member's efforts are synchronised towards a common finish line.

Equally vital to this endeavour is establishing the conditions of satisfaction, which define the blueprint of success for the task at hand. When you specify, "The report should be in Word format, include all departmental data, and be proofread for accuracy," you're setting a standard of excellence. It's like giving your team a map with a detailed legend and clear landmarks. These conditions are a beacon of clarity in the often murky waters of project completion, guiding your team's efforts not just to reach the destination, but to do so with a mark of quality and thoroughness.

Together, these two factors transform vague directives into powerful missions. Setting a deadline infuses the work with importance and momentum, compelling team members to align their time and resources towards achieving the goal. Meanwhile, defining the conditions of satisfaction ensures that the end result not only arrives on time but also meets or exceeds the expected quality standards. This dual focus on timing and quality reinforces accountability, encourages meticulous attention to detail, and fosters a culture of high performance and pride in workmanship.

Moreover, this clear framework supports the growth of team members by challenging them to manage their time effectively and strive for excellence in their output. It's a lesson in discipline and ambition, wrapped in the simple packaging of deadlines and standards.

In essence, setting a deadline and defining conditions of satisfaction are not just administrative tasks; they are acts of leadership that inspire, challenge, and guide your team towards collective and individual triumphs. These conversations are the threads that weave the tapestry of successful projects, vibrant team dynamics, and the relentless pursuit of excellence.

Each of these conversations is a thread in the fabric of leadership, weaving together a tapestry of commitment, clarity, and cooperation. By adopting this framework, you empower your team to navigate challenges with confidence, foster a culture of accountability, and collectively march towards achieving the envisioned success. Let this be your guide to not just directing but inspiring, not merely assigning but engaging, ensuring that every step taken is a stride towards the collective goal.

5. Completion Assurance Conversation: Ensuring Integrity and Fulfilment.

The "Completion Assurance Conversation" is a pivotal tool in the leadership toolkit. It transcends the typical oversight of tasks and enters the realm of fostering commitment and ensuring integrity in every promise made within your team. This conversation is not merely a checkpoint, but a profound engagement that reassures team members of the significance of their commitments. It's a dialogue that underlines the essence of leadership: guiding your team not by overseeing their tasks but by safeguarding the promises that drive towards a common goal.

Imagine the scenario: a teammate has pledged to deliver the monthly performance report by a certain deadline. The Completion Assurance Conversation comes into play not as a reminder of the task but as a reaffirmation of the commitment. By engaging in discussions before the deadline, you're not merely checking on progress; you're reinforcing the trust and reliance placed in each team member's word. It's a testament to the belief that integrity and effectiveness are paramount, surpassing the mere completion of activities.

Such conversations are underpinned by two core principles: integrity and completion. Integrity, in this context, means ensuring that every action aligns with the commitments made, providing a solid foundation upon which trust and effectiveness are built. Completion, on the other hand, signifies a definitive end to a task where nothing remains to be done. It's the recognition that a task is fully accomplished, embodying the commitment to fulfil what has been promised, or acknowledging that no further action can be taken.

This distinction between completing and ending a task is crucial. It elevates the task's conclusion from being merely about reaching an end to fulfilling a promise with thoroughness and integrity. When a deadline arrives, what matters is not just the work handed in but the fulfilment of the pledge made, embodying the true spirit of completion.

In nurturing the Completion Assurance Conversation within your team, you're fostering a culture where promises are kept, commitments are valued, and every task is brought to its rightful conclusion. It's a practice that goes beyond the boundaries of work, instilling values of trust, responsibility, and integrity—qualities that define not just exceptional leaders but also cohesive and successful teams.

6. Conversation for Transforming Breakdowns: Navigating Through Challenges Together

In the journey of leadership and teamwork, encountering breakdowns is inevitable. It's not the absence of challenges that define a team's strength, but its ability to transform these breakdowns into breakthroughs. This pivotal process is facilitated through a specific type of dialogue we call the "Conversation for Transforming Breakdowns."

This conversation is an essential tool for any leader and team, serving as a bridge from encountering a problem to finding a solution collaboratively. It's about collectively acknowledging the breakdown, understanding its nature, and then systematically working through it to not only solve the immediate issue but also to emerge stronger and more unified.

The steps to this transformative conversation echo the principles outlined in Chapter 6 - Weathering The Storms. They involve recognising the breakdown, assessing its impact without the cloud of negative emotions, identifying what has worked and what hasn't, and redefining the path forward. However, what sets this conversation apart is its collaborative nature. It's not just about one person navigating through the storm; it's about the key team members sailing the ship together.

Engaging in this dialogue means fostering an environment of openness, trust, and mutual respect. It encourages each team member to bring their unique perspectives to the table, ensuring that every voice is heard and valued. Through this collective effort, the team doesn't just find a way out of the immediate crisis; it builds a stronger foundation for facing future challenges.

The "Conversation for Transforming Breakdowns" is a testament to the power of unity in adversity. It underscores the importance of not just working alongside each other, but truly working with each other. By committing to this process, teams can turn their weakest moments into their greatest victories, forging a path of continuous growth and improvement.

For a deeper dive into the specifics of this transformative process, refer back to Chapter 6 - Weathering The Storms. There, you'll find a comprehensive guide to navigating through breakdowns, detailed steps for turning challenges into opportunities for growth, and the importance of collective effort in achieving success.

Increasing Communication Skills: The Foundation of Transformation

At the heart of leadership, relationships, and indeed every aspect of life, lies communication. It's not just a skill to be honed for business success; it's a daily practice that nurtures relationships, boosts confidence, and forms the bedrock of our interactions. This final section is a deep dive into cultivating effective communication, a trait that, when mastered, has the power to transform.

Listen Intently

The cornerstone of effective communication is listening. It's about truly hearing what others have to say, engaging with their words, and showing genuine interest. By listening more than you speak, you not only gain insights but also make others feel valued and understood. Remember, every conversation is an opportunity to connect on a deeper level.

Adapt Your Communication

Tailoring your language and approach to the person you're interacting with is crucial. Effective communication is not one-size-fits-all; it's about understanding the unique perspective of your conversational partner and adjusting accordingly. Whether it's a family member, a friend, or a colleague, ensuring your message resonates with them strengthens the bond and enhances mutual understanding.

The Power of Body Language

Non-verbal cues play a significant role in how our messages are received. An open posture, steady eye contact, and an engaged demeanour signal attentiveness and respect. Even in the digital age, where face-to-face interactions may be limited, the principles of positive body language remain pivotal in fostering connections.

Clarity and Brevity

Getting to the point without unnecessary digressions makes your communication effective and respectful of others' time. Whether it's verbal or written, being concise yet thorough ensures your message is understood and appreciated.

Equality in Interaction

Respect is the foundation of positive communication. Treating everyone with equal regard, regardless of the context, not only reflects your values but also encourages an environment of mutual respect and openness.

Taking Notes

In meetings or conversations, jotting down key points signifies engagement and helps in following up on discussions effectively. It's a simple yet impactful way to demonstrate your involvement and ensure no detail is missed.

Maintain Positivity

A positive demeanour, even in challenging situations, can greatly influence the outcome of your interactions. Smiling, even when you're on the phone, can alter your tone, making your communication more pleasant and effective.

Think Before You Speak

Pause and reflect on your words before you let them out. This mindfulness can prevent misunderstandings and ensure your message is both thoughtful and appropriate. Planning your response can turn potentially contentious conversations into productive dialogues.

Incorporating these practices into your daily life enriches every interaction. Whether it's with family, friends, or colleagues, effective communication is transformative. It builds bridges, resolves conflicts, and forges strong bonds. As we conclude this chapter on leadership and communication, remember that the journey to becoming a compelling communicator is continuous. Each conversation, whether it's at home, in the community, or at work, is an opportunity to practise, learn, and grow.

By embracing these principles, you're not just improving your ability to convey ideas; you're shaping the world around you. You're building a legacy of meaningful relationships, inspiring leadership, and impactful interactions. The journey of a thousand miles begins with a single step, and in the realm of communication, every word counts. Let your words be the light that guides you and others towards a brighter, more connected future.

In essence, communication is the soul of leadership and the heart of human connection. It's what transforms ambition into action, challenges into opportunities, and groups of individuals into cohesive, purpose-driven teams. As you close this chapter, remember that the journey to becoming an adept communicator is ongoing—a path of continuous learning, adapting, and growing. Armed with these skills, you're not just prepared to lead; you're ready to make a meaningful difference in every aspect of your life.

Being the Captain

The Power of Leadership in Action

The Rugby World Cup final of 2003 was more than just a match for Sir Clive Woodward and his team—it was the culmination of years of vision, strategy, and unwavering belief in the power of great leadership. The road to that moment had been long and filled with challenges, but Woodward's clarity of purpose, his ability to inspire through vision, and his determination to make the process enjoyable brought the team to the brink of greatness.

As England faced Australia in the World Cup final, every ounce of preparation, every moment of training, and every conversation of belief came to a head. The match was a gruelling test of endurance, skill, and mental resilience. Both teams fought with everything they had, yet there was something about the way England held their composure under immense pressure that showed the depth of their preparation. In extra time, with the scores tied and only minutes left, England remained resolute. They knew they had the tools, the confidence, and the leadership to seize victory.

In that defining moment, as the team surged forward, Jonny Wilkinson received the ball. The stadium fell into a breathless silence as he steadied himself, took the kick, and watched the ball sail through the posts. The stadium erupted in a roar of joy as the final whistle blew—England had won their first Rugby World Cup.

It wasn't just the final kick that secured their victory; it was the culmination of leadership in action. Woodward's ability to bring clarity to the team's vision had kept them focused through the highs and lows of their campaign. His insistence on enjoyment—creating a culture where hard work was both challenging and rewarding—had kept the players fully engaged, willing to push themselves beyond their limits. And his strategic brilliance, combined with trust in his players, allowed them to rise to the occasion with calm confidence, even under the weight of immense pressure.

As the players gathered on the field, their faces lit up with a mixture of exhaustion and exhilaration, they hoisted the trophy high above their heads. The sight of the England team, champions of the world, reflected the power of Woodward's leadership. The fans roared in unison, their voices rising to the sky, as England celebrated their historic achievement. It was a moment that symbolised what is possible when a leader brings vision, clarity, and enjoyment to a team.

Woodward's leadership had inspired his players to go the extra mile—not just in that final match, but throughout their entire journey. They didn't just play rugby; they believed in a greater purpose, a shared goal that had been clearly communicated and consistently reinforced. They worked hard, but they enjoyed the process, knowing that each step brought them closer to their dream.

In business, sport, or life, the lessons from that World Cup victory are clear. When leaders provide clarity of vision, trust in their team's abilities, and make the process of achieving goals engaging and enjoyable, extraordinary results are possible. The England rugby team's triumph serves as a reminder that great leadership is not just about directing people—it's about inspiring them to believe in something bigger than themselves and to give everything they have to make it a reality.

In the end, it wasn't just the trophy that mattered, but the journey to lift it—the way a team came together, led by vision, fuelled by trust, and strengthened by the joy of the work itself.

Final Words: A Blueprint for Transformational Success

As we conclude this journey through the keys to transformational success, it's important to reflect on the essence of what has been shared. These principles, while straightforward at their core, demand dedication, resilience, and a commitment to continuous growth. This final chapter serves as both a recap and a rallying cry, a reminder that the power to change and achieve lies within your grasp.

Game On!

Gamification transforms mundane tasks into engaging, goal-oriented challenges, fostering motivation, achievement, and collaboration. By integrating carefully chosen game elements, work becomes not just about completing tasks, but enjoying the process, creating a life that is both fun and productive.

Rise Up, Self!

Your transformation begins with a spark—a purpose that lights up your path. Finding and nurturing this purpose is your first step towards meaningful change, whether in your personal endeavours or professional ventures.

Charting Course

Knowing your destination is crucial, but plotting the course to get there is what brings your dreams into the realm of possibility. Goal setting transforms aspirations into actionable plans, guiding your journey step by step.

Eating the Elephant

Mastering time management is akin to learning how to eat an elephant—one bite at a time. Transforming time into productivity allows you to make the most of every day, propelling you closer to your goals with each disciplined action.

Setting the Sails

Decisiveness is your compass in the sea of life. It's about making choices that align with your purpose and navigating through uncertainty with confidence and clarity.

Soaring Higher

The pursuit of personal improvement is an endless ascent. Staying committed to learning and growing ensures that you are always equipped to face new challenges and seize opportunities.

Weathering the Storms

Adversity is inevitable, but your response to it defines your journey. Viewing obstacles as stepping stones rather than roadblocks allows you to emerge stronger and more resilient.

Final Words: A Blueprint for Transformational Success

Being the Captain

Leadership is not reserved for the select few; it's a quality that can be cultivated by anyone willing to connect, communicate, and inspire. Transforming chaotic management into effective leadership through clear and compassionate communication is the key to guiding your team to success.

Remember, the journey towards transformational success is not just about reaching a destination. It's about the growth, learning, and joy that come from the journey itself. Embrace fun, play, and enjoyment as integral parts of this process. They not only elevate your spirits but also inspire those around you to engage fully in the collective mission.

As you move forward, I invite you to explore the interactive journal created as a companion to this book. It offers exercises, reflections, and resources designed to deepen your understanding and application of the concepts discussed. Visit www.chanthology.com/wtgjournal/ to begin this extended journey.

Challenges will arise. There will be moments of doubt and difficulty. In those times, pause, reflect on your purpose, and remind yourself of the strength and resilience within you. It is through embracing these challenges and moving forward with determination that true transformation occurs.

This book is not just a collection of strategies; it's a guide to creating a life and business that reflect your deepest values and ambitions. Use it as a starting point, adapt its lessons to your unique path, and never stop striving for excellence.

Your transformational success is not a question of if, but when. With each step taken, each decision made, and each challenge overcome, you are not just playing the game—you are winning it. Onward to a future of boundless potential and unprecedented achievement.

Harnessing Joy: A Journey Back from Failure

The fall was as rapid as it was unexpected. After years of riding the crest of success, I found myself grappling with a reality I had never imagined: my business had failed. It was a harsh awakening from a dream of invincibility. This failure cost me nearly everything—my home, my car, and even the everyday presence of my children. Bankruptcy was not just a financial status; it became a stark label of my personal and professional life.

In the aftermath, I made a solemn vow to rebuild. But this resolve focused solely on regaining lost financial ground and prestige. I was determined, yet blind to the fundamental flaw in my plan—I had excluded joy from my blueprint for recovery.

My initial business success was fuelled not just by smart strategies but by a genuine passion for the work. In my relentless pursuit to rebuild, I had neglected this essential ingredient. My days were grey, my tasks joyless. I understood success strategies intellectually, but failed to apply them effectively because I wasn't enjoying the journey.

Realisation dawned gradually. My former business hadn't just been about profits; it was driven by enthusiasm and the sheer pleasure of entrepreneurship. Recapturing this joy became my new mission. I started integrating small, enjoyable rewards into my daily routine, allowing myself moments of leisure even amidst austerity.

I reshaped my daily life to include activities that brought happiness. Simple joys like a walk in the park, a yoga class, or sitting and drawing—activities that cost little but offered rich emotional dividends—became part of my schedule.

This infusion of fun transformed my approach. Tasks were no longer just milestones to be achieved; they became steps in a fulfilling journey. My productivity and creativity surged. Solutions came easier, and obstacles became less daunting.

The impact was profound and multi-dimensional. Not only did my professional endeavours begin to thrive again, but my personal life also saw remarkable improvements. I was happier, more engaged with my family, and found myself living a life rich with emotional wealth.

The measure of my success shifted dramatically. No longer based on financial metrics, it expanded to include the quality of my relationships and the contentment in my daily life. This holistic approach to success—rooted in joy and engagement—turned out to be far more sustainable and rewarding.

As you apply the principles laid out in this book, from goal-setting and time management to decision-making and leadership, remember to weave joy and passion into the fabric of your endeavours. Success isn't just about the outcomes you achieve; it's also about how you achieve them. Let fun and joy be not just the seasonings, but essential ingredients in your recipe for a fulfilling life.

Remember, a truly successful life is rich not just in material wealth, but in laughter, love, and contentment. As you close this chapter and set forth on your journey, carry with you the lesson that joy is not just a companion to success—it's a vital catalyst. Make joy a priority, and watch as the world opens up in ways you never imagined. This isn't just how to succeed; it's how to live profoundly.

Always Play to Win

In life, as in any game, the difference between merely surviving and truly thriving lies in our intention to play to win. This doesn't mean stepping over others to reach the top; rather, it's about embracing each day with zest, making conscious decisions that align with your deepest values, and relentlessly pursuing your passions.

Winning in life means crafting a journey filled with purpose, joy, and fulfilment. It's not about the accolades you gather, but the laughter you share, the challenges you overcome, and the peace you find. As you move forward, remember that the most rewarding wins are those that bring not just success, but happiness and a profound sense of satisfaction.

Armed with the tools and understanding from this book, step forth with the courage to implement what you've learned. Transform your goals into achievements, your challenges into opportunities, and your dreams into realities. Remember, the best time to plant a tree was twenty years ago; the second best time is now.

Thank you for sharing this journey with me. Let's continue to grow, inspire, and lead a life of impactful success. Remember, it's not just about winning the game—it's about loving the play.

Take the Leap: Join the Journey to Mastery

As we turn the final page of this guide, remember that the journey towards transformational success is ongoing. The principles and strategies laid out in these chapters are just the beginning. To continue growing and achieving, I invite you to connect with me further.

For continuous learning and deeper engagement, subscribe to my newsletter at chrisball.com. Here, I share regular insights, resources, and strategies that extend beyond what we've covered. Each newsletter is designed to help you refine your skills, discover new perspectives, and stay inspired on your path to success.

Final Words: A Blueprint for Transformational Success

Let's also connect on LinkedIn at linkedin.com/in/cjball/. Join a community of like-minded individuals who are all striving to play the game of life not just to participate but to truly win.

If this book has impacted your journey, please consider leaving a review on Amazon or Goodreads (or both). Your feedback not only helps me serve you better but also assists others in deciding how this book might help them achieve their own goals. Share your story, your successes, and how you've applied the lessons learned. Let your insights inspire others to embark on their journey to transformational success.

As you continue to navigate your path, keep these resources and connections at your fingertips to ensure you are never alone in your quest for greatness. Let's make your game one for the history books. Play boldly, play wisely, and most importantly, play joyfully.

Acknowledgements

First and foremost, to my unwavering pillar, my wife – the bedrock of this entire endeavour. Her steadfast determination in nudging me to commence writing, followed by countless revisions, was instrumental in shaping this book. It's one thing to express myself, but another to communicate in a manner that resonates with a wider audience, and she ensured I bridged that gap. Serving both as an ardent supporter and a stringent reviewer, she's been the driving force behind every sentence that made the cut.

To my children, my unwitting mentors. Observing the world through their innocent, playful, and, at times, humorous lens has been enlightening. Their candid, jovial, and occasionally slapstick outlook has been a continuous source of wonder to me. Through their eyes, I've learned to find fun in the serious and gain wisdom from the absurd. Their genuine love and trust have always been a beacon, guiding me towards bettering myself, not just as a parent, but as a human being. My son Josh, whose perseverance and determination in creating his own game inspire me to push further and aim higher every day. My daughter Emy, whose unwavering pursuit of purpose and fulfilment, along with her invaluable recommendations, has been a constant source of inspiration throughout my journey.

Importantly, to my Mum. She epitomised the spirit of chasing one's dreams against all odds. Watching her life unfurl, split between societal expectations in her early years and then, as if reborn, diving headfirst into her true passion, has been both a lesson and an inspiration. Her artist's soul found its canvas, painting pictures and colouring the essence of her existence. While her works might not have brought her financial riches, they did something far more valuable - they painted her days with pure, unadulterated joy. Every brushstroke, every piece she sold in her quaint shop, was a testament to her indomitable spirit. Through her, I learnt that true wealth isn't gauged by a bank balance but by the contentment in one's heart. And she, with her gleaming eyes and hands stained with paint, was a living embodiment of that joy. She instilled in me a fundamental truth - to ardently follow my passions, carve out my niche, and to mould those passions into a life rich in purpose and happiness.

There is one final acknowledgement that I wish to make, one that has perhaps had the greatest impact on this book: to God. This journey began almost twenty years ago, with many moments of progress and equally many of hesitation. Time and again, I set this work aside, unsure of its direction or purpose. But a few years ago, everything changed. I began walking through life with God as my guide and my support. In doing so, I discovered a new source of inspiration, one that brought clarity and strength where there was once uncertainty. Through this divine partnership, I found the resolve to finish this project, and the words flowed in ways I could not have imagined. Every sentence, every idea within these pages is dedicated to the hope that this book may offer encouragement to anyone seeking a better, more fulfilled life. It is through prayer, meditation, and a deep connection with God that I have been able to create this. My intention has always been to help you—the reader—on your journey, as you search for your own path towards a richer, more meaningful existence.

www.ingramcontent.com/pod-product-compliance
Lightning Source LLC
Chambersburg PA
CBHW052011070526
44584CB00016B/1699

THE UNIVERSITY of LIFE and HOW I GRADUATED FREE

JOAN MILLER

DISCLAIMER

To the readers of my book, I wish to advise that I am not a qualified medical practitioner. The path you choose to take, I leave to your own discretion and understanding.

I intend to present you with information and learning gained from my own experience. I offer this as a spiritual feast with the sincere hope that the words I have written will edify you and light a path of peace and love before you.

For forty-four years, I have practised as a clairvoyant-medium/hypnotherapist. For many years I conducted a Transpersonal School, educating students in inner-peace, self-awareness, and psychic abilities.

In 1991, I gained a Diploma of Clinical Hypnotherapy, including Psychology and Clinical Procedures, from The NSW School Of Hypnotic Sciences.

As this is part memoir, I have relied on my memories and intuitions to relay my life's story. In no way do I wish to cause discomfort to any persons mentioned. To respect privacy, I have used pseudonyms where appropriate.

DEDICATION

I dedicate this book to:

My grandmother, Louisa Daisy, who suffered because of
her God-given gifts.
May my words give vindication to her spirit.

My little brother Bob, who passed
to spirit in 2020 after a long battle
with Alzheimer's and Parkinson's Disease.

Dr Matthew Scott-Young, the amazingly gifted
neurosurgeon who gave me a life in 2014
with his skill and compassion.
God bless you.

And to all who have been my teachers through life.

ACKNOWLEDGEMENTS

My life has been rich with people who have taught me in both negative and positive ways. There are far too many to name. However, at this time, I would like to acknowledge the following:

My dearest friend Denny, a published author, for her untiring work in getting this book to finality. The love she has shown me by spending so many hours communicating long-distance on our computers and phones is a gift I shall always cherish. Not only a gift to me but to all who read the following words for which Denny acted as a brilliant midwife.

Denny's editor-aunt Laurel, who taught her many skills in the writing of her book, *Still Standing: A Mother's Raw Journey From the Shadows of Loss to the Dawning of Hope*. www.dennymeek.com.au.

To my excellent editor, Marion, my wonderful proofreader, Charlie, Linda, and the entire team at Aurora House; I owe you my deepest gratitude for all your hard work.

To my older sister Gladys, for collaborating on childhood memories. You and our younger brother Bob play an integral part in this book.

Dr Stanislav Grof and his late wife, Christina (founders of Transpersonal Psychology). Stan, you helped me to find 'The Holy Grail'. You once told me my book was ahead of time. Well, 'the time has come, the walrus said.'

The late Professor John Mack for his belief in my abduction stories after meeting the Grofs. In John's words, 'They put a hole in my psyche, and the UFOs flew in.'

Finally, the late Dr John Whitman Ray, pioneer of Body Electronics and the Science of Regeneration. You were not only a very qualified practitioner but also a visionary. Dear John, you were a man ahead of time.

CONTENTS

Testimonials	xi
Prelude	xiii
Overview: The University of Life – Psycho-spiritual Progression for Humanity	xv
PART ONE: My Life, My Journey	1
1. My Childhood	3
2. My Teen Years	37
3. Work Experience	47
4. Marriage	55
5. New Guinea	69
6. Back In Australia	81
7. A New Awareness	87
8. A Reprieve	101
9. My Psychic Career Begins	107
10. A Visit To My New Guinea Village	109
11. Legal Decisions And Change	117

PART TWO: Lessons from the University of Life — 147

12. Grandma Daisy — 149
13. Auras And Energies — 157
14. Body, Mind & Spirit — 167
15. Kundalini — 175
16. Psyches, Trips, 'Empty Houses' & Exorcisms — 183
17. Haunted Houses — 195
18. Fear Is Just A Four-Letter Word — 199
19. Death As A Birth To Another Reality — 203
20. Near-Death Experiences (Ndes) — 213
21. Messages From 'The Other Side' — 215
22. Albert Einstein — 237
23. Connecting With Our Own God Within — 239
24. Sai Baba: A Call To India — 243
25. Muslim Prophecy For End Days — 271
26. My Extraterrestrial Experience — 273
27. Prophecies — 283

Epilogue — 305

About The Author — 309

TESTIMONIALS

There are many things previously unknown that are now commonplace. As we question the very nature of the universe as a holographic quantum projection that our minds are proving to be, then we start to question our very essence that may have commonality in the zero-point field beyond the speed of light, where all is connected. Are some of us more able to perceive the information available in the 'field'?

In this light, I would recommend you consider the words of such a formidable lady where pleasure and pain combined to open her mind to all possibilities.

Dr. Jacqueline Boustany MBBS,
Dip Paeds, MPH

You are truly a gifted soul. Thank you for sharing your gift! Every time I see you, I leave feeling refreshed and connected with my beloved soulmate, Glenn. The things you can tell me are spot on without fail, and you have helped me through some of my darkest times since losing him. Thank you for helping me to start healing! Thank you for helping me realise I am not going crazy when I think Glenn is talking to me or sending me signs.

I am blessed to have met you, for you have opened my mind to the other side – something I always hoped was real and now know is.

Mel

You have helped me immeasurably. I really appreciate what you have done for me through your reading. I can now see a new realm of possibility for continuation of the soul after the physical body is not functioning anymore and this has brought me comfort beyond words. I am no longer heavy in grief because 'they' clearly conveyed their messages through you, and you were able to pass things on that no one else could have told you other than my family on the 'other side'. This proved to me that their spirits are still with me, and they haven't left just because their body has. And that is so cool!! Thank you so much.

Jacqui

I just wanted to send you a message of love in these wild times. I hope life is still beautiful for you and you are coping with everything that is going on. I often think about you and the impact you had on me believing in magic. That one small moment I experienced with you has still, to this day, given me so much strength and courage to have faith and trust the process. I, for one, know I could sit and listen to your stories and wisdom all day. Eternally grateful.

Ange

I have known Joan for almost forty years, and in that time, she has read successfully not only for myself but also for many of my friends and family. She has always been 'spot on' with relaying quirky sayings and things only I would have known about my passed-over loved ones.

In the last seven years, since my dear husband's passing, I have made a point of having Joan read for me on his birthday. He comes through without fail, along with many other departed loved ones, and it has helped me to feel not so lonely. I truly feel connected with him again, and it has given me such peace to know that he is always with me and protecting and guiding his loved ones from the other side. Blessings.

Marjie P

PRELUDE

While I have never formally attended a university, I have had many wonderful teachers. Some of these teachers were linked with the medical profession, the alternate medical profession, and many more with *The University of Life*. The lessons from the latter involved no outlay of cash but, in deep retrospect, were a valuable asset to my spiritual growth and evolvement.

During my fifties and sixties, I undertook studies with Dr Stanislav Grof, who, with his late wife Christina, pioneered the Spiritual Emergence Network and Holotropic Breathwork. Dr Grof is a Czech-born psychiatrist with over sixty years' experience in researching non-ordinary states of consciousness. He is also a founder, and chief theoretician, of Transpersonal Psychology. In addition to his research, practice, and teaching in the USA, Stan has travelled and taught in many countries around the world. He has written many books and articles and received numerous awards.

In my fifties, I attended a Transpersonal Conference in Brisbane where Dr Grof and many other interesting lecturers spoke. That day was a doorway out of 'dark' into 'light' for me. At the end of the conference, I hugged Stan, telling him he had just helped me find the Holy Grail.

The late Dr John Whitman-Ray was another of my teachers and mentors. He and one of his colleagues held workshops at the Transpersonal Centre I directed. Dr John pioneered Body Electronics, a method where a group of people holding points on meridians in a patient's body could facilitate healing, a little like charging a flat battery. Dr John also taught nutrition and iridology.

All my life, I have been an inveterate seeker of the truth and a fighter against injustice.

My eternal gratitude goes out to my mentors and teachers for sharing their research and learning with me and many others.

My eternal gratitude goes out to the many students who have trusted me to lead them, and to my many clients who have allowed me a space in their lives through my Reading for them.

My eternal gratitude especially goes out to the people who were my 'hard and unwitting teachers'; they who, having led me into dark places, forced me to look for the doorway to the light and the road less travelled.

OVERVIEW

THE UNIVERSITY OF LIFE:
PSYCHO-SPIRITUAL PROGRESSION FOR HUMANITY

WELCOME TO THE MOMENT OF ORIENTATION TO THE UNIVERSITY OF LIFE! May you graduate with flying colours, a happy heart, and 'the peace of mind that passes all understanding'.

You may have been fortunate enough to have attended the greatest universities on planet Earth, have attained the highest degrees – doctorates, professorships, bursaries. All these great attainments do not bring with them the recipe for a happy, peaceful, fulfilled life if *The University of Life* is neglected or remains unrecognised.

I believe that every soul chooses to incarnate into a physical body on planet Earth in order to experience a range of modalities, i.e., physical, mental, emotional, spiritual, and creative. This is what I have termed *The University of Life*. Each consecutive incarnation is designed to advance the soul to a higher order of being if the soul recognises the truth and purpose of the incarnation.

At the time of merging with the physical/Earth body, the soul brings with it the accumulated memories of past lives and a variable outline of the life ahead. This merging can occur in utero or at the moment of birth. Being as ether, these memories – which are like a vast library, encyclopaedic in nature – bathe themselves in the crystal membrane of every single cell of the human body.

How unfortunate it is that the early church doctrine of Christianity outlawed these very concepts. Instead, for a person to be considered a Christian, they are asked to adhere to the precepts of the church, estranging them from their individual soul's purpose. My considered opinion is that allowing a cross to be marked upon the third eye at baptism, confirmation, or such occasions is an act of 'crossing out' or negating that person's spiritual birthright.

In history, how many poor souls were burnt at the stake or tortured because they had a greater spiritual link with the universal God than their tormentors had?

Giordano Bruno was an Italian Dominican friar, philosopher, mathematician, poet, cosmological theorist, and Hermetic occultist in the sixteenth century. He is known for his cosmological theories, which conceptually extended the Copernican model. At age fifty-two, he was publicly tortured and burned at the stake. His crime? He was a brilliant psychic!

I also query words from the Holy Communion service: 'The blood of our Lord Jesus Christ which was shed for thee, preserve thy body and soul unto everlasting life.' These words are spoken countless times daily throughout the world. The *Book of Common Prayer* contains the Order for Burial prayers in which it is stated: 'We therefore commit this body to the ground, earth to earth, ashes to ashes, dust to dust.' Is there not some dichotomy in these statements? At death, the cells of the physical body die and decompose. How is it possible to 'preserve' our bodies 'unto everlasting life'? 'As above – so below'. The 'God' or Electromagnetic Energy – the power of the soul returns from whence it came at the point of death of the human body.

One of the biblical stories that I have pondered since my teen years has been the story of Adam and Eve. The expectation that one should believe in a snake or serpent with the power of speech is nothing short of preposterous! A fairy-tale? A misinterpretation? In my opinion, possibly both.

Modern research and archaeological discoveries are unravelling the mysteries of the ancient past. Darwin's theory of natural evolution no longer holds ground. In recorded history, our physical bodies have not mutated to a 'higher order'.

According to Mesopotamian tradition, thousands of years ago the gods descended from the heavens and, by way of genetic engineering, upgraded the human species. From the area we now know as Iraq, once known as Sumer or Sumeria, come stories of the Anunnaki, an advanced race of human-like extraterrestrials who brought with them advanced technology. It is my firm belief that the Anunnaki created the Garden of Eden with the help of the original inhabitants of planet Earth. The 'Adams' and 'Eves', a more primitive form of mankind, existed when the Anunnaki arrived. Through genetic manipulation, the Anunnaki upgraded these beings, making them 50% more intelligent than primates and able to be servants to their benefactors.

The tree of life referred to in the Adam and Eve story is, to my mind, an allegory to describe the Kabbalistic Tree of Life consisting of the Kundalini, the chakras, and the pathway of spiritual growth. The 'fruit of the tree' – the apple

– is the attainment of spiritual knowledge. The serpent is a representation of the Kundalini energy. When the created servants became as knowledgeable as their masters, they were banished from the Garden of Eden.

With the help of satellites, it is now possible to explore beneath the surface of the planet. Many antediluvian civilisations are being discovered. Remains of giants that once inhabited our Earth. Proof of advanced technology.

With the invention of CAT scans, PET machines and more, it is possible to explore the anatomy of the human body in detail. In my opinion, there needs to be more understanding of the role the Kundalini plays in our physical health and well-being. Although the physical anatomy is well taught, in Western culture, little is taught of the psychic anatomy, the path of the Kundalini, auras, and how to recognise the correlation between the conscious and unconscious minds.

The cerebral spinal fluid, as it moves along the spinal channels, follows the path of the Kundalini and passes through the chakras or, what I have termed, the Spiritual Stations. These stations hold within them an indication of our levels of spiritual unfoldment or understanding. They can also contain blockages on an emotional level, inhibiting the progress of the soul upon its journey and affecting the health of the individual. Many children, and some adults, suffer from gut problems, and this is often because of unresolved emotional problems from either the present life or carried over from past lives. (See Chapter 6: Kundalini).

If the psycho-spiritual energies become blocked on the lower chakras, gut pains or other ill health can manifest, as can violent or anti-social behaviours. Once the energies are unblocked by way of spiritual practice, counselling, or acupuncture, the force or power can move up through the heart chakra. Once achieved, love for self and all of creation can be experienced, and self-healing and compassion for others begins. Once the energy reaches the pineal, the crystalline energy of that chakra aligns with the universal crystalline energy and that energy, in turn, permeates the liquid crystal energy of every cell in the body, healing on a physical, mental, and spiritual level.

Never in the history of the world has there been such a feat of engineering as the human body. Never has there been manufactured such an intricate masterpiece as the human brain. Great progress has been made over recent years in electronics, computers, and robotics, but none of these are as perfect and foolproof as the full potential of the human brain. Human beings are not born with a user manual. We must access our intellect to understand our own being and solve situations we face throughout life.

History is full of the exploits of great explorers whose fearless journeys have opened up new vistas on planet Earth. Men have walked on the moon; plans are underway to visit Mars and beyond. But we all have the potential to be explorers of our innermost beings, opening up new portals to enrich our lives.

Most people utilise only a small percentage of their brainpower (approx. 10%). The left-hand side of the brain (the rational side) is constantly in use in most people, while the right-hand side (the creative side) is vastly neglected. We were all born with a left leg and a right leg but do not hop around on our left leg all our lives. Why then be satisfied with using less than the full potential of the brain?

The unconscious mind is a vast repository of all that we have learned, experienced, and witnessed, not only in our present existence but also by way of the soul memory from past incarnations. Both pleasant and unpleasant experiences and emotions are stored in the unconscious mind. In most cases, the unpleasant, negative records are such a heavy burden upon the person that they inhibit the mind from being able to control the physical body in a healthy condition.

In the case of extremely sensitive people, worries, responsibilities, or emotional traumas can become such a burden in the unconscious mind as to trigger a spiritual emergence. Hand in hand with this altered state comes new paradigms of awareness, journeys into yet unexplored psychic realms, channelled creativity, automatic writing, clairvoyance, clairaudience, etc. To the uninformed, the birth of these new abilities at a time of physical or mental vulnerability only creates further confusion. In many cases, spiritual emergence becomes fragmented over a period of years because of unconscious fears of the change deep within the psyche. The disintegrated energy, striving for inclusion, can sometimes be felt as pain in different parts of the body. There will be no evident physical cause, but the pain is what I have termed 'psychic-somatic' by nature.

The most common area of the anatomy where these 'psychic-somatic' pains are felt is the area of the umbilical. This area corresponds to the solar plexus, where any emotional blockages are held. Through deep hypnotic regression, I have found that some of these blockages have been carried over from past incarnations. If in a past life a person was incarcerated or burnt at the stake as a so-called 'witch', the painful soul memory would hesitate to allow the spiritual/psychic energy to advance, fearing a repetition of abuse. Unresolved past-life traumas are sometimes carried over to a subsequent life, undiagnosable pain being the soul memory of the cause of death from a spear or bullet wound in a previous life.

Drug therapy, while a temporary solution to allay the process, is not the total long-term answer. Shock treatment or electroconvulsive therapy does not remove the energy or discontinue the process completely. Rather, the energy can become disorientated, with what I have termed a 'scrambled-egg' psychic result. At this epoch, the use of illicit drugs is prominent. From my point of view, there is danger in experimenting, particularly in the case of a juvenile brain. I feel that imbibing drugs in youth will put a spanner in the works, causing confusion between both hemispheres of the brain.

It is my considered opinion that bipolar situations are the result of both hemispheres of the brain wanting to perform at the same time. Conversely, I feel that autistic and so-called 'idiot savants' are more linked to the psychic world than the physical, operating more with the right hemisphere of the brain, rather than with both left and right hemispheres.

At times of spiritual emergence, it is as though a veritable Pandora's box is opened on a subconscious level. Random memories of the past and precognition of events still to happen can be disgorged in what appears to be a state of psychosis. A paradigm shift can occur where a person believes themselves to be in a different time frame. This can be confusing to the patient but also to some of the medical professions lacking knowledge of the spiritual ramifications.

I believe that deep down in the human psyche, there is a longing for such an initiation, which, if not supervised by experienced teachers, can lead to an 'Alice in Wonderland' type journey.

REBIRTH OF SELF

Last night I heard a cry from past, beyond.
So sad, beseeching; I could not abscond.
The cry I heard held such familiarity
And yet, confused, it lacked a clarity.
'Come back! Come back! And hold me in your warm embrace.
Do not forever turn away and hide your face,
For I am part of all you've been and are
And properly recognised can be your Guiding Star.'
I turned, with faltering steps retraced my path.
So tremulous and fearing so an aftermath.
Did nest from past a savage eagle hold,
Ensnaring me, its talons stretched to steal my soul?
'Come back! Come back! I know you hear my cries.
Come back! I'll give you truth in place of lies
For 'tho with age, your sight grows dim,
The windows of your soul show light within.'
I wrestled with my counterparts
Of common sense and aching heart
And knew to bring my soul to perfect peace,
I must return, the mystery bird release.
O'er craggy mountains and through tortuous streams
I struggled, the while releasing hidden dreams
That hovered like some ghostly forms
Accepted hitherto in life as 'norm'.
Aghast, I froze as 'neath my feet a boulder fell
Into a crevice deeper than my mind could tell.
But then my Guardian Angel spurred me on
And warmed me with his love, his spirit song.
'The path of faith allows no fall

If with pure love you heed the call
To go beyond the realms that you've perceived,
To shed more light on where you've grieved.'
'Come back! Come back! I cannot wait!
Your journey to me seals your fate
And 'tho you fear the sight of me,
Your journey here will set you free.'
The calling tugged upon my heart.
I noticed not how jagged rocks my feet did smart,
Or how the tears that fell upon my cheek
Told word that hitherto I could not speak.
'Oh God! I need to find that bird:
Compulsion draws me to the past, to the absurd
And 'tho I fear it could devour me,
To find soul's peace, I'll set it free.'
The pathway dwindled from the lofty heights:
A meadow sweet and green was my respite.
The anxious cry 'Come back!' had died away
And in its place a whispered 'Come and play.'
My fervent wish the bird to free
By then was mixed with dire curiosity.
Forgotten then those feet were torn
As I returned towards whence I was born.
To heed 'Come back!' that fervent plea
From something, somehow part of me,
I searched with passion in that leafy glade,
Rewarded as discovery 'Fear' there slayed.
No eagle, raven black as coal
In wait to take my very soul:
Oh God! I recognised a vital part
Of me, abandoned at the very start.

A tiny bird, unable yet to fly.
My heart sang out, my soul began to cry.
Why did I fear to see this bird?
And why so long was it unheard?
If recognised in times before
Could not this bird have learnt to soar?
My guardian angel touched my head.
'Let not the past now make your bed.
Enough that you have heard the cries
From past and did cognise.
Sweet slumber, dreams sublime.
Time will soothe you from your tortuous climb.
The little bird you've helped to fly
So be at peace – no more to cry.'

There is nothing sacrilegious in using the 'gifts of the Holy Spirit' as stated in Corinthians 1:12, as long as these gifts are used for the betterment of self and mankind. Few people are aware of the edicts set down by the early church at the Council of Nicaea (AD 325), by which all recognition of reincarnation and spiritual/psychic gifts was outlawed.

In my opinion, states of schizophrenia, anorexia, bulimia, post-natal depression, and bipolar can be the result of a 'fractured spiritual emergence'. It is feasible to suggest that spinal misalignments can, in some cases, allow these conditions to manifest.

It has been proven that flashing lights can trigger a fit in the case of epileptics. But repeated flashing lights, as in computer games and more, can also induce psychic openings.

Spiritual information I have received gives me the understanding that if a soul has been born many times over in the one gender, a future incarnation in a body of the opposite sex defies the nature and pattern that has been lived many times in the past or the most recent incarnation. At this transitioning time of planet Earth, many souls are clamouring to incarnate, regardless of the gender of the body they incarnate into. Soulmates are seeking the partner they began their journey with eons ago and forming loving relationships regardless of sexual orientation.

The solar flares are exacerbating electromagnetic energies, and those of us who are sensitive to them are feeling the escalation. Vivid dreams are becoming more common, as are psychic synchronicities.

As we are, in a collective consciousness way, 'God', thought transference or psychic synchronicity on a large scale is possible. It all depends on which level it takes place. Fearful thoughts emanating from lower levels of consciousness are transmitted very fast, causing mass panic. Most churches are found to be domains of peace. The possibility there lies in the fact that visitors to such places have their minds centred on their reverence for God. This is usually the heavenly God described in the Holy Bible, many not realising that they are indeed part of God.

At this time of change, it is important that we take time to meditate and endeavour to connect with our higher selves – our 'God-selves'. Although we can obtain learning and guidance from books and the internet, connection with our higher consciousness is the only way we can gain tailor-made information to serve our lives in the best way possible.

PART ONE

My Life: My Journey

1 > MY CHILDHOOD

How can I describe my early life? A kaleidoscope of fractured colours, a tapestry of light and dark? Or, as I reflect over the years, a karmic journey, a postulate to prepare me for the years ahead of me. And yes! An apprenticeship for my successful career as a clairvoyant-medium, counsellor-hypnotherapist, and spiritualist minister.

By relating my experiences, I am not trying to convey a sense of 'poor me,' nor am I portraying myself as a martyr. In bold contrast, it is a story of how pain, utilised in a positive manner, can build a much stronger constitution than a life without challenges. By relating my experiences, I hope to encourage those of you who are reading my words to realise that there is a deeper meaning to suffering or painful experiences. Each moment of life is precious! LEARN TO LIVE IN THE NOW!

A TOAST TO TOMORROW

On yesterday I've shut the door.
I've ceased to wonder evermore
Why pain and hurts have crossed my path
Leaving heartache as their aftermath.
I'M HERE, TODAY, ALIVE AND WELL

And yesterday's an empty shell.
My future can fulfil my needs
As nourishment from a gourmet feed.
If I can but foresee my road,
Shed worries to enlight my load,
Seek happiness in each new day,
Trust God, believe and try to pray,
Convince myself I'm here and now,
The days ahead I'll live – I vow.
Each wasted day I'll not retrieve.
When autumn comes then I'll not grieve
But think of all the joys I've had.
Remember my good life and be glad.

There have been many times when I have diligently prayed for answers and have been rewarded by way of scenarios, parables, and poems. For example, 'Tempering! The steel of a warrior's sword must be heated then struck with a hammer repeatedly to temper and strengthen the steel.' It is no strange coincidence then that I see a connection between the sword and the path of the Kundalini as it travels upward on the human spine.

The beautiful marble statues carved by Michelangelo were shown to me. Everything has energy and consciousness, even marble. Each strike of the hammer, the bite of the chisel changes, fashions the stone. Time is of the essence. No great statue of note was ever finished in days. But with time, patience, and inspiration, a product of grandeur is created.

Before we are born into our human bodies, a higher force is involved with the pattern our lives will take. The greater challenge we choose for our life path dictates a greater strength on our soul level. Karmic retribution is enabled. Negative actions we have perpetrated against others in a previous life can be negated by us agreeing to accept penance and related experience in the life to come.

The human memory bank is a vast library of experiences. Many are educational, and with pertinent training, skills learned in previous lives can be accessed. Amnesia and Alzheimer's disease seem to be able to separate people from painful memories. Painful memories from the past can inflict suffering upon the present until we address the past. These heartfelt memories can affect our present lives if we do not recognise that we chose these situations in order to learn.

It is true that 'no man is an island'. Forgiving the perpetrator, realising that a good or godly person, or a person of sane mind, would not willingly inflict mental or physical suffering upon another soul, can be a powerful healing tool for painful memories.

I will not waste my time ruminating on bitterness, regrets, or guilt. Each moment of my life is precious to fulfilling my karmic journey, a journey that has taken me to the depths of the darkest valleys and the highs of the highest mountains.

There will always be critics, but in a positive vein, criticism can be utilised to reappraise our lives and our path. There will always be jealousies from those who have not been prepared to exert the efforts we have in order to succeed.

The human brain is like a laboratory: every thought and every action has a chemical reaction, which in turn determines the state of our health and wellbeing. It has been suggested that the quality of life and demeanour of extremely ill people can be improved by watching happy or fun movies. In a humorous vein, I once told a young man who was very depressed that he should watch happy movies as his brain would then respond by producing endorphins, one of the 'happy hormones' that are created by glands in the human body. Sometime later, he approached me and asked, 'What are the DOLPHINS you told me about?' I guess there is a correlation between endorphins and dolphins, as I see them as one of the happiest and carefree creations of the animal kingdom.

Another young man who managed a service station asked me why his bosses treated him like 'shit' when he worked so hard. 'If your bosses drove into the service station and handed you a cap full of "shit", would you put it on?' I asked him.

Of course, his answer was 'No!'

'But,' said I, 'you are putting on a "verbal cap of shit" when you accept undue criticism.' The young man was becoming very depressed and unwell. After some counselling, he changed his job! His new boss really appreciated his work efforts, and his whole demeanour and health rapidly improved.

It is true that our best teachers are our hardest teachers. During my school years, the cane was the instrument of control for the teachers. I am pleased to relate that I was never the victim of a school caning. However, I do remember boys picking the lovely pink peppercorns off a tree overhanging a fence near our school, supposedly to dull the pain of a strike from a cane. Fear of a caning was the best ostensible motive to be on best behaviour.

My mother's choice of punishment apparatus was a leather belt complete with a metal buckle or, at times, a cane-handled feather duster. And although at the time of punishment the world seems very dark, the strength and determination bred from such situations is a reward in itself.

Shakespeare wrote, 'All the world's a stage,' and that is true in that in a good play, there must be both villains and heroes.

And so it is in the Game of Life. It is important we accept that we chose to perform a certain role when we incarnated. Equally important is to accept that those who perpetrated misdeeds upon us were indeed our best teachers.

My childhood was a nightmare, my teenage a torment, but the ensuing years led me into even darker times. My life was dictated by what my mother wanted. Whatever I did to try to please her was never appreciated. She was manic and, in her final years before her passing at ninety-one, said, 'I would be so angry that I would belt and belt until I almost blacked out myself.' If you were to ask me who was my best teacher, in an oblique way, I would have to say, my mother. For the first nineteen years of my life, she both painfully tested and traumatised my life and yet, through the pain, there was born a deep introspection and querying of the meaning of life. During my mother's later years, I came to pity her for the path of unhappiness she had left behind her. There were times that I sewed for her and made her beautifully decorated birthday cakes. In these later years, my mother was sitting with my older sister, watching a television program on child abuse. My sister later told me how aghast our mother was as she commented, 'Oh ... I used to do that.'

It is difficult to feel loving towards people who have not shown love to you. From experience, I have taught students to adopt a perspective of mentally divorcing themselves from a relationship connection and then seeing that person as another creation of God. Without the expectation of relationship love, it becomes much easier to associate with that person.

In reverie, I travel back to my childhood: lying on the grass, watching the clouds scudding across the sky, I would question where I came from. I always felt somehow different from others. Whatever leisure time I had was filled with drawing, writing, or reading countless books.

It was only in recent years, after studying blood groups, that I realised the blood groups of my mother and the man I believed to be my father would not make my rare blood type. On questioning my older sister, the truth began to surface, and I was able to make sense of some of the traumatic incidences of my childhood. I gained insight into why my mother often referred to me as being 'different' from her other children. Maybe in my imaginative, creative ways, I was different. Or was it a hidden admission that the man I called 'Dad' was not, in fact, the man who fathered me? On her death bed, my mother confessed to an affair during her marriage. This was the man who was my father. She kept his love letters until a few years before her passing. My niece, who was present at the time of my mother's demise, told me that from lying prone, very ill, she sat bolt upright exclaiming 'Gordon!' as she took her last breath. I guess he was my father, although the man who worked hard to put food on the table is the man I will always lovingly remember as my father.

Having studied Transpersonal Psychology, I can, in retrospect, make some sense of my mother's irrational behaviour. I feel she would fit the criteria for 'scrambled-egg' or 'half-baked' psychic. In her teens and early twenties, she became a champion springboard diver, a sport rare for a female in the 1920s. She suffered from migraine headaches and pain in the neck area, and I am of the opinion that pressure on the cervical spine from diving could have caused damage that affected the pathway of the Kundalini. If blocked, the Kundalini, being a powerful force, can precipitate violent behaviour patterns.

My parent's first child, a son named Keith, was born when my mother was twenty-six. His birth was a difficult one, exacerbated by a condition known as placenta previa, in which the placenta blocks the birth canal. A teething gel used widely in the 1930s contained mercury and it was not until some years later it was discovered that it caused pink disease. It was estimated that 1 in 500 children were affected by this gel. My brother was one of them. In September 1935, Keith died, aged eighteen months; at the same time, my mother realised that she was pregnant with my older sister.

The following January my sister was born; however, our mother was diagnosed with a goitre, necessitating surgery. Surgery, along with post-natal depression, made caring for a baby non-viable. So, my father's sister took care of my sister until our mother was well enough to care for her. Childbirth and grief can be two precipitators of spiritual emergence. Both conditions affect the hormones and metabolism of a woman.

There was a certain coldness to my mother's demeanour, an inability to show love, and a determination that she would 'win the toss' regardless of what it took. Before her passing, my mother admitted to her marriage being a 'marriage of convenience' and that she didn't know how to love as she had never been shown love. I do not believe that to be true. I was told stories of how my grandfather took my mother, the youngest of three daughters, to stage shows and accompanied her to diving competitions. In reality, I feel the coldness of my mother's emotions was born from unrequited love.

When I was about four, my father got a little ginger Foxie dog for my older sister and me. We called him Timmy. He was a very playful pup. We loved him, and he was protective of us.

And that was his downfall. Every time our mother lashed out at my sister and me, Timmy would attack her. Needless to say, he was not around for long.

Then there was the cat. I can't remember how the cat came into our lives, but I do remember how it went out – horrifically! This black and white feline gave birth to six kittens. There and then, my mother decided to get rid of the lot. Unbeknown to us children, she tied the legs of the mother cat together and put her and her kittens in a hessian bag. They were thrown into a nearby canal, my mother thinking she had closed that chapter. Next morning, upon opening the front door, we found the mother cat with a kitten in her mouth, dragging her poor body along with her back legs still tied together. She had escaped death that time, but I guess another of her 'nine lives' was imminently doomed.

There were no Steggles Chicken or KFC outlets around in the 1940s. Chicken for dinner was a luxury. But to get a bargain meant buying a live chook and killing it. This was a chore that my mother handled with aplomb, but not so for us children. We were made to hold the poor creature while its head was severed. Something in the nervous system of a chicken gives it the ability to run around for a short time after its head is chopped off. That was nightmare stuff for young children.

It is hurtful for any child to be told they were a 'mistake'. But it was more than just words. There seemed to be innate jealousy of any success I gained or of compliments I received from others. More than once, my mother told me I was a 'busted Frenchie baby'. To an innocent child, that meant nothing. Around the time of the coronation of Queen Elizabeth II, some neighbours stopped to chat. The subject of the new queen arose; my mother described her as a beautiful young woman. The neighbour retorted, 'But you have a beautiful young daughter. Just look at her lovely hair.' I was fourteen, slim with long, dark curls. Within hours, my mother had somehow persuaded an older, heavily built cousin to hold me down while she attempted to cut my hair off. To this day, I do not know how I fought the two of them off! Maybe the strength of the Tiger and the Bull. (Astrologically, I am a Taurean Tiger.) My older sister related a story my mother had told her some years ago. My grandmother, in a fit of rage, had gone to my mother's wardrobe and taken scissors to her frocks, leaving them all in tatters. Such destructive 'scrambled-egg' behaviour and obviously a behavioural pattern in no way foreign to my mother.

My maternal grandmother, having gone through a broken marriage, was committed to the Ararat Mental Asylum because she saw 'dead' people and heard voices. My grandmother's story is related later in the book.

For the first three years of my life, my parents, my older sister and I lived in a rented home two doors down from my paternal grandmother and aunty. My mother really didn't see eye to eye with her in-laws. However, my older sister and I enjoyed spending time with our grandmother, aunt, and cousins.

My early memories are of family get-togethers each weekend. My widowed grandmother, aunties, and uncles sat with a cigarette in mouth and a beer in hand, listening to the horse races. Across the laneway from Grandma's house, there was a millet broom factory, a front for an SP bookie depot. TAB centres were still a long way into the future, and off-course betting was illegal. The role of placing the bets usually fell to my older sister, and as for me, to this day, I cannot stand the sound of horse racing being called. Having owned and loved a few beautiful horses, it repulses me to see these beautiful animals exploited for financial gain by humans.

When I was two years of age, a doctor advised that my older sister have her tonsils and adenoids removed. For no reason, I also had my tonsils and adenoids removed. The operation was carried out in a big Catholic hospital where the nuns wore the all-enclosing black or white habit. As a mask for anaesthetic was placed over my face, I thought a nun in black was sitting on me, smothering me. That left me fearful of nuns for some time. Nerve damage from a tonsillectomy at such a young age left me with a deep voice. At age seven, this deep voice pointed me out as the victim. A few girls were talking in class, and I was one of them. The teacher, with her back turned to the pupils, heard only the deep voice. My punishment: standing in a corner, wearing a dunce's hat, bandages tied around my mouth. There was no Department of Community Services to protect children in those days. Nor were any questions asked of the bruises we wore around our legs.

The opportunity to buy a home came when my father obtained compensation for injuries he had received when he had some fingers almost amputated when stumbling against an electric fan in his factory workshop. He was a blacksmith, working long hours on the war effort, and if it weren't for the fact his brother-in-law was the first aid man, he would have had his fingers amputated. My uncle persuaded doctors to attempt surgery, knowing that not being able to play piano would devastate my father. Many stitches, splints, and bandages later, my father's fingers were healed, albeit a bit crookedly. Soon after, during a fishing trip, my sister and I were swimming beside the jetty where our father was fishing. Suddenly I was caught in a rip losing my footing and in danger of drowning. My older sister was unable to help me as she too was struggling against the current. To this day, I remember the feelings of firstly fear, then calm and peace. My sister's screams alerted our father. Instinctively he dived into the water to save me without realising that for a man, the water was only waist-deep. The splints and bandages were wet, but my life was saved.

At age three, we moved into a two-bedroom brick home on a new suburban estate. A main road lay directly opposite our home, and although quite a distance away, the headlights of the cars would stream through my parents' bedroom window at night, casting shadows down the hallway. These moving, ghostly shapes were the cause of much fear and trepidation for my sister and me.

There was no sewerage available, so our toilet was the old pan system. Weekly, the night soil truck, colloquially referred to as 'the dunny truck', would arrive, the pan being collected and renewed. Toilet tissue on a roll was a luxury still far into the future, so squares of newspaper would be cut and threaded on a string, then hung on a hook on the toilet wall. Preparing the toilet paper was one of the chores allotted to my older sister and me.

My mother's threats could instil fear into our hearts. We were constantly made emotional victims by her threats. One of the most horrific was: 'I am going to get the "dunny man" to take you away.' In retrospect, this is one of the most memorable times that fear pushed my spirit out of my tiny physical body. Aged four, sitting on the pan toilet, daydreaming as I often did to escape reality, the door was suddenly reefed open.

There, illumined by the sunlight behind him, stood a very big, tall man with a black, tar-coated pan perched upon one shoulder. Almost eighty years later, the memory is still vivid and indelible. I screamed and collapsed on the floor. A being that I later associated with Jesus Christ tenderly lifted me up and took me to a most beautiful garden saying, 'Child, you can relieve yourself anywhere you like here.' Sometime later, I returned to physical consciousness to find the pans had been exchanged, but I was left lying on the floor of the toilet.

Our home was in a cul-de-sac, at the end of which were paddocks and a canal. Horses would often be left in the paddocks to graze. Having no fear of these beautiful creatures, I one day peddled a small, dinky bike in among the herd. My mother appeared, yelling and screaming at me. This spooked the herd of horses sending them into a stampede. The fear I felt was bad enough without the belting I received.

A new home was being built next door. My sister had started school, and being lonely for company, I soon became friends with the tradesmen. At times they even shared their morning tea with me, a freckle-faced tot with Shirley Temple curls. Even at a young age, I loved to learn, to find out how things were done. A tiler soon took me under his wing, allowing me to hand him the different coloured tiles he needed for a bathroom floor. Floor tiles were not sold in sheets in those days, but each pattern or colour singularly in their own boxes, the tiler creating a pattern as he worked.

At age four years and nine months, I was accepted into kindergarten and, as a keen student, mostly topped my classes in exams throughout my school years. One of my favourite subjects was art, closely followed by composition. It was a challenge for me to seek out 'big' words from the dictionary to embroider my literary works. From my love of books sprang the nickname 'Bookworm'. All throughout my life, I have been an avid reader and collector of books. One of my most treasured possessions is a Sunday school prize from my fourth year. It is a book of the Lord's Prayer for children, the cover illustrated with children of many nations dancing hand-in-hand in a circle.

As a child, I saw fairies and later wrote poetry and stories about them. At about age five, I saw fairies disappear into the side of a hill where a group of children were playing. Wanting to see more of them, I began digging, only to be ridiculed when I explained what I was doing. The word 'liar' soon taught me the safety of introversion.

FAIRY TAILS
by Joan, aged 13

Said the witch to the wizard,
As she sat on a lizard,
'The fairies are down in the dell.
Of course, it is drastic and almost fantastic
The elfins are ringing the bell.
Yes, they're ringing the bell
And running pell-mell
To a party for their Fairy Queen.
There's eats, yes, they're treats,
Ginger pop and such sweets
And a cake just as big as you've seen.
There's plenty for all

And there's also a ball
To be held by the light of the moon.
Do you think we could sneak,
And take a quick peek at the proceeds?
They'll be there quite soon.'
So down crept the pair,
With their straggly hair
All hanging by their wizened faces.
The sight that they saw
Made them hold their jaw
For the fairies had taken their places
And were dancing around
On the dew-dewy ground
While the pipers played tunes soft and low.
And so, this kept on right into the dawn
Till the sun was just shedding its glow
And the witch and the wizard
Had gone via lizard to their caverns
Built far down below.
Then fairies and elves
They crept from the dells
And were gone till the moon it grew round.
Then once more they would dance
And how they would prance
On their moonlit fairyland mound.

With an understanding of spiritual dimensions and psychic phenomena, I can reflect on situations that were amazing but confusing to me as a child, and source of amusement to those around me. Not everyone saw what I saw. One instance that still stands tall in my memory is of an incident the night

I played the part of a Hindu princess in a Sunday school play. I guess I was about five at the time, dressed, awaiting my turn to go on stage. The view from an open window afforded viewing accessibility to the historic old church and an expansive graveyard. As I looked down from the first storey room, I saw a brilliant, luminous blue light hovering above one of the graves. Fascinated by this light, I called to some of the older children to come and see. None of them saw anything but darkness. Many years later, I came to understand that what I saw was the spirit of the deceased, apparently reticent to leave the mortal remains behind.

Nothing my older sister and I did ever pleased our mother. After saving a few pence from selling seedlings gathered from our father's garden, we would buy small gifts for her birthday or Mother's Day, only to have them thrown back at us with the retort, 'I don't want anything from naughty girls!' We were not naughty, rather, we lived most of the time in fear, and I now believe we became adrenaline junkies.

Our mother held innate superstition of many kinds. Spilt salt necessitated throwing more of it over your shoulder to avoid bad luck. The colour green was a harbinger of death; 'Out of green into mourning.' And in art class at school, the rule was 'blue and green should never be seen'. So shortsighted, when perfection in God's creation is the combination of green pastures and azure blue skies.

Another of Mum's superstitions was one we most vehemently welcomed. To see a white horse could bring good luck but not without another part of the 'play'. A white horse encountered, the magic words to be said were, 'Criss-cross lucky white horse, bring me good luck today or tomorrow.' Then silence had to be maintained until the second part of the play came into view: a black dog! Then the magic spell would be sealed with one word – 'Swift'! So seriously did our mother take this superstition that it carried through her entire life. Her superstition was our good luck, as her fears of bad luck gave us respite from her tongue-lashings. In fact, on our rare excursions out, we were always on the lookout for a white horse.

About once a year we travelled by bus and train to the beach. I can still remember the delightful smell of salt-sea air and the splendid vision of the ocean as we walked from the railway station. Occasionally my parents would go fishing from the rocky banks of rivers. When there were oysters on the rocks, my father would gather some. The rivers were clean in those days.

Another incident that saw my mother dumbstruck was an exploding pressure cooker. My older sister was on the receiving end of hot verbal abuse in our kitchen. A pressure cooker full of minced beef and onions was simmering away on the stove when somehow it malfunctioned. The lid blew off, spewing hot mince towards the kitchen ceiling, the shock and the mess putting a stop to the angry melee.

My father's refuge – his garden – was always a picture. I remember his Ranunculus, Anemones, poppies, Primulas, stately Delphiniums, stocks, and sweet-smelling Phlox. I remember picking the flowers off the regal snapdragons, pretending they were little puppies. And the Zinnias provoke a memory of bees. The blue bag, a chemical agent that was added to whiten washing, was brought out quite often when my sister and I caught bees as they buzzed around collecting pollen. Somehow the blue bag relieved the pain of the sting. Devoid of pets, the bees were at least a living thing to be observed. Looking back, the stings we got from the bees were warranted for our putting an end to these marvellous creatures.

At the side of our home was a gas meter covered with a wooden box. I still remember in preschool, being fascinated by the little white fluffy balls I found under the wooden box. Of course, I had no knowledge that they were the eggs of the poisonous redback spider. Maybe the belting I got then saved my life from spider venom.

Our backyard was always a trove of vegetables, from tomatoes to pumpkins. Each bed was edged with a gutter about eight centimetres in width, and it is of these gutters that an episode of sweet retribution surfaces from my memories. Endeavouring to escape a thrashing with a leather belt, my sister and I ran into the backyard with our very angry mother hot on our heels. It had been raining, so the gutters edging the gardens were filled with water. In her anger, our mother forgot that she was wearing her new pink slippers with pom-poms on the front. As she lashed out at us, the edge of a gutter gave way, and she found herself ankle-deep in mud. As usual, our misdemeanour had been minor. Because of our mother's lack of foresight, and the laughter we were unable to hide, our punishment was doubled.

One of the highlights of our year was Bonfire Night in late May. For weeks before, all the children in our street would salvage whatever dry, combustible materials they could, piling them in a tepee shape in a neighbouring paddock. In a joint effort, a clown-type figure would be fashioned and sat atop the dry fuel. If we were lucky, we would be given some pocket money to buy 'penny bungers', a sky rocket, 'raining cascade', or a powerful 'double bunger'. Aged about eight, I was enjoying the thrill of the blazing fire when one of the local boys tossed a double bunger in my direction. In a split second, a hole was burned in my dressing gown. Not my mistake or my action, but I bore the punishment.

About the only sneaky thing we did behind our mother's back was to make toffee when she wasn't home. My sister was an expert at it, even learning that adding bicarb soda would make honeycomb. Our sweet treats devoured, we had to be most careful to clean up all evidence before our mother returned.

Our mother had a sweet tooth, so cakes and sweets were often prepared. I recall coconut slices, baked custards, and a dish we called 'dead dog'! The latter was concocted of stale bread soaked in sweetened milk and egg to which was added sultanas and currants before being baked. I guess that sweet earned its nickname because of its heavy consistency and the dried fruit resembling flies. Once cakes had been placed in the oven, my older sister and I would compete for permission to scrape the mixing bowl. By the time the scraping had been done, the bowls were almost clean enough to not need washing.

From an early age, we had our chores. Washing and drying the dishes, cleaning the bathroom tiles with kerosene, polishing the silverware and cutlery, polishing the linoleum flooring, and, as mentioned before, cutting newspapers into squares. In retrospect, polishing the floors was probably one of the most enjoyable chores, as once we had laboriously applied the floor wax to the linoleum, we would skate around with rags tied to our feet until the floors shone.

Once a week, my older sister and I walked about two kilometres to Mr Hill's grocery shop to hand in a grocery list to be delivered. Of course, supermarkets were still a long way into the future, as were family cars and home phones for those not well-off. The shelves of the grocery shop were arrayed with jars and tins containing produce to be decanted into brown paper bags. Big square tins adorned with a Rosella, the Arnott's biscuit logo, were lined up. The order would go as such: six Digestive Ovals, six Ginger Nuts, six Nice, etc., being placed in a brown paper bag. If we were lucky, we had a reward for walking to the grocery shop. We got to see a pet monkey that was owned by a man living near the shop. There was also a little time for playing in the nearby park.

The trip to the butcher shop was another story. It was also about two kilometres from home but at the end of a road leading up a very steep hill. Our father usually walked that path with us, his incentive that we might find some coins if we kept a sharp eye out. Of course, he would deftly throw a penny or threepence ahead of us, encouraging us to treasure hunt for ourselves.

The luxuries of the twenty-first century were non-existent when I was a child. My family bought our first kerosene refrigerator when I was ten. Magic! We could make ice blocks! Hot water for our baths was generated by a chip heater, with wood chips being fed into the heater.

My older sister and I would sit on the floor in front of a big radio listening to programs such as *The Search for The Golden Boomerang* and a comedy show called *Yes – What?* A radio program featuring 'Old Nancy – the Witch' instilled so much fear in us that it was with great trepidation that we moved from the lounge room to our bedroom. By the time my teens were reached, radiograms were the in thing, and vinyl records, containing the favourite singers of the day, dance music, and 'orchestrals' were available. While boarding with my aunt,

I was able to play albums of vinyl records that my cousin, a sailor, had brought from overseas, losing myself in reverie.

Pre-packaging was way into the future in the 1940s. A billycan would be placed outside the front door for the milkman to fill with fresh milk. Our baker transported his wares in a pony cart. Another horse-drawn cart was laden with earthenware jars filled with Horehound, a delicious drink enjoyed before the days of bottled sodas. And way before the advent of the Hill's Hoist clothesline, the propman would traverse the streets with his call of 'props, props!' The props of cut saplings were used to hoist up a wire or rope clothesline.

The chore that was the most repugnant to us, and to this day viewed as repulsive, was to have to empty the chamber pot of our parents. Mostly filled to the brim with urine, cigarette butts and whatever, in turn, we were forced to carry this portable latrine from the bedroom to the outdoor toilet. Spills drew punishment.

During the years of World War II, my father worked overtime as a blacksmith. In his absence, my mother was able to give vent to her rages, frustrations, and temper – the object of these being my older sister and me. Many evenings were spent locked in our bedroom, the light bulb removed, our only comfort that we were both suffering together.

Thrashings with a leather belt or a cane were commonplace, leaving bruises that today would have been questioned by school staff. Holding my sister and me by our hair, my mother would smash our heads together until we almost blacked out. I have come to realise that at that young age, my spirit left my body, leaving a limp, lifeless body to be ill-treated. Before spinal surgery at age seventy-six, x-rays showed a deformity in my cervical spine, the curvature of my neck abnormal from a young age.

My father's sister May, and her family, lived about three kilometres from our home. One dark, rainy night, my mother decided we would visit my aunt. My sister and I wore Red Riding Hood type pixie capes made of cotton, lined with rubber, a pre-plastic invention being the choice for rain protection. I was about five years old, tired, and crying that I couldn't walk any further. I felt a hard whack across my back, catapulting me from the footpath into a gutter. A sharp pain struck my face, and blood blinded my left eye. I had landed face down in a pile of broken glass, the glass causing a deep gash under my left eye. When my mother failed to stop the bleeding, she began to panic. The nearby shops were closed, but she knew that one of the shop owners lived in a dwelling above their business. Frantic knocking on the door brought help with bandages and sticking plaster. There were no stitches, and to this day, a scar remains as a reminder of that dark, rainy night.

My deep voice and a cackling laugh were fuel for my Aunty May's wry sense of humour. She would tickle me until I cried out for her to stop, then she would produce an egg and tell me I had laid it. Another trick was to convince my older sister and me that our freckled faces would be made pristine by allowing the 'peed' napkins of our baby cousins to be rubbed across our faces. Not very pleasant for my sister and me, but certainly supplying great humour for the onlookers.

I guess Aunty May's sense of humour was her saving grace. Her husband had been crippled in a mining accident and remained mostly bedridden for many years till his death. Meanwhile, May reared two boys, tended her vegetable garden, and placed horse racing bets with the SP bookies. I remember accompanying her to an SP bookie's home to place a bet, illegal those days. Approaching our destination, we saw a policeman standing at the gateway we were about to enter. May quickly took out the paper with the required bets noted on it, chewed it up and swallowed it. Certainly, there was no way evidence could be found.

After May's husband died, she holidayed with us a few times. She grew great big cabbages and ate great plates of the same. The times May came to stay with us, my sister and I were forced to share a double bed with her. That was not very welcome to us children as May's flatulence was unbridled.

My father's younger sister Beryl was married to a truck driver. He bought a big old mourning coach, a vehicle built to convey mourners to funerals and, in a way, something like a modern minibus. Occasionally my family would travel with him to the countryside southwest of Sydney. There, in vast paddocks surrounding a Catholic monastery, we would gather beautiful mushrooms by the bucketful. There were a few close calls when angry bulls objected to being disturbed. I recall lying on the grass when quite young, questioning where I had come from and what was the purpose of my existence. I found solace in writing poetry and drawing.

When I was four, my sister had left her schoolbag at a friend's home a couple of streets away. A paddock at the back of our home afforded a shortcut to the friend's home. My mother decided that I was to go to collect the bag, dropping me over the back fence instead of traversing the streets. Alas, there were broken bottles hidden in the long grass. I was wearing thin shoes, but they proved no protection from the broken glass that cut through the insteps of my feet. My feet were bandaged up and left to heal without medical intervention, a later diagnosis being that some tendons had been cut. Over the next few years, I had trouble with my feet and ankles when I got out of bed in the morning. This problem was observed by a visiting school doctor. A course of physiotherapy was advised, and special heavy boots to be worn were supposed to strengthen my ankles. A course of weekly orthopaedic sessions was arranged. This necessitated catching a bus after school, travelling about ten kilometres, then changing to another bus for a further twenty-kilometre journey. At seven to eight years old, that was quite a challenge. But a further challenge was the ridicule I received from other children because of the ungainly boots I wore.

My father's escape from domestic unrest was in his garden and his music. He took pride in his lovely flower garden and in growing vegetables. As a self-taught but competent pianist, he was always welcome to play piano at Masonic Lodge functions and even at school events. His sedative of choice: beer and cigarettes. He was a good man but allowed my mother to dominate him to the point of submission. Twice he sought legal separation but didn't follow through on it.

At age five, I began piano lessons. My older sister had already been learning piano for some time. Six months later, lessons were terminated. This was a great disappointment to me even though our piano teacher was armed with a stick that was not amiss to landing on knuckles. By the time I was eleven years of age, I had taught myself to read music and play piano. Music theory I know very little of; however, I play well enough to have entertained people in nursing homes, played old-time music for dances, and played a few tunes on two cruise ships.

My sister and I had a two-kilometre walk to and from school, mostly uphill. My most vivid memories are of walking under the overhanging branches of Peppercorn trees laden with silvery pink berries, picking small, pink briar roses for my teacher and walking across a railway bridge as the steam train chugged by underneath, expelling a cloud of warm smoke so welcome in winter.

At about age seven, I found an apple lying on the classroom floor. Of course, I ate it! But I really paid the price for my sweet enjoyment. One of my classmates reported that she had lost an apple. What followed was nothing short of a major inquisition, my sister, being summoned to give credence to whether or not we had brought an apple to school. A whack of the ruler and having to stand in the corner of the room with my back to the class for the rest of the day was the punishment metered out to me. Two of my young classmates showed compassion beyond their years, each giving me a penny to buy more fruit.

The government supplied small bottles of milk to school students during the 1940s. Each morning, a man accompanied by a teenage boy would deliver crates of bottles to our classroom. The teenage boy was different and, as I later realised, had Down Syndrome. He was a happy-go-lucky young man who liked nothing better than to invoke laughter from the class by pulling faces and doing funny dances.

A few times a year, my primary school would have 'Doll Shows' where students would bring their prized dolls to vie for a small prize. The dolls I had as a child were a rag doll, a rag doll with a pseudo-china-head, and a little black doll. Oh, how I yearned for a doll like some of my peers. Sometimes my sister and I would snavel some of our mother's wooden dolly pegs, drawing faces on them and dressing them in scraps of material.

My mother was a competent knitter. After diligently watching her expertise, I too became a competent knitter at quite a young age. Although my doll was nothing spectacular, her clothes were beautifully knitted in patterns.

My Aunty Beryl had a big 'Baby Betty' china doll, packed away until she had a daughter. Alas, the daughter never came. My aunt mothered three sons. But at times, 'Big Sister', as her doll was lovingly called, would be brought out to play with.

Hell-bent on having a lovely doll, I ran messages for neighbours and saved the grand sum of four pounds and five shillings. At last, I bought my own beautiful doll. Not made of china but of a pseudo-composite material, with rope-like hair. But she had sleeping eyes, a beautiful dress, and a poke bonnet. And alas – as with my aunt – my first three children were boys. And by the time my boys were born, plastic had been invented, relegating china dolls to the category of antiques.

The doll I paid four pounds, five shillings for, eventually gained me a handsome profit. After keeping her for over sixty years, during which time we lived in New Guinea and different towns in Australia, I sold her to a doll collector for eighty dollars!

Oh plastic! From my carpet bag of memories, another incident, though a catastrophe at the time, I now see as quite humorous. Plastic was a new invention when I was about twelve years old, and my maternal grandfather bought my siblings and me little plastic egg cups. They had a marbled, colourful appearance and an attached saucer.

Mum was making steak and kidney pies while we children were eagerly awaiting the leftover pastry to make 'dough men' – little balls of pastry with matchsticks for arms and legs. Our creations achieved, we placed our dough men on the egg cups and put them in the oven next to the steak and kidney pie. Before long, the kitchen was awash with the most pungent smell, and as the oven door was opened, the reason was obvious. The plastic egg cups had melted, releasing the chemicals they were composed of and leaving a gooey, melted mess throughout the oven. Even worse was the fact that the steak and kidney pie was ruined as the smell of burning plastic had permeated every little bite of it. Of course, the naïveté and ignorance of we children was no deterrent to a belting.

On reflection, most of the years I spent at school were very enjoyable, the only downside being jealousy from some of my peers because of my good grades. It was so easy for those not putting in as much effort as I did to label me with the name 'Teacher's Pet'.

Each morning before class, the kindergarten and primary school students would line up in the school quadrangle before our headmistress to sing 'God Save The King' and a hymn called 'Just for Today'. The words of that hymn are still indelible in my mind and have sprung forth to comfort me when times were dark and overbearing.

JUST FOR TODAY

Lord, for tomorrow and its needs, I do not pray.
Keep me, my god, from stain of sin just for today.
Let me both diligently work, and duly pray.
Let me be kind in word and deed, just for today.
Let me be slow to do my will, prompt to obey.
Help me to sacrifice myself just for today.

Let me no wrong or idle word unthinking say;
Set thou a seal upon my lips just for today.
And if today my tide of life should ebb away,
Give me thy Sacraments divine, Sweet Lord today.
So, for tomorrow and its needs I do not pray,
But keep me, guide me, love me, Lord, just for today.

And for the world, the years of my early childhood were dark and overbearing. WWII was raging, and although Australia remained unscathed save for a Japanese mini submarine entering Sydney Harbor and an attack on Darwin, we remained relatively safe. Of course, drills were taught and practised in schools, ensuring that should there be an enemy attack on our part of Australia, we would know how to practice safety.

Although there were many painful times in my youth, nothing compares to the suffering experienced by a family who moved into our neighbourhood post-war. The family were Hungarian Jews, survivors of the horrific Nazi death camp, Auschwitz. Most of the family had been killed in the notorious gas chambers leaving only the mother and her two daughters, who married and came to Australia after being liberated by the American servicemen. The two young couples each had a child, one a boy and one a girl. My older sister and I just loved visiting the family, playing with the young boy, and basking in the smell of the divine strudels that the older woman would bake and share with us. We taught them some English words; they taught us a smattering of Hungarian. The older lady had been a teacher of languages before the war, mastering seven languages.

When I was about eight years old, new neighbours arrived. One was a boy roughly my age. Scavenging whatever bits of wool or string we could, we would create giant 'cat's cradles', a game played by criss-crossing the twine into patterns, all the while balancing atop a fence.

A few times a year, we were given sixpence to go to the movies, again a two-kilometre walk from home. Walking to and from the movie theatre allowed us enough money to buy a sweet – a slate pencil aniseed stick or a 'Bobby' or 'Curl' toffee. One movie that is etched in my mind is a Tarzan movie with Johnny Weissmuller as the star. Tarzan, or it may have been his partner Jane, swam underwater for some time, breathing through a hollow reed, as a primitive prototype for a snorkel. I freaked out, and my sister had to leave the theatre with me. The memory of previously almost drowning was still indelible in my mind.

Dad's pay-night was something to look forward to. My older sister, younger sister, and I would receive a meringue sprinkled with hundreds and thousands, while Dad's gift to our mother was a box of chocolates. If we were lucky, we would get a chocolate. One morning, after eating our meringues, my younger sister was urinating what appeared to be blood. Then came the realisation that too much red cochineal had been used in the meringues.

My life was a series of humiliation after humiliation. At age eight, my school was attending a swimming carnival. I was not competing but attending as a spectator with those in the class also not competing. I think I had a cold at the time, but not sick enough to be absent from school. To be travelling to the venue by bus was exciting, but my mother put a very heavy premise on my attendance. I had to attend wearing brown paper pinned inside my clothes. Of course, the paper crackled when I moved, making me the butt of much amusement for the other children.

That same year I had to have a molar removed at the dentist. I believe the dental injections those days were based on cocaine. Years later, I was told I was allergic to opiates, which explained a severe reaction I had to the drug. Along with delirium from the drug, the bleeding would not stop. I just got weaker and weaker until my paternal grandmother arrived and ordered that I be taken to a doctor. Although foreign to me at the time, my memory affords me insight into astral travel that took place at times of illness when a child. I would awake from what I felt was sleep, expecting to find a book or some other object in my hand, but there were none. Learned insight now shows me that my spirit was astral travelling as an escape from painful episodes.

With so much media education in the twentieth century, it seems almost preposterous to think that a nine year old girl still believed babies grew in gardens. But that is what I was told. And that is what I believed! And my father grew huge vegetable marrows in our yard. Although I was oblivious to the fact that my mother was pregnant, I did realise she was getting fatter. One of our girl cousins was staying for a few days as it was school holidays. So there we were, four little girls begging for a biscuit. Mother was in one of her dark moods. Picking up the biscuit tin, she slammed it against her protruding stomach, angrily reprimanding us for being hungry.

A week later, on the baby's due date, my mother had my older sister place a toy trumpet on her abdomen to listen for heartbeats. But there were none. Two more weeks passed. My Aunty May suggested a big dose of castor oil. By the next morning, the baby was delivered ... dead. The baby was a boy.

Although I was innocent of how babies were made and delivered, I knew there should have been a baby brought home from the hospital. And yet there was none. My mother was angry at herself for the damage she admitted she had done, but also angry with all around her. Again, clear to me now that she was suffering from post-natal depression and grief.

My three year old sister and I were shown the now rotting vegetable marrow down the yard and told, 'God sent you a dead baby because you are naughty girls.' Whoa! What a heavy emotional burden for young children to carry.

Around that time, I was given a book of Danish writer, Hans Christian Andersen's fairy tales. One of the stories in the book was titled 'The Storks'. It told how storks delivered babies to their new families, and before sexual enlightenment, that was widely taught and believed by children. A really dark part of the story detailed how the babies were kept in a pond awaiting delivery. Some of the babies in the pond were dead, and horrifically, they were delivered to the families where the children had been naughty. Of course, I had that pointed out to me. I guess my mother felt a little easier if she shifted the blame.

In my fifties, during studies in Transpersonal Psychology conducted by Dr Stan Grof, my class was guided into regression techniques. The memory of the grief and blame that had been unjustly placed upon me surfaced, exploding with suppressed emotions. Clear justification that I had nothing to do with the death of my baby brother registered, and the scales of justice became a little lighter.

My mother, with her talent for knitting and crochet, was at one time paid for crocheting baby clothes. My mother once knitted peach pink dresses for her daughters, aged ten, eight, and two. They were very pretty, and in hindsight, I can imagine the anger my mother must have felt when another child pushed a bike I was sitting on, the wheel tearing into the skirt of my new dress. Again, not my deed, but I received the punishment.

My sister and I honed our skills in dressmaking from a very early age. Gold taffeta curtains had been discarded. We saw an opportunity to create something wonderful from them: a fairy dress for the little boy next door! We cut and stitched the dress on an old treadle machine. The special trims were silver stars cut from thin metal salvaged from building rubble and fashioned with tin snips. We were so proud of our achievement. Disappointingly for us, the boy's mother was not impressed. A few years later, the same neighbour was indirectly responsible for an action that almost cost me my life. She asked me to tell her eight year old son to come home for dinner. I was ten at the time, and although I was a bit bigger than the boy, was caught unaware by his actions. A swift kick to the stomach from him doubled me up in pain that refused to go away.

The next day a week-long family holiday was planned. Throughout the week, I was wracked with pain and vomiting, but this got me no sympathy from my mother, only accusations that I was trying to sabotage the holiday for the family. Upon returning home, still in bad pain, I had a high fever. At last, I was taken to a doctor who ordered immediate surgery to avoid a burst appendix. The only available hospital was over ten kilometres away from my home. Bus and train were the only means of reaching that destination.

By the time we reached Saint Joseph's Hospital, my condition had deteriorated. I was immediately prepared for surgery and wheeled on a gurney into a waiting room adjacent to an operating theatre. The sounds and smells coming from the operating theatre were disconcerting to me, especially when a nurse walked past me carrying a jar with a 'specimen' freshly removed from a patient. Always curious, I asked what was in the jar. 'Appendix,' replied the nurse.

Post-surgery I was put to bed in a huge sixteen-bed ward. The woman in the bed next to me was drawing much attention from the nurses. I overheard one of them say that she was a 'Fortune Teller' and that she would give the nurses who were attentive to her some predictions about their future. This felt a little scary to me then; however, thirty years later, my abilities as a clairvoyant-medium blossomed. In my relative opinion, the name 'Fortune Teller' severely debases a God-given gift, and it is a title that I vehemently abhor. Beds were in short supply. A few days after surgery, I was placed in a bed in a dark corridor of the old hospital. My family didn't own a car, and my mother had my four year old sister to contend with, so I had no visitors. A kindly Catholic nun took me under her wing, finding me a bed in a much brighter ward, albeit a men's ward. She even brought me chocolates!

Ten days after surgery, I was discharged from the hospital. The manner in which I was discharged fills me with disbelief to this day. My twelve year old sister was sent to fetch me. With me dressed in pyjamas, a dressing gown, and slippers, we travelled by train and bus to our home.

One week later, a sticky substance began oozing from the appendix operation wound. Nothing was done about that, and in retrospect, I feel I was fortunate not to have succumbed to septicaemia. Many years later, following abdominal surgery, a surgeon commented that 'the appendix operation must have been a bad one because it had left severe adhesions.'

When I was eleven, we moved from Sydney to a small town on the NSW central coast. Two years after delivering a stillborn boy, my mother had given birth to my brother, and our family had outgrown a two-bedroom house. My mother's superstitious nature placed the colour green as a bad omen. 'Out of green into mourning'. As if a colour had anything to do with someone dying! However, the most affordable home my parents could find was ironically clad with green fibro.

My father had a much bigger backyard to plant vegetable gardens. And we two oldest girls had much bigger chores manning the spear pump to daily water Dad's gardens after school. I guess that is where I developed my love of growing ornamentals and vegetables.

2 > MY TEEN YEARS

For the first three months of high school, I attended a Sydney girls' school, so transitioning to a country co-ed school was quite confronting. The younger teachers at my school had difficulty controlling some of the boys who, at times, relished in outrageous behaviour. Christmas beetles tied to a piece of string buzzing around. A blue-tongued lizard secretly placed in someone's school case. And one of the boys, trained by his ventriloquist father, 'throwing' his voice to send our poor teachers searching for a non-existent newcomer.

My first Holy Communion at age twelve found me wearing shoes that were far too big, the toes stuffed with newspaper. My sister had a new veil to wear, but I wore the mosquito net off my baby brother's cot. The service was held in a tiny, weatherboard Anglican Church. A few years later, I became the organist at that church, pumping out hymns on an ancient but ornate pedal organ. The music books at the church were quite old, so it was quite common for city visitors to sing to a different tune while I pumped out the old melodies. I also taught Sunday school.

At age thirteen, a reward for topping my exams was the opportunity to go on a school excursion to Sydney. The criterion was that the school uniform was to be worn. My mother found an old school hat minus the band and to that added a navy suit coat of my father's. He being so much bigger than I, made the coat look ridiculous. My mother only offered her permission for me to go on the excursion if I wore the attire she chose. Fortunately, my headmaster and his wife borrowed a fitting uniform, and I enjoyed my excursion.

Sometime later, another excursion to the art gallery and museum in Sydney was planned. My mother refused to give permission for me to go. My mathematics teacher took pity on me and paid my mother a visit to persuade her to change her mind. Her excuses for not allowing me to go on the excursion poured forth, one of them being financial. But the following weekend it was planned that I travel by bus and train to Sydney to deliver some goods to the home of my father's brother. My mathematics teacher immediately saw a loophole! He was driving to Sydney that weekend and would take me as a passenger, thus saving the bus and train fare to be used for the excursion.

To the best of my recollection, my teacher drove a Morris sports car. The road from the central coast to Sydney those days was a tortuously winding road, and I was very prone to car sickness. Nowadays, the country is graced with an immense, multi-laned freeway, but in those days, the single north and southbound lanes wove their way through the mountains. About an hour into the journey, car sickness reared its ugly head. To compound matters, it started to rain. Poor me! I sat by the roadside, heaving while my concerned teacher tried to protect me from the rain by draping a towel over my head. Embarrassment would be an understatement. Mortification more to the point. Nevertheless, the weekend passed with business attended to, and I had the money saved from that journey to pay my way for the school excursion.

Towards the end of Intermediate year, I was nominated to attend a special Rotary dinner, having earned the privilege by coming first in my art class and dux of the school. The guest speaker was Pixie O'Harris, quite a famous artist and well-known writer of the day. Her beautiful illustrations and poems graced our school magazines, her murals adorned the walls of our school assembly hall and the walls of the Camperdown Children's Hospital in Sydney. Throughout the dinner, Pixie kept looking my way and smiling. Formalities over, Pixie approached me, calling me 'Shirley' (again, a reference to Shirley Temple because of my curls). For a moment, I stood transfixed, completely overwhelmed by someone I idolised. Then, bursting into tears, I ran outside! The next day I wrote to Pixie, enclosing some of my poems about fairies and some of my drawings. She replied with a drawing of a mermaid and a lovely letter. Many years passed: sorting through a collection of my poetry, I obtained Pixie's address from her publisher, Angus & Robertson, and we corresponded. And now, so many years later, her drawing and letters are precious to me and my memory.

Having started school younger than most, I was always the baby of the class and embarrassingly shy and naïve. The older girls' conversations about their sexual exploitations with holidaying boys were nothing less than confusing to me. By age fourteen, the only flirtation I had was when the son of our local policeman began to throw his artwork my way or come and sit near me at the movie theatre. That flirtation was short-lived as one of my friends became pregnant by him while I was off school ill. It was with a heavy heart that I watched as another rushed shotgun wedding took place. So-called shotgun weddings were commonplace in those days. To have an affair outside of marriage could label a girl a 'scarlet woman'. I must say that modern-day 'try before you buy' relationships make more sense than a forced or convenient marriage.

Synchronicity is so mysterious! A few months ago, I was talking about old times with the postmistress at the local post office in my northern NSW town. Jenny asked me where I had lived as a child and teenager. Like the links of a chain being put together, we came to realise that Jenny's dad was the older brother of my first crush, another son of the local policeman.

Later in life, as an ordained Spiritualist minister, I married many couples. I cannot recall any who were not already what was once called 'living in sin'. As a matter of fact, most couples had their own homemade page boys and flower girls.

I was always apprehensive about bringing friends to my home as I never knew what kind of mood my mother would display. There was gossip around town that the mother of a school friend had been having an affair while her husband was away on Air Force duty. My friend came to call on me but hurriedly left as my mother retorted, 'You are not having that daughter of a whore in this house.' Embarrassment! Hurt! Not just for me but for my friend. My friend's mother was a most attractive woman, very much like Princess Grace of Monaco. I think there was an element of jealousy there!

By the time I was twelve, I had found part-time work as a babysitter for the local grocer, work in a milk bar, and even gathering horse manure from the local bottle yard for three pence a barrow full. The old man and his crone of a sister who lived in the bottle yard with their two big Clydesdale horses who pulled the bottle wagon were scary people. My father needed horse manure for his garden, and I needed money to buy clothes.

As I overcame my trepidation at entering the bottle yard to collect manure, I realised that the old lady was virtually crippled. Her only outings were sitting on the bottle cart. Under the old felt hat she wore, her hair was straggly and matted. It appeared as though most of her teeth were missing, and her skin was the texture of old leather, burned by the sun. I took her any leftover food I could find, and so one of the strangest friendships I have ever had began.

Another source of pocket money in my early teens was painting bouquets of flowers on the dressing table mirrors of neighbours. Mixing watercolour paints with white shoe cleaner cream produced a great consistency for the work, and I eagerly changed the décor every few weeks for a few shillings.

There was a horse riding school in the vicinity of our home, and as I love animals, I started to invest four shillings for an hour of hiring a horse. In retrospect, I realise that most of the horses were tired old nags who, left to their own will, would make straight for a nearby swamp to fill their belly with water. That was of little consequence to me as just to sit atop these beautiful creatures, to stroke them, feel their warmth, and be in harmony with them was enough for me. I fed them apples and ignored my father's humour when he exclaimed, 'That one will never win the Melbourne Cup, love.'

Dad's humour in regard to horses didn't end there. My older sister had a new boyfriend who rode horses. One day he cheekily rode down the paddock past our kitchen window, throwing 'Conversation Lollies' over our fence, hoping my sister would retrieve them. Dad was a witness to this act and called out, 'The Indians went the other way.' My sister was mortified that her new beau had been ridiculed. The lollies inscribed 'I love you!' and 'Can we date?' were never eaten. Why? The young man was an offsider on the proverbial 'dunny cart'.

Around this time, my younger sister was about six years old. My mother was after her for some minor wrongdoing. To escape, my sister crawled under a neighbour's house, not worrying whether there were spiders or even snakes in the darkness. When my mother found her, I was ordered to strip down to my undies and drag my sister out so that she could be punished. The house sat barely thirty centimetres off the ground and was strewn with broken rubble. Needless to say, I shared in my sister's punishment, both physically with grazes and emotionally, by being made to strip publicly, and knowing that I delivered her to punishment.

Mortification is not a strong enough word to describe being ordered to lie on a bed face down, knickers discarded, while your father is ordered to spank you with his big, heavy hands. And for what was probably a minor misdemeanour. With tears running from his eyes, my father did as he was ordered, being goaded by my mother with exclamations of 'harder, harder!' It is only now, as I write my memoirs, that my older sister tells me she received the same treatment more than once.

Of course, neighbours were aware of my mother's treatment of us. One, an old Welshman, even threatened to call the police when my mother tied my two year old brother to a tree on a length of rope because he had climbed the front fence. But no one ever acted upon their threats.

Although our home was set a little off the ground, there was a year when floods totally surrounded the house. Again, we lacked the luxury of a sewer toilet. To my mind springs the sight of a 'dunny pan' floating out of the outhouse and being swept away in the swirling floodwaters. Through playing in the dirty water, my little brother ended up with a severe ear infection which was to cause him serious problems in the years to come. Another mishap for him was a collision with the 'dunny truck'. While walking with an older cousin beside a local road, my brother suddenly ran onto the roadway. The 'dunny truck' swerved to miss the young child, but a collision was unavoidable. Fortunately, my brother escaped with severe grazes. There were no broken bones. The doctor who attended to his injuries gave the job of applying Friar's Balsam to his wounds to my cousin's partner, who was a male nurse in the Australian Navy. Friar's Balsam really stung, and the doctor decided he didn't want to be blamed for causing my brother more pain.

    A short distance from our home, there was an abandoned airstrip that had been built during WWII. My older sister and I took turns doubling on an old pushbike, traversing the length of the airstrip, which then led to a great surf beach. There we would swim and sunbake till we were as red as lobsters, not realising that years later, skin cancer would be a major problem. Then, after the sunburned, blistered skin had subsided, we would take turns peeling the sloughed off skin from each other's backs.

    Then there were hikes up into the surrounding mountains where we swam in the freshwater pools at the foot of cascading waterfalls. The occasional eel appearing sometimes cut short our fun. A mountain with a walking track to the summit was in close proximity to our home and competing to see who could reach the top the quickest was a regular happening. At times, my father would allow my older sister and me to use his rowing dinghy. In the dinghy, we would adventure out into the Brisbane waters, setting ashore on massive sandbanks that many years later would be developed into prime real estate.

All throughout my schooling I really excelled. First or second place was the norm except for one year when I was ill and gained ninth place in one of my exams.

My mother promised me a watch if I gained first place in the Intermediate Exam – the final before leaving school. When I did gain first place – dux of the school at age fourteen – my mother took me to a 'hock' shop (second-hand dealer) and bought a shabby old gold watch where the numbers had almost worn off. There was no band on it, so she tied a piece of black velvet ribbon to the watch. Of course, my schoolmates were all asking to see the watch I had been promised. Embarrassment forced me to lie to them by saying that it was too valuable to take to school. My father was obviously aware of my disappointment as once I started to work, he gave me some money towards a new watch that I bought. It was gold with tiny turquoise jewels denoting the hours.

The Presentation Night at my school was a disaster for me. Some hours before, I witnessed a violent attack on my older sister. My mother had beaten her to the floor and was belting her with a straw broom and kicking her. I was screaming for her to stop but was helpless to intervene. Thankfully, our father arrived home from work and swiftly put a stop to the belting. I ran down a nearby lane to a spot where I often found peace. A small creek surrounded by trees and wildflowers.

Evening came. We arrived at my school. I was both excited and nervous to walk up to the stage but also still shaken from the afternoon's violent episode. My name was called and announced as having achieved dux of the school. The headmaster handed me my prize and congratulated me on being the youngest student to achieve that status. Into my mind came the words to respond; however, they were never spoken as my legs buckled beneath me and I fell to the stage. I later learned that it was hysterical paralysis. We had no car and lived about a kilometre from my school, so my father piggy-backed me all the way home.

3 WORK EXPERIENCE

With my Intermediate education complete, my teachers begged my mother to let me go on to tertiary education. She bluntly refused. The only other alternative was to travel two hours morning and night to Sydney to work in an office. The old 'Puffing Billy' steam trains were the mode of transport to Hornsby station, where a change was made to electric trains to Sydney. My older sister and I would be awake no later than 6 am. After a hasty breakfast, we would catch a bus to the railway station. Miss the bus and the train would be missed unless some kind soul came to our rescue. In the three years of that sojourn, I reached the railway station in many varied manners. A motorbike, a horse and cart, a garbage truck, and even a hearse.

Pantyhose were still a long way away as far as innovations were concerned. Stockings were held up with suspenders attached to an elasticised body stocking called 'step-ins' worn under one's knickers. I guess a late night the previous evening meant me being half asleep as I dressed for work, oblivious of what was missing until a cold draft reminded me. My workplace was only minutes away when I realised that I had forgotten to don the knickers. A quick trip to a nearby shop saved my dignity but cost me money for a pair of granny pants.

One fun journey on the old 'Puffing Billy' train springs to mind. My sister, her future husband, and I were travelling from Central Railway station to our hometown. The old story of 'three is a crowd' came into play, and my sister suggested that it would be fun to travel home in the cab of the engine driver and fireman. My sister knew the fireman of that train and he willingly agreed to allow me to travel 'up front'. I would have been sixteen. Halfway up the line the fireman called to me. For the next hour, I had the most exciting journey, feeling the wind in my hair, and watching the fireman stoke the fire that fuelled the boilers for steam. As the blackness of tunnels approached, the driver allowed me to pull the cord that blew the whistle. Then when my home station was reached, the engine had overshot the station. The kindly fireman helped me from the engine and lifted me up onto the railway station. Reaching the bus, I sought out my sister and her boyfriend, at the same time wondering why all around me looked either shocked or amused. Then the truth dawned! I was covered with soot – the legacy of my most exciting journey. The abuse I got from my mother when I arrived home did nothing to quell the enjoyment I had had with the unusual way I had travelled home.

Two evenings each week I attended the Ultimo Technical College, training to be a stenographer by learning typing and shorthand. These days Pittman's Shorthand is a thing of the past, technology has phased it out over the years.

Four months before I turned fifteen, I began my career as a typist-switchboard operator at a theatre advertising company. Of course, I was the baby of the staff and the butt of a very conceited older girl. Her comments of, 'I want to teach little country girls how to dress and wear make-up' were hurtful, her actions much worse.

Brassieres in those days were quite fundamental, composed of cotton, elastic and sometimes embellished with a little lace. Nylon and 'padded bras' were yet to be invented. Miss Bliss had her own method of being upfront with the salesmen who periodically came in and out of the office. She padded her bra with what were known as 'falsies', lumps of moulded rubber made to be placed inside the bra and later called 'chicken fillets'. For some unknown reason, Miss Bliss removed the foreign bodies one day and, unbeknown to me, hid them in the drawer of my desk, which contained receipt books used by the salesmen.

The switchboard lights were buzzing, bells were ringing, and I was in the middle of sorting out cords to telephone extensions when the most humiliating embarrassment almost floored me. A salesman opened the drawer of my desk and two 'falsies' flew through the air, landing at his feet. I was too dumbfounded to plead my innocence and too busy taking care of incoming calls, so I just had to bear the ridicule thrown my way.

Twelve months after beginning work, I gained employment as a Junior Typist at the State Public Service Office, my pay almost double that of my previous job. The Chairman of the State Public Service Office those days was Sir Wallace Wurth, a kindly gentleman. At times he left his office and the boardroom looking in on the other offices under his domain. Before long he took a liking to me, calling me 'Shirley'. Again, referring to Shirley Temple, the curly-headed child star of the 1940s.

Sir Wallace arranged with my boss for me to serve morning and afternoon tea to visiting dignitaries rather than have the resident tea lady handle the service. For a time, I served tea or coffee to prime ministers, presidents, and others to whom I did not relegate importance at the time.

Eighteen months after starting work, travelling for four hours daily to work in Sydney, my health began to suffer. At age sixteen, I was diagnosed with a duodenal ulcer, and at seventeen, painful ear abscesses.

For a short time, I boarded with my mother's sister in Sydney. It was during this time that I fell ill with jaundice. My mother, not being on speaking terms with her sister, engaged a young man to drive her to my aunt's home. Together they bodily dragged me through the bedroom window and transported me to my parents' home.

The only bright side to my life at that time was my love of ice skating. Friday and Saturday nights, I would attend the skating rink in Sydney. The only condition that my mother would agree to me boarding with her sister was for me to catch the 'paper train' to the family home after Saturday night skating. That meant arriving at my hometown at about 3 am on Sunday, only to leave for Sydney on Monday at 6.30 am. Also travelling on the paper train were quite a few shift-working men from my town. After a time, the railway guards got to know me and would choose a safe cabin for me to travel in. Large cylinders filled with chemicals that heated with the movement of the train would be placed on the floor of the cabins, and in winter they were more than welcome. If I happened to fall asleep during the journey, it didn't matter as one of the local men would always call to me. But on one occasion, no one did. I awoke, looking out the train window at a strange station. About one hour later I disembarked from the train, carrying my white skating boots, just as dawn was breaking. My family had no phone, but I was able to phone a friend who relayed a message to my mother. My homecoming was filled with anger rather than understanding.

When I was seventeen, a friend at ice skating introduced me to her boyfriend's mate, Teddy, a handsome twenty-one year old Air Force recruit. For six months, we had a beautiful romance, Teddy respecting my moral values of no sex before marriage, coming to stay at my parents' home and loving me unconditionally.

Teddy received a posting to an RAAF base near Darwin, asking me to wait for him. My mother refused to let me continue the romance, telling me I was too young. That was heartbreaking to me as Teddy was the only person who had ever shown me love, caring, and trust.

While boarding with my aunt, my cousin, a chief petty officer in the Australian Navy, bought some young Canadian sailors to his mother's home. One young man, Clarrie, asked me to be his penfriend. Being fond of writing, I agreed. There was no romance with Clarrie; however, exchanging letters bought some light into my life.

Knowing that I loved ice skating, Clarrie's family offered for me to visit them in Ontario, Canada. I was working as a secretary but took on extra work as an usherette at Hoyt's Cinema, and a waitress in a coffee lounge. The proviso from my mother was that if I wanted to visit Canada, I had to pay for my return journey by ship. Air travel was only for the rich in those days.

Within six months, I had paid for my return passage to Canada, made a wardrobe of warm winter clothes and obtained a passport. Only one thing remained. Underage in those days, a traveller needed a parent's permission and signature to leave Australia. Knowing how hard I had worked to secure my journey, my mother laughed and tore up the papers I wanted her to sign, saying, 'You are not going anywhere.'

The following year, just weeks before I married Des, my aunt and a friend told me that my mother had got Clarrie's address from my belongings and had written a scathing letter to him, his family, and even the captain of his ship. That explained the letter from Clarrie telling me I was not welcome.

Fortunately, I recovered the money I had paid for my trip to Canada. An uncle, who unknown to me at the time, knew why I wasn't travelling, suggested he help me buy a car and get a licence. My little four year old British car brought some joy into my life. I had paid £800 cash for it.

Dad, or the man I believed to be my father, was alcoholic but non-violent. My mother was manic, had a fearful temper and, at times, could be quite violent. As mentioned, beatings and yelling were commonplace in our family household during my childhood and youth. But when my brother was seven years old, the violence became quite serious.

My brother had been playing with a balloon. Unintentionally it had knocked a cheap, plaster duck ornament off the wall, smashing it. I heard the belting and screaming in an adjacent room but then began to feel alarmed when I heard strange, gurgling noises. As I rushed to my brother's aid, I was shocked to find my mother sitting straddled across him, her hands around his neck, strangling him. Angry red welts were raised across his seven year old chest where she had whipped him with an electrical cord. I immediately grabbed my brother and ran to my car, intending to take him to a doctor to be checked out. On driving to the corner of our street, Dad alighted from a bus. 'Where are you going?' he asked. I begged him to look at the damage Mum had done to my little brother and asked if he wanted to accompany us to the doctor. 'You can't do that!

She's your mother.' And with that, Mother got away with it, only to further abuse my brother.

Three years later, I was in hospital, having just given birth to my first son. My mother entered the ward where I lay, to tell me that my young brother was having brain surgery. The birth of my son had been distressing enough without having that knowledge imparted on me. With great aplomb, my mother related what led to my brother needing surgery. Sometime before, my brother had swum in floodwater resulting in an ear infection. The infection, in time, had caused a mastoid and a brain tumour.

Again, my mother's temper had been poured out on my brother. She herself related to me that she had been hitting him around the head and felt he was staring at her in defiance, but he had lapsed into a coma. That really brought her to the realisation of the damage her temper could inflict and the necessity to seek medical help.

One vivid memory is of my father walking through the door quite inebriated. My mother was preparing the evening meal and had a big knife in her hand. As she raged towards my father, knife held aloft, he was obliged to hit her to stop a stabbing. Whether it was from a nosebleed or a cut from the knife, I'm not sure; I remember blood on the wall and floor.

4 > MARRIAGE

When I was eighteen and three months, my older sister was getting married. Her fiancé's mate, Des, was his best man. Des had visited our family home on numerous occasions, but there was no attraction for either of us.

Des's parents were invited to my sister's wedding. They immediately took a liking to me. I was slim and attractive with long, dark, curly hair. Before the wedding was over, they had invited me to a weekend away at Ocean Beach, and Des's mother begged me to be the daughter she never had. Des's father even coined the nickname 'Cuddles' for me.

Within the next few months, Des was posted to Cribb Island Navy Base in national service. That meant six months on the south coast of Victoria. His mother pushed for an engagement – even came up with the money – and drove us to Wollongong to buy the ring. Her niece had married a jeweller, so a sale on a Sunday was no big deal.

During the seven months we were engaged, Des continually tried to coerce me into having sex, but I remained stoic in my moral beliefs. He had never had a girlfriend, and stories his mother told me, and the homosexual fishing mates he had, led me in later life to believe his sexual preferences were dubious.

About six months after I had bought my first car, it developed some mechanical problems. I knew nothing of mechanics and soon allowed myself to be talked into buying a new car – a car that I would have to pay off another £400. The same make of car, just a newer model.

Around that time, I met Teddy's mate Alan, also a member of the RAAF. He told me Teddy had had an accident on the tarmac at the RAAF base where he was stationed and asked if I would write to him. I did, sending photos of my sister's wedding.

Teddy was to arrive back in Sydney a few months before my marriage to Des and asked if we could meet him at Mascot. Teddy had met Des a few times, so was no stranger to him. He didn't arrive at Mascot, so Des and I returned to our respective homes. Imagine my surprise when I found that Teddy had already arrived at my parents' home, having caught an RAAF flight. Teddy had bought my mother flowers and cigarettes, and suddenly she seemed to be favouring him as a match for me.

With my two younger siblings in tow, Teddy and I drove off to the newsagents to buy the daily paper for my father. While away, Des rang and my mother told him I had gone out with Teddy. Not exactly the truth as I had my brother and sister with me and was only gone for about fifteen minutes. Des's mother rang and insisted on knowing what was going on. I was on the verge of taking off the engagement ring, grabbing whatever I could, and running away with Teddy. I had had enough of living in a dysfunctional household. But sadly, I lacked the courage to please myself.

Thirty-nine years later, having been married to my second husband for almost twenty years and working as a professional psychic, I was 'told' from Spirit that Teddy was dying. He had held a soft spot in my heart over those many years, so I decided to search for the truth.

During the time we kept company, Teddy told me about his family's farm and his sister, who was the same age as me. My first call was to Telstra. I requested the name and phone number of an old established family in the small country town. I got it! Next, I phoned the number, which was answered by what sounded to be an elderly farmer. After deliberations with his wife, he remembered the name of the man Teddy's sister had married. I called her, and after explaining that I was a clairvoyant-medium, and the long-lost connection with her brother, the dear lady told me her brother was dying from a terminal illness. Full credit to my then-husband, who drove me hundreds of kilometres, and then left me for a short time to reminisce and say my farewells to the only real love of my life.

As my wedding day approached, my mother met my future in-laws a few times. She seemed to become quite jealous of the fact that my future mother-in-law wore expensive clothes and fur stoles. This resulted in my mother stating that she would only pay for sandwiches at my wedding. If I wanted more, I would have to help out financially.

The material had been bought for my bridesmaid and flower girl dresses, and the dressmaker arranged to sew them. I had saved money to buy the material for my wedding dress but had to abandon the idea as I had to pay money towards my wedding breakfast. Hearing of my predicament, a distant relative lent me a beautiful wedding gown and veil for what I hoped would be a special day.

Wedding day: 1 June 1957. It was arranged that my brother-in-law would drive my parents to the church in my car. This did not satisfy my mother. My future father-in-law and his brother owned Ford Fairlanes, which were being used for the bridal cars. My mother insisted she be transported to the church in a Fairlane, throwing schedules out so that I was late for my wedding.

The wedding over, Des and I spent the first night as husband and wife at the small flat we had rented. It was nothing flash; the doors didn't even lock properly.

I guess every bride dreams of her wedding night being romantic – that is, if she hasn't already had sexual relations. The night of 1 June 1957 was the start of eighteen years of sexual abuse for me. Abuse that I kept secret or covered up out of sheer embarrassment. A night of sexual frenzy followed by a 'honeymoon' that was nothing short of sexual abuse. Nothing romantic. I was sexually naïve, innocent, knew nothing of lubricants and had never seen an adult man totally naked until my wedding night. His sexual appetite satiated, Des would light up a cigarette and completely ignore me.

We spent two weeks in a flat at Coolangatta. In a flat next door was a family with two small children. As an escape from repeated sex, I encouraged the children to be around me. They had no car, so we took the family out to the Currumbin Bird Sanctuary in my car. As a car floor mat moved, confetti became evident. They were apologetic as they had no idea we were on our honeymoon. I greatly welcomed their company.

Returning to Sydney, we learned that an old family friend had had a heart attack, leaving his wife to round up a herd of cattle and see to the milking of the cows. My in-laws were heading to Bega, and Des was insistent that we also go. We had had little sleep, and I was already feeling very unwell.

My mother-in-law later told me that she had gone to the flat to inspect the bed, my nightclothes etc., after we had left for a honeymoon, looking for proof of my virginity. Such antiquated and unjust behaviour from a woman who had been a nurse.

Within weeks I was diagnosed with cystitis, having to take vile medication that was green and yellow. Although I was really suffering, there was no abatement from Des's sexual appetite. Eight weeks after the marriage, I was too ill to go to work as a secretary and even too ill at times to leave the bed. However, in my weakened state, I could not fight off sexual abuse. My mother-in-law, a trained nurse, saw evidence of this but did nothing to defend or protect me.

Three months into the marriage, my mother insisted that I visit my father for Father's Day as I had been too ill to visit for his August birthday. Our car was being worked on, so we borrowed my mother-in-law's small car for the journey.

On arriving at my parents' home, my thirteen year old sister and her friends were playing 'spirit in the glass', a homemade version of a Ouija board – a method used to contact the spirits of deceased persons. They invited me to join, which I sceptically did.

A doctor acting as a locum for my general practitioner had told me I should go back to work the next day. I felt so ill that I very much doubted I would be able to. Tongue in cheek, so to speak, I asked the Ouija board whether I would return to work as told. Immediately the stylus started to move crazily around the board, spelling out the letters 'H O S P', at which stage we were all too freaked out to continue.

That night I became so ill that I thought I was dying. As morning broke, I asked my mother to call a doctor to the home. As hours passed and no doctor arrived, I said she should call a minister! Eventually, a doctor arrived and ordered that I be taken to a hospital immediately. Within hours I was admitted to the Prince Henry Hospital in intensive care with pyelonephritis, paralysed down one side with infection and in danger of my kidneys failing. For two weeks I lay in hospital on drips and medication to fight the infection that threatened my life.

The illness and medication had taken their toll on my beautiful, curly hair. At age fourteen, I had escaped the scissors my mother wielded in an attempt to cut my hair because neighbours had admired my curls. But at nineteen, I had never had my long hair cut. Sympathetically, my sister took me to a hairdresser for my first haircut.

On my return to the flat, Des was lying on the bed. His reaction when I walked in with a new hairstyle: 'Get out – you are not my wife. My wife has long hair!'

Weekends were a welcome respite for me. Des went fishing with his mates.

A few months after the marriage, I was coerced into selling my car. It was not accepted that the car was in my name or that it was only a small sedan. Des wanted a bigger, flashier car, and as his father, a mechanic, worked part-time for a car dealer, it was arranged. My car was sold to my father-in-law's doctor. Five pounds was all I received after the balance of the loan was paid out, meaning I had lost almost a thousand pounds of hard-earned money.

About a year after the marriage, I had a miscarriage while getting ready for work. I was alone, in shock, and called out for my landlady next door to help me. The pregnancy was the result of unprotected, unwanted sex being forced on me. A gynaecological specialist I was sent to see examined me and told me I would never carry or bear a baby as my uterus was that of a ten year old child. That was a shock! I wanted to be a mum! A sympathetic doctor offered to help me with hormone treatment – newly discovered technology.

Many years later, during my studies in psychology and mind conditioning, I questioned whether conditioning in my early teens had led to an 'infantile uterus'. In her darker moods, my mother would tell me that my gay cousin was turning into a female and that I was becoming male. Although that was confusing to me, I did consider that I had dark, hairy legs and a deep voice. At times I would pin my long hair across my face to resemble a beard and moustache. Nevertheless, I was a girly teenager who loved pretty clothes.

There was always a bargain to be met with Des. If I wanted to have a baby, I had to agree to him borrowing money to buy a sleek black Riley with a chrome swan on front. Of course, Des got his Riley and a fishing dinghy.

The red leather seats of the Riley were very worn, so I offered to reupholster them, not with leather as the original, but with red faux leather. It was quite a difficult job as the backs of the seats were fluted. I got the job completed along with new door liners to match. As Des began to install the door liners in the Riley, he struck a problem. His temper exploded, and so did the glass window in the door as he slammed it. I suppressed laughter as I realised that Des was his own worst enemy.

Eighteen months after marriage, I again fell pregnant, a pregnancy that was fraught with severe morning sickness. In spite of the illness and medication, I worked as a secretary until, at four months, I had to be hospitalised with a threatened miscarriage.

My mother-in-law had asked me to make tailored covers for her lounge suite while she was away on holidays. I guess moving the heavy chairs around didn't help the pregnancy much.

The due date for my first baby to be born came and went. The hospital admitted me with false labour and then sent me home. With the baby ten days overdue, I was not feeling well. I had been advised that I was not to be left alone, so Des and I moved to his parents' home.

My mother-in-law told me that I should get more active if I wanted the baby to be born and told me to help rub back the paint on a car my father-in-law was restoring. That was hard work as I was really suffering.

That night labour hit with a vengeance, so advanced that I could not even sit down in the car but had to lean over the seat in front of me. I had been attending the public section of a large Catholic hospital and did not have my own doctor to attend the birth. When we reached the hospital, a Catholic nun said, 'Oh, your baby is nearly here.' Not so! Eight hours later, Dean was stuck in the birth canal, and we were both in a bad way. Without a word, chloroform was put over my nose, and the baby was pulled out with forceps, his head very much bullet-shaped through being stuck in the birth canal for so long.

Maternity wards operated in a different manner in those days. New mums were bound around the abdomen and the breasts until the milk came in. Hospital stays were usually seven to ten days, with a bed-stay for the first three to four.

Something was wrong, and I was unsure of just what it was. A lady in the neighbouring bed suggested I take a mirror to the bathroom and have a look. I was twenty-one and had never seen my own or another female's anatomy. I was still confused. The head surgeon of the hospital was summoned and performed surgery on me in the ward. The instruments that had been used to deliver my baby had caused damage. Further pain was caused by my milk coming in, necessitating excess milk to be removed by electric breast pumps.

Home from hospital, there was not an ounce of respect or compassion shown to me for the fragile state I was in. The sexual abuse continued regardless.

The Riley became expensive to repair, so decisions were made to sell it. I made a deal with Des: if we didn't pay another car off, I would go back to work as a secretary when Dean was ten months old and save for a block of land.

A crèche was arranged, but my mother-in-law refused to let her only grandchild go to a crèche. Instead, I was to pay her a third of my wages to mind Dean, with him being delivered and collected from her home and his food supplied. This was more costly than the crèche. As usual, I agreed. Anything to avoid conflict.

For the next two years, I worked as a top-flight secretary, my workload being such at times that taking a typewriter home and working until late at night became a necessity. An efficiency expert was called into a removalist company I worked for and ordered the manager to pay me double wages for the amount of work I was doing. Unfortunately, within weeks the business closed down due to two of the four owners enjoying golf more than the business. But my references were great, and I was never out of work.

My health began to suffer. Firstly, I was diagnosed with pneumonia, but then it became questionable as to whether or not I had tuberculosis. After clinical tests and more medication, I was cleared of that diagnosis.

While visiting some new friends at Port Hacking, I noticed a real estate advertisement for land on a peninsula with a state forest nearby. Although Des was unenthusiastic, I really put my foot down and finally signed a contract on a tree-studded double block of land with sandstone outcrops. At £3,500, it was a bargain.

Three months after Dean turned three, I became pregnant with Eric and worked as long as I could to pay off our beautiful, big block of land. My father was a member of the Druid's Lodge, through which he was able to arrange a loan to pay off a small balance of money we owed on the land and to build a three-bedroom weatherboard house.

Three weeks before Eric was born, we moved to our new home. Not being able to afford carpet throughout the house, we opted to have the floors sanded and estapoled. While the workmen worked on the floors, I sat in the kitchen watching cakes cook in the oven; the first oven I had with a window in the door!

While I was pregnant with Eric, Dean being a very bright child, kept asking questions about my growing girth and the movements of the baby in my womb. At that time, there was a very popular educational book called *Where Did You Come From?* Des was going shopping one day, and I asked him to buy a copy of the book for Dean. Imagine my shock when instead of the book for Dean, Des came home with books on pornography and homosexuality.

Post-pregnancy with Eric, Des started to complain that I was no good sexually to him anymore. Doing my best to be a good wife, I made an appointment to see a urologist, wondering whether the kidney and urinary problems I'd had were causing a sexual problem. When the specialist asked me for my referral, I just burst out crying. I didn't realise I had to have one. Taking pity on me, he offered to treat me with a series of dilatations of the ureter. That was a most uncomfortable, miserable treatment and, in retrospect, totally unnecessary.

With Des still complaining that I had sexual problems, I attended the outpatient department of a large hospital. I think that day goes down in memory as one of the most traumatic. The gynaecologist wasn't the only one to internally examine me. Without warning or permission, six student doctors were ordered to examine me. And for what?? The verdict was that I had no problems. Des was experiencing impotency and found it easier to blame me, who was very unworldly.

When a house was built next door, the owner was an openly bisexual woman who had affairs with women while her husband was working away. Des started to accuse me of having an affair with her. Lesbianism is something that has never interested me.

Being in very acute abdominal pain, a doctor was summoned to our home. The lady doctor at first suspected an ectopic pregnancy. After an internal examination, she diagnosed a big ovarian cyst. Just the matter of a lady doctor examining me sparked Des off with accusations of lesbianism.

Two years after Eric was born, we had our third son, John. Once again, I endured a very difficult birth. John came into the world two weeks early, the cord tangled around his neck. I had a very good, caring gynaecologist. When he realised there was a problem, he pushed on my abdomen with all his worth, forcing the baby down. John was born a bit blue and spent the first couple of days in an incubator. Meanwhile, through the pressure of labour, I had bitten down on an abscessed molar, so had to leave the hospital for a few hours to have the bad tooth extracted. Two extractions in twenty-four hours!

We had lived in our new home for over two years, having to endure a 'dunny pan' as there was no sewerage connection, and we could not afford a septic system. With the toilet being on a lower level than the home, this was very inconvenient, especially with three young children.

The memory of a lucky escape springs to mind. While waiting for Des to arrive home from an afternoon shift, I dozed off watching television. Fortunately for me, it was a bright moonlit night. As I walked towards the toilet, I saw movement through the open door. In front of the pan, there was a snake rearing up. I frantically banged on the front door of a neighbour who killed the snake – a tiger snake, highly venomous.

Des already had a fibreglass dinghy but decided he would like to have a Fly-Bridge Cruiser custom built. This he did, in marine ply. The basic shell having been built, it was transported to our backyard for us to fit out with polished wood, a brass ships wheel, galley with a small refrigerator, toilet, double bunk in the front, and two single bunks at the rear. Des fitted a Holden motor with a shaft attached to the propeller while I painted anti-fouling paint. The instructions on the tin stated, 'toxic on skin', but it was difficult to avoid getting painted. I helped paint the boat and added the signwriting of *Jeda*. I sewed the vinyl mattresses with fishing line in lieu of cotton so that the seams would remain strong.

All up, the boat and trailer cost us over $3,000, ten times the cost of a septic tank system. Money became so short with the cost of the boat that I sewed curtains and cushions to make ends meet. Then as Christmas approached with no money to spare for toys for the children, I obtained six weeks work at a local hotel, working as a barmaid. Before that time, I had only been in hotels twice in my life. I enjoyed the work immensely and the company of my fellow workers. There was a day when we bar people were sworn to secrecy as to who was manually operating the beer pumps. The motor had blown, and the local 'dunny man' offered to man the pumps in return for a few schooners.

At last, the boat was ready to be launched. She was launched in the Georges River and moored to a leased mooring. The day started well, but before it was done, there was turmoil, and Des was in tears.

Des worked at a large factory, sharing shifts with an older homosexual man, George, who began lending Des books on homosexuality. At times they seemed to get along well, but trouble began brewing when a not so clever surprise was sprung on George. Des had put a dead mouse in George's sandwiches; George had a heart attack. This did not go down well with his fellow workers.

The company had plans to build a factory in Lae, Papua-New Guinea, and invited applications from tradesmen. Des was an electrician, not happy with his present position, so he applied for a position. That was some months before the launching of the boat, and I think Des was of the opinion that he didn't have a chance of getting the job in Lae.

Arriving home from launching the boat, we were confronted by a telegram announcing, 'Be in Lae, New Guinea, within six weeks.' Although the option of changing work sites pleased Des, he was distraught at the thought of leaving his new boat behind. Indulgent sex seemed to be the panacea to most of his problems, so I suffered abuse. Forced, unprotected sex resulted in a pregnancy and, in the middle of packing up and preparing for the big move, a miscarriage.

Somehow, we managed to borrow money to build a timber cradle for the boat and pay insurance and freight as on-deck cargo to Lae, Papua New Guinea.

5 > NEW GUINEA

With our exodus from Australia, a new chapter of our lives began. Des, our three young sons, and I boarded a plane at Mascot Airport. Destination: the tropical township of Lae, Papua New Guinea.

Not long before we were to board our plane, my mother raced into the terminal, telling me I was a wicked girl for leaving the country and that I would never see my father again. My father had had a heart attack but lived on for another ten years.

The plane journey was new and exciting; flying over the Whitsunday Islands and gaining a new perspective of the world. As we emerged from the plane at Port Moresby Airport, the humidity hit full force, and I wondered how I would cope in this new climate.

The fence bordering the airport terminal at Port Moresby was lined with local people, all curious to see white people arriving in their country. Being in the presence of dark-skinned locals was new to me and a trite unnerving for my three young boys.

Presenting to customs in the airport terminal, we were asked to open our suitcases for inspection. In filling out a customs declaration, we had declared that we were carrying playing cards – prohibited in those days due to locals becoming violent if not happy with who won a game. The locks on the new suitcases refused to open. The cards remained in the suitcases and in our possession when we reached Lae.

The company Des worked for made us feel most welcome, delivering us to our new home, a three-bedroom duplex, high-set overlooking a palm-fringed beach and the beautiful Huon Gulf. The view from our home took in the coastal mountains and, with the neighbouring main shipping wharves, an interesting procession of overseas cargo ships.

A few days after moving into our new home, our shipping container full of belongings arrived. This was in no way unnoticed by the locals, in particular a young boy of about seventeen called Bwani.

Bwani approached me with a request to employ him as a houseboy, which was the custom for all expatriates in those days. Wages were cheap, and the company supplied accommodation in a 'boy house' for the young men who mostly had left their villages for the first time.

Bwani spoke a smattering of English, his dialect, and of course, the common language of Pidgin English. In due course, I became fluent in the strange language of Pidgin English, although I found it a bit confronting to start.

Bwani, eyeing the contents of the shipping containers, said, 'Mi laik kissim Missus.' 'Kissim Missus?' That left me wondering what in the world Bwani meant, until I was told that 'kissim' meant to 'fetch something'. Bwani just wanted to be helpful in unpacking numerous cartons. He was a good boy and eventually became like one of the family, having meals with us and cleaning up afterwards, which was much appreciated.

The day the container full of our belongings arrived, lots of 'gut samtings' (good things) were unpacked and scrutinised by lots of dark eyes. The floor polisher was a new 'samting' and immediately had to be demonstrated. A few days later, I heard a piercing scream from Bwani. The bolt holding the handle of the polisher to the base had fallen out. The base and brushes were running around the room attached to the electric cord while poor Bwani was convinced that the 'debil' was to blame.

A few weeks later, I answered another anxious call for 'Missus!', only to find that Bwani had somehow gotten his shirt caught in the electric wringer of the washing machine and was convinced that the washing machine was trying to eat him.

As I made friends with the locals, I regularly made big batches of rock cakes to share with them. One day, in the middle of measuring out ingredients, I received an urgent phone call to go to town. My in-laws were visiting at the time.

Bwani was a wizard at cleaning up the kitchen. Cooking was such a delight with someone to clean up the mess for me. Bwani had never cooked. After I had been gone for a while, Bwani decided he would finish mixing the batter for the rock cakes even though my mother-in-law tried to persuade him to wait for me. The ingredients were in the bowl. The electric mixer was turned on full pelt. I walked through the door to see Bwani's brown face covered in flour and batter, and batter dripping from the kitchen walls and windows.

Within weeks of arriving in Lae, I was offered a part-time job: three days a week managing the office of a local builder. Jack employed all local carpenters in his building business. Their wages were a pittance, while the company accommodation amounted to nothing more than some shanty-style sheds.

Within a few months, *Jeda* arrived, was delivered and set down in her cradle, still needing a trailer to transport her to the sea. With the trailer built, the company offered payment for use of the boat to tow the sewer line from the new factory out into the gulf.

The big day arrived! The new white bosses were giving orders. The crew of local boys, most unschooled in English, were running around excited and confused. A case of 'too many chiefs and not enough Indians'.

Jeda slid from the trailer into the water prematurely, the rudder hitting the beach. As Des at the wheel tried to steer the boat into deeper water, *Jeda* began to wheel around in circles. The wreck of a small WWII Japanese ship lay in the shallow water, *Jeda* drifting perilously close to it. The only way to avoid a collision was to beach the marine-ply boat.

For the next few weeks, life with Des became unbearable. The only solution was to pay for repairs to *Jeda*, become a member of the Lae Yacht Club, and pay for a mooring at Voco Point, which we did.

A few weeks later, I went to check on *Jeda* at her mooring only to find her partly submerged in the water. Locals had tied a ferry boat up to our boat and as the tide receded, *Jeda* was dragged onto her side, allowing the sea to enter via the exhaust and the toilet outlet. Damage was done and Des was most irate! He was being pressured to get electrical installations completed in the new factory, was angry with company management, and his dream boat was sinking in more ways than one.

There was so much damage done to the boat, and it was not covered by insurance. So, after all the hard work and money spent on *Jeda*, she was sold for $900.

Des's anger and depression were really getting to me. I remember falling to my knees and asking if he wanted a divorce. When he angrily answered 'No!', I told him that I had given him all I could and that all I had left was my life. On reflection, I realise that was a crazy offer. Life had become intolerable.

Around the same time, the shire council where our home in Australia was situated, contacted us with a proposition. A new subdivision had been approved, and it entailed cutting off 150 feet of our 300 feet deep block of land. The council suggested that, as we were not in Australia to negotiate, they would offer us $3,500 in agreement to them purchasing the 150 feet of land. Of course, we agreed.

Most of the money received from the council was spent on a twenty-one foot cathedral 'V' fibreglass runabout boat with a 125hp Johnson motor to propel it. This boat was imported from America and christened *Sesema*, meaning 'quick' in the Yahapa dialect. *Sesema* was a sporty looking boat with a walk-through windscreen and extra seats in the prow. The hood was the fold-down type. With what money was left, I bought an electric organ.

My new friends

By the time we bought *Sesema*, I had become friends with local people from a village called Labu Talli, situated about twelve miles down the coast. Their journey to Lae to sell yams, coconuts, sago, fish, and betel nut could take hours if there was not enough wind to fill the sails of their lakatoi canoes.

In my endeavour to get to know these beautiful local people, I would take lemon ice blocks and cold water down to the beach and ferry women, children, and some of their cargo to the local markets. I could not bear to watch the women carrying heavy bilums (string bags) of produce on their backs and strung from a band over their heads. Some even carried a baby in another bilum hung in front of them.

Before long, I had started a free taxi service every Friday, the old Land Rover running multiple trips to the market. From the beach to the market was less than two kilometres: easy to drive but heavy going by foot. Sometimes the journey would be to the Haus Sik (hospital), as Labu Talli had no access to medical aid.

It was not long until a few of the Labu people – mainly young men – would pay us a visit on Friday nights. I would bake dozens of rock cakes. The young men would bring their guitars. I would play music on the electronic organ, and entertainment would be assured. They were happy times for me, despite Des becoming very jealous of my popularity.

The village elders were told stories about the 'Missus' who helped the people, and it was not too long before I was invited to travel by lakatoi to the village. But before I made that journey, one of the youths from the village insisted on teaching me some of the village dialect so that I could surprise the elders with my greetings.

For a few weeks before my special journey, Angi, the young man from the village, would have an evening meal with my family, then tutor me in his local dialect. It really surprised me how quickly I mastered this strange language. Although it is many years since I have conversed in the Yahapa dialect, in my mind it is still very fluent.

A perfect day dawned for my first trip to Labu Talli. The waters of the Huon Gulf were tranquil, the surrounding mountains and the white clouds above perfectly reflected. Des had to work. So, our three sons, three of the villagers who lived in Lae, Angi – who was the organiser and 'Captain' of the lakatoi – and I made the journey. Lakatois varied in size from one-man canoes with a small sail, to huge dugouts about twenty foot long with twin sails. The lakatoi we travelled on that day was the larger variety, and Angi certainly lived up to his reputation as 'namba one cowboy bilong lakatoi'.

Labu Talli will always live in my mind as an island paradise. Imagine rows of coconut palms fringing sandy beaches, crystal clear lagoons with sago palms dipping their fronds in the waters, rows of thatched houses surrounded by colourful gardens, and happy smiling faces lining up to welcome me.

After being led to the centre of the village, I was escorted to a clearing that had been prepared for my arrival. A chair was placed before me. I declined and insisted on sitting on the sand along with the villagers. Food was offered to me, speeches made in Pidgin English, and I, with my newfound skills, answered in dialect to the delight of all that were there.

A duckling and a bag of turtle eggs were presented to me as a token of esteem. I decided that as turtle eggs were a saleable product for my newfound friends, they should not be wasted. So, on my return to Lae, I experimented by baking a coffee cake with turtle eggs instead of chicken eggs. I had expected turtle eggs to smell fishy and was surprised to find the only difference from chicken eggs was that the white component was of a denser consistency. There was no smell at all. As for the cake, an ordinary coffee cake came out of my oven as the best I had ever made. And Pavlovas made from the whites of turtle eggs were the best ever!

The company manager's wife commented on the texture of one of my coffee cakes, so I introduced her to turtle eggs.

Some of my guests, and hers, seemed a bit hesitant to try the beautiful cakes. Once the psychological barrier was broken, they were enjoyed by all.

As my friendship with the people of Labu Talli deepened, they insisted that we build a weekender in the village. A prime spot overlooking the Huon Gulf with a crystal-clear creek running at the rear was allocated to us. Through the building company I managed, I obtained banks of second-hand cooper louvres and discounted roofing and cladding materials. From a nearby plywood mill, I bought logs for two dollars apiece. They became stumps to support our island retreat.

The men of the village all helped with construction, perching our holiday house on high stumps to allow social meetings to be held on the beach beneath the house. The floorboards, built from packing cases that had housed factory machinery, were laid with a gap of about twelve centimetres all around. My native 'Poppa', Yacku, explained the gap was convenient for visitors to spit out their betel nut.

The view from our house was stunning! Looking out across the Huon Gulf we could see smoke from the factory chimneys way, way in the distance. Coconut trees flanked our house and my dear friends planted gardens all around with the most colourful tropical plants. At night the sound of waves on the beach was our lullaby.

Yacku would lead us to one of the lagoons and show us the best way to catch the many big fish that lived there. He was a master carver and carved me wooden dishes shaped like fish.

Many times, the young girls of the village took me on small canoes to catch fish in a way quite alien to me. Having reached the palm-fringed lagoon, the girls would loudly smack the surface of the water. This somehow caused the fish to swim to the surface enabling the girls to throw a net over them.

The women of the village also taught me to collect sago from the sago palms. The tree having been felled, the pulp from the trunk would be saturated with water, then kneaded and pounded until the white powdered sago was released. The water and sago would then run down a chute fashioned from a palm frond, collecting in a container at the bottom, the sago powder eventually being separated from the water. A lot of hard work, and I can't say I enjoyed eating the end product. From my childhood, I had memories of sago puddings, the raw sago looking like little balls. Cooked with sugar and maybe custard, that sago was a delicacy. Raw ... ugh!

With our acquisition of *Sesema*, we made the journey from Lae to Labu Talli in about twenty minutes. Some of the men of the village would stand at the mouth of the creek awaiting a tidal surge, then beckon Des to steer the boat over the bar and into the lagoon. From the lagoon we would travel up the creek, tying our boat up on a Pandanus tree at the back door of our holiday haven.

After cooking an evening meal, we would place the cooking utensils in the freshwater creek. A few hours later, freshwater prawns were there for the taking. The local boys made us small spears to ensure a catch.

We bought a generator to supply power for our holiday home and a movie projector that supplied Saturday night entertainment for the whole village. There was no need for a constant supply of new movies; the villagers were well satisfied with watching the same ones over and over. And the actors in the movies? Well, of course, the villagers themselves. Saturday nights after sundown, the villagers, dressed in their best, would assemble beside our small holiday home. As the movies were projected on the fibro wall of our home, there were squeals of delight as our friends watched images of themselves dancing, cooking, and sailing lakatois.

So many stories to tell of my adventures in New Guinea and the beautiful bonds I made with the people there. These stories are the laughter and tears that are the subjects of another book I am writing, *A Gateway Called Lae*.

Jappy, one of the young villagers, became quite proficient at handling our boat. News had got around town about *Sesema* and soon reached the ears of the harbourmaster. Cargo ships were constantly entering the harbour and berthing at the wharves close to our home. There was trouble with the harbourmaster's boat, so I was approached to come to the rescue. Des was unable to leave work. Jappy and I were enticed to run trips out to the ships so that the harbourmaster and quarantine officer could fill in the necessary paperwork before the ship berthed. For most of the year, the waters of the Huon Gulf are very still, so 'heaving to' beside a massive cargo ship was no problem. The harbourmaster and quarantine officer climbed the ladder leaving Jappy and me to await their return. Little did we know that we were afloat right under the heads. It was not only shock that hit us! Needless to say, one trip was enough. No amount of money could entice us to repeat our water taxi service.

About six months after our village house was completed, there was an accident at the company factory. A young local man was electrocuted. Sadly, it was my young friend Angi. Although many years have flown by, I still remember the feeling of disbelief when told of Angi's passing. He was such a gentle, friendly young man. His tribal name was Hukulu.

ANGI - HUKULU

'Though he was of a different race,
He dark of skin, I light of face,
He was, as my brother true, was Hukulu.
And now that he has 'gone to sleep',
A memory of him I'll keep.
He was such a gentle boy:
'Nambawan cowboy bilong lakatoi'.

Angi's family had adopted me as a daughter, so I shared their grief intensely. To help, I had a bronze plaque made and inscribed, and bought bags of cement and white marble chips to build a gravesite at the village cemetery. Before we left New Guinea, I dug up two red rose bushes that some other friends had given me. These were planted beside Angi's grave.

One week after the accident I was flown to Sydney for surgery. A cyst on my right ovary and prolapse from difficult pregnancies were causing me intense pain. Three weeks away from my beautiful friends who were in deep mourning made the loss easier to bear.

My gynaecologist decided that I was too young to undergo a hysterectomy but warned that another pregnancy could be life-threatening. With my sewing skills, I had made many beautiful dresses for little Australian and New Guinean girls and really craved a baby girl. Without question, my gynaecologist signed papers for me to submit to adoption authorities.

A court case that followed the accident was quite a trial for Des, he being the head electrician. Des's mental health began to decline, and his legs broke out in tropical ulcers. We spent weeks in the village, which was enjoyable to the boys and me, but in retrospect, I realise it must have been emotionally difficult for Des.

During the eight weeks we spent at Labu, I home schooled my boys and offered to teach the village children basic English, maths, and songs. This I did in the village church, a large building with waist-high walls that opened to the roof. Many of the village women would stand outside the church, joining in with the singing. Some of the young men would play guitars. They were such happy times.

With Des's mental health not improving after two months, we were told we were to be transferred back to Australia. This news really upset my new friends. Crowds of them sat near the manager's home, letting him know that they were not happy with the decision.

The Huon Gulf, being rather sheltered, rarely sees rough seas. The day we had planned a final trip to the village, the seas were turbulent, and no place for our boat to travel. Still, I had to have one last look at the village that had found a soft spot in my heart.

Someone suggested I hire a light plane to fly over the village: a great idea! Des had to attend a meeting, so my three boys and I drove to the local airport to at least have an aerial view of Labu. As we climbed aboard the small plane, the pilot introduced himself. 'Good morning. My name is Geoff Slaughter.' Not the best name for a pilot. He satisfied our needs by 'buzzing' the village as the villagers ran to the beach and waved their goodbyes.

6 > BACK IN AUSTRALIA

Arriving back in Australia, we were confronted with our home in shambles. A family friend had begged us to rent our home to his brother, who, with his wife, had three children. Agreeing, we placed the responsibility for rent and care with local real estate agents. The estate agents left in control did not do the inspections as agreed. On our return, the damage and neglect inflicted on our home was unbelievable. Although we were legally granted some compensation for damage, the repair and clean up before we could settle into our home was very taxing.

A building company where my sister was employed needed a secretary, so I was able to get employment as soon as we had settled back into our home. Thinking that adoption procedures would be lengthy, I restrained from telling my boss of my adoption plans. Three months after I had taken up the position as secretary, a surprise phone call changed everything.

'How would you like a baby girl for Christmas?' Wow! What a surprise that was! I had prepared a cradle and some baby clothes but no napkins, bottles, etc. My sister and I raced to a shopping centre as soon as our workdays were complete. The door of a clothing shop was closed, but the owners were still working inside. Their response to 'Please help me, I am having a baby tomorrow' was utter confusion, but they kindly obliged and sold me all that was necessary.

Jade was the most wonderful Christmas present you could ever imagine. A three week old chubby baby with dark, curly hair. The hospital nurses had tied pink bows among her curls. A real bonus was that she was a really placid little baby.

With the three boys and a baby to care for, work for me became redundant. The owner of the building company was a most caring man. He had agreed to take on a New Guinean man as an apprentice builder and, knowing that I had lived in Papua New Guinea, asked me if I was interested in taking the young man in as a boarder. With four children in a three-bedroom home, I was reticent to agree. My parents lived close to the building firm, so I approached my mother with the suggestion that she take on the young New Guinean man as a boarder. Well, she agreed on the proviso that he have separate bed linen, towels, china, and cutlery to her. She was extremely racially prejudiced. So, I made room for the young man, who proved to be an absolute delight. About five months after Jade came into our family, I instinctively knew I was pregnant. Even when there was proof that I was indeed pregnant, Des forbade me to tell anyone. As the pregnancy progressed, Des started to accuse me of having sex with another man, denying he was the father of the child I was carrying. That was absolutely untrue!

My gynaecologist advised termination of the pregnancy. When I declined that suggestion, he offered to monitor my health and help with the delivery of the baby in the best way possible. Fourteen months after my first daughter came into my life, Emma was born with the help of an epidural injection and some surgery.

With five children, our three-bedroom home became totally inadequate. Des was extremely unhappy in his work situation, and there was a vacancy for a worker with his qualifications in Brisbane.

In the middle of an extremely hot summer and with the birth of my baby imminent, we put up the For Sale sign on the house we had built ten years before. A lot of blood, sweat, and tears had gone into creating lovely sandstone paths and gardens in that home. But there had also been a lot of heartache.

To Brisbane

Six weeks after giving birth to Emma, our home was sold, and we packed up our household goods and shipped them off to Brisbane. With *Sesema* in tow, Des drove to Brisbane with the three boys while I flew with the two babies.

Rentals were in short supply, so the first week in Brisbane was spent in a caravan park, seven of us packed in like sardines. That week was nothing short of a nightmare! With crying babies and nappies stained with black grease from dirty washing machines, I was at my wits' end. Then we managed to rent a two-bedroom cottage in a Bayside village about a kilometre from a beautiful block of land that we bought. Property in Queensland was much cheaper than property close to Sydney in those days.

Within the next few months, we had contracted a builder to build a two-storeyed home with plenty of room to cater to our family. To save money, I would ride one of the boy's bikes to the building site and do whatever labouring I could.

Meanwhile, Des was resisting starting work in Brisbane. Firstly, he asked permission to delay commencement of work, but then things went from bad to worse. Each morning I would cook his breakfast, pack his lunch, and see him off to work, only to have him return within the hour stating that he couldn't face it. With only six weeks to go until he qualified for long service pay, Des quit his job, losing quite a lot of money.

Work at a local brick factory proved to be too exhausting for Des, so that lasted less than a day. He left without pay. After a few weeks without pay and building costs mounting, Des finally realised he would be better off with his original employer. Unfortunately, the long service pay could not be reinstated, but he was employed again.

We finally moved into our beautiful, new home overlooking the bay. Life should have been good, but Des's mental condition was deteriorating. He began ordering brown paper parcels from sex shops, pouring over pornographic papers and becoming much rougher with his sexual demands. Des's moods were becoming intolerable! It was hard enough for me to care for our three boys and two baby girls without the man of the house acting like a child when he didn't get his own way. I could not leave the children to their own devices in order to satisfy his insatiable sexual urges. Quite possibly because of the garbage he was reading, he began demanding sex on the front lawn and even in the back of our station wagon parked alongside a main road.

It was clear to me that he was having a mental breakdown. His mother had been hospitalised with mental problems a few times over the previous years, and I could see a pattern emerging with Des. Finally, he agreed to see a doctor. An appointment was made with a psychiatrist. Des, our two little girls, and I presented in the office of the psychiatrist. Des was dressed in one of the safari suits I had tailor-made for him, I was dressed smartly, and as usual, our two girls were beautifully dressed in clothes I had sewn for them. The psychiatrist began to question Des as to why he was so depressed. I was a good cook, sewed for the whole family, reupholstered furniture to save money, did most of the gardening, and did my best to satisfy Des's unreasonable sexual demands, which were more mechanical than romantic. Once he got what he wanted, he would light up a cigarette and forget that I lay beside him.

The psychiatrist looked long and hard at Des. 'I can find no reason why you are so unhappy,' he said. Des retorted, 'She won't perform oral sex on me!' Most unprofessionally, the psychiatrist began to laugh. Although I did not find the situation funny, I did find Des's accusations very unfair. He was uncircumcised and a very heavy smoker. His whole body smelt of nicotine. Needless to say, further visits to the psychiatrist were refused.

7 A NEW AWARENESS

My quiet time was after 11 pm when the rest of the household was in bed. Time for a cuppa and to put my feet up after another busy day. Walking into our bedroom, I was confronted by what appeared to be Des naked on the bed surrounded by fire. Within seconds, common sense told me that was not the case. Not understanding spiritual phenomena, I had no idea that it was his angry aura that was visible to me.

At the end of my tether, I did the only thing left to me. I placed my hand on Des's back and prayed to God to help him. Hours seemed to pass by. I felt exhausted. Then like a bolt of lightning, a surge of electricity passed through my body, then I felt at peace and slept soundly for the rest of the night.

Des had been on sick leave from work once again but woke up the next morning telling me he felt better and would go to work. After I had made his breakfast and he had left for work, I went to go downstairs; however, I blacked out and fell the whole flight of stairs, unconscious. Bruised but with no bones broken, I rang an older friend to come help me with the two girls. Jill happened to be a Spiritualist and, after questioning me as to what had happened, informed me that I had given

Des a 'spiritual healing' but had drained myself of energy in the process.

After confiding the visions I had been having to Jill, she suggested she take me to see a clairvoyant-medium who was visiting from Melbourne. She also arranged with another friend to take me to a Spiritualist church the following Sunday evening. I will forever be grateful to the wonderful medium who conducted the services in that church. Sometime later, I became the organist and would attend Sunday evenings with my two little girls in tow.

Some months later, Margo, the medium from Melbourne, visited our home for a week. Driving past an old, abandoned farm homestead, she suggested we enter and explore. This seemed a bit scary at first, but with great trepidation, I followed her. Squatters had left their mark both in rubbish and in damage they had done to the old home. I picked up an old Bible, finding pages of it scattered in different rooms.

Des was a professed atheist, so I carefully wrapped the old Bible in a baby napkin and hid it in our walk-in wardrobe. I was told from Spirit that there was a message on a page marked with a blue cross. Once found, the message gave me great peace of mind.

'My soul doth magnify the Lord, and my spirit hath rejoiced in God my Saviour. For He hath regarded the lowliness of his handmaiden.'

At a later date, I checked the contents of Morning Prayer in the Bible. It mentioned Queen Victoria, Prince Albert, and some of their children from which I deduced it was printed in approximately 1840.

The following poem was channelled.

THE PRAYER BOOK

The old house stood forlornly in a field where tall grass bowed
Tho' I'd passed it almost daily, no trespass I'd allowed
Till a strange impulse compelled me to wander from the road
Across the red soil paddocks which for many years were ploughed
While the house it was decrepit, all around was atmosphere
And the ghosts of many gone before I felt were very near.
As I trod the broken floorboards of the once fine balcony,
I looked out across the grasses to the sparkling jewelled sea.
But once inside the doorway, a gloomy, black contrast
For some who'd come before me had helped destroy the past.
Where once a warming fire had glowed inside the hearth,
Lay piles of filth and rubbish, 'the spoiler's aftermath'.
In every room and hallway there lay grim evidence
Of vagrants and their chattels strewn with glass that had been rent
'Tho they'd stripped the walls of lining, searched for spoils in every nook,
The most priceless thing they'd left there was an age-old prayer book
The vandals and the looters had done their job so well,
No thoughts for them of Heaven, just a prophecy of Hell!
It lay with yellowed pages 'midst the rubble and the dirt:
As I thought about the bygones, the present really hurt.
For that book had borne a witness to each death and each new birth.
Had been used for wedding service and seen guests display their mirth.
Maybe comforted in sickness, consoled when death came near.
Had united many families and many people cheered.
It amazed me as I started, how the pages seemed to fit

For I'd found them widely scattered but picked up most every bit.
As I lovingly constructed, bridged a century and a half,
I realised I'd found the treasure, had had a cosmic laugh.
For those who'd walked before me had looked with eyes of greed.
They'd stripped the brass and copper for that fulfilled their need.
But can their finds be measured by any rule or rod?
Sure ... they gained a little treasure, but they missed the Word of God.

Dark days and nights

In an endeavour to save a failing marriage, Jill kindly offered to mind the five children for a week, giving Des and me a holiday on the Gold Coast. Money was short. After much searching, we managed to find a reasonably cheap motel.

Les Girls, featuring the beautiful and talented transsexual Carlotta, was playing at a nearby hotel, so we booked in for dinner and a show. I dressed in a smart suit I had made, pinned my long hair up in a bunch of curls, put on my make-up and set off for what I thought would be a great evening.

The evening was a disaster. After Carlotta's set was finished, Des left me sitting alone and went to her table, offering to buy her drinks and showering her with compliments. Her manager, noticing what was happening, took pity on me, asking me why I was allowing my husband to behave that way. After the show, Des told me that he felt a strong attraction to Carlotta.

After returning home, we visited Jill's house with gifts of gratitude. When I began talking about the Spiritualist church, Jill's daughter, Tina, asked if she could accompany me the next Sunday evening. I felt almost dumbfounded when Des suggested he would like to go to the service. He had stated to me that he was an atheist, so I suddenly hoped he had had a change of heart.

There was a new speaker at the church service that Sunday evening. He was giving glowing accounts of his meditation classes, encouraging more people to attend. The three of us agreed to attend the next class the following week. During the class I felt a strange uneasiness; no spiritual peace at all. No surprise then when I received a phone call from the minister of the church to warn me that this man was working with the 'dark side' of Spirit and that I shouldn't attend his classes. Relating what the minister told me to Des, was answered with 'Rubbish!' Des and Tina continued to go to classes every Thursday night. Despite Tina being openly lesbian, Des kept proclaiming to me that he could convince her she really was heterosexual. I eventually got sick of hearing the same story, packed a bag, and told him to go away with her. At least I would have a break. Des even borrowed the sports sedan of our eldest son.

Des was still having problems with work, extended sick leave being questioned by management. Someone suggested that hypnotherapy might be the answer to his problems. Desperate to find an answer, I found a hypnotherapist named Carl and made an appointment. His advice was that he wanted Des and me to attend sessions every evening for a month. This proved quite expensive, and my father-in-law eventually offered to lend us some money.

In retrospect, agreeing to treatments from Carl only added fuel to the fire of disasters that were plaguing my marriage. Repeated hypnosis was opening up my psychic centres. I told Carl I knew his real name (not the name he used for his business). I had also begun to have spiritual visions. On relating some of these to Carl, he said, 'She has the brain of a genius;

I just hope I haven't jiggered it up!' But he had actually gained powerful control over my mind.

Des had been a heavy smoker since his teen years. During one hypnotic session, Carl added the suggestion that if Des didn't give up smoking, it would jigger up his sex life. Big mistake. That only caused further problems that had to be overcome.

During a session with Carl, he told us about a social club he conducted, recommending that we join to share times with other families. I remember signing a paper, but in retrospect, realise I was still under the influence of hypnotic suggestion when doing so. Although I remembered signing a paper, I could not remember any of the details printed on that paper.

We were struggling financially. I had begun taking in mending and sewing to make ends meet. Explaining this to Carl, he made a suggestion. He needed a receptionist at one of his clinics and, as I had office experience, asked whether I was interested in taking the position. Des, being on extended sick leave, agreed to mind the two girls if I would work for Carl.

During a lull in patients, Carl suggested he hypnotise me, and I agreed. I surfaced from a hypnotic trance to find Carl having sex with me. Years later when I studied hypnotherapy, I was told by my teachers that I was a very obedient hypnotic subject. Carl was not an attractive man, doughy faced and overweight, and I had strict moral principles. I was shocked beyond belief! Carl's reaction to my shock was to laugh, which upset me more. He asked if I intended to tell Des what had happened and when I answered in the affirmative, he just laughed. 'He already knows!' was his answer. I had been set up.

In the years that followed, I heard numerous stories about Carl's improprieties with clients. His 'social club' was in no way a family orientated club but, in fact, for people wanting to be in open sexual relationships. His modus operandi was to entice patients to join for his financial benefit.

Carl began to lend Des pornographic movies, which he shared with a family friend. They would spend hours locked in the main bedroom projecting the movies on the wall. A few minutes of one was enough for me as I found nothing entertaining in hard-core pornography. The family friend arrived one morning after the night-before viewing and attempted to rape me. He was a strong, younger man. I somehow talked my way out of the situation the first time, but not the second.

Caught unawares, I was rough-handled and thrown onto a bed, an arm across my throat stopping me from screaming and cutting off my breathing. I could hear one of my girls crying in her cot in the next bedroom but was no match for the brute strength of that man. Raped, in pain and utter disbelief, I collapsed in the shower, sitting under the warm water, physically and mentally unable to go to my girls. I should have rung the police, but embarrassment had won out. Some years later, I was told the man who raped me was in jail on charges of bigamy.

When Des arrived home that afternoon, I was still very upset. I expected him to be angry with the perpetrator and sympathetic to me, his wife. All he said was, 'Maybe I should go and take his wife now.' The former family friend stopped calling around to watch porn.

I decided that I would study for entrance to university with hopes of gaining diplomas in psychology and anthropology. With five children and a big home to care for, study was mostly done late at night. Money was short, so there were no visits to the movies or dinner at restaurants.

When Des told me that one of the men from the meditation group he attended had invited us to his fortieth birthday party, I agreed to go. In retrospect, I very much doubt the 'meditation group' was in any way spiritual.

Des parked the car in a near-city suburb, and we walked to the house where the party was being held. In response to Des ringing the doorbell, a man dressed in a sarong opened the door and then, once we had entered the house, securely locked and bolted the door. A sense of fear began overcoming me. As we followed the man, we were led into a huge room lit by dim blue lights. Mattresses were all around the room, with beach umbrellas tilted over them and couples engaging in sex on the mattresses. In shock, I wanted to throw up and asked to use the bathroom. I could not believe that Des had duped me into entering such a horrible place. Locked in the bathroom, I became hysterical while Des came knocking on the bathroom door demanding that I come out. When I did, I demanded that we leave immediately. Realising that his guests were becoming alarmed at my behaviour, the man unlocked the door allowing Des and me to leave.

I was extremely angry and upset, but not as angry as Des. He hit and kicked me as we walked back to our car, calling me a party pooper and many unmentionable names. When Des was angry, he was prone to driving fast. The trip home only added more anxiety to what I was already feeling.

Des had a way of making me feel sorry for him. I guess I had never felt love, so I mistook obedience for love. When he put it to me that if I wanted to help him feel better, I should accompany him to a nudist park, I finally succumbed with the proviso that it would be a weekday and a quiet park. This was done. There were only a few people at the park, which consisted of paddocks and a netball setup. I sat with my two little girls away from the rest, trying to concentrate on my studies. I was neither happy nor amused.

A few weeks later, Des told me to pack up a picnic lunch as he wanted to take me and the girls out for the day. The boys were old enough to care for themselves. The picnic lunch venue turned out to be another nudist park. Grudgingly and to please Des, I stripped off as was the rule of the park. A week later, a family we had met came to visit. The husband had taken videos of me bending over, tending to my little girls, and found humour in invading my privacy. I was enraged! There were to be no more nudist parks for me.

Des was quite angry at my reticence to attend nudist parks, so he suggested we attend a council swimming pool that was open to nudists one night per week. After much arguing, I conceded. Within minutes of entering the pool area, I saw a middle-aged man touching a young teenager inappropriately. I left immediately.

Des told me that a family from Carl's social club had contacted him and asked to come spend a weekend at our home. He handled all the arrangements, even arranging with his parents to have the five children stay over at their place. This was confusing to me as I expected there would be children coming to socialise with our children. That was when I was told that I had signed a paper, while still under hypnotic suggestion, agreeing to be a 'swinger' – taking part in an open marriage. The realisation that I had once again been duped upset me greatly. Amid my tears and protestations, I was given an alcoholic drink. I have never tolerated alcohol well, and I suspect there was a drug of some kind mixed with the drink. I awoke to find I was in bed with the visiting man.

My protestations that I was being forced into adultery were counteracted with accusations that I was selfish and a prude. As I left to go to church with my two little girls, I was mocked with 'Holy Mary's going to church!'

One Thursday night, I was cooking biscuits in the kitchen when Des walked in with a hippy-looking couple. They disappeared into the main bedroom while I continued with my cooking. Shortly after, the hippy male came into the kitchen, took hold of my hair and forced me into the main bedroom, forcing me to my knees to watch my husband engaging in sex with the woman. Having just recovered from pneumonia, I was feeling very weak and no match for the man who held me down. Des was very nonchalant to my protestations.

Another Thursday night, Des arrived home with a blonde woman telling me that she had agreed to have a sexual threesome. She had agreed, but I certainly had not. I had serious doubts about his Thursday night 'meditations'.

Des's brother arrived at our home one day to find me in tears. When I showed him stacks of newspapers called *Bawdy* and *King's Cross Whisper*, he took them away, leaving me to face my husband's anger. I didn't want to have that garbage lying around with my three young sons in the home.

There were many Sunday evenings when I walked into the Spiritualist church, hand in hand with my two little girls, tears streaming down my cheeks. The minister, an amazing medium, was tuned in to my dilemma and was always there for me.

There were more surprises to come when I found out that Des was meeting a woman for sex in her mobile home during his lunch break from work. When challenged, he did not deny it.

Enough was enough! I had reached the end of my tether! There was nothing in the way of government family support in those days. I moved into my sewing room, telling Des he could do as he wished as his idea of living was certainly not mine. Undaunted, Des invited the woman he had been seeing, and others, into his bed, while I slept in the adjoining room. Sad to say, I wish I had phoned his parents to come and see what was happening. I should have packed Des's bags and thrown him out.

Each time he met with this new woman, he would taunt me with declarations that she could satisfy his sexual needs better than I ever had. He told me she had given birth to twins, which led me to question Des's boasting. Finally, I came to realise they were having an unnatural sexual relationship.

Should I have called for help from my teenage sons who slept downstairs? Hindsight is quite a revelation, but it doesn't change the past.

Months before, Des had returned from work very angry with his bosses. He took his anger out on me by anally raping me, causing me a lot of pain which he totally ignored. We had arranged to go camping the following morning, more to satisfy Des's want to go fishing than for the children and me to have a holiday.

Funds were short. I had managed to buy a cheap three-metre square tent, sewing an annexe onto it with my trusty sewing machine. The tent would at least be large enough for two adults and two little ones to sleep in, and the boys could sleep in the station wagon. Our belongings were then stored in the annexe.

For two days, I suffered from the injuries Des had caused me until he at last took notice and agreed to return home so that I could visit my doctor. Immediate hospitalisation was recommended. It was Christmas Eve, and even though I was in acute pain, I wanted to be with my children on Christmas morning. My doctor left the responsibility to me after I agreed to go to hospital late on Christmas Day.

Boxing Day, as I emerged from the fog of anaesthetic, I was confronted with Des telling me he couldn't manage the children. His mother had at first offered to help but then changed her mind. To keep the peace, I finally signed myself out of the hospital and returned to domesticity.

Following a hysterectomy earlier that year, I had to return home to cope with a busy household on my own. My older sister lived interstate. The wife of Des's cousin occasionally came to my rescue.

Des had total disregard for my health or safety. When I told him that I felt the brakes of the station wagon I was driving were not working properly, he put it down to my imagination. One week later, as I was driving down the highway with my three year old daughter in a children's car seat behind me, my fears became a reality. As I approached a busy intersection with traffic lights, the brake pedal made no response to my action. Feeling danger if I continued through the intersection against the red light, I turned into a small parking lot surrounded by shops. As I screamed a warning to people standing in my path, I steered towards a steel pole outside a TAB shop. Fortunately, the car slowed down enough to gently nudge the steel post.

In desperation, I made an appointment to see my doctor to get his advice. Unfortunately, he was on holidays, and the doctor I saw happened to be my father-in-law's doctor. Not being aware of that, I began telling him about the unbearable situation I had been experiencing, including my father-in-law calling on me and touching me in a most unfatherly way. The doctor asked whether my father-in-law still lived in the district, to which I replied in the affirmative.

By this time, my mediumship was emerging. With five children to love and care for, I could not afford to have a nervous breakdown. Instead, I had a 'psychic breakthrough'.

A neighbour who was interested in psychic phenomena meditated with me a couple of times a week. The first time I experienced trance channelling was when her English grandfather began to speak through me with a voice that was reminiscent of Sir Winston Churchill.

At one of our sessions, we both intuitively got a message that I should not be at home that night. Although the reason for the warning was not evident at the time, I did take it seriously, and so did my neighbour.

The evening meal over, I bathed the girls, put them to bed, and went to my neighbour's home. We sat on her verandah, the lights out. Within an hour, my father-in-law's car arrived, followed by a white car, headlights blinking. I stayed at my neighbour's home until late that night despite one of my sons being sent to order me to return home.

The next morning Des came to the door of my sewing room where I was sleeping and called me a 'cunning bitch'. I feel there had been an attempt to commit me to a mental institution. The home and the children were well cared for; I sewed, I cooked, I cleaned. Although I was aware psychically, at no time did I feel mentally incompetent.

As outlined in a previous chapter, spiritual emergence will bring with it testing that is not always pleasant. Not all 'voices' belong to angels. And there was one such occasion that really shook me up.

My in-laws had taken the two girls out for the afternoon to give me time to rest. Disposable baby napkins were not available then, so I was hanging cloth napkins on the clothesline when a voice that sounded angelic spoke to me. 'There is going to be a terrible accident, and you will never see your two dear little girls again. But never mind, dear, we will be here to help you.' I remember falling to the ground and screaming, 'God – what more can you do to me?' When the girls were delivered home, safe and sound, I began to question the validity of the 'voices'.

Visions of Des's sexual adventures were being shown to me psychically. When I related them to him, I was accused of being crazy. This concerned me so much that I sought advice from a solicitor who advised me to move interstate.

The solicitor had been working for a client who had been incarcerated in a mental institution for three months before psychiatrists determined the state of his mental condition. The patient was a high school teacher. His wife, being involved in a clandestine affair, wanted him out of the way. Fortunately, the truth became known; however, the poor man went unheard with his pleadings for three months.

There is an old saying, 'What doesn't kill you makes you stronger', I certainly adjure to that one.

8 › A REPRIEVE

The final blows to staying in the household came within one week. I began getting strange phone calls – no vocals, just heavy breathing. Then a voice warning me that if I didn't do as I was told, I would be found floating down the bay. I immediately rang the local police, who came to my home and took the two girls and me to the police station to make a statement. Nothing was done.

Two days later, another phone call was from an openly gay man who claimed he could keep my husband happier than I could. It was all too much for me! I collapsed on the floor in the corner of the kitchen, feeling so defiled by the man I had married.

Quite by chance, a friend happened to call, letting herself into the home when she heard my crying. The truth of what I had been enduring exploded from me, leaving her totally shocked. Within hours she and her husband had packed my baby girl and me up and set us up in a granny flat at their home. We met my middle son off the school bus. Des, realising what I was doing, went out of his way to collect the other children.

The woman Des had been meeting apparently lived on acreage. He told our youngest son and eldest daughter that he would buy each of them a horse if they went with him to live on 'Aunty Lee's' property. The horses never eventuated, and the relationship was short-lived.

The first night in the granny flat was full of fear. Each noise made my heart beat a little faster. My hosts had forgotten to tell me that there were often bush rats in the ceiling. My son slept with a bush knife beside his bed.

A bunch of house keys had been lost. Des had the only set of keys. The children and I needed clothes, so I climbed a ladder and made my way into my home by way of a first-storey window.

Fear and the advice I had received from the solicitor were ever-present in my mind. Des refused to let me have the other two children, the eldest being old enough to please himself.

Eventually, I reached the conclusion that I would be better off staying with relatives on the New South Wales Central Coast. With my Falcon station wagon packed, I set off on a long journey south.

Psychic synchronicity seemed to be answering my prayers for safety. As I approached the small village of Failford, I felt a fear that I was being warned of danger. The Ford Falcon had been leaking oil. Was I being given a message that the Ford would 'fail'?

A previous journey over the Bulahdelah Range, just south of Failford, had proved hazardous. Heavy rain and roadworks made the going tough. Little did I realise that the Bulahdelah upgrade had produced a very good road; however, remembering the past scared me. After sitting in the car for some time, I asked a nearby farmer to check the oil leak for me to ascertain if it had affected the brakes. The responsibility of caring for the two children that were with me weighed heavily on me. Eventually, assured that the car was safe to drive, we set off, crossing the range and eventually arrived at my cousins' home.

My cousin and his wife were beautiful, spiritual people and made us very welcome. Their thirty-two year old son lived with them in the lovely waterfront home that my cousin, a builder, had built. They were very quiet people in the habit of reading books at night. Moving in with a fifteen year old son who played electric guitar and a three year old daughter must have been quite an assault to their senses.

Although I appreciated their hospitality, I insisted on being independent. At my urging, my cousin found me a cheap rental close by their home. It was a deceased estate that had been empty for some time and was in poor repair. But it was to become our home for a few months.

Words spoken by the Spiritualist minister in the Brisbane church where I was organist sprang to mind. 'Never mind, dear. Let it all go. Up ahead, you will be walking on carpet.'

Trying not to sound facetious, I wrote to her telling her that not only was there no carpet on the floors but that I could not even walk on the linoleum tiles. The kitchen had somehow been flooded, causing the square tiles to curl up around the edges. Once the tiles were removed, we walked on bare boards.

In an attempt to restore some normality to the life of the two children with me, and for me, I decided to drive back to Queensland to gather my sewing machine and many other personal essentials. The journey back was without incident, and we settled for a few nights in the granny flat at my friends' house.

My sewing machine and bundles of material were an important priority as they would enable me to earn some money. I expected I would have to once again climb a ladder to enter my home. I found the front door unlocked and made my way upstairs. The sound of a female voice coming from the main bedroom startled me. However, even more shocking was the realisation that the woman was a person I had been counselling. She was married to a much older man and was not happy. She obviously felt she owed me an explanation for being in bed in a home that was still legally mine. Her excuse was that she had come to the home to see me, not knowing that I had moved out, and had been suddenly struck down with a migraine headache. Her defence of her situation was that Des had told her to pop into bed.

'Dinner is on the table,' my friend called. She had warned me not to leave the keys in my car, but so much was turning over in my mind that I completely forgot. Big mistake! No sooner had we sat down to dinner than we heard a car scream to a sudden stop outside.

Des, at the wheel, ordered our eighteen year old son to steal my car. He was slightly built and no match for my host, who, years before, had enjoyed a successful wrestling career. Although enraged at the way I was being treated, my host walked away, afraid of the damage he would do if he tackled my son.

Des had sold the boat, replacing it with a red Charger, complete with a foxtail flying from the aerial. There was no need for him to steal my car. There was also a Vauxhall Viva sedan, all registrations in Des's name. I was later told that he sold one of the cars for $200. The other? He gave it away!

With no vehicle, we were forced to travel by coach back to the NSW Central Coast, freighting our belongings. It was difficult for a three year old to understand why her father had taken our car, leaving us to walk everywhere. It was nothing less than spite!

Surviving on a government pension while renting a home was extremely difficult. Des contributed nothing towards the children's keep. To make ends meet, I sewed clothes for a nearby boutique, sitting at my sewing machine till the early hours of the morning most nights.

Christmas was approaching. My cousin had found beds, a refrigerator, and a television for us, and I was determined to create a comfortable home for us for Christmas.

While walking through a fabric shop, I saw some beautiful upholstery material at a very cheap price. In a Salvation Army op shop next door, I spotted a comfortable lounge suite that, with a little effort, could be made like new. When I offered a deposit to hold the lounge suite, I was told that they did not accept lay-bys. An avalanche of tears that had been brewing burst forth as I felt defeat once again. Once again, my cousin came to my rescue, lending me the money to buy the lounge suite and material, and with my upholstery efforts complete, we had a comfortable lounge room for Christmas.

A few days before Christmas, I answered a knock on the front door only to find Des's parents carrying a carton of beer and wine. I have never been an alcohol drinker, so I have no idea why they decided to offer alcohol as a gift. Food would have been more acceptable, as I had to be careful of costs at all times. Once inside the home that had become my refuge, my in-laws begged me to return to their son in Queensland. After the torment I had been through, that was the last thing I wanted to do.

Back to Queensland

We three celebrated Christmas with my wonderful cousins. Then as the new year began to unfold, my son decided that he wanted to return to his school in Queensland. Todd, another one of my cousins, had built a home for his family right next door to the marital home that I had left. On his way back to Queensland after visiting his mother in Sydney, he called in to visit. A few years before, I had done all the organising of buying the land for him and arranging for my builder to build a big two-storeyed home similar to mine for his family.

Todd graciously offered for me and my two children to occupy the downstairs rooms of his home until we could find other accommodation. Being a strongly built truck driver, he assured me I would be safe.

Although my cousin and his wife made me very welcome, living next door to Des and our three children that were still with him, was very stressful. Des had moved a woman and her two children into the home, and although his mother insisted the woman was just a housekeeper, I knew differently. In fact, once our divorce became final, they married and a few years later went to live in a nudist park. The marriage broke up soon after.

9 > MY PSYCHIC CAREER BEGINS

Stress was pushing my psychic buttons, and I found I could 'read' for friends. My accuracy amazed me! One of my friends mentioned my expertise to an older clairvoyant who expressed a wish to meet me.

Jenny, the clairvoyant, was a Reader in a tea lounge in Brisbane CBD every Tuesday. She wanted to take a break and recommended that I take over the position. Although apprehensive, I needed the money. And so, my career as a clairvoyant-medium was born.

As Des had stolen my car, I had a long bus trip to the city. Between the hours of 9 am and 5 pm, I would read teacups for payment of 50 cents per cup. The owner of the tea lounge kept up my sustenance with tea, coffee, and scones with jam and cream. With the constant stream of customers, I rarely had time to visit the ladies' room. I was often prone to dozing off on the long bus trip back to my cousin's home.

Clairvoyance was classified as illegal in 1978. The ordinance was listed under the Vagrancy Act. A vagrant in the Oxford dictionary is defined as a homeless person; however, I had a home. To overcome the illegality, the proprietors of tea lounges displayed the following sign:

> *WE DO NOT PROFESS TO TELL FORTUNES*
> *WE ARE MERELY ENTERTAINING*

Shortly after commencing work at the tea lounge, I felt the need for a home of my own. Daily there were sarcastic and ridiculing remarks coming from next door. One of my clients in the tea lounge remarked that I looked worried and asked whether she could help. And help she did! Marie and her husband had a very big home they wanted to rent. It contained a small flat they allowed me to sublet, an office and double garage downstairs, and a lovely tree-fringed yard at the back. And it was situated only fifteen minutes by bus from the city.

Within months I had established a clientele for Readings along with some house cleaning for one of my clients. Without a car, I walked my young daughter to school and was waiting at the school each afternoon to walk her home.

The downstairs office came in handy for my Readings, while two university students became my tenants in the flat. Then I was offered a secretarial job at a much better wage than the tea lounge. Money from the sale of my home became available, enabling me to buy a neat little sedan. My life was slowly getting back on track.

10   A VISIT TO MY NEW GUINEA VILLAGE

The love and peace I had felt among my friends in New Guinea years before whet my longing for normality. When I suggested a trip to the New Guinea village to my fifteen year old son, he asked me whether his schoolmate and his mother could make the trip with us.

My connection for correspondence with the New Guinea village was with one of the tribesmen who had attained the position of a senior member of local government in Lae. My request to visit the village was received with great aplomb and excitement.

The minister at the Spiritualist church announced to the congregation that I intended to take toys and clothes to my friends in the New Guinea village. An avalanche of goods began to flood in. I also approached a large toy store that graciously supplied inflatable beach balls and floats and dolls. A biscuit factory donated tins of shortbread biscuits.

My kitchen became a workshop as friends helped me to cut out and sew finger puppets and rag dolls. My office began to fill with boxes of goods.

A few days before we were to fly to Lae, the manager of Air New Guinea phoned me. At the time of booking flights for our party, I had asked permission to take a few boxes of toys for the children. My friends were so excited. They were planning a big welcome ceremony. 'I am very sorry to have to inform you that we have had to cancel the flight your party is booked on.' Shock! Tears! And, I had to tell him that a few boxes had grown to eight large cartons. The manager of the airline, sensing my predicament, assured me he would look for a solution and phone me back.

In a state of total disbelief, the only thing left was to pray. 'Dear God', I prayed, 'I am not asking you to move mountains. I just want to move these cartons to New Guinea.' I continued to pray the same words over and over until I was jolted out of my reverie by the sound of the phone ringing.

Qantas had a half empty plane flying to Lae and the manager of that airline was quite happy to take us as passengers and the Christmas boxes as cargo. With faith restored, we set about pasting Father Christmas pictures on the boxes and packed our bags to travel to the best Christmas celebration I have ever experienced.

Years before, when my family and I were residents in New Guinea, I helped plan a Christmas party for the Australian expatriates. With my trusty sewing machine, red material, and white cotton wool, I fashioned the traditional Father Christmas suit. I took a few metres of nylon anchor rope from our boat, teased it and made it into a magnificent beard. With black gumboots, the suit was complete. One of the young Aussie men played the part well. He looked more like the Pied Piper as hordes of adult natives followed him down a path in the Lae Botanic Gardens, no doubt thinking that the Aussie had gone 'long long' (crazy) for dressing that way in the tropical heat.

As my two children, two friends, and I emerged from the arrival terminal about thirty kilometres out of Lae, we were met by an avalanche of people. News of my imminent arrival had spread, and truckloads of locals had travelled to greet us.

The Christmas cargo was unloaded, much to the delight of all onlookers. So great was the excitement that a few suitcases not belonging to us somehow got mixed up and taken. These had to be delivered back to travel agents the next day.

We five Aussies were driven to Lae and set up in a flat owned by the South Pacific Brewery. One of my local 'brothers' was a foreman at the factory, had gained permission for us to stay in the flat, and to be guests of honour at a big gathering and celebration on the company sports ground.

My son's mate remarked that I was being treated like Queen Elizabeth. 'Oh no!' I retorted. Queen Elizabeth wouldn't know all the people at such gatherings. 'I am being treated better. All of these people are my friends.'

With hundreds of people milling around us, we were escorted to a table and chairs placed in the middle of the oval. The table was set with tropical flowers, bowls of chicken pieces, chips, and bottles of beer and lemonade. We had recently eaten a meal on the Qantas flight but could not even consider insulting these beautiful people by refusing to eat the food proffered to us. Then I remembered the tins of shortbread biscuits that had been donated. The two boys fished them out of the cargo, and the children devoured them 'quick time'.

After the years of unhappiness and suffering I had survived, the loving reception I was given filled my heart to overflowing. Words could not express my feelings. The answer came by way of a hymn. Thanks to God for leading me back to spend time with my special friends. I began singing The Doxology: 'Praise

God from whom all blessings flow.' Those in the congregation who were familiar with the words joined in.

We spent the night in the Brewery flat with two men rostered to sit outside the door to ensure our safety. My friends had filled the refrigerator with bacon and eggs, bread, milk, and breakfast foods.

My village friends had upgraded their mode of transport from Lae to the village, managing to buy a small ferry boat. Once offshore from the village, we were transferred to lakatois to make the final journey to shore. The beat of the kundu drums rang out as we were ushered up the beach to a welcoming ceremony that was prepared for us.

Preparations were underway for a big Christmas party. I had given the tribal elders money to buy rice, tins of mackerel in tomato sauce, bread and butter, soft drinks, cordial, and a few cartons of beer for the older men.

I borrowed a primus stove and Phyl, the mother of my son's mate, helped me to make pancakes with turtle eggs, toffees, and gallons of custard made with powdered milk.

On the afternoon of Christmas Eve, and with our cooking done, we were sitting on the verandah of our new island dwelling. The front of the house looked out over the Gulf, while the back verandah overlooked a delightful, crystal-clear creek edged with palms and native Hibiscus.

When we had returned to Australia seven years before, I told my local friends to share the holiday house they had helped us to build beachside. This they did. They 'shared' it. Some members of the tribe got some of the roofing iron, others banks of cooper louvres, some got flooring and so on.

When news of our proposed visit was received, they built us a delightful local-style thatched house just above the high-tide mark of the sea. A verandah overlooked a crystal-clear creek that carried water from a waterfall.

While holidaying years before, we had explained to some of the village men the method of building a septic tank type toilet by way of cutting the ends out of 44-gallon drums and stacking them in a big dug-out. Being so close to the sea, the toilet would flush when the tide changed. And so, our tropical, thatched house was complete with a thatched toilet, built to the design to which we had introduced them.

Accompanied by squeals of delight from the children, two small lakatoi canoes approached. The onboard cargo: two fat pigs. Horrified, we watched as the pigs were slaughtered and their bristles singed over a fire. A hock was offered to us, but we politely refused.

Christmas Day dawned to the sound of a WWII bombshell being struck like a gong to signal the beginning of a church service. Due to the many visitors in the village, the service was held underneath the coconut palms between the sea and the creek. The village church was not big enough to accommodate the crowd.

As well as the new dolls in the cargo brought from Australia, there was a big doll with blonde hair and only one eye. One of my daughters had removed an eye from the doll that had been hers.

An altar was set up, complete with candles and orchids. An empty beer carton lined with straw became a manger for the blonde, one-eyed doll that was representing baby Jesus.

Among clothes I had brought from Australia was a beautiful white blouse with flowing sleeves. This was worn by my 'sister', Watuna, who perched in a tree while shining a torch on the proceedings. She announced that she was Archangel Gabriel.

Red crepe paper that I had bought for decorations was cut into strips and became leg bindings for some of the young men who played biblical parts.

To the accompaniment of guitars, heavenly voices rang out. Island people certainly have a gift for music.

I suddenly became aware that Phyl was becoming quite agitated and turned to her with a quizzical look. Then she brought my attention to the altar. A candle was very close to catching alight the hair of the 'Jesus' doll. With the village dogs running around and underneath the altar, the box had moved.

Following the Christmas Service, toys and clothes were laid out in bundles in the Men's Meeting House, a big open-sided building with a thatched roof. The head chief of the village honoured me by allowing me, a woman, to enter this building in order to supervise the handing out of the Christmas gifts.

Anticipating my visit, the village people had been busy making their gifts for me to take back to Australia. There were wooden carvings of lakatois, strings of colourful beads, woven bags and bilums (string bags). Some of the gifts had to spend time in quarantine but were highly appreciated by all recipients.

In my reverie, I see the joy on the faces of the children as they played with their new toys and the excitement of the adults at receiving new clothes. The plastic floats were soon inflated. The waves off the beach were dotted with little naked children afloat on colourful floats while the older boys played with new footballs and cricket sets.

The youth of the village had set up a long bamboo trestle, shaded with thatch, for the food to be set out on. Excitement filled the air. We were asked to wear native clothes of lap-lap and a meri smock or shirt adorned with beautiful frangipani leis.

Once the food was set out on the long tables, the village pastor blessed it, then began to lead a procession with us following. On our plates, the girls placed bread and butter, rice, tarot, mackerel in tomato sauce, pork, toffees, and sago cakes and were about to pour custard over the lot! Phyl and I had made the custard to sweeten up the rice and sago, and we swiftly made them understand that.

The feast and the speeches over, we retired to our tropical beach house for our last night in Paradise. THAT was the most unusual Christmas I have ever experienced, but one that is etched in my mind and my heart forever.

Leaving such a tropical paradise for the second time was very difficult. It was a very tempting thought to divorce myself from all mod-cons and become native in such a peaceful place. My friends begged me to stay. But I had to consider the education of my children. Sadly, we said our farewells.

11   LEGAL DECISIONS AND CHANGE

A notification requesting my attendance at Family Law Court arrived in the mail. When I mentioned this and the ordeal I had been through to my newfound local doctor, he insisted I engage his personal law firm to act for me.

When I arrived at the Family Law Court on the day of the hearing, I found the law firm had sent one of their junior staff to represent me, who had a serious lack of aplomb. One of Des's cohorts had arranged for him to be represented by one of Brisbane's leading criminal lawyers, who some years later was found to be guilty of a crime himself.

Being absent from two of the dependent children for one night was classed as 'desertion', an unfair accusation that my representative miserably failed to defend. Had I the fortitude that I have today, I would have gladly risked acting in contempt of court in order that the truth be told. The fact that Des was addicted to pornography and had been referred to a psychiatrist was never mentioned.

The court recommended that to seek custody of the two children in Des's charge, I should seek further representation to approach The Family Law Court. That would have cost me every cent I had. During meditation, Spirit advised me to save the money to buy land where I could build a new home.

THE COUNTRY LIFE

I am a country girl at heart
But wasn't always from the start.
I've left behind cement and tar.
I've even thrown away me bra!
I used to work among big wheels.
I tottered 'round in high, high heels.
Typed letters – mornings, afternoons.
Announced 'The boss will see you soon.'
My filing work was just a breeze.
My typing done with expertise.
My working hours – nine to five
And for perfection I would strive.
The city air was less than pure,
In fact, it stank worse than a sewer
And everyone seemed in a hurry
Or saddled with a load of worry.
One day I came to common senses
And left suburbia with all its fences.
Threw high heels, bras into a bin
And left 'Big Smoke' without chagrin.
I bought myself some Wellingtons
And overalls with buckles on
But if from Heaven the sun doth shine,
I find for work, bare skin is fine.
More overalls I just won't buy
'Cause bare skin takes less time to dry.
Up in the hills I took my stand
Secure on my piece of land
But then I found to my chagrin
A farmer works through thick and thin.

I bought myself a Jersey Cow,
A Cattle Dog, a pig, a sow,
A horse – I never rode before
And – Oh my God! – Was my bum sore!
The cow – her name was Bloody Mary,
At milking times was quite contrary.
She'd butt her head and flick her tail
And knock me off my milking pail.
Before too long I just assumed
Manure's not a bad perfume.
Because cows don't go to the 'loo',
It doesn't take long to accrue.
To be realistic, not remiss,
On farms it's very hard to miss.
Manure has that rustic charm
That labels you 'Lives on a farm'.
My first milk episode took hours
And Bloody Mary had the scours.
I found with one teat milk would run
From the other three I just got none
Until I played a music score
Then Bloody Mary leaked all four.
Twelve quarts of milk each day I gleaned
Until my fridge was full of cream
And buttermilk and home-made cheese.
All that from four teats and a squeeze.
The pig and sow soon went to work,
Their family duties didn't shirk.
I called the pigs Sal and Big Ben.
In time they multiplied to ten.
I don't think pigs have inhibitions.
Their progeny won exhibitions.

I don't think Sal was very shy
When giving Ben the old pig eye.
In time their expertise with pork
Of country shows became the talk.
Each time I carried 'piggy swill',
I thought of dollars in the till.
My cattle dog was very smart.
His name? Oh, I just called him Bart.
He wasn't pure bred you see
But he knew how to use a tree.
They say a dog is man's best friend
And to that I will condescend
But not if there's a bitch on heat
At another farm just down the street.
I built a house thanks to ham on hocks.
Down the yard I built a thunder box
And open fires can be good
If somebody else chops the bloody wood!
Yes, country life is really grand.
You'll never get me off the land.
I persevere with saddle sores
And socialise with sows and boars.
I'm sure Big Ben and Sal won't squeal
If I don't appear decked in high heels.
While Mary and I – we both agree ...
It's great to let your tits hang free!

(Note: There were no pigs. Lots of inspiration from my initiation to life on a farm.)

During a further meditation session, I was told from Spirit to buy land close to Mount Warning in northern NSW. Further, I was instructed to place an advertisement in a Lismore newspaper requesting acreage to buy. A phone call to the Lismore Chamber of Commerce led me to the office of the *Northern Star* newspaper.

A couple, newly ensconced on a large acreage in the Nightcap Range, answered my ad. They had bought the acreage thinking that the sale of their Brisbane suburban property was secure. That proved not to be the case. Their solution was to subdivide their large acreage and sell portions of it.

The home I rented in Brisbane sported a huge choko vine, a vegetable that I really relish. Strangely, it was the fruit of the vine that helped me to make the vital decision to buy land from these people. With a prayer for confirmation that I was doing the 'right thing', I planted two chokos at the entrance to the property. If they were still growing when I returned the following week, I would buy the property.

One week later I drove down from Brisbane, heading straight for the property and the spot where I had planted the chokos. Yes! They were still growing! The land was to be mine.

The offer was put to me that if I was willing to hand over half of my money to pay for the subdivision, I would be sold acreage at the price of $1,000 per acre. I had $9,000! Dutifully I handed over $4,500. When the surveyors appraised the land, the smallest piece of land they could split off covered ten and a half acres. With council approval and another $4,500 handed over, the land was mine.

The property had been used for beef cattle for many years and, apart from a tree line bordering the dirt road, was bare, with only remnants of trees, dead stumps. There was a small spring-fed creek and the most majestic views of Mount Warning to the north and a backdrop of the Nightcap Range to the south.

A family who had been my close neighbours in Sydney many years before had settled on a property in Kyogle about forty minutes' drive from my new land. They were very pleased to see me and invited me to stay. After a lovely dinner and a lot of catching up, I retired to bed. Weary from a long drive, I soon fell into a deep sleep. A blinding light and deafening roar woke me with a start. My friends had forgotten to warn me that their farm was bordered by the interstate railway line. Until a few hundred metres from their home, the rails lined up with the bedroom in which I was sleeping, before veering off on a tangent.

On my second visit to Kyogle, my friends told me that an acquaintance of their neighbours wanted to meet me. The neighbouring man drove me to meet Mike, who lived in a ramshackle, derelict old house set in bushland beside a creek. Most of the windows were broken, and electricity was non-existent.

Following that visit, Mike began writing to me. Not owning a car or even a driving licence, Mike hitchhiked to the rail station and came up to visit me in Brisbane.

My clairvoyant friend, Jenny, expressed a wish to view the land I had bought and suggested we visit Mike unannounced. She suggested that we take inflatable mattresses and warm blankets as it was winter, and I had warned her about Mike's abode. We also took loads of food which I think was more warmly welcomed than we two women.

When Jenny and I prepared to leave Mike's place, he asked to accompany us firstly to see my new property, then to spend a few days in Brisbane. As the three of us walked over my newly acquired acreage, Mike spied a small dwelling on the neighbouring property. It was very unkempt but, as with my new land, had a magic view.

After a few enquiries and an introduction to the owner of the land, I arranged for Mike to move next door for the rental sum of $8 per week. There was no electricity, bathroom, or toilet, but compared to Mike's Kyogle accommodation, it was a bargain.

Mike was twenty-six. I was forty years old, and although both of a spiritual persuasion, our lives had been on totally different paths. Mike's father was a very successful businessman and although his parents divorced when he was in his late teens, he and his older brother had a very comfortable life.

Around the time of examinations for graduation from high school, Mike and his brother were involved in a serious car accident. They had been to a cousin's wedding. Mike ended up with a broken leg and a sliver of glass right at the spot where the Third Eye is located. Mike spent the next few years in Sydney, then hit the road travelling hippy-style, up and down the east coast of Australia.

A few weeks after Mike had made his move, I travelled to Grafton to do clairvoyant Readings at the Jacaranda Festival. This had been organised by a well-known television personality (I shall call her Anne), who begged me to share the Readings with her.

Half of the takings were to go to charity; half we were to share. I told Anne that because of the family upheavals, I did not want any publicity. It came as quite a shock to me then that as soon as we arrived at the Grafton showgrounds, I was led to a caravan where the local radio announcer began to interview Anne about clairvoyance.

We were hired for a three-day stint of Readings, the charity arranging for the two of us to stay at a local motel. The night before our 'performance', Anne asked me to teach her to read Tarot Cards. At that late stage, it was impossible! Agreeing with me, she stated that she would just work with psychometry. We were set up in a big tent divided down the middle. As we both started to read for customers, I overheard Anne becoming quite annoyed with a young girl. The girl vehemently disagreed with what Anne was telling her had happened in her past. Quite loudly, Anne exclaimed, 'Well you can keep your little secrets if you want!' and stormed out of the tent.

Returning to the tent, Anne suggested that I do the Readings, and she would be the spruiker and money collector. But worse was yet to come. Anne spent each night at the poker machines and the bar, and a lot of money became unaccountable. She befriended a racehorse owner and his team at the bar and persuaded me to join them. I was drinking lemon squash, but the rest of the party was drinking to celebrate a race win. Anne, having had one too many drinks, started to act out the story of the recent path my life had taken, including having met a much younger man. Feeling cruelly betrayed and let down, I ran sobbing to the motel room. The racehorse owner followed me. He asked me what I was doing accompanying Anne and handed me his business card, telling me to phone him if I was ever in his hometown.

On my journey back north, I called in to see how Mike was settling in. He told me how keen he was to help me develop my new acreage and finally persuaded me to bring my youngest daughter to live in the cabin with him while organising the building.

Mike was spiritual, handsome, and very persuasive! My mind ran in circles as I drove back to Brisbane. Should I leave a comfortable home to live in a shack?

The two students had vacated the flat I was subletting, and the daughter and son-in-law of my clairvoyant friend, Jenny, had moved in while they were building a new home. Greg was a senior bank manager, and he had employed my son, Eric, in his bank. This lovely couple encouraged me to move closer to my new property and assured me they would care for Eric. At age sixteen, Eric was quite mature. As well as his bank work, he worked casually as a disc jockey at the local roller skating rink and played keyboard in his band.

With what I could fit into my car, including a fold-up bed, Emma and I left suburbia and headed to the country for a new start. The cabin had no electricity, no bathroom and only a pit toilet, but the scenery was magnificent.

The first night at the cabin, Emma fell asleep on an old lounge chair, and I intended to let her stay there, preparing to sleep in the fold-up bed myself. Mike lifted Emma into the fold-up bed and told me I could share the double mattress he slept on. For three weeks, we shared a bed platonically, bathed under a local waterfall while we waited for the washing we had done to dry, and sat by a fire at night watching the stars in the clear unpolluted sky.

The cabin had been derelict and unoccupied for some years. The only furniture was a table fashioned from an old tree stump that stood on a small verandah.

A few days after moving in, I found a ring set with a big orange stone sitting on the table. On questioning Mike, he had no knowledge of the ring and had not seen it only hours before. I asked Spirit where the ring had come from and was surprised to be answered with, 'It is a gift from the Prince of Peace.' Really!!

The following Sunday we attended a service at a Gold Coast Spiritualist church. Helen was an excellent medium who gave overhead Readings in the church. Handing her the ring, I asked her what she felt about it. 'Oh,' she exclaimed, 'that ring is a spiritual apport.' Now that was a word I had to look up in the Oxford Dictionary. I had never heard it before. The meaning: a spiritual manifestation.

In Brisbane, we had acquired a young pup, and being loathe to leave her, I also packed her into my car. Unfortunately, the arrival of a dog on a cattle property did not go down well with the owner of the cabin. Neither did the fact that an older woman was shacked up with a young man. Fortunately, the vendor of my property had an old dairy building on her land next to my new property. And yes, she was willing for us three to live in the old dairy. Our dog, alas, went back to Brisbane.

The old dairy sported a sound water tank, but the guttering of the old building leaked badly. I found a solution by melting plastic bottles over a fire, creating a kind of bog that filled the holes and allowed the tank to fill with water.

The copper insert from an old boiler became a handy bath, and although small, sitting in a small bath under a starry sky was a pleasant experience.

Day by day, my mind was oscillating about whether to stay or not. I loved my new property and was eager to start working on it. Mike informed me that he had been cut off from social security because he had refused to travel south to pick fruit. My money was our sole source of income, my vehicle the only car to drive. Mike had never owned a car, let alone a driver's licence. Nor was he making any effort to find paid work. After living in sub-standard accommodation for a month, I told Mike that Emma and I would be moving back to Brisbane. He promptly told Emma to go for a walk, picked me up, threw me on the bed and made love to me. Then he asked me to marry him.

The more I talked about travelling back to Brisbane, the more Mike became excitably persuasive about the plans he had to help me develop my property. The previous years had taken their toll on me. I was tired of change and upheavals. Eventually, I succumbed to Mike's persuasions and agreed to stay.

The following week I drove Mike and Emma to Sydney to meet Mike's family. It was not the family welcome I expected. Mike's father eventually became a good friend, but his initial reaction to news of an impending wedding was, 'Darl, don't marry my son. Just shack up!'

Mike's mother looked gobsmacked but decided we would dine out to celebrate. Mike's older single brother, Evan, declined an invitation to dine with us but was happy for me to chauffeur him to surf beaches. His reaction to the dinner invitation was, 'Sorry, I don't want to be part of something I don't believe in.' And he didn't believe in clairvoyants, at least not at that time.

Within twenty-four hours, there was a twist to the dinner guests. I happened to know a very pretty young lady in Sydney who was also a clairvoyant. She agreed to accompany Evan to the dinner party. In a borrowed car, Evan drove the young lady home, stopped the car, and asked her to marry him. She laughed. Evan ordered her to get out of the car and see herself to the door.

Driving back from Sydney, I decided to phone the racehorse owner who had been kind to me sometime before. He arranged for us to have a drink with him and asked where we were staying for the night. When we told him that we intended to continue driving a few more hours to home, he went off and booked us a luxury unit at the hotel, wishing us well for our impending wedding.

Plans for the wedding went ahead with a Spiritualist minister I had worked with, also named Joan, agreeing to officiate. Deciding to be independent and situate on my new property, we borrowed a large tent from a friend, bridging it with a tarpaulin to a large lawn locker. Mike and I built a shelter to cover an old fuel stove and make-do kitchen. We even added a bathroom.

I had added roof racks to my sporty, little sedan and, having been told about the bargains at a local tip, bought a brand new bathtub, albeit a little chipped. The journey home was most comical. The bathtub lashed to the roof racks of my car was fine for a while; however, at a sharp bend in the road, the ties broke and the bathtub ended up ceremoniously in the middle of the road.

With the bathtub installed in our make-do bathroom, I took an old cream can to an engineering workshop and had a long pipe and tap welded into the can. This was a great solution. As we cooked dinner on the old fuel stove, we also heated our bathwater.

Our tent home was furnished with a double bed, two old lounge chairs, and benches built out of planks we had found. The lawn locker was furnished with double bunks, a desk for Emma, and a table for my old non-electric sewing machine. My wedding dress, Emma's flower girl dress, and a pink silk wedding shirt for Mike were sewn on that trusty, old machine. Uniforms for Emma's new school were also made with it.

A few days before our wedding, we three went to stay with my friend, the minister. In her kitchen, I made the wedding cake and iced it with bridal trimmings, and cooked as many dishes as I could, supplementing them with bought chicken and salads.

Having been taught some skills in floral art, I also made bouquets for my matron of honour, Emma, and me. As a matter of fact, as the guests were arriving at the church next door to the minister's home, I was sitting dressed in shorts, putting the finishing touches on bouquets.

My son Eric gave me away and presented Mike and me with silver ingots engraved with the message 'Love'. The nuptials complete, about eighty family and friends joined us in the church hall for a feast.

For some time, I had shared the duties of organist at a Brisbane Spiritualist church with a young man. He kindly offered to load his electric organ into his van, bring it to the wedding venue and supply the music for us. He, being much younger than I, didn't know the old-time dance music. So I kicked off my shoes and got foot tapping with all the old music I knew.

A few of the teenage guests set to work writing 'Just Married' on my car and putting coins in the hub caps. Placating their efforts, my bank manager friend, who was acting as Master of Ceremonies, asked where we were spending the night. When I answered that we couldn't afford a hotel, he kindly went off and bought us a night at a flash hotel. The gift came with a condition, though. Mike had to carry me over the threshold and through the foyer of the hotel. That did not happen! Mike parked the car at the rear of the hotel and quickly made his way through the back door with me following.

The wedding over, Mike and I settled into working on the property. Having been used as a cattle property for many years, it was devoid of trees except for the road boundary. There were dead trees and stumps that we cleared to make a 'canvas' for what eventually became a spectacular garden paradise.

Although Mike worked well with me on the property, he showed no interest whatsoever in finding paid work. My work was the only source of income and assured us a building loan. Whenever I broached the subject of Mike finding paid work, his answer was, 'Oh well ... I will go and join the Army. Then you will have to chop the wood for the fuel stove yourself.' I was totally unaware at the time that men with a police record were banned from joining the Armed Forces.

Our wedding was quickly followed by Christmas. Emma was intent on having a pony, and as she was being tolerant of our makeshift living arrangements, I felt she deserved her wish.

A Shetland-Welsh pony, yarded about an hour from our property, was advertised for sale. 'Tiny' and another pony had been used for kiddie rides and their owner was proving to be quite cruel to these beautiful animals. A few days before Christmas, I drove with Mike, Emma, and her girlfriend to buy Tiny complete with saddle and tack. The old man who was selling Tiny was willing to deliver him to our property but only after he had had his fill at the local hotel's happy hour. Leaving Mike with the old man, the two girls and I travelled home.

Night fell. Emma went to bed, and I sat before a fire I had lit. Hours passed. Then at about 1 am, I heard an almighty commotion at the front entrance to the property. A huge Pantech truck was parked at the entrance. Two long planks connected the truck to the road and not one, but two Shetland-Welsh ponies were being coerced into walking the planks. The old man had sure had his skinful of booze, and as Mike did not drive, the old fellow had driven the big Pantech with two Shetland-Welsh ponies on a long winding country road. When I questioned why he had brought two ponies, he told me he thought the two would balance better in the truck. But what of the journey home?

We sat around the fire eating corn fritters and drinking coffee for hours. Not even cups of coffee sobered the old man up. So we decided he had better sleep in the bunks that were in the lawn locker, and Emma slept near us in the tent.

Morning dawned, and Emma was ecstatic at her Christmas gift. The old man suggested that we take the two horses for a swim at a nearby swimming hole, and in the middle of summer, the cool water was welcome not only to ourselves but to the ponies.

A couple of days passed, and the old man made no effort to leave. I guess good cooking and company were even more enticing than his local pub. In the end, I had to send him on his way with $750 for the purchase of Tiny.

Tiny proved to be a lovable, old rogue. In a good mood, he would allow two or even three young children to ride on his back. On some rare occasions, when he was not in the mood, he would 'pig root' until the children fell off. Luckily, because of his small stature, the ground was not far from his back.

There were often patches of magic mushrooms springing up on the property: hallucinogenic fungi. One day I found Tiny standing among a patch of chewed up mushrooms, his head swaying from side to side almost as if he was trying to dance.

A couple of years later, living in our new home, I agreed to host a pyjama party for Emma's birthday. I baked a big chocolate cake, fashioning it into a gabled house with smarties for shingles. Hours of work went into the creation. A couple of hours before the guests arrived, I remembered that I needed more soft drinks. The weather being rather warm, I locked the wire screen door, leaving the big glass doors unlocked. Can you imagine my reaction when, returning home, I found Tiny in the kitchen happily munching on the delicious birthday cake? He had escaped from his paddock, bumped on the wire screen doors until they jumped the runners, and invited himself to a party of his own.

A couple of months after our wedding, Mike and I left off working on the land to have lunch in the tent. As I began to eat a sandwich, a big red-bellied black snake came sliding toward me. In retrospect, I can laugh at what must have seemed comical. But at that moment, sheer terror consumed me. I crouched on the back of an old lounge chair, looking like a scared monkey, while Mike calmly munched on his peanut and beetroot sandwich. Mike's Siamese cat lay sleeping on the bed. He picked the cat up and threw it towards the snake, hoping the cat would attack the snake. The cat was too tired. Needless to say, the snake escaped.

Only weeks before, my New Guinea 'Poppa', who had passed to Spirit, warned me, 'Big Fella black snake. Give you big scare.' And I thought he was joking!

The next day I laboriously set to work with sheet iron and tin cutters fashioning fortress walls to surround the tent and shed. Being so new to living on the land, the snake incident had left me quite nervous.

In the close neighbourhood, there was an old farmhouse that was sound but quite derelict. I managed to track down the owner through his daughter who lived nearby, and God bless the dear man; he allowed us to move in rent-free if we cleaned the place up.

The housing loan approved, we engaged a builder to build us a modest two-bedroom home. The footings were dug, cement poured, and then the builder vanished, leaving us to pay the suppliers. He apparently saw an opportunity to make big money in a town that had been ravaged by a storm.

My brother, a builder, took pity on us and offered to build for us, with Mike and me assisting as labourers. Eventually we had our home, complete with a cosy fireplace and combustion stove. We planted fruit trees of every kind, a large vegetable garden, and herb gardens. Our bountiful harvests of fruit were shared with all who visited.

With a little practice, I became quite adept at milking the cows and making ice cream, cottage cheese, and yoghurt. The saddest part of owning milking cows, was having to send their calves to the abattoirs. The beef property next door ran cattle of a different breed, and the farmer did not want young bulls mixing with his herd.

And the sheep! One of my clients asked if we would take a young ram as they were moving house and would not have a paddock. So 'Lambert' was added to our menagerie. Thinking Lambert might like some company, we bought a young ewe. Lambert had never seen another sheep, and to begin with he was scared of the ewe. But not for long. The next morning, we found the ewe dead in the paddock!

Lambert matured and grew big curly horns. His favourite pastime seemed to be chasing me. But I was not the only prospective victim of Lambert. Responding to a loud bellowing from down the yard, I found that one of my bull calves had become tangled in the fencing wire, and Lambert was trying hard to mount the poor creature.

Suffering from a migraine headache, I decided not to accompany Mike, Emma, and a friend on their outing to the beach. As I lay in a dark room, I realised my instructions to unplug the phone and lock the glass doors had been ignored. Walking into the living room to answer the phone, I was confronted by Lambert, who had knocked the screen doors down to take up position in the middle of the living room.

Like a gladiator in an arena, I began to do battle with Lambert, eventually getting him through the door and locking the big glass doors. As defiant as ever, Lambert began butting on the glass doors. Armed with a broom, I did battle with that sheep until Mike returned.

By this time, I was feeling quite ill with the migraine and decided to see a doctor. Before leaving the property, we tied Lambert up to a post, mixed some sleeping pills in a bottle of red wine and, with the aid of a funnel, poured the mixture down his throat. Two hours passed. I returned to the property sedated from an injection. But Lambert, after all that had been poured into him, was straining at the rope to butt me. We bade him farewell.

ODE TO LAMBERT OF LATE

Lambert was a sheepish sheep,
A ram in backyard reared.
His owners when they moved their house
Said that they'd like him spared

From abattoirs and chopping blocks
Because they loved him so.
'Could we a home to Lambert give
Where greener pastures grow?'
There at my feet in our old truck
Lambert journeyed home.
Maybe a lady sheep we'd buy
'Cause he looked so alone.
Next day – excitement in the air –
We went to buy a ewe
Expecting Lambert would supply
Romantic overtures.
We took the little lady sheep
And put her in the yard
But Lambert wanted none of her,
That crazy sheep just B-A-A-A-D.
He came and hid behind my skirts:
Believe me it was panic.
He didn't know he was a sheep:
Poor fellow – he was manic!
We left two sheep down in the yard:
I'm not sure what occurred.
The next day lady sheep was dead,
The following interred.
To Fudge, the cow, our Lambert then
Turned passionate intention.
Good gracious me. What would you call
A sheep and cow invention?
As Lambert grew his horns became
As sharp as any knife.
His hormones also rattled up

And he desired a wife.
Would you believe I then became
The object of his desire?
My running skills improved somewhat
To miss a fate most dire.
Old Lambert wouldn't be outdone,
He butted on my door.
The plate glass trembled with each blow.
I couldn't take much more.
'We'll be humane,' My husband said.
'This is a crazy sheep.
I wouldn't pull a gun on him
But we'll put the sheep to sleep.'
A bottle of the roughest red
Lay on my pantry shelf:
When mixed with twenty sleeping pills,
Was a weapon of great stealth.
My nerves were shattered, and I shook
From this taxing episode:
For help, my husband took me to
A doctor down the road.
A needle in the arm and then
My nerves were more composed
Yet in the car I counted sheep
As peacefully I dozed.
And Lambert I was sure would be
Right through the Pearly Gates
But as our doorway we approached
Lambert stood in wait.
The rough red and the sleeping pills
Killed not this sheep's desire:

My legs were weak as through the fog
I saw him strain the wire.
The closing of this story now
I really can't relate.
Suffice to say that crazy sheep
Is Lambert now of 'late'.

Then there were the little lambs. One of my clients gave me four of the most beautiful little lambs, one grey with a black nose, one brown with white patches, and another two caramel coloured. Our paddocks were lush after rain, and I felt so benevolent placing our new pets in a paddock full of food. I knew nothing of bloat resulting from too-rich pastures. The cure is to stab the animal in the flank to relieve the pressure, but by the time I found the poor little lambs, it was too late.

We also had chickens. During a cold winter, I brought some week-old chickens into the house by the fire at night. One of them almost drowned, falling into a pond, but I patiently tended to him until he was strong. He grew into a very big rooster with a bright red comb and big spurs on his feet. He showed no gratitude to me for saving his life but instead took to flying onto my back whenever he caught me in the garden, chasing me up the block until I escaped into the house exhausted. The rooster didn't stay around for long. Being a vegetarian, I had no need for a rebellious rooster, although neighbours welcomed him.

There were many times when goannas attempted to gain access to the chook pen to steal the eggs. Our first efforts to combat their attempts were to paint small stones white to resemble eggs. Unbelievably, the goannas actually picked up the stones and began carrying them away. Eventually we totally roofed the chicken pen with wire netting.

When gifted some doves and Peach-Faced Lovebirds, we built a lovely bird arbour. Hungry goannas soon tracked that down too. We found that goannas could break through wire to secure a feed.

In time, Emma's pony Tiny was joined by two other horses, one a part Arab, white with pink freckles, and the other an ex-trotter, chestnut, tall and regal. We bought saddles and tack to suit and frequently enjoyed riding up in the hills for the next few years.

One mid-summer morning, Mike came to me with the sad news that our part Arab steed had fallen on a steep incline and died from a broken neck. Some years later, having acquired a bobcat machine, I dug many a grave for local animals. With nothing more than shovels, digging a grave for a large animal seemed a daunting task. Cremation was the only solution.

Our enjoyment riding horses came to an abrupt halt when someone stole our saddles and tack from our shed. I think our beautiful ex-trotter Phelspar missed being ridden and lacked exercise. I was later told that horses used to exercise can develop fat around the heart when not so active. As I walked down the paddock, I would call to him, and he would whinny in answer. One sad day as Phelspar came trotting to me to partake of some treats, he started to falter, eventually falling to the ground. There have been times when I have been able to communicate with animals. In desperation, I asked this beautiful creature what was wrong. With his head on my knees, he looked up at me and communicated, 'I have had a heart attack. I am leaving the body.' Then, my beloved Phelspar heaved a last breath and was physically gone.

And what of Tiny? The Shetland-Welsh pony, the loveable rogue, was part of our family for some years until he escaped from our paddocks, walked into a neighbour's dam and got bogged in the mud. That led to his demise.

Over the years, beautiful dogs joined our family, German shepherds, Labradors, and bitzers. Jack and Jill were two cavalier King Charles spaniels from the same litter. Adorable little bundles of fur, ginger and white with freckled noses. Their stay with us was sadly short-lived. In a season rife with ticks, they both succumbed very quickly to tick bites and died.

Then there were the cats, one black Burmese and one tortoiseshell. Hazel, the tortoiseshell, had a habit of wanting to share her catches of mice with me and would ceremoniously drop her catches at my feet. One day I was in the process of doing a clairvoyant Reading for a client, all being diligently recorded for posterity. Hazel ran under the table and dropped a partly chewed mouse at my feet. Taken by surprise and with all being recorded, I exclaimed, 'Oh, you dirty little bitch, Hazel. Why did you have to do that?' Hours later, I realised my client was named Hazel. That client recently phoned me after quite a few years, and we laughed as we reminisced.

And the residents in the wild! My beloved friends, the wallabies. Each morning and evening they would congregate on the flats of the property to graze. By offering treats of fruit, they would allow me to get close to them, their joeys peeking out from mum's pouch to view the outside world and to nibble at some tender grass shoots.

The present owner of the property allows me to visit. Recently, two of my friends accompanied me on a breakfast picnic. Just as in the past, the wallabies arrived to graze on the flats. It gladdens my heart to know that the present owner loves them just as much as I do.

Sharp 'tap, tap, taps' on the glass door of our bedroom was the signal that the wild wood ducks were waiting for a breakfast handout. The laughter of the kookaburras was always a source of cheer. The screeching of the black cockatoos was often a signal that rain was approaching. And the rainbow lorikeets and rosellas were always a blaze of glory. A family of frogmouth owls nested in their special tree year after year.

Over a period of twenty-seven years, Mike and I worked to turn a barren cow paddock into an absolute paradise. We planted fruit trees of every kind: nut trees, Jacarandas, Poincianas, flame trees, palms, and different varieties of orchids nestled in the branches of the trees. There was a sunken rose garden complete with a miniature waterfall. A fishpond with a fountain, and the centrepiece of the driveway featured a beautiful statue spouting water in the middle of a multi-coloured floral display.

Once we had acquired a bobcat, we built a roadway down to the creek, with a picnic table and a fire pit. Many meditations were enjoyed there in the secluded peace of nature, the only sound the babbling creek and small birds.

A few years after our home was built, my brother helped us to build a seminar centre. Small groups attended weekend classes in self-awareness, inner peace, and psychic development. They were wonderful years. Unfortunately, they came to an end when alcohol began to rule Mike's life.

Mike's father passed, leaving us a much-appreciated legacy. As I had financed the initial set-up of the property and had been the major breadwinner, I insisted on buying tickets for an around-the-world trip. The experience was great, but Mike's indulgence in alcohol was growing out of control.

The final years spent in my mountain retreat were difficult, to say the least. Mike quit work, and alcohol slowly took its toll. There were two car crashes, the first where he sustained only minor injuries. The second, when he smashed into an oncoming cattle truck while in an alcoholic stupor, almost cost him his life.

Divorce was inevitable. With a generous payout, Mike left the property. The upkeep of the magnificent spectacle we had created was far too much for me to manage. Sadly, I listed my beloved property on the real estate market, left the rural peace, and built a new home for myself in a nearby country town.

In the middle of unsettlement, I found comfort in meditation and feeling the presence of my spirit guides. The most profound visions and information bolstered my confidence and assured me the changes taking place were in line with my karmic journey.

One day, while in deep meditation, I found my 'spiritual self' in a most magnificent cathedral. I looked up at the high vaulted ceilings, the brilliant stained glass windows and a myriad of angels floating above me. Before me stood a massive throne; seated on the throne was a giant being, and although I could not see the face of this person, I could make out long white hair, a beard, and the folds of a long white satin garment. My feelings of astonishment were exacerbated when I looked down at my own body and saw that I was totally unclothed, with long, dark, curly hair reminiscent of my teens. And yet, amid the astonishment I felt a profound sense of peace and tranquillity. From the being on the throne, a voice issued forth: 'You now stand naked and unashamed before the throne of

God.' And from my eyes sprang tears of joy. Sometime after, I experienced a second similar visit.

In the years following my exit from the peaceful mountains, I built two homes and renovated a third within seven years. Quite a bit of the hard labour was carried out by me. To save money, I painted and landscaped. Tiling has always been a passion I enjoy.

At age seventy-five, I tiled about half of a big home and painted it throughout. This was before the spinal surgery that saved me. The pain in my body was unbelievable, but being the stubborn Taurean I am, I persevered. At 2 pm, the day before surgery was scheduled, I completed the tiling. Then, feeling satisfied that I had accomplished my mission, a friend drove me to the hospital to prepare for surgery the following day.

In September 2017, I travelled to Machu Picchu, Lake Titicaca, and Easter Island, intrinsically drawn by visions of the past. Shortly after my return, I was called to be a contestant on *Who Wants to Be a Millionaire*. That was a surprise as I had applied to be a contestant quite a time before.

The flight to Melbourne and the accommodation in a lovely hotel all went smoothly. Then at 1.30 am on the morning of the television recording, an alarm clock rang out in the room next door. I had slept for only three hours, after which sleep evaded me.

After a morning of group rehearsals, all was a go for recording. It was my good fortune to win $1,000 in 'Fastest Finger' questions, giving me bargaining leverage. That came in handy on the second last question, reducing the four possible answers to two. I guessed the correct one!

Being involved in psychic work for many years, I am somewhat conversant in astrology. Whether it was good fortune or divine intervention is debatable, but the outcome certainly gave me the resources to explore many of the ancient cultures and ruins I had been directed to.

The final question before me:

Alpha Centauri is –

1. A Star System
2. A black hole
3. A comet
4. A nebula

I answered, 'A Star System'. At age seventy-nine, I won enough money to travel where Spirit directed me. If you're interested in seeing my episode of Millionaire Hot Seat, it is available on YouTube.

Millionaire Hot Seat, Episode 194 (21 November 2017)
https://www.youtube.com/watch?v=TijUF18sIlE

As I visited each of the ancient sites that had been destroyed by wars, earthquakes, or floods, I was admonished that the ruins were the result of 'mankind going astray' in the far-distant past.

Craig, a surrogate son, was working for an airline. He was based in Abu Dhabi and was able to arrange some flights that enabled me to visit him and his wife and to travel extensively. A long-time friend was living in Italy, which became a jumping-off destination between other countries.

Over the next two years, I travelled to Egypt, climbed the Great Pyramid of Giza, and sailed down the Nile. Visiting the temples and the Valley of The Kings satiated a long-held wish for me. The end of that journey culminated in being hospitalised in Abu Dhabi with severe viral influenza. Craig travelled back to Australia with me. Before being hospitalised, I had visited the magnificent Sheikh Zayed Grand Mosque, the Dubai Mall, and the Palm Jumeirah.

A prediction I had made for a young client named Graham had come true. He scored a position working in Washington DC and urged me to come and visit. Oh, how I loved Washington DC. It was heartbreaking to see the riots in that beautiful city when Donald Trump lost the presidency.

The Washington DC Aeronautical Museum, with its IMAX theatre, intrigued me so much that I visited seven times. On the seventh visit, the attendant refused my entry fee and just waved me in with a big smile. Darling! From Washington DC, I travelled to New York, attended three stage shows on Broadway, and then travelled on to the magnificent Niagara Falls. Back to Washington DC, which became a springboard for the next leg of my journey: Los Angeles, Disneyland, Las Vegas, Grand Canyon, and many other sites before landing in San Francisco.

In 2019 I travelled to Paris, visiting many cities and rural areas between there and Rome. In Civitavecchia (the seaport of Rome), I joined a Norwegian cruise ship and cruised the Mediterranean for two weeks visiting the islands of Santorini, Delos, Pompeii, and many other ancient sites and ruins.

History and archaeology have always held a fascination for me. The workmanship displayed in some of the ruins is exquisite! Some of the tourist brochures state that invasions were the cause of some ruins. I'm inclined to think the major cause of the majority has been volcanoes, earthquakes, and tsunamis.

As I travelled and viewed the grandeur that had been, Spirit reminded me of what had been and the possibility of repetition of the same to come. Life is like a patchwork quilt or a Persian carpet. The dull, difficult times help one to appreciate the bright, joyful times.

And YES .... As in the UNIVERSITY OF LIFE, there are lessons in ALL!

PART TWO

LESSONS FROM THE UNIVERSITY OF LIFE

12 GRANDMA DAISY

A lone figure sits on a stone wall at the edge of the beach at St. Kilda, Victoria. The date is 21 December 1937. A member of the public feels something strange and calls the police. Constable Reginald Bensley arrives and approaches this lone woman, enquiring about her belongings and her intentions, to which she replies: 'Yes. I have had a call from the Highest Authority to do that. I am waiting for another call, and it will depend on that what I do next.'

Constable Bensley observes the woman for one hour 'during which time she walked chest high into the sea and was brought out by a sea bather'. Constable Bensley then takes the woman into custody. When taken for medical assessment, the woman is charged with 'delusional insanity' and given orders for her to be committed to a mental asylum.

The woman was my maternal grandmother, Louisa Daisy Younghusband, known as Daisy. Daisy was born on 14 February 1879 – Valentine's Day. At the time of her committal, she was fifty-nine years old and spent the next eleven years of her life incarcerated in horrific conditions. Her initial commitment was in the Kew Mental Hospital, from which ten months later, she was transferred to the Ararat Mental Hospital.

On 18 October 1898, age nineteen, Daisy married my grandfather, Sydney Charles Carrington Younghusband. The marriage began with a rocky start. Before the year had ended, Daisy gave birth to a stillborn baby. Three daughters followed: the youngest, my mother Julie, was born in 1907.

In the early 1900s, my grandfather and his brother set up a jewellery shop in George Street, Sydney. The shop, 'Harry Young - The Jeweller', was quite a prosperous business until the start of the Great Depression in 1920. By 1924 the business had closed.

The Great Depression brought hardship to many who had been in business, and I guess jewellery was one of the most unnecessary commodities of that time. In 1924 my mother and her parents moved from Sydney to Glenelg, South Australia. My grandparents' two older daughters had married young and left home. Sydney and Daisy set up home in an old miner's cottage. Their marriage was already on rocky ground; my grandfather spent many hours accompanying my mother to swimming lessons and competitions.

In 1927 my mother left home, and that same year, her parents' marriage ended. Daisy then moved to Victoria to start a new life. Nothing much is known about the life my grandmother experienced during the next ten years; however, I feel sure she finally fell victim to the emotional suffering she had experienced.

Daisy had been separated from my grandfather for ten years. Her explanation for the clothing, etc., on the path was that she 'wanted people to take them' in order to make a new life for herself. She told the doctors she heard voices and saw people who had died some years before.

Daisy described visions of Jesus Christ on the cross, quoted passages from the Bible and felt that she had been chosen by God to reveal to the world the New Era and ways for wrongs to be righted. Feeling that God has chosen one for a special role is paradigmatic of someone experiencing Spiritual Emergence. Unburdening oneself of material things is another aspect.

She had not harmed another soul, had committed no crime and yet was locked away from society and treated in a most inhumane manner for eleven years. Although Daisy had trained as a nurse, she was allocated work in the asylum laundry.

Through the Freedom of Information Act, my sister obtained the medical records relating to Daisy. These are shocking, to say the least! One comment stated that Daisy asked for sixpence to buy a tin of treacle but was refused. If she became too agitated, she was locked in a cell.

My grandmother Daisy was not alone in being misjudged. The famous South African president, Nelson Mandela, was arrested in 1962 and spent the first eighteen years of his twenty-seven years in jail in the brutal Robben Island Prison, a former leper colony off the coast of Cape Town, where he was confined to a small cell without a bed or plumbing and compelled to do hard labour in a lime quarry. Nelson Mandela was only allowed to see his wife, the mother of his two daughters, once every six months. He was routinely subjected to inhumane punishments for the slightest offences. Among other atrocities, there were reports of guards burying inmates in the ground up to their necks and urinating on them. Nelson's crime? His following words: 'I have cherished the ideal of a democratic and free society in which all persons live together in harmony and with equal opportunities. It is an ideal which I hope to live for and to achieve. But if needs be, it is an ideal for which I am prepared to die.'

While in confinement, Mandela earned a Bachelor of Law degree from the University of London. He also smuggled out of prison a draft of his autobiography, *Long Walk to Freedom*, published five years after his release. Mandela was granted the Nobel Peace Prize in December 1993 and on 26 April 1994, he was elected as the first black president of South Africa.

Fortunately, Nelson Mandela had the backing of thousands of anti-apartheid campaigners, his visions of a better, more just society becoming a reality for him. Another visionary with spiritual ideals, Martin Luther King, was assassinated for preaching peace. Many will remember a peaceful march in Washington DC and the speech he delivered to 250,000 people: 'I have a dream'.

Unfortunately, my grandmother languished in the most shocking conditions because no one was willing to help her. In answer to doctors enquiring about the possibility of releasing her, my mother wrote the following:

> *Dear Doctors, I was very grateful to hear from you and news of my mother. Believe me, if ever opportunity arises and better fortune comes my way, I would come and take her home. But at present, I am the poorest member of the family with three children under nine. My elder sister is quite comfortable, all her family grown up and married except one. But she is very selfish and would not dream of helping.*

Sadly, I never got to meet Grandma Daisy. In my childish way, at age eight, I wrote her letters. Her gratitude to me was shown by way of a couple of small felt toys and, once, a bunch of pheasant feathers and colourful seeds.

Fast forward seventy-two years: a lovely young man I call my surrogate son or Luke arranged for us to join a ghost tour. The venue for the ghost tour was the Aradale Lunatic Asylum, the prison for 'mental people' my grandma had been incarcerated in.

It was dusk as we arrived to join eight others and the leader of the tour. The Aradale Lunatic Asylum proved to be quite a large estate. The impressive three-storey façade set on large grounds meandered into many adjoining wings and outhouses. The torches we held revealed dilapidation and disrepair in most of the areas. As I walked along the driveway, I picked up pheasant feathers and thought of Grandma Daisy's gifts to me.

Our guide for the evening's tour provided us with Electromagnetic Frequency Meters (EMFs) so that we could endeavour to communicate with spirits of the deceased. These are battery powered and contact with the frequency of disembodied spirits is obtained via messages communicated by way of flashing lights. The holder of the meter asks whether any spirits would like to communicate. To validate a 'Yes', the requisite is one flash of the meter. To answer 'No' to a question, two flashes are requested. The efficacy of these meters is such that I later purchased two.

Our group walked through the many buildings being led by torchlight. We visited the morgue, the laundries, the common room, and a large block of small cells. As we stopped at certain locations, our EMFs livened up with their flashes. Our questions came thick and fast, as did the flashing answers.

There were not only spirits of 'mentally disturbed patients' still wandering around attached to the old premises, but also doctors and staff who had been employed there many years before. As a medium, I had the advantage of being able to hear the voices of spirits who wanted to communicate and was able to answer them.

Many of the spirits who remained attached, earthbound, to the asylum stated they were unaware they could leave the bounds where they had physically been incarcerated for years. Many felt that because no one cared about them on the Earth plane, there would be no one to care for in the spirit world.

Although doubtful that the spirit of my Grandma Daisy could be found, I nevertheless called out to her as we wandered through the sprawling buildings. Imagine my surprise when, as we walked up and down the line of cells where inmates were sometimes locked at night, I made contact with my grandmother. Because she had felt that no one wanted her in their lives, because she felt no one loved her, her spirit had stayed bound to her prison. She was unaware that her spirit would be welcomed in another dimension.

As with other trapped spirits, I told her she could leave the place of torment she had suffered in for the last ten years of her life, detach from the Earth plane and be welcomed into a higher spiritual dimension. I called upon the tour group to pour out their love on the spirit of Daisy and was rewarded by euphoria as I saw a ball of light rise up and disappear through the ceiling. Daisy was not the only earthbound spirit released from Aradale that night. In fact, I wondered how successful the 'ghost tours' would be after that night.

It saddens me to think that I was unable to help Daisy before her passing in 1949. However, my birth came just months after her incarceration and, as a young child, all I could offer her were a few childish notes.

And now, as I write this testimonial to the torment that my grandmother, Louisa Daisy, suffered, I feel her presence. There are tingles up and down my spine. I can hear my heartbeat and know that she, and many others who were treated as she was, are from the spirit realm, urging reform of the treatment of 'mental disorders'.

13   AURAS AND ENERGIES

The brain is made up of millions of nerve cells called neurons. These cells generate electrical impulses and messages to produce thoughts, feelings, sensations, movement, and control our body functions.

Thoughts are the language of the brain. Thoughts have frequency, vibration, and resonance. Positive thoughts are like a magnet to the Universal Energy.

Feelings are the language of the body, received and taken by the consciousness of the brain into every cell of our bodies. Feelings of fear, depression, and anxiety have the power to transmute the energy of the cells of our body into a negative state, causing lethargy and ill-health. Whereas happiness and joy flood positive energy into our cells. This can become obvious when witnessing the human aura.

The cerebrum section of the brain is divided into two major parts: the right and the left cerebral hemispheres. The hemispheres communicate with each other through the corpus callosum, which is a bundle of fibres sitting between the hemispheres. The left side of the brain is responsible for controlling the right side of the body. It also performs tasks that have to do with logic, such as in science, mathematics, and major decisions. On the other hand, the right hemisphere coordinates the left side of the body and performs tasks that have to do with creativity and the arts.

Most people utilise only a small percentage of their brainpower (approx. 10%). While awake, the left-hand side of the brain is constantly in use in most people, while the right-hand side is vastly neglected. We were born with a left leg and a right leg but do not hop around on our left leg all our lives. Why then be satisfied with using less than the full potential of the brain? I believe it is most important to exercise the right side of the brain by way of performing creative acts such as art, painting, music, dancing, sewing, etc. It has been found that students of music also excel in mathematics and literature.

The millions of cells in our bodies are in constant flux, dying and being reproduced, many of them constantly, some every few months. The new cell that is reproduced is a clone of the old cell, whereby the feeling or message of the cell is replicated into the new cell. Hence, if a negative state of mind is affecting a certain cell, causing a state of ill-health, the new cell will inherit the same aspects if the mindset is not altered. Psychology is not only connected to the brain but to every cell of our body.

Every cell in the human body has a two-metre strand of DNA carrying our genetic blueprint. In our body, we have enough DNA strands that, if stretched out, would reach the sun and back 129 times! Every cell in our body has its own divine intellect and is a miniature cosmic library.

History is full of the exploits of great explorers whose fearless journeys have opened up new vistas on planet Earth. Men have walked on the moon. Plans are underway to visit Mars and beyond. But we all have the potential to be explorers of our innermost and cosmic beings, opening up new portals to enrich our lives.

Great progress has been made over recent years in the fields of electronics, computers, and robotics, but none of these is as perfect and foolproof as the full potential of the human brain. The field of Artificial Intelligence is growing exponentially; however, I feel there is danger in trusting a non-human intellect to make serious decisions.

The unconscious mind is a vast repository of all that we have learned, experienced, and witnessed not only in our present existence but also by way of the soul memory from past lives.

The Kundalini, as described in yoga literature, is said to be an 'energy coiled up like a serpent at the base of the spine'. When this energy is awakened, it rises up along the spine, passing through chakras or energy centres. I have likened the path of the Kundalini to a railway line with the chakras as stations. Each station reached brings with it an opportunity to release past restrictions and embrace a new, higher state of awareness.

As these chakras – or stations – are vivified or energised by the power of the rising Kundalini, they become receptors and distributors of inflowing cosmic energy for the body. These chakras are located near major nerve plexuses and coincide more or less with the glands of our endocrine system. When these centres are energised, they affect the endocrine glands and, through them, our behaviour and physical functioning. (See *Stalking the Wild Pendulum*, Itzhak Bentov, 1988.)

I have found that the most pertinent times for Kundalini arousal have been the time when the endocrine system is in flux. Here I am referring to puberty, menopause, post-natal, and times of extreme stress. Titles such as 'puberty blues', 'change of life', and 'post-natal depression' don't seem to reach the root of the problem.

There is nothing sacrilegious in using the gifts of the Holy Spirit, as stated in 1 Corinthians 12, as long as these gifts are used for the betterment of self and mankind. Few people are aware of the edicts set down by the early Catholic Church at the Council of Nicea (AD 325), by which all recognition of reincarnation and spiritual/psychic gifts was outlawed.

Few people would doubt that we are at present living in the epoch described by John the Divine in Revelation, the last chapter of the Holy Bible. Prophet Joel also channelled from God:

> *After I have poured out my rains again, I will pour out my Spirit upon all of you! Your sons and daughters will prophesy; your old men will dream dreams and your young men will see visions. And I will pour out my Spirit even on your slaves, men and women alike and put strange symbols in the earth and the sky – blood and fire and pillars of smoke.*
> **(Joel 2:28-29)**

Is it unreasonable to expect that this prophecy is now taking place? If prophecy was accepted in biblical times, why not in modern times when there has been so much mental stimulation from television, computers, and all manner of modern learning aids and techniques?

We, living in our so-called 'sophisticated society', exemplify the protection and nurturing of our children, shielding them from worrying or unpleasant experiences until WE feel that they are able to cope on their own. By the time adulthood has been attained, the 'big, wide world' suddenly becomes an effrontery to the senses.

Many native cultures practice initiation with their youth while they are still in the protection and care of their families. The mode of initiation may entail experiences of fear, pain, hunger, deprivation of company or such, pushing the consciousness of the youth through a barrier to adulthood by a knowingness and learning to make personal decisions without parental or elder guidance.

I believe that deep down in the human psyche, there is a longing for such an initiation, which, if not supervised by experienced teachers, can lead to an Alice in Wonderland type journey.

It is quite concerning that the use of hallucinogens has become so widespread among teenagers. Many seeking an altered state of consciousness or an escape from the realities of the world use marijuana, ice, and many other drugs. There is danger in experimentation at any time but particularly in the case of a juvenile brain. I feel that imbibing drugs in youth can put a spanner in the works, causing confusion between both hemispheres of the brain.

A crude terminology I have affixed to an interrupted or incomplete spiritual emergence is 'half-baked' or 'scrambled egg' psychic. There are some instances when it is quite difficult to reverse the situation. It can be best explained by the analogy of mixing the wrong ingredients in the batter for a cake and then trying to extract them.

My understanding of bipolar disorder is that the left-hand and the right-hand sides of the brain are either in conflict or both trying to operate at once. The on/off switch between the two hemispheres of the prefrontal cortex of the brain may not be operating as it should, resulting in confusion and, at times, irrational behaviour patterns. It has recently been found that the pathology of bipolar is unstable Na/K channels on cell membranes that flood these ions back and forth in cyclic ebbs and flows.

To my mind, autism is the result of a soul not being properly locked into the physical body, creating a fear of the surrounds. Autistic people usually have a very strong link with Spirit, at times excelling in art and music. A commonly known sub-category of the autism spectrum is Asperger's Syndrome. People with Asperger's are less socially adept, although, at the same time, have above-average intelligence. Although I am not able to prove the fact, I have wondered if a genetic predisposition renders the child susceptible to autism being triggered with the MMR vaccination for babies.

The Oxford Dictionary defines the term 'idiot savant' as follows:

> *A person who has a mental disability or learning difficulties but is extremely gifted in a particular way, such as the performing of feats of memory or calculation. A person who is extremely unworldly but displays natural wisdom and insight.*

To me, the term 'idiot savant' is disgustingly antiquated and insulting. These people are probably more closely linked with the God energy than others. Their intellect is more attuned to the Akashic Records, albeit at the expense of their physical persona.

During my first experiences of trance channelling in my late thirties, my body exhibited all the signs of an epileptic fit. These experiences were totally spontaneous and, to begin with, very scary. Once the shaking and partial loss of consciousness passed, I felt imbued with a wonderful peace and became the channel for the disembodied spirit to communicate through.

The first spirit I channelled was the English grandfather of a friend. I remember how my body felt as though it was expanding and then the voice issuing forth from my vocal cords. I was told the Englishman was a large being when in body. His voice, which I could hear although in a trance, sounded very much like that of Sir Winston Churchill, prime minister of Britain during WWII.

Over the years, I have surmised whether epilepsy is related to spiritual emergence. Understandably, some epileptic conditions can be caused by diseases of the brain. As epileptic seizures are caused by a disruption of the normal electrochemical activity of the brain, I question whether there is a psycho-spiritual basis for them. It has been proven that flashing lights can trigger a 'fit' in the case of epileptics. But repeated flashing lights, as in computer games and such, can also induce psychic openings. Many people diagnosed as epileptics experience seizures at times of stress or trauma. My theory is that the spiritual consciousness separates from the physical body in order to escape from a situation that the person finds abhorrent.

In recent years I have experienced what is termed myoclonic seizures, sudden jerks of the body as I have been falling asleep. These seizures are classified as normal. I feel they are part of a temporary separation of the spiritual body from the physical body preceding astral travel or the spirit travelling to other dimensions.

My above theories extend to some cases of SIDS or sudden infant death syndrome. A young baby, the spirit having recently arrived from a spiritual dimension and with the fontanelle (cranial bones) still unfused, maintains a close link with the world they have left. It is not uncommon to witness a young infant smile and laugh at an unseen presence. These babies have the ability to see spirits. At the time of passing, the spirit of the deceased leaves the physical body through the Crown Chakra, during which process the cord connecting the physical with spirit breaks. Although there has been much research into the cause of SIDS, there has been little concrete proof of the cause of the infant's death. My theory: if, while the spirit of the baby is astral travelling, there is a loud noise or disturbance, I feel it is possible that the etheric cord may break due to a feeling of trauma.

Some years ago, I was Reading for the wife of an anaesthetist. She related how she had astral travelled during surgery, witnessing doctors performing an operation on her as she hovered above them. On sharing this experience with her husband, he told her she had been hallucinating. I have had such experiences myself and feel it was due to my physical body being sensitive and intolerant to the medical drugs administered to me.

Alcohol has never played a part in my life, and although I enjoy an occasional social drink, I know my limits. The overconsumption of a delicious drink called Blackberry Nip became a scary episode for me. A client had given me the bottle as a gift. After I had imbibed a few glasses of the delicious nectar, I found my spirit-self floating above my physical body, trying desperately to reconnect.

At this time, with the influx of so many hallucinogenic drugs, I feel many people are experiencing the same effect. The danger is that dark entities, or what I have termed 'little dark fleas', are ever ready to inhabit the body that is left vacant.

Each day we take an average of 28,000 breaths, breathing in approximately fourteen kilograms of oxygen. Carbon dioxide is made in our bodies as cells do their jobs. Our lungs and respiratory system allow oxygen in the air to be taken into the body while also letting the body rid itself of carbon dioxide in the air we breathe out. The cells in our body need oxygen to stay alive.

It is interesting to note that people who suffer migraine headaches can often see auras. There seems to be much conjecture as to the cause of migraine attacks, and treatment by administering oxygen seems to give relief. In my experience, I have found that people who suffer migraine headaches are also extremely psychic. Another aspect is that the period of suffering usually coincides with hormonal activity, i.e., puberty to menopause.

From puberty to my mid-fifties, I suffered unbearable migraine headaches. As heavy pain medication caused side effects, my only relief was to take medication to induce sleep.

Within my hypnotherapy practice, I can gauge the depth of the hypnotic state of a patient by observing their aura. As the physical body relaxes, the aura displays brighter and wider. It is almost as though the tension of the physical body is strangling the spiritual body.

As a young child, I could see auras. I imagined these colours were rainbows dancing around people, animals, trees and plants. During the years I conducted workshops and seminars, a friend who owned a special camera took photos of attendees that showed their auras. So much can be told about the state of physical and mental health of people from the human aura.

My method for guiding my students to see the aura of other students was to have the subject stand in front of a bright light. The light will show the aura. When I have attended a ballet or stage show, apart from being entertained by the dancers and actors, I am also impressed by the auras of the people on stage. With the spotlights on them and their enthusiasm for their performance, their auras really shine.

A method for seeing one's own aura is to look in the mirror of your bathroom when it is nicely misted up after you have taken a shower. You will usually see a band of either clear or coloured light surrounding your physical body. One of my clients was so excited when she realised that she could see her aura that she ran out of the bathroom to share this information with the rest of the class who were having a meal. In her excitement, she forgot she was naked!

Some people may not see an aura around another person but feel the kind of energy that person is emitting. This is what either draws one person to another or repels them, what causes an attraction to or a fear of the other person.

14 BODY, MIND & SPIRIT

I am ever mindful that we incarnated as spirits into a physical body, or vehicle for Spirit, to enable us to have a physical or human experience, and for this reason, I feel it most important to nurture the physical body. This is not based on factors such as vanity or ego but respect for the body that is the vehicle for Spirit.

Throughout my early life, there have been physical anomalies that have not satisfied me. One in point has been my prominent nose – an inheritance from my Jewish ancestry. My first husband exacerbated my dissatisfaction by referring to my 'Jew's conk' whenever he was in a depressed or angry state, seeking to bring me down to his level. Many times I researched rhinoplasty: surgical reconstruction of my nose. Once I realised that my spirit was the prime traveller, physical dissatisfaction dissolved, and I found comfort in the body in which my spirit resides.

I do believe that respect for the physical body, both in appearance and health, should be of the utmost importance. It has always been my practice to pay attention to dress and hairdo, and I have a ritual of using a facial moisturiser morning and night and applying some of my favourite perfume and some lippy after my morning shower. This ritual happens whether or not I am socialising with other people. After all, if our body was a motor vehicle and it was carrying a spiritual VIP around, we would, out of respect, do our best to keep the vehicle in prime condition. Now in my early eighties, my physical appearance is not neglected, and I am content with my reflection in the mirror.

Since the mid-1990s, food choices have changed drastically, mostly due to the influence of immigrants. Introduction to European and Asian cuisine has certainly improved the variation in our diet. On a negative note, the proliferation of fast food outlets and the temptation of pre-cooked and packaged food are placing our younger generation on a dietary road to disaster. Juvenile obesity and even diabetes are fast becoming medical problems.

So many chemicals are used in agriculture these days, and the long-term effect on our physical bodies is unknown in many cases. I grow whatever food I can organically. Picking salad vegetables and herbs from my own garden and eating them with a fresh vibration, knowing they were grown and tended with love, is pure joy.

It is not only in the food choices that I see problems but in the manner in which the food is prepared and eaten. Food prepared with love carries a loving vibration into the physical body. What is known about the preparation of ready-made meals?

Religious fervour is waning! Rarely is grace said before a meal is eaten, yet I do not necessarily link the saying of grace or blessing the food to a religious viewpoint, but rather to imbue the food to be eaten with good, positive energy and gratitude that we have food to eat.

For a good deal of my life, pure water has not been a favourite drink for me. Adulterating water with a diet cordial made water more palatable to me. A few years ago, I bought a book titled *The True Power of Water* by Masaru Emoto. In his book, he discusses the consciousness of water and illustrates this theory with photos of water crystals influenced by external good or bad opinions. The photos displayed in his book are truly amazing. As an example: water in a jar with the word 'happiness' written on a label produced a beautiful, symmetrical crystal. Conversely, water in a jar with the word 'unhappy' produced an incomplete, weak crystal. The influence of Masaru Emoto's book set me thinking about my aversion to drinking pure water. It is now my habit to bless the water that I drink and even to thank it for nourishing my body.

The human body is composed of approximately 70% water, tissue, bones, and blood contributing to the whole. If water has enough consciousness to be affected by verbal or written opinions, then to keep 70% of our body healthy, we must pay closer attention to the water we imbibe. And what of the water we exude by way of perspiration, sneezing, tears? Surely there must be emotions contained within those tiny droplets. Can the emotions held in our perspiration affect the odour of such? Is this what animals can sense?

Based on the saying, 'As above, so below', I have jokingly commented that for all we know, we may be a bug in the gut of God. I am sure there are many thousands of microbes in our physical body that think their host (ourselves) is one vast universe. A human body is said to consist of approximately 30 trillion human cells. Cells are in constant flux, with dead or worn-out cells being discarded and new cells taking their place.

Each cell bears a similarity to a uterus filled with amniotic fluid, our DNA and RNA being as a foetus that is nourished by our input of food and drink. Bearing in mind the research of Masaru Emoto, it is imperative that the fluid in each tiny cell is at its optimum state. As each cell is cloned in the renewal process, the paradigm of the discarding cell is the pattern for the new cell. If the cell that is being discarded is a sick or toxic cell, the replacing cell will carry on the program.

The main categories of cells are: stem cells, red blood cells, white blood cells, platelets, nerve cells, neuroglial cells, muscle cells, and cartilage cells.

There are over 200 different cell types in the human body, each with their own particular function solely but usually by forming a particular tissue. Different tissues then combine and form specific organs, where the organ is like a factory where every type of cell has its own job.

Red blood cells and cornified cells (which are found in hair, skin, and nails) do not contain a nucleus or DNA. All red blood cells and cornified cells must start with DNA, as DNA contains a code that tells each cell how to construct itself in the first place. Human red blood cells and cornified cells simply destroy their nucleus once it is no longer needed as part of the maturation process.

Stem cells are amazing! They have the potential to become any type of cell in the body. These incredible cells are the ancestors of all cells in the body, from simple skin cells to complex neurons. Over recent years, research and use of stem cells in the medical field have produced wonderful results.

Collagen is the glue that, along with electromagnetic energy, helps to hold the body together. It is the most abundant protein found in our body.

While on the subject of cells, I would be remiss not to relate an interesting experience I have had to do with cells. During my seventy-sixth year, an amazing neurosurgeon named Matthew performed surgery on my spine. For many years I had been in acute cervical spine pain; a fall on a travelator in the Bangkok Airport increased the pressure until the pain was almost unbearable. Finding my surgeon was nothing short of a miracle, as was the success of his surgical skills. The spinal discs were taken out, minced up with my bone, donor bone and cement, and replaced along with metal cages from C1 to C7. Screws hold the cages in place, along with two screws into my skull. My neck is rigid, with no side movement, which is a small price to pay for freedom from pain, and well-being. I will forever bless and be grateful to dear Matthew.

There is a strange side factor to my spinal surgery. Pre-surgery, I had a rather quiet, shy demeanour. A good talker? Yes! But outspoken? Never! Following my surgery, I noticed quite a change in my persona. I found strength in speaking my mind, albeit cautiously, and found that instead of taking life too seriously, I began to see the funny side of life.

As each cell of the body has its own consciousness, I really do believe that my donor bone was harvested from a male cadaver who, in life, possessed a wry sense of humour. After all, there have been stories of people having heart-transplant operations then craving beer and food that they would not have eaten pre-operation.

At an advanced age, I found success as a stand-up comedian, writing my own material. This career began with my winning a comedy competition on a cruise ship, followed by two more wins, the judges giving me a score of 12 out of 10.

The mind can be a factor in the healing process of the physical body. As a clinical hypnotherapist for over forty years, I have assisted patients to better health through positive visualisation and meditation. Proverbs 23:7 in The Holy Bible states: 'For as a man thinketh in his heart so is he.'

And as for the mind, from the time of conception until our death, when our spirit leaves the body, our heart is continually beating, our organs and mind processing without leave. A mechanical motor would be hard-pressed to operate without failing for that long.

Therefore, it is beneficial to our health to make daily meditation a habit, whether it be for five minutes or an hour. As the meditative state is reached, the systolic blood pressure can decrease by up to 10% or more. With meditation, muscles relax, releasing the build-up of lactic acid caused by stress or excess exercise. An excess of lactic acid in the joints of the body can contribute to causing arthritis.

And now to the subject of Spirit. Acknowledgment of our spirit, or our god-self, is most important. It is our spirit who, at the end of the journey (death of the body), will pass back into the Spirit realm either satisfied or dissatisfied with what it has learned or achieved. Our own personal journey is all that matters. We can help, care for, serve or love others, but we cannot carry them on their spiritual journey. Each of us has our own race to run.

Some time ago, I channelled the following Universal Prayer and religiously recite it silently to myself first thing on waking and just before settling down to sleep at night:

Lord God of the Universe,
Lord God of the Solar system,

Lord God of Planet Earth and everything created thereon,
Lord God of my Being, my Beloved Atma (Higher Self)
I love you with all that I am, with every atom of my Being. And I thank you for all the lessons that I have had in the past – the good and the bad – that have brought me to this point in time. I thank you for (the warm bed that I am in, the food that I have eaten, the wonderful day that I have had ... whatever you feel).
And I thank you for all the wonderful things that you are bringing into my life to fulfil my purpose.
Good Health.
Prosperity.
Great opportunities.
Loving people.
Success.
Peace ... etc.
And I send out peace, light and love to all who have wronged me, have been deceitful or cruel to me, and I forgive them.
And I send peace, light, love, and healing to ... (any family or friends who need help with healing).
And I thank you for all the goodness that is coming into my life.
Amen.

It is my belief that God is the life force of the universe. When our physical body dies, our spirit or god-self is released back into the realms of Spirit to either remain there or to await rebirth or reincarnation according to the level that our spirit has attained through birth and rebirth.

The time when our spirit enters our physical body can vary. This can be any time in utero, and most times is associated with what is termed 'the quickening'. This is the time during a pregnancy when the movement of the baby is felt within the mother's body.

At the moment of death, the spirit leaves the body through the Crown Chakra, carrying with it the spiritual energy and the aura. During our lifetime, we can view our physical body by its reflection in a mirror, determining whether or not to make changes to our hairstyle, our fashion, etc. It is the spiritual body that is the most important factor in our life, for it dwells in every atom of our being, and our demeanour is the outward result of our thoughts, our feelings, and our sense of well-being.

15   KUNDALINI

When I was first experiencing spiritual emergence in my late thirties, I was often drawn to the symbol seen on medical papers – the caduceus: a winged rod with two snakes entwined. Being curious of the meaning, I wrote to the Australian Medical Association and received some papers from their library on Greek Mythology. To this day, I doubt that many medical professionals understand the real meaning of the symbol.

I now know the caduceus to be the symbol of Hermes or Mercury in Greek, Roman, and Greco-Egyptian mythology. The myth tells the story of how Mercury once attempted to stop a fight between two snakes by throwing his rod at them, at which time they entwined themselves around the rod. This symbol was also carried by heralds, including Iris, messenger of Hera.

Asclepius was the ancient Greek god of medicine and healing, symbolised by a staff entwined by a single snake. Due to documented mistakes and confusion, the caduceus was adopted in the USA as a symbol of medicine during the late nineteenth and early twentieth century. The two-snake caduceus design has ancient and continual associations with trade, eloquence, negotiation, alchemy, and wisdom, but also with thievery, lying and the passage to the underworld. When will the true meaning be recognised?

Through studies and experience over the past forty years, I have become comprehensive in an understanding of the meaning of the caduceus and its relationship to the Kundalini pathway of 'Ida' and 'Pingala'. In my endeavour to simplify the understanding of Kundalini arousal, I may seem to differ from Eastern explanations. Pursuit of the spiritual result is the manifest goal.

We are not just the physical body. There are many layers to our make-up, just like an onion. Eight layers correspond to the make-up of the auric and physical body. For now, I shall just concentrate on explaining the chakras and the path of the Kundalini as it traverses them.

The seven fundamental chakras:

1. Muladhara: situated at the perineum, the space between the anal outlet and the genital organ.
2. Swadhisthana: just above the genital organ.
3. Manipuraka: just below the navel.
4. Anahata: just beneath where the rib cage meets.
5. Vishuddhi: at the base of the throat.
6. Ajna: between the eyebrows.
7. Brahmarandra: at the top of the head.

Chakras have more than one dimension to them. One dimension is their physical existence, but they also have a spiritual dimension, and this is what I want to focus on.

Once the Kundalini energy reaches the level of Brahmarandra, it is possible for a state of Sahasrara to be attained. But there is no particular way. One has to either jump or fall into a bottomless pit. This is called falling upward or the process of spiritual emergence.

Meditating on 'Ajna', or the Third Eye, can bring peace into one's life; however, to have the courage to pursue or accidentally find oneself thrown into the process of achieving Sahasrara can bring one the 'peace that passeth all understanding'.

Sahasrara reached, can really change a person's life. Discernment becomes easier. Accessing the Universal Library called the Akashic Records opens up new vistas. Creative abilities are enhanced, and mental equilibrium can be attained.

You can become ecstatic, so ecstatic that the whole world becomes nothing more than a play in your understanding and experience. Everything that is serious for everyone is just a joke for you. Facetiously, I have come to call living in the physical world today the 'cosmic comedy cock-up'! I no longer worry about things but trust, and if I cannot immediately see an answer, just say 'que sera sera' and hand any problems to the Universal God Energy.

The process of Kundalini arousal can happen voluntarily or, as in my own case, forced because of my Taurean determination not to have a 'nervous breakdown' but a 'nervous breakthrough'. Unfortunately, I had no guru, no expert to guide me through the process and was only able to understand the path my life and energies had taken when at a later date, I met mentors who had an understanding of the process.

The rod in the symbol of the caduceus, to me, is symbolic of strength like tempered steel once the Kundalini energy is fully integrated. At times when I was severely tested on my spiritual path, I questioned 'Why?' At first, I was repeatedly shown a steel sword being placed in a fire, heated, then struck with a hammer, the process repeating until tempering was achieved. Further, as an answer to my questioning, I was shown a marble statue like the Pieta. A sculptor with a hammer and chisel would be chipping away. I was told everything has a consciousness, even marble. Every blow of the hammer and bite of the blade is felt by the marble, but the end result of the beautiful statue is perfection.

Winding upwards from Muladhara, or perineum area, are two channels of energy called Ida (female) and Pingala (male). Picture the human spine as a railway line, with the chakras as stations. At each of these stations, the Ida and Pingala meet and cross to the opposite side of the railway track.

Many and varied emotions are involved at each of these chakras or stations: blockages not released in this life and, indeed, on a soul level from past lives. In order to complete the journey, one must endeavour to clear the blockages and continue on to the next station along the line.

Energies associated with Muladhara and Swadihistana are usually of a sexual nature. There can be blockages associated with sexual fears or frustrations or past abuse, or even unhealthy sexual perversions. But as these centres become charged with energy, there can be a strong craving for sexual activity.

At the level of Manipuraka – around the level of the solar plexus – it is most common for emotional blockages to be held. This is why belly aches of an emotional kind are often experienced in childhood. To move forward from this level, it must be understood that all that remains of the experience is cellular memories, and traumatic memories can only hurt if one relives the experience or triggers open the doorway to their unhealed past. If one has been hurt or caused pain and does not release the emotions caused by that pain, then they are allowing themselves to suffer while the perpetrator of that emotional injury 'suffers not'.

Many people with undiagnosable illnesses are classified as psychosomatic, i.e., a physical illness or other condition caused or aggravated by a mental factor such as internal conflict or stress. I have coined the word 'psychicsomatic' as it is my belief that for many illnesses, the causality factor is a blockage on the chakra levels.

The Anahata chakra can be affected by unresolved emotional matters of the heart, e.g., loss of a loved one, broken marriage or relationship or even a lack of love for self. As the Kundalini energy rises to this level, a person can feel an overwhelming love for all of humanity and even responsibility for the welfare of all of creation. It is at this level that a subject having the experience can believe that they are meant to be a saviour for the world – another Jesus Christ. There have even been cases where people have felt it necessary to sacrifice themselves, believing it was a necessity to save others.

The term 'broken heart' does not in any way refer to a physical anomaly, for the physical heart does not break because of an emotion. It is a term that more closely describes the emotional/Kundalini situation. A physical malfunction of the human heart has nothing whatsoever to do with Kundalini.

Visshudi: The Throat Chakra station greatly affects one's ability to express themselves verbally, with honesty, clarity, and integrity. Blockages on this level come about when people are fearful of expressing their truth, contradicting others for fear of reprisal, or fear of offending others with conflicting opinions. Deep breathing exercises, singing, and public speaking can help at this stage.

Ajna: The Third Eye Chakra. Many people experience severe headaches when the third eye begins to open. At this stage, clairvoyant visions become the norm. Great care must be taken to discern the true and proper meaning of each vision. Many can be metaphysical.

One of the first spiritual books I read was titled *Autobiography of a Yogi*. The author described how a young Tibetan monk would have his third eye punctured by a small shard of a special wood, the wound bound up and left for a while to facilitate the opening.

Bramarandrah: The Crown Chakra. This is the doorway to enlightenment! This is also the doorway through which the spirit leaves the physical body on the point of death. Headaches and a floating feeling around the top of the skull can be felt when this chakra is activated. Metamorphosis is achieved: the aspirant emerges from the Cocoon of Translation and becomes the butterfly that can rise above all.

My understanding of many mental illnesses is that they usually manifest at puberty, at the onset of hormonal changes that affect the pituitary and pineal glands (psychic centres). This is when an initiatory spiritual emergence – the rising of the Kundalini – is activated. This emergence is the spiritual birthright of all beings.

Many native tribes are aware of the Kundalini process and practice initiation rites to openly facilitate it. An interrupted or incomplete spiritual emergence in puberty can be likened to a storm triggering the fruit to fall from the tree before it is ripe.

The physical, mental, and emotional changes that take place during puberty are difficult at any time. Fear, anxieties, and traumas at this stage of an adolescent's life can veritably shake the tree – the 'Tree of Life'.

In this unsettled state, challenging energy is more able to permeate the aura, creating a state of neurosis. Mediumship can begin to be experienced; however, if there is not sufficient understanding of the spiritual emergence process, low-level voices can bring torment to the adolescent.

In the case of anorexia, a controlling 'voice' can coerce the adolescent into starvation by convincing them that they are fat when in actual fact, they may be mere skin and bone. Some refer to these 'voices' as 'the Boss' or 'the General'. I have even known some victims to have been convinced into thinking that the voice controlling them is God – not their own god-self but a higher entity that must be obeyed.

Portia de Rossi, the beautiful and talented wife of TV star Ellen DeGeneres, describes being plagued by a 'drill sergeant' of a voice that barked orders at her, demeaning and tormenting her for years. Her book, *Unbearable Lightness*, is a must for those wanting to relate to others who've suffered from anorexia or bulimia.

Although prescription medication may be needed, it is not the only answer. I feel a greater understanding of the Kundalini process is necessary and appropriate support given to a sufferer to complete the process of spiritual emergence in order to return them to the wholeness of their life.

16 PSYCHES, TRIPS, 'EMPTY HOUSES' & EXORCISMS

'There are more things in Heaven and Earth, Horatio, than are dreamt of in your philosophy.' From Hamlet by William Shakespeare.

There are many dimensions – seen and unseen – and many entities that dwell in the unseen. Not all of these entities are 'angelic' – as a matter of fact, there are many demonic entities hell-bent on creating havoc, torment, and disruption. Although the Holy Bible and scriptures speak of Satan or the Devil, I prefer to call discarnate spirits (i.e., those spirits no longer inhabiting a physical body), who cause torment and disruption, 'dark fleas'. Although I have found drugs and alcohol to be the main doorway for these spirits to invade the consciousness of physical beings, they also seek opportune times when people are experiencing spiritual emergence – entering non-ordinary states.

These dark entities are able to attach to a physical being regardless of their character or spirituality. The danger of not being consciously present because of overconsumption of alcohol or drugs is that these dark fleas will seek an opportunity to move in – become squatters for a time – have their own party and cause havoc.

The danger comes not only because of alcohol or drugs but also because of factors such as life becoming so unbearable that the spirit separates from the physical, leaving what can be termed as an empty shell.

Many times, I have questioned Multiple Personality Disorder as a splitting of the psyche. I am more inclined to think that emotional trauma causes the spiritual essence of a person to temporarily vacate the physical leaving the body as a veritable stage for untoward actors.

Although I have never partaken of drugs and rarely alcohol, I have, during the time of spiritual emergence in my late thirties, experienced quite traumatic torment because of my ignorance of these beings at the time.

With five young children, two of them under four, and a marriage falling apart, I was experiencing what I term a 'psychic breakthrough', as being a strong Taurean/Tiger, I would not allow myself to have a 'nervous breakdown'.

In a sensitive state, it is quite easy to be deceived by dark forces masquerading as angels. As previously mentioned, I was tested in this manner when a voice said to me, 'There is going to be a terrible accident, and you will never see your two dear little girls again. But never mind, dear, we will be here to look after you.' After an anguished hour, my two little girls, returned safely home, began climbing our stairs. It was then that I began to question the validity of the angelic-sounding voices and to realise that no one is safe from these onslaughts. We all need to develop spiritual discernment. If in doubt, question.

Many times, I have thought of the biblical story of Satan tempting the Lord Jesus, adjuring him to turn stones into bread if he was the Son of God. Or to throw himself off the steeple of a temple and many other tests. And I have found, over many years as a medium, that many souls who have left their mortal form by suicide have done so by being girded on by dark fleas.

How many times has it been heard from the dock in a court of law, 'The voices told me to commit the crime'? And an old excuse for wrongdoing: 'The Devil made me do it!' The more a person succumbs to the voices of darkness, the more dark energy wields control over them. Their spirit-body, finding the drugs offensive, leaves the body as an empty house enabling the darkness to enter and play havoc.

Although the prisoner at the bar can plead diminished responsibility due to temporary insanity, they still have to accept accountability for choosing the drug that allows in the dark fleas in the first place. Many jailed prisoners have found God once locked away from society and illicit drugs. When deprived of drugs, the essence of their true identity is reinstated and wholeness is possible.

We live in a three-dimensional world, but there are many dimensions higher and lower than ours. There are higher angelic realms but also lower energies inhabited by dark fleas.

As I add to this chapter, while a patient in a hospital with a lung infection, a young nurse, having been told of my gift, came begging me for help. Her deceased grandfather immediately communicated with me, naming himself and family members. The young nurse is concerned for her brother's health as since mid-teens, he has been having psychotic episodes following imbibing marijuana and other drugs. At age twenty-two, he has a record of being involved in violent fights and having to be restrained by police at his home. His loving parents and sister are desperately looking for a solution to his problem.

Once a physical being becomes infected by these malevolent dark fleas, it is almost comparable to a physical body being infected by candida albicans: a type of yeast infection that can invade most parts of the body, causing havoc to the health of the host.

As with candida albicans, a very clean diet is part of the solution, as is abstinence from all drugs apart from prescribed tranquilisers or the like to assist a transition. Alternate therapies such as acupuncture, osteopathy, massage, hypnotherapy, and meditation can play an integral part.

Dr Stan Grof pioneered a treatment of psychotic patients by administering, under supervision, doses of drugs such as LSD. I feel these treatments allowed the patients to complete their metamorphosis into a higher level of consciousness instead of remaining as what I describe as 'half-baked psychics' or 'scrambled egg psychics'.

During the years I directed a Transpersonal Centre, I had experiences that I would have ascribed to Hollywood thrill seeking. Being involved with the individuals who came seeking help, I can honestly report these happenings as factual truth.

One Saturday afternoon in spring, I was working in my garden when a car carrying three young people pulled into my driveway. There were two males and one female, all in their mid-twenties, all seeming quite distraught and disturbed. They begged me to help them, so, putting aside my gardening, I led them into my healing sanctuary.

The three young people sat on a settee as I sat opposite them in a rocking chair. As their story unfolded, they seemed to become more and more agitated. One of the young men had heard of my centre and was desperately trying to help his mates. The young couple seeking help had been to a party the night before and had consumed not just alcohol but LSD and marijuana. Within hours of leaving the party, they began hearing voices tormenting them and goading them into actions normally untoward to them. Out of fear, they sought the help of their mate, who drove them to see me.

About fifteen minutes into discussion, I noticed the expressions on their faces seemed to change, and then suddenly, two sets of hands lunged towards my throat, accompanied by guttural growls. Their mate let out a yell while I called upon my spirit guides and angels to protect me from the darkness that was manifesting. Then as suddenly as the action had begun, it ceased, the two bursting into tears, sobbing fearfully and begging me to help them. The male told me the voices were telling him to kill me, but he knew I was endeavouring to help them and wished me no harm.

The young male victim asked me to tie him and his girlfriend up so that they could not be activated into harming me. Although I thought this idea quite preposterous, I walked towards the door leading into my living quarters to search for suitable bindings. Behind me I heard, 'Please don't leave us. We don't feel safe without you.'

The laundry was next door to my healing centre. I had, the day before, returned from travelling, and the only binds I could find were black pantyhose. My centre had piles of mattresses that were used for meditation classes. So, within minutes the two young people were restrained with pantyhose bindings and were lying on mattresses with tears streaming down their cheeks.

For an hour, I called upon the Lord Jesus Christ, the angels and archangels, my beloved spirit guides, and all the spiritual energy I could muster to drive out the dark fleas that were tormenting the two young people. Another Spiritualist lived nearby, and I called out for her help along with my husband, who had returned home. We lit incense, and we prayed. About three hours passed. The change of energy became palpable. The two young people asked to be untied. Sobbing more passively, they walked outside to the lawn and began heaving up slimy mucous. They both vehemently vowed never again to partake of drugs or alcohol. The young woman, having been alienated from her parents, then asked permission to phone her mother. She tearfully asked forgiveness for any stress she had caused her mother.

Feeling that normalcy had been achieved, I opened the door for the three young people to leave. A look of fear came over them as they were reluctant to leave my centre. So, after phoning a doctor friend, I allowed them to stay. I had recently been hospitalised with atrial fibrillation and prescribed tranquillisers which I had not needed. At my doctor friend's advice, I gave each of the young people a pill and directed them to see him the next morning.

Many years ago, I began working with a teenage girl who had become catatonic after being sexually assaulted. She was very withdrawn and non-verbal to begin with. As I believe emotional stresses can block the path of the Kundalini, I had an osteopath friend treat her. Another friend, an acupuncture therapist, also began treatment to help the 'qi' (pronounced *chee*) or 'life-force' flow more easily.

One day she locked herself in the bathroom of her home and, responding to the 'voices', rubbed her faeces through her hair. The voices told her to anoint herself with her faeces. That same evening, without warning and obviously being possessed by a dark flea, she kicked me violently in the shin. Blood began to run down my leg. As swiftly as she had delivered the offending kick, her demeanour changed. She looked horrified at my injury and said, 'Oh, your poor leg. Who did that to you?'

At times when I was counselling this girl, she would put her fingers in her ears and say, 'God is telling me not to listen to you.' Of such is the counselling of the darker forces!

About thirty years ago, I visited this same young woman, along with her new baby, in a mental hospital. Her mother asked me to accompany her to a common room to discuss her daughter in private. A heavily built woman came charging into the room screaming, 'Help me, help me. Get me out of here. I am going to get burnt to death here.' I put my hand out to offer comfort to the woman, but my offer was returned with an angry outburst of 'YOU DON'T KNOW!!!' Two wardsmen took hold of the woman and placed her in a padded room. I did not think the woman was delusional. I feel the poor soul was another case of a 'half-baked' psychic.

Two nights later, I convened a meeting at my home to discuss how the young woman and her baby could be helped. Her parents and the therapists who had been working with me attended. The divorced parents of the girl were in total disagreement as to what treatment their daughter needed. Amid some heated discussions at about 11 pm, I had a vision of the girl calling for help and asked the group to pray for her safety. The next morning her mother phoned me to tell me that her daughter had been locked up in a padded room next to the woman who had been so agitated, and those wards had caught on fire. And yes, the woman who had predicted that she would get burnt to death did, in fact, die.

One well-known example of dark psychic empowerment is the life of Adolph Hitler. Being born in Austria in 1889 to a single mother must have attracted some emotional stigma considering the opinions of that time. The conditions of hardship, ridicule, and introversion can be fertile grounds for psychic unfoldment. Adolph Hitler certainly carried within him charisma and strong psychic power, albeit of a darker force or nature. Most interesting is that throughout his life, Adolph Hitler suffered from gut problems. Adolph Hitler was a vegan and a brilliant artist. As for his close confederates, I believe it is possible for the dark fleas to contaminate people in close alliance. And what 'sane' or 'uncontaminated' people would perform the wicked experimental surgeries that were done on prisoners? It is beyond belief that Adolph Hitler and his generals were able to put to death over 11 million Jews, innocent people, and not be questioned by psychiatric or judiciary bodies of the day.

Yet another example is that of Charles Manson. He was born to a sixteen year old single mother, never knowing his father. Much of his juvenile life was spent in reformatories or prison, mostly for robbery. By the time he reached his mid-thirties, he had gathered around him a group known as 'The Family', who saw him as something of a messiah. The group used drugs and studied science fiction, the occult, and fringe psychology. Like a cauldron of poison energy, the group descended into darkness until a horrific group murder, including that of a pregnant film star, Sharon Tate, was viewed by them as nothing more than a fun day out. Unbelievable!

Many young people who wander the streets despoiling buildings etc., with graffiti could probably be found to be brilliant artists if their energies were guided in a holistic manner. There may be among these young people latent Michelangelos or Leonardo da Vincis.

On an artistic note, Vincent van Gogh was a brilliant nineteenth-century Dutch artist. It has been recorded that he had periods of madness, periods of unconsciousness. He is quoted as saying, 'Normality is a paved road. It's comfortable to walk, but no flowers grow on it.' Vincent van Gogh was a talented but sensitive man. He was from a religious background and had altruistic ideas. He had ideas of establishing an artists' community at his house in Arles, in the south of France. For a short time, all was well. Then following a disagreement with Gauguin, it was believed that Vincent severed his left ear, wrapped the ear in newspaper and delivered it to a young lady who worked at a local brothel. Was this self-mutilation the result of urging from dark fleas? Would a person deliberately do such a thing unless instructed by a dark entity? Vincent eventually agreed to be admitted to a mental asylum, where he spent a year. Within a year of leaving the mental asylum, and aged thirty-seven years, he shot himself. A medical diagnosis was never conclusive. Suggestions were manic depression or alcoholic poisoning. Vincent was addicted to drinking absinthe, which in large quantities can induce psychosis.

And on a more humorous and personal note, I will relate a true story involving my parents. About thirty-five years ago, my parents, then in their seventies, moved from suburban Sydney to semi-rural Brisbane. My mother loved gathering and cooking mushrooms. Unfortunately, the mushrooms she collected one day were not the safe edible kind. I guess they were magic mushrooms, a psychedelic species whose principal active compounds are psilocybin and psilocin. These mushrooms are also known as 'gold tops'. My mother cooked up a great meal of steak, onions, and mushrooms, sharing it with my father and their overweight poodle dog. My brother, who lived with my parents, did not like mushrooms, so opted out from eating them. About an hour after the meal, my mother started to experience what my brother described as the horrors. In a totally different vein, my father began to joyfully sing all of the old-time songs that he usually played on the piano. Meanwhile, Coco the old overweight poodle, was cavorting around the room like a two year old.

My brother watched on for a short time, totally confused at the happenings, until he walked into the kitchen and began to realise that the mushrooms must have been responsible. Upon this realisation, he rang an ambulance. My parents were transported to a major hospital, where they were kept under observation overnight. Word soon got around, and a Brisbane newspaper printed the story along with photos of my parents with the caption 'The oldest hippies yet'. My mother told the reporters that she felt the mushrooms had cured her arthritis. Quite possibly a temporary drug-induced euphoria.

My theory on obsessive-compulsive disorder is that, in an effort to tidy up a 'scrambled egg' mind, the need is translated into physical action. One of my hypnotherapy patients kept repeating the childhood nursery rhyme: 'One, two: buckle my shoe. Three, four: shut the door. Five, six: pick up sticks.'

Over many years I have counselled families where children have become quite disturbed because an adult living in the home partook of drugs. I am convinced the dark energy attracted by the drug-taking adult had a negative effect on the children. Concurrently, I have treated patients who were affected by entities brought home by their adult children.

A very attractive, creative businesswoman in her fifties contacted me in a very distraught state. She had begun meditating and hearing voices that were giving her very troublesome information. In her vocation, looks were important, so when she was told that she would be involved in a horrific accident and be horribly disfigured, it was more than unnerving to her. During a further meditation, she was told that she had terminal cancer with only months to live. None of this was true. The dark fleas were lying to her.

My client had three sons, one of whom I knew to be a partaker of drugs. He had lived away from home for some years and had recently moved back in with his parents. Just as someone sharing a dwelling can pass on measles or a virus, the dark fleas had infiltrated the consciousness of the mother.

I am also inclined to think that Tourette's Syndrome is a form of possession state, a dark entity tormenting the host with 'tics' and tiresome body movements. Offensive language is part of the syndrome. If such foul language is not part of the daily norm for a family, then where does it originate? A weakened physical or neurological state could also leave the subject open to psychic invasion.

It could be said that demonic possession by authorities was a major practice from the twelfth to the early nineteenth century. During that time, the 'Holy Inquisitions' were a group of institutions within the Catholic Church whose aim was to combat heresy − a belief or practice contrary to orthodox doctrine. Penances were exacted on those judged to be heretics. They could take many forms, the most severe being life sentences or execution for unrepented heretics. Thousands of 'heretics' or so-called 'witches' were burned at the stake because of their beliefs. I was ONE of them!!

As mentioned, Giordano Bruno was an Italian Dominican friar, philosopher, mathematician, poet, cosmological theorist, and Hermetic occultist in the sixteenth century. He is known for his cosmological theories, which conceptually extended the Copernican model. At age fifty-two, he was tried for heresy by the Roman Inquisition on charges of denial of several core Catholic doctrines, including eternal damnation, the Trinity, the divinity of Christ, the virginity of Mary, and transubstantiation. For this, and his theories on the infinite universe, the multiplicity of worlds, and the sun-centred theory, he was publicly tortured and burned at the stake.

As he was led to his death, Giordano stated the following:

'Truth does not change because it is, or is not, believed by a majority of the people. Maybe you who condemn me are in greater fear than I who am condemned.'

Giordano's crime? He was a brilliant psychic!

17 > HAUNTED HOUSES

Over many years I have been called upon to do a spiritual clearance on so-called 'haunted houses'. Many of these abodes are occupied by the earthbound spirits of former owners who either have not accepted their death or have unresolved earthly problems.

Lily, a young, single mother of two girls, bought herself a modest weatherboard cottage in an attempt to make a new life for herself and children following a divorce. Being a creative soul, she set up a spare room with a sewing machine and all of her artistic accoutrements. Each time the young lady left the room and turned the light off, it would immediately turn back on. On occasions, the smell of rose perfume would come wafting into the room.

Lily approached me for help to find answers, so I travelled to her suburban home, asked her to take her children out for the evening and set about endeavouring to contact the spirit responsible for the disturbance. As darkness fell, I sat in the sewing room, calling upon spiritual protection and an answer to the conundrum. About an hour passed. The light began to flick on then off a number of times. At last, I was able to make contact with the spirit of an elderly lady who had once owned the home. She was a tormented, earthbound spirit and kept repeating to me, 'My son Henry will go to the Devil for what he did to me.' Then, 'The purse in the back garden is rusting!'

Lily and her girls returned home late that night, and after a discussion of the message from Spirit, we became convinced that the purse in the back garden was probably a tin containing money that the old lady had buried. At midnight, and by moonlight, Lily and I started searching the yard but to no avail.

After that night, the interference with the light ceased. Lily began researching among long-standing neighbours and in the local cemetery for a background to the mystery. Eventually, the story unfolded. The old lady had been bedbound, her son Henry being her sole carer. She had been prescribed drugs for her illness that required her to drink large quantities of water to avoid toxicity in her body. Her son apparently gave her the medicines but not the water, toxicity being the cause of her death.

And as for Henry? Lily researched until she found family links, and in the local cemetery laid the graves of the old lady side by side with her son Henry. Henry survived his mother by less than a year.

A surrogate son and his partner recently took me to stay at Australia's most haunted house, Monte Cristo, in Junee NSW. The widowed owner of this most majestic two-storeyed home related some historical stories to me. When she and her husband bought the Monte Cristo property in the 1960s, the house was very derelict. Her husband worked on restoring the house to its former glory. Returning home from town one night, they saw that the whole building was lit up inside. Impossible! There was no electricity connected to the building, and they possessed only one kerosene lamp to light the way for the family.

We three travelling together decided to sleep in the same room, they in an old four-poster bed and me in a single. The reason for these arrangements was not that I was in fear. Rather I was intrigued.

Immediately after we began to unpack our clothes, a young girl came to me from the spirit world. She told me she had died in that room while giving birth to a baby. The owner's son confirmed this was true: a young maid employed by the original owners of Monte Cristo had become pregnant to the man of the house and had died giving birth to a baby.

Monte Cristo is quite famous for its ghost tours and has featured in movies in the past. I felt totally at peace while there. My feeling is that the ghostly presences that inhabit this grand old home enjoy the film star role of entertaining the guests.

If a medical patient shows evidence of swelling, a rash, a fever or such, a diagnosis is relatively simple. Blood tests can show much about the health of a person. The human mind is so very deep and probing what is hidden or not volunteered by the patient makes diagnosis quite difficult.

A sensitive person, ignorant of ways to spiritually protect themselves from perverse spirits, can be like a lamb among wolves. The most usual form of communication I receive from Spirit is by way of telepathy, not aurally. Because of this, discernment is an important factor.

There have been times when I have been requested to accompany a client on a visit to a relative who was a patient in a mental hospital. Mostly these have been teenagers and all, most probably, experiencing spiritual emergence. And all of them exhibited extraordinary abilities to write poetry or songs.

Most schools educate their students on acceptable behaviour and personal cleanliness, hygiene, and stranger danger. But what about mental hygiene and dark flea danger? In this present age, with so many young people experimenting with drugs, I would welcome the opportunity to lecture on the danger of possession states as a result of imbibing illicit drugs.

18   FEAR IS JUST A FOUR-LETTER WORD

The very word FEAR equates with 'negative', with 'failure'.

Fear of failure, fear of the opinion of others, fear of losing. The aforementioned by themselves designate failure. Many inventors, authors, and millionaires have had many failures before they found success. For if you've never failed, you've never tried anything new.

Failures are the building blocks for success. When you have faith in your own divine being, you will not fear the opinion of others. The great captains and explorers of history journeyed across unchartered oceans without fear. Even in archaic times when it was believed the Earth was flat. Their lives, and the lives of those whom they paved the way for, were better because of their fearless actions.

HOPE is also a four-letter word. Better to venture out into the unknown with faith in yourself and hope your journey will bring success. And 'if at first, you don't succeed – then try, try again'. The very least you will gain are knowledge, experience, and learning to light your way with subsequent ventures.

There is a famous story I have always loved. It is a tale told about Robert the Bruce, King of Scots, from

1306-1329. A humble spider inspired Robert the Bruce to overcome fear.

In 1314, at the Battle of Bannockburn, Bruce's army of 5,000 defeated Edward II's much larger army of 20,000, driving the English finally and firmly out of Scotland. Previously, King Edward I of England defeated Robert the Bruce six times, hunting him down and slaying many of his countrymen. For three months, Robert took refuge in a cave on the island of Rathlin, off the Irish coast. An earthen floor and a straw pallet were not kingly surroundings. However, it was not his surroundings or the chill wind of winter that bothered Robert the Bruce. As Robert sought an answer, his eye was drawn to a spider attempting to attach its silken thread to an overhead beam in order to spin a web. Six times the spider tried but fell.

'Six times have I fought against the English and failed,' thought Robert. 'Now, if this spider falls again on the seventh attempt, I will give up the fight for Scotland. But if it succeeds, I shall try again.' The tiny spider, with all its strength, tried for the seventh time and succeeded in fastening the first line of the web it was trying to make.

The tiny spider knew no fear of failure and so taught a mighty king to overcome his fear of failure. Robert the Bruce set out for Scotland again and continued his fight against the English for the next eight years, defeating them and finally driving them out of Scotland in 1314 at the Battle of Bannockburn.

In my fifties, I encountered a situation that compelled me to seek a place of peace and isolation for a few days. A few years before, I had read for a man who, although he had presented incognito, I intuitively knew was a Catholic priest. He was a beautiful soul and listened intently to a message from his deceased aunt telling him of a spiritual retreat he would build. This retreat did come to pass.

I phoned the priest, asking if a broad-minded, non-Catholic would be welcome at his retreat. Alas, all of the regular cabins were full, so he offered me the use of his own humble retreat deep in a rainforest.

Two priests drove me, in a four-wheel drive vehicle, along tracks in a rainforest, finally stopping at a tiny, corrugated iron hut close to a magnificent waterfall. The bed was built of chicken wire strung between chunks of logs. There was a fireplace made of corrugated iron, and the only method of lighting was from a gaslight. The priest questioned me as to whether I would fear being alone, to which I answered that I was never alone as long as God was with me. He then assured me that I would probably have the company of a mouse.

Darkness falls very early in a rainforest. I tried, tried, and tried again to light the gas lamp. From the dark recesses of my memory sprung pictures of a teenage friend trying to light a kerosene lamp, spilling kerosene and fire across the floor of her parents' temporary dwelling. In the fragile state I was in, I allowed fear to win! I decided to retire to bed early.

The next afternoon, as darkness ensued, I again attempted to light the gas lamp. After a few frustrating attempts, I sat down and cried out to Spirit for help. Instantly to my mind sprang the following: 'How can you expect to become enlightened if you can't even light the lamp?' True!! Courage to overcome fear eventually got the lamp lit. By lamplight, I cooked myself a meal on the fire, then sat and watched a small mouse as it explored the cabin.

For those of you who have visited one of the Disneyland parks, you will understand the feeling of exuberance I felt when I visited Disneyland, first at age sixty, then again at age eighty. For those days I was a six year old, and an eight year old. And yet Walt Disney, the dear man who created these extravaganzas, was fired from a newspaper job for lacking imagination and having no original ideas. Had he allowed fear to triumph, millions of people, both children and adults, would not have enjoyed his most wonderful creations.

And in the words of Albert Einstein: 'Stay away from negative people. They have a problem for every solution.'

19 DEATH AS A BIRTH TO ANOTHER REALITY

How strange it is that the birth of a baby is celebrated, but the death of a person is mourned. The time has come for a re-examination and re-education of this phenomenon.

Throughout my life, I have been present at the birth of babies, my own and others, while facilitating 'Hypno-births' with the use of hypnotherapy to relax the woman in labour. Even with the assistance of hypnotherapy, birth is still a painful experience. The mother-to-be can tell her story of labour pain, but what about the experience of the baby?

During my studies on mind, I was educated in perinatal experiences, the journey taking place at birth not just by the mother but also by the baby being delivered. Leaving the blissful confines floating in amniotic fluid to travel down the birth canal, the uterine and pelvic muscles squashing, squeezing against the tender body and the cranial bones. In order that the passage through the birth canal can be facilitated, a baby's cranial bones remain flexible and may not be totally fused until around eighteen months to two years of age.

The baby, relating to the only human it knows, can associate pain or pleasure with the mother. My first child was ten days overdue and stuck in the birth canal for eight hours, then ripped out with instruments as his heart rate was faltering. His attitude towards me throughout life has been fraught with anger, regardless of my love and care for him.

Can you imagine how it would feel for your head to be placed in a vice, the screws tightened, the experience of being crushed, perhaps a headache, and desperately seeking a way out? Might you want to seek revenge against the person causing you pain?

Reliving my own birth was equally traumatic but for a different reason. My mother was most unwell at the time she became pregnant with me and admitted that my conception was a mistake. Reliving being in utero, I felt that I was living in a sewer and could not wait to get out. As soon as I was delivered, my soul wanted to crawl away from my mother's anger, but of course, that was impossible in a newborn's body.

Many years later, as mentioned earlier, after alternate studies covering blood groups, I realised that my mother's blood group and that of the man I loved as my father could not have produced my rare blood group. Further, moments before her passing at age ninety-one, my mother sat bolt upright, arms outstretched and called out the name of her lover. She had kept his love letters until she was ninety.

Many times over my career, I have been questioned on the subject of miscarriages, stillbirths, and infant mortalities. Miscarriages and stillbirths do happen because of physical deformities or anomalies. But there is sometimes a much deeper spiritual reason behind these happenings.

Our soul, in the spiritual realm before our earthly birth, is given some choice on the earthly pathway that is set before us.

I have been told young souls who pass before taking a breath or at a very early age, incarnate as teachers in order to give experience to those involved, i.e., parents, family, and medical staff. The same applies to souls who choose to incarnate into a physically deformed body or with severe mental retardation. In most cases, these souls are spiritually evolved and have spiritual fortitude to endure the physical journey, which in most cases frees them from the cycle of rebirth into physical bodies.

At physical birth, the baby journeys down the mother's birth canal, most times the process taking hours and being the cause of pain to both the mother and the baby. When faced with death, leaving the physical vehicle, the soul vacates the physical body through the Crown Chakra at the top of the head. The process of dying may be extrapolated because of fear of the unknown or of a reticence to leave loved ones behind. Once the process is finished, I am assured by most who have communicated with me that their completed journey has been one of total joy and wonderment. There are usually groups of loved ones who have passed beforehand, waiting to welcome the deceased into their new world.

Tradition tells us that the Book of Ecclesiastes in the Holy Bible was written by King Solomon. Ecclesiastes 3:1-8 is centred on the theory that there is a pre-ordained time for everything.

'There is a time for everything and a season for every activity under Heaven.
A time to be born and a time to die.
A time to plant and a time to uproot.
A time to kill and a time to heal.
A time to tear down and a time to build.

A time to weep and a time to laugh.
A time to mourn and a time to dance.
A time to scatter stones and a time to gather them.
A time to embrace and a time to refrain.
A time to search and a time to give up.
A time to keep and a time to throw away.
A time to tear and a time to mend.
A time to be silent and a time to speak.
A time to love and a time to hate.
A time for war and a time for peace.'

Birth and death are inevitable for all living beings. A sense of loss or loneliness is a natural emotional state. However, the stigma of death being only a time of darkness must be addressed. Given time and appropriate support, the darkness of sorrow can naturally give way to enjoyment of happy memories shared.

Death is but a turning point upon the path that the soul journeys on, an ascension for the soul when the experience and learning that we came into the physical body for has been gained. When the time is right, we can graduate from the vast University of Life and ascend to a higher order that we have rightfully earned.

Always remember, the soul is infinite, and love shared between souls can never die. The mortal form may wear, perish, or be cast off like a garment that is worn or no longer needed, but the soul lives on.

Although we who are left may miss seeing the mortal form of a loved one, they are able to visit us on the Earth plane. And when our time to graduate to a higher-order arrives, there will be wonderful reunions with those who journeyed before us.

At the present time, there seems to be a proliferation of Alzheimer's disease. Maybe modern chemicals have an influence? Maybe it is a way of unconsciously escaping a life that has become lonely or unbearable. It has become quite common for me to contact the spirit of a person who is suffering from Alzheimer's disease as though they have already passed away. My opinion is that the spirit is more closely linked with another dimension, but the heart or physical body is loath to let go of the physical dimension.

I am a spiritually-minded person, and it is my wish to run my race to the end of my karmically-allotted years. Nevertheless, I am accepting of the practice of euthanasia. Our physical being is the one thing that we totally own. Therefore, we, if sound of mind and with medical and psychological support, should have the choice to exit this dimension when we wish.

A recent documentary called *Laura's Choice* beautifully documented Laura's efforts to end her earthly journey when she was eighty-eight years old. Laura was not ill but was tired and felt she had had enough of life. Her efforts to seek euthanasia in Australia failed. By the time she turned ninety, Laura had found a clinic legally offering euthanasia in Switzerland.

Laura, her daughter, and granddaughter made the journey to Switzerland, spent some quality time travelling together then, at an arranged time and with medical supervision, Laura made her final journey with love and peace around her.

Contrary to some religious beliefs, suicide does not bring damnation on a soul. Again, which path a soul takes with the physical body is their own choice. I am in regular communication with souls who have taken leave of this dimension because living in it has become unbearable. These souls are always relieved to be able to communicate to their loved ones through me, assuring them that they are happy in a new dimension but still able to visit the world they have left.

Death is not an ending! Just as exiting our mother's womb at birth is a new beginning, death into another dimension is a new beginning, a new adventure. Never once, in over forty years as a medium, have I heard a person in spirit say they want to come back to Earth.

If it could be proved beyond doubt and in an entirely convincing way, if it could be proved scientifically that life and love are eternal:

Would your love be enhanced?

Would your fears vanish?

Would your purpose in life be magnified?

Would you no longer fear death?

How would life be different for you if you knew that just as patterns of dynamic light from distant stars continue to expand into the universe, our light, our dynamic information and energy, our soul and spirit not only continue to expand into the universe but live and grow just as we do on Earth? That the living soul can be likened to a dynamic living rainbow, a vibrating spectrum of visible and invisible energies that shimmer and shine forever?

Consider a time when eternal life is an accepted part of our universe. Imagine a time when the continuum for all of our human relationships can be extended beyond the physical years spent on Earth.

In the many years that I conducted funeral services I encouraged the families of the deceased to make the service a celebration of the life the deceased had lived. To ceaselessly grieve a departed loved one can hold that spirit back from their spiritual journey. The most beautiful and selfless act we can carry out is to wish our loved one 'Godspeed' and accept that their karmic role on planet Earth has been fulfilled.

Burial or cremation after death is a very personal choice. The choice may sometimes be dictated by religious ethics. My personal choice would be cremation. Graveyards have been notoriously associated with ghosts, and there is some basis for this. If, at the time of death, a spirit is loath to leave the physical body, the presence of that spirit can be felt or seen in close proximity to the deceased body.

There are many other reasons why a spirit stays earthbound. Murder victims sometimes hang around the site of their demise, hoping to help solve the crime.

Cremation is the choice of many indigenous peoples. Probably the best known are the cremation sites around the River Ganges. Typically, up to 300 bodies are brought daily to Varanasi for cremation. Hindu belief holds that a person cremated around the River Ganges will be freed from the cycle of rebirth.

Regardless of burial or cremation choices, I see the physical body metaphysically as a pair of shoes that has worn out. The spirit body, once separated from the worn-out body, can journey on to higher dimensions, to higher consciousness.

Jesus Christ said, 'In my Father's Home, there are many mansions.' My personal opinion is that 'many mansions' refers to different levels of the spiritual realm. While I personally do not adhere to the notion of 'hell' or 'purgatory', I do believe there are lower levels of the spiritual realm where the souls of people who have led a less than altruistic life find themselves after their demise. Love and compassion are keynotes of the higher realms, offering ascension to these realms to souls that have left the Earth plane in troubled circumstances.

MANY MANSIONS

Live life and enjoy it each night and each day:
Give love and give kindness as you can on the way.
But should Death come and beckon to a loved one or you,
Then face it with knowledge that Christ's words were true.
'Many mansions are there in the Heavenly Home.'
Were the words of The Christ when on Earth he did roam.
To the thief that was hanging on the cross by His side
He gave solace and comfort and told him abide
By the words that He spoke, with glad tears in His eyes,
'You'll be with me again in The Lord's Paradise.'
For the garment we're given to wear at our birth
Is the home for the soul as we walk on this Earth.
But the body's of man, while the soul is of God:
The soul goes back to Heaven; the flesh goes to the sod.
For the soul is immortal and will be evermore,
While the body can suffer, be painful and sore.
But we all must remember, through the pain and the dross,
Those encouraging words Jesus spoke from the cross.
For the world is a school we have come to, to learn.
If we make some mistakes, I am sure we won't burn.
For we're made by a God of compassion and love
Who in time will return us to His Heaven above
Where we'll meet with the loved ones who've gone on before.
So be not afraid to pass on through the door
To a world free from sorrow, a world free from pain,
To a world free from greed and earthly disdain.
When our faults and our misdeeds we have lain at His feet,
We can pass on unburdened and our journey complete.
Have no fear that your loved ones are lost or alone,

They'll have many to greet them when at last they've reached
Home.
And think of the wonderful freedom they'll feel
When freed of a body no mortal could heal.
So look to the flowers, the moon and the sun
And believe that God knows we are here, every one
And will gather us up when our journey is through
And will take us to Heaven, for I know this is true.

FOR NOEL

Heaven is the 'place along the road'
Where God decrees we leave our heavy load,
Take off the mantle of this Earth,
Find peace and joy in Heavenly birth.
And who are we as mortal men
To say our journey's nine or ten
Or fifty or one hundred miles:
'Tis when God smiles,
Decrees our journey is complete
And calls us to His Blessed Feet.
And those of us who stay behind
Must strive to see God's mystic signs:
Be comforted that loved ones now reside
In Heaven where The Christ abides.
Know love, once given birth, can't die.
Though hearts and souls in anguish cry.
Some people travel lonely down Life's Road
With naught but emptiness and heavy loads.
But how much greater Heaven's Door
When love and friendships filled Life's Store.

A couple of friends in their sixties asked me to officiate at their wedding. Ted was a heavy smoker, and I felt concerned about a persistent cough he had. I suggested to Ted he should try to give up cigarettes, to which he replied, 'The bloody things haven't killed me yet.' A few weeks later, he coughed up blood and went down very quickly with lung cancer.

On his death bed, Ted hung in and hung in. I felt that there was a fear of dying. Relatives and friends who had previously passed to Spirit began to appear to me, and as I began to name those waiting for Ted, I could see his spirit separating from his physical body more rapidly. I felt as though Ted began to have a feeling of being safe like a child when their parents are there to take them home.

It was 11 pm when I left Ted's home. It took me thirty minutes to travel to my home. Minutes after I arrived, Ted's wife rang to tell me that Ted had passed fifteen minutes after I had left their home.

20 > NEAR-DEATH EXPERIENCES (NDES)

Although I feel I had more than one near-death experience (NDE) in my childhood, I have experienced two that I recall in my later life.

Following an operation in my fifties, I began to have heart pains and atrial fibrillation. On advice from a friend who was a doctor, I asked my husband to take me to the local hospital. On the way to the hospital, I felt a massive 'bang' through my heart. I was out of my body, and I seemed to be floating up a golden staircase. A being that appeared to be Jesus Christ was at the top of the stairs. He handed me a white gown and a golden cord. Into my consciousness came the words 'Daughter, your earthly days are finished. You have permission to stay.'

On reflection, I feel I had the audacity to argue my case, so retorted: 'No. I don't want to stay here. Spirit has sent me so many people needing help that I haven't had time to write my books yet.' Into my mind flashed a message warning me that if I went back into my body, there was a risk of having a stroke and ending up in a wheelchair. For the next few days in hospital, I was connected to heart monitors and experienced a temporary paralysis of my left leg. I left hospital completely well, remembering my near-death as a beautiful experience and knowing that I will never fear death.

Seven years ago, following a five-hour spinal operation, I had another NDE. As hospital staff returned me to my ward, I could hear, see, but could not feel my physical body. A voice called for a doctor announcing that I had just 'crashed'.

The level of Spirit I found myself transported to was one that was completely foreign to me. The surroundings felt cold and misty. Out of the mist, my mother appeared to me. She had passed about seventeen years before. The damage to my spine had been caused during childhood, exacerbated due to age and arthritis. My mother acknowledged the cause of spinal damage and vehemently apologised and begged forgiveness from me. I forgave her, and we travelled together to a much nicer level of Spirit, where I left her and returned to my physical body.

21 MESSAGES FROM 'THE OTHER SIDE'

Over the many years of my career, there have been many memorable messages from 'the other side'. Some have been indelibly etched in my mind, and from this vast reservoir, I shall quote just a few.

The following poem was channelled from a little girl who had died after losing her battle with cancer.

FROM A LITTLE ANGEL

God lent me to my earthly Mother
And to my fair-haired, blue-eyed brother
And Daddy with the curly hair
Who bought my big, pink teddy bear.

My teddy bear lost all his hair,
But still I gave him all my care
'Till sad to say I left him – 'Where?'
My dear, old, cuddly teddy bear.

My Mummy said I mustn't cry,
She'd buy a new one by and by;
That perhaps another little girl
With big, blue eyes and lots of curls

Found and loved my teddy bear
That I mislaid – I don't know where.

The doctor came when I was ill
And tried to give me lots of pills.
I heard them say that I was sick
And that a bed they'd have to pick
In that big place where I was born.
My Mummy's face looked sad and worn.

The nurses came and 'needled' me
And said how big I was for three.
I couldn't count like my big brother
And like my darling Dad and Mother.

My tummy 'sicked' and hurt a lot
And all those lights were awfully hot.
The little curls around my head
They all fell off across the bed.

My Mummy said I still looked fair
Without my golden, curly hair
And that she'd love me all the time
As I loved that teddy bear of mine.

My Daddy didn't talk a lot
And seemed to think the room was hot.
He went outside when Mummy cried.
I know his face he had to hide.

My brother tried to cheer me up
By sitting down and jumping up.
He poked a funny face at me.
Yes, he was six and I was three.

One day I just grew very tired.
I heard them all say I had died
But I was with my newfound friends,
The Angel Babes that dear God lends.

My Mummy knows she gave me care
And loved me like I loved my bear
And yet she cries much more than me
When I lost my bear when I was three.

But like that other little girl
With big, blue eyes and lots of curls,
Who found my bear when I was three,
My Angel friends took care of me
And brushed the hair that grew on me
And said how big I was for three.

I want my family to know
That God is everywhere I go;
That He is with them night and day
And listens to them when they pray.

Perhaps one day God does intend
To lend another Angel friend
To Mummy, Daddy, and big brother:
God Bless that boy, Dad, and dear Mother.

Many years ago, a fourteen year old girl who lived on a country estate in the area I lived in was knocked down and killed by a car. She had excitedly run behind her school bus to meet a friend without checking the traffic. Although I did not know the family personally, I was given the following poem from Spirit and guided to find her family home to deliver the message.

A FLOWER CALLED ANGELA

Be sure your child now walks in peace.
No need your brow be ever creased.
She serves with angels from above
Who come to visit charged with love.
'Though she was true and fair of face,
She's been granted Lord God's Grace
And cast off great and heavy loads
That burden us upon Life's Road.
A girl alive with bloom of youth
And yet to God a living proof
That she was fit to be with Him
'Though each one left felt their light dim.
If in our gardens we all grew
Roses of the finest hues,
Were asked to choose not two but one
For God's bouquet, would we choose none?
The choice my loves not ours to make,
'Though parting makes the heartstrings quake.
But comfort comes from knowing true
That God's bouquet holds part of you.

While a patient in a country hospital many years ago, I witnessed a young spirit boy walking beside a nurse who was attending to me. When I mentioned the boy to another nurse, I was told the boy I was seeing was the son of the first nurse. Although I cannot remember how old the boy was when he passed, I remember that his name was Greg, and he had lost his battle with cancer. The following poem was channelled from Greg.

FROM GREG WITH LOVE

Remember Greg when sun is shining.
Remember how you did my ironing
And iced my cake at birthday time.
Remember how you bought me cars.
When I played sport, the gay 'Hurrahs!'
Remember waking up to find
What Father Christmas left behind.
Remember how we used to sing.
Forget the sad and bitter sting
For I'm not lost, I'm still your boy.
I'm still around to share your joy.
Remember how I used to run
With bare feet in the morning sun
And how I'd paddle in a stream
When tadpoles were a young boy's dream?
For shoes I did not care a lot
If they were hot or hurt a lot
And so, it was with mortal frame
That suffered and was wracked with pain.

I run in Spirit in the sun.
I walk in clear streams – Oh what fun!
And as the tadpoles slowly grow
From fish into the frogs, you know
I've grown, I am a man you see
With company Oh most Heavenly.
But I am with you everywhere
To share your worries, share your cares.
I come to hold your hand at night.
I come to bring you peace and light,
To wipe your tears, to bring you smile
As you did for me over all our trials.
Rejoice I've overcome my pain.
Rejoice for I am whole again.
I've made it to the other side
Where there is no bad news to hide.
Don't let the love that you all gave
Be wasted in a manner grave.
Let it burn on and brighter be
And know my IMMORTALITY.

My dear friend Denny lost two of her children to teen suicide and, previously, a baby boy born with a heart abnormality. Her triumph over pain and her efforts to write a book that has recently been published has been the impetus that has goaded me to finish my book. Her book *Still Standing* is a true testimony to how the pain of loss can be overcome by an understanding of death and the realisation that the spirits of loved ones are still alive in another dimension. It has been, and still is, my privilege to be the 'telephone' that connects Denny to her beloved children.

When Simon, Denny's eighteen year old son, passed from suicide, I was asked to conduct the funeral service at the gravesite. He was a very sensitive young man who found Earth too painful a place to live.

During the service, Simon's mother read a children's story, partly to assuage her younger son's grief, about a water bug traversing from below the lily pond to the world above. It was unknowing of what the world above held but discovered that its new body included wings to fly.

As my friend began to read the dragonfly story, a dragonfly began to circle her head, staying until the story had been read. The dragonfly has become a family favourite symbol and is an outstanding feature on the cover of Denny's book.

On the passing of other creatures

Over the many years of my career, I have been the communicator to bring solace to the owners of beloved pets that have died. The God-force is in all living beings; their journey does not end with the demise of the physical shell.

Dian Fossey was an American primatologist and conservationist known for undertaking an extensive study of mountain gorillas from 1966 until her 1985 murder.

Living in the jungle of Rwanda, gorilla colonies became as family to Dian. Over the many years she dedicated to campaigning for the protection of gorillas from poachers, Dian became particularly close to a gorilla named Digit, so named because one of his fingers was missing. Digit grew into a magnificent silverback but was unfortunately murdered by poachers, as was Dian sometime later. As the news of these murders became known to me, the following poem channelled through to me.

THE SUBJECT OF THE SOUL

There are many schools of thought my friends
On the subject of the soul.
And whether we as humans
Are closer to God's goal.
But I believe sincerely
Each soul by breath of God is kissed
From the weevil to the walrus
And gorillas in the mist.

It matters not if creature
Is mammoth in its size
Or tiniest of insects
With beady, little eyes.
Why would our Loving Father God
From Heavenly plan desist;
Make soulless dogs and cats and geese
And gorillas in the mist?

When this truth is comprehended
All embracing love begins.
And I'm sure Mankind's made more mistakes
And more than any creature's sinned.
The lowliest of creations
These souls we should assist
From the rhinos to the dolphins
And gorillas in the mist.

And if my self-importance
Should lead me from God's goal

And I mistakenly confer
More importance to my soul,
I ask that God will lead me
Up from that dark abyss
And show me other souls He made
Like gorillas in the mist.

Over the many years of mediumship, I have made confirmed contact with the beloved pets of my clients. Horses, dogs, cats, rabbits, birds, and believe it or not, even silkworms. A heavily built nineteen year old sat opposite me as I tuned in. In a vision before me, I saw a mass of silkworms crawling around the table. In utter confusion, I asked the girl if she could identify with what I was seeing. She burst out crying. Once composed, she told me that she had rolled out of bed on top of her box of silkworms when she was about eleven years old. As most of them were squashed and died, she had carried the guilt of killing them, albeit accidentally, for eight years. I guess seeing the silkworms alive in spirit was a way of assuaging her guilty conscience.

There have been times when animals who have had to be euthanised by veterinarians have communicated their love and gratitude to their beloved owners. It is very hard for an animal to totally express the pain that they are suffering. There have been times when an animal has told me that they were ready and willing to leave the physical body.

Since I was a young child, I have been averse to eating meat because I felt it was cruel to kill animals to eat. While I do not condemn meat eaters if that is their choice, I have not eaten beef or lamb for over forty years. Even chicken has recently disappeared off my dinner plate. I am almost vegan, growing my own vegetables when possible and eating seafood. After all, cows and sheep are vegans, and they are healthy!

With the advent of modern medicines, vitamins and treatments, labour-saving devices and such, people are living to a greater age than previous generations. But what good is a longer life if the quality of life is afflicted? With the incidence of diseases such as Alzheimer's and Parkinson's on the rise, the probability that these are the result of manufactured food or domestic chemicals unknown a century or more ago must be a consideration.

In my early forties, I was helping a young girl to understand her psychic abilities. Her boyfriend had a relative who worked for an agency handling world-famous speakers and had bought her two tickets to be in the audience of the famous English medium, Doris Stokes. The young lady had intended to take her mother to the venue, but after a quarrel with her mum, she invited me to go along. That was no surprise as I had been told psychically that I would meet Doris Stokes but could not understand at the time how this would come about. We were seated in the front row of the Brisbane City Hall theatre; Doris stood right above us on the stage. Following her demonstrations of mediumship, Doris asked whether any of the audience had questions for her.

I spoke. 'Doris, you are a well-known psychic and author and have been a practising medium for years. I am rather new at mediumship and find it very hard to 'cut off' after Readings.'

'Oh dear,' said Doris. 'Even if I finish a session late at night, I put something on the telly to take my mind off my work.' Over forty years have passed, and I often think back to that night and the books written by Doris that are on my bookshelves.

While an organist at a Spiritualist church in Brisbane around 1977, I was told about a famous spiritual artist named Coral Polge. She lived in England, but for a small fee, would draw spirit guides, relatives etc. I promptly sent off some money and very little information about me. My main concern and questioning were that the stress I was experiencing from a marriage that was in tatters was opening up my psychic channels, and I wished to know my guides and helpers. Coral executed some amazing drawings: my guides were White Feather, an American Indian; Gorolon, a young Tibetan Monk; Ailsa, a Catholic Nun; and Bernard, who was blind when on Earth. Then there was a remarkable likeness of my Uncle Bill and grandmother-in-law Janet and a drawing of a young child – possibly miscarried from life – the image of my boys when they were young. The details were astounding. Many years later, a friend studying at the Psychic College in London managed to organise a meeting with Coral and her husband Thomas, also a psychic.

As a loving, caring medium, I am very loath to shut the door to people suffering bereavement. As a matter of fact, as I write this chapter, I am a patient in hospital with a lung infection.

Five days ago, I was transferred by ambulance from a public hospital to a private hospital of my choice to be attended by a lung specialist who had cared for me once before. As the ambulance pulled away from the public hospital, the female paramedic recognised my name and said, 'You read for me thirty years ago after my dad died. You connected with him, and he said I would have a daughter. Doctors told me I would never have children, but now I have a twenty-five year old daughter.' She asked for my business card, then, with great care, handed me over to the private hospital. Two days later the paramedic rushed into my isolation room in a state of agitation. 'I forgot your card was in my uniform pocket and it got chewed up in the washing machine. Can I please have another?'

There are so many stories that I could tell of my mediumship connecting spirits with parents, children and even police in murder cases. I shall relate just a few that come to mind.

A broken-hearted young mum (I will call her Jane) came to me after delivering a stillborn baby boy. She had two daughters and, being overjoyed that the last planned was a boy, had decked out the nursery in blue. Alas, her baby boy died before birth. She agonised, casting blame upon herself for not having given up smoking, for climbing a ladder when pregnant and for any other blame she could think of. The soul of the baby told her it was a karmic exercise and that if she could accept that explanation, another baby boy would be born to her.

Counselling and hypnotherapy made good progress with Jane over the ensuing few months. Spirit advised me to tell Jane to buy a beautiful rose bush to plant in her lovely garden, and we could hold a little ceremony and dedicate the rose bush to her spirit baby so that she could release her grief and help the spirit baby. So we did.

As I began the ceremony with Jane and her husband, I saw an older spirit man with a toddler boy in hand smile, then walk from the garden. Within weeks Jane was pregnant again and gave birth to a healthy baby boy to enjoy the beautiful nursery. The following poem was channelled for Jane and her family.

THE ROSE IN GOD'S GARDEN

Bless the Little Soul who chose
To come from Heaven like a rose;
To bloom within the garden
'Neath his mother's heart
And yet of family playtime
Never be a part.
Bless this Little Soul
For he has blessed you all.
True Teacher, tiny as he be,
Who felt your love
Although you could not see
The dear, small face,
The tiny hands, the heart
Before he left so swiftly
And once more in God's Garden
Plays a part.
If we who love can love a child unborn
And for his earthly presence mourn,
Then he has shown us love beyond compare
That once we realise
We can share with all Mankind,
Though to their faces we are blind.
The tiny babes who're born
Into a world full of despair
And cry for food, or gasp for air.
Just know that on his journey
To God's Garden high above
He's taken part of you,
Your special love.

That as God pauses
By that special rose
He'll know that with your love
You helped it grow.

And in response to my officiating at a service for a man named Paul:

> *Dearest Joan,*
>
> *Thank you again so much for holding such a beautiful service to celebrate Paul's life.*
>
> *The memory of that day is such a treasure to me and the children and also to our friends who were there.*
>
> *The words were such a fitting description of the man. The surroundings were such a reflection of all he loved.*
>
> *I will always have you in my heart – you are woven into the fabric of our life now – for always. With love, the 'M' family.*

FROM PAUL

A window views the outer world
As the final chapter on Earth unfolds.
A sanctuary of Peace and Love.
From all around, the touch of velvet glove.
The sun on mountains in the early morn
So fresh and bright just as a babe that's newly born.
Dark shadows as the night inclines.
The closing days on Earth a soul reminds.
Close by to where I lay my head,

On pillows piled upon my bed,
The White Magnolia touched by Spirit's Grace,
So white and perfect cupped by purple lace.
And yet it is a stark reality
That once from cup the petals can be free,
The tree that held the flowers stands so bare,
But you remember beauty that is rare.
The journey to the mountain high,
The wind that echoed every sigh,
The spoken words, the roses red,
For me created sacred bed.
But now from Earth my soul is free
And yet in all remains a part of me.
The bed, the window mountains, sea:
And yes! – the White Magnolia tree.

Many years ago, a lady I shall call Anne came to me for a Reading. I connected with a little girl who had died in an accident. Her daughter, about five years old, had broken away from her grip and ran to her death in front of a big truck. I saw a little spirit girl with blonde, curly hair and a big smile. As I described the child to the mother, she would not acknowledge that it was her daughter. Yes, the child had blonde, curly hair but was a Down's syndrome child. I explained to the mother that once in spirit, all was perfect. I asked if she would have let her daughter be taken to another country to be healed, but with the proviso that she would not see her again for a long time. She answered in the negative. I then explained that that was not a kind consideration for the child who had to live with a disability and told her to think along the lines that her daughter was in perfect condition but living in a faraway country.

One of my nephews met a girl who had two dependent children. Phil had a grown daughter from a previous marriage. Together they had a beautiful, blonde-haired daughter. Sadly, when the child was about three years old, she drowned. My nephew, then a bikie, travelled hundreds of miles with his partner and some friends to seek help from me. I was told from Spirit they would have another little girl within a year who looked identical to their lost child, but she would be born with a fiery spirit. In the meantime, a popular Australian magazine heard the story of their heartbreak and supplied a memorial for the lost child and financed a lovely wedding for the couple, including the story in their magazine. And within a year, another little blonde-haired girl became part of their family, and she is a fiery, high-spirited girl.

About six years ago, the deceased husband of my client, Bec, came through from Spirit. His name was Jason, and his ex-wife had contacted Bec, suggesting she come to see me. He sent love to Bec and said he hoped all would go well with her pregnancy. Unknown to me, she was his partner when he was killed in a freak auto accident. At that time, Bec was quite an obese girl, and it was impossible to tell she was pregnant by looks, nor did I know how she had heard about my work. Bec already had a young son with Jason.

Jason came through, and although there were floods of tears, there was a lot of relief. A second baby boy was born some months later, and the local newspaper printed a front page cover of mother and child with the caption, 'Jason's Legacy'. Bec asked me to officiate at a ceremony to scatter the ashes in the sea at Byron Bay. When photos were printed, there appeared many beautiful coloured orbs in the air around us. Proof that there were many unseen also at the service.

About two years later, Bec asked me to perform a christening service for her two little boys at a lovely local venue. Jason's ex-wife also attended with the son she had earlier born to Jason. As I conducted the ceremony, purple balloons were released. Three of them drifted slowly upwards and bunched together under the fronds of a tall palm tree. Jason said it was a sign that he was watching over and cradling his three sons. Bec married again and had a baby girl.

Many, many times, I have made contact with the spirits of people who have been killed in horrific accidents. Although the surviving relatives agonise over the pain the victims must have experienced at the time of their death, the truth is different in most cases. As the spirit of the victim intuits the closeness of leaving the mortal body, it separates itself from the mortal body. Then it is as if an empty shell, the physical body, with no sensitive consciousness, is left to face the blow.

Over many years I have found the spirits of accident victims will find any way they can to communicate with their earthly loved ones to tell them they arrived in the afterworld safely and are with loved ones there.

A headmaster of a big country town school has been a client of mine for many years. As I was Reading for him about four years ago, two young spirit men named themselves and told me they had been killed in a road accident the day before. Peter looked shocked! These two young men had been students of his the year before. On his return home, Peter learned the information given to me was actually correct. From Peter's Reading, a chain reaction followed, with relatives and friends travelling a long way to make contact with the boys.

In October 2006, another car accident claimed the lives of four young teenage boys. They had met for a Chinese meal then decided to go for a drive to a beachside region for some excitement. A fifth boy, the driver, survived. Many family and friends have made contact with the boys through me since. The father of one of the boys was instrumental in creating a driver education centre to teach safe driving practices to young people. What a wonderful legacy!

When I asked my client why she was worried about her daughter, who was a nurse, she burst into tears. I had a vision of her daughter working in an overseas hospital among dark-skinned people, and I felt that she was pregnant. And that, dear readers, was the cause of tears. Her daughter Kerry was in a very happy relationship with a young indigenous man, but her mother sadly was very racially prejudiced.

My client's mother had passed to Spirit and related the following to me:

> *Do you remember the panda bear toy I bought for Kerry when she was a little girl? Well, in six months' time, there will be another little panda for you to cuddle. She will be half black and half white and you will love her as much as Jane loved her toy. But the little panda that is to arrive in six months' time will be your beloved granddaughter.*

A beloved friend recently lost her daughter 'J' after a long battle with cancer. J's father had died some years before, and her husband had passed about five years ago after suffering from motor neurone disease for some years. Before

J passed, I shared lunch with her and her beloved mum. I knew then that her time on the Earth plane was short, for as well as we three around the table, there were many visiting from Spirit.

After J passed, she showed me that at the time of passing, she was looking in a big, oval mirror and knowing that she no longer wanted to be in that body. Her father and husband appeared from Spirit and lifted her out of her physical body. They carried her over a rainbow bridge to Spirit. A few days later, J communicated to me that at passing she felt like Dorothy in The Wizard of Oz and that Toto was there to meet her. She laughed about funeral services for goldfish.

My notes on the day of J's funeral service:

This morning, the voice of a lady in spirit told me she had been a florist. (I did not know until the eulogy was read that J had been a florist in her younger days.) She told me to pick three white magnolia grandiflora from my garden. Then she asked if I would please pick some of my Singapore orchids from my deck. At the service, as I placed the flowers beside her casket, J told me that the three magnolias were symbolic of her three daughters. The orchids represented her son, her two little grandsons, and the grandchildren yet to come.

As the service began, I saw a man, who I realised was J's dad, walking down the aisle of the chapel with J dressed in white beside him. Her husband was standing beside the casket, waiting for her. I didn't know until I was later told that her husband's ashes were in an urn on the top of J's casket. J had said to me, 'It was not a funeral but a spiritual marriage.'

Throughout the service, I was having visions. J's father was standing outside his milking shed calling the cows to him. Then the cows turned into the people in the chapel, and buckets of milk were set out before them. (Milk is symbolic of prosperity, purity and loyalty – the 'milk of kindness'.) The chapel was crowded with long-standing family friends, many linked by a common factor, the dairy industry. As the rain fell upon the roof of the chapel, a raindrop fell on the head of each one present. As it did, the person became like a crystal drop of water. The crystal water flowed down the aisle, forming a beautiful crystal pool. (The crystal pool is from a meditation I channelled, in which it contained all the goodness your God wants you to have.) The pool was alive with loving energy. J stepped into the pool like an excited child, splashing around.

J named many people, family and friends, who were waiting to welcome her into her new home. She told me, 'The excitement I found was like looking for and finding the sixpences in the Christmas puddings (an old custom). And, 'Please tell my darling mum I am so proud of her.' I later wrote to my dear friend:

> *At a marriage, the parents give their daughter away to her husband. My dear 'M' – you handing your beloved daughter's spirit into the care of her loved ones on the other side was most beautiful and courageous. I am so proud to call you a beloved friend.*

A reference from M is on file in my office:

> *I have known Joan for almost forty years, and in that time, she has read successfully not only for me but also for many of my friends and family. She has always been spot-on with relaying quirky sayings and things only I would have known*

about my passed-over loved ones. In the last seven years, since my dear husband's passing, I have made a point of having Joan read for me on his birthday. He comes through without fail, along with many other departed loved ones, and it has helped me to feel not so lonely. I truly feel connected with him again and, it has given me such peace to know that he is always with me and protecting and guiding his loved ones from the other side.

Blessings, M

22 ALBERT EINSTEIN

*A*lbert Einstein (1879-1955) was a German-born physicist who developed the special and general theories of relativity and won the Nobel Prize for Physics in 1921 for his explanation of the photoelectric effect. He is generally considered the most influential physicist of the twentieth century. And yet Einstein did not talk until he was almost four years old. He adored playing the violin and said that if he had not gone into physics, he likely would have become a musician. His encounter with a compass at age five left him mystified by the fact that invisible forces could deflect the needle. This led to a life-long fascination with invisible forces.

He became deeply religious at age twelve, composing songs of praise to God. As he delved further into science, he found science contradicted his religious beliefs.

During his schooling, one of his teachers told him that he would never amount to anything. Einstein excelled in science and mathematics. He graduated from university in 1900 but was unpopular with some of his professors because of his habit of seeking answers for himself. After being denied a letter of recommendation, Einstein was turned down for every academic position he applied for.

Albert Einstein went on to become a world-renowned physicist, the successor to Isaac Newtown. He lectured around the world and, in 1921, received the Nobel Prize for Physics. He became famous for his theory of relativity.

Einstein also launched the new science of cosmology. His equations predicted the universe was dynamic – expanding or contracting. This contradicted the prevailing view that the universe was static, so he reluctantly introduced a cosmological term to stabilise his model of the universe. In 1929 astronomer Edwin Hubble found that the universe was indeed expanding, therefore confirming Einstein's earlier work.

On the subject of God, Einstein wrote that he believed there was an 'old one' who was the ultimate lawgiver. He stated he did not believe in a personal God that intervened in human affairs but in a God of harmony and beauty. His task, he believed, was to formulate a master theory that would allow him to 'read the mind of God'.

Einstein wrote:

> *I am not an atheist, and I don't think I can call myself a pantheist. We are in the position of a little child entering a huge library filled with books in many different languages. The child dimly suspects a mysterious order in the arrangement of the books but doesn't know what it is. That, it seems to me, is the attitude of even the most intelligent human being toward God.*

Einstein posited many theories such as wormholes, higher dimensions, the possibility of time travel, the existence of black holes, and the creation of the universe. Today many leading physicists are trying to finish Einstein's ultimate dream of a 'theory of everything'.

23 CONNECTING WITH OUR OWN GOD WITHIN

For many years I conducted a Transpersonal Research Centre, guiding my students in meditation procedures and exploring and developing their own psychic abilities. Looking back through a photo album of classes, it is interesting to see that some of those students have gone forward to forge their own psycho-spiritual paths. Many of them still maintain a loving connection with me.

Some snippets of notes from my students:

'I want to express my appreciation for the guidance you have given me. You have helped me to open my eyes and look beyond. I am happy to be travelling on my new-found road!'

'Thank you for a wonderful weekend. My batteries are fully charged, and the lift in consciousness was wonderful. As I travelled home with my two friends, I had, for the first time (with my eyes open) floods of beautiful purple colour. I thought my sunglasses were reacting with the windscreen in the car at first, so I removed them, and sure enough, it kept happening all the way home.'

'Many thanks for the enlightenment and power to retrieve. For the first time in months, I feel sane and comforted. This weekend was sheer bliss!'

'What a rejuvenating, inspirational weekend. Thank you for welcoming me into your classroom of love and sharing your knowledge.'

'You opened my eyes at forty-five! It has been wonderful for me. Thank you for all you have done.'

'Thank you once again for a relaxing weekend. My life has taken on a new path filled with love and happiness, and I extend that love to you.'

'Many thanks for making the start of my journey so memorable and valuable.'

Never in my years of teaching did I hand out diplomas or worthless pieces of paper. My tribute to the weekend classes was a key for each student. On each key, I engraved the name of the student along with a card bearing a channelled poem pertinent to that person. The name-engraved key was a symbol that within each of us, we have the key to unlock doors to the seemingly impossible if we believe in and connect with our own God-within.

Over recent years, many old souls have entered the world through newborn babies. Some call these children the 'Indigo Children'. The energy and spirituality of these souls are sorely needed to guide humanity through dark days.

I will close this chapter with a beautiful channelling. I had hopes that some musician would feel compelled to put music to the lyrics, but to this date that has not happened. 'Mr Music, are you out there somewhere?'

LULLABY FOR A NEW-AGE CHILD

My child, you look around you
At a world by violence torn.

In time you may well question
The reason you were born.
Lay down your head in slumber,
Now close your sleepy eyes
And let your spirit wander
To the stars up in the skies.

CHORUS

So, sleep and dream of beauty,
Of harmony and peace:
A new world you'll be making
Where joys will never cease.

The light of love surrounds you,
With love, your spirit grows.
The seeds of hope are in your heart.
They'll grow one day I know.
Bright eyes now closed in slumber
Will see a brave, new day
Where all folk live in harmony,
Where children laugh and play.

My child you lay a-sleeping
In a bed so safe and warm.
The light of love surrounds you,
Protects you from the storm.
In dreams you'll fly on moonbeams,
Bright stars you'll wish upon
And know your wishes will come true
For that's why you were born.

24 SAI BABA: A CALL TO INDIA

A few years after Mike and I married, we were wandering along the streets of Nimbin, a quaint hippy town in northern NSW. There were notices posted in the window of the neighbourhood centre and we paused for a moment to check out anything of interest. On display was a notice inviting people to attend films named *The Lost Years of Jesus Christ* and *Sathya Sai Baba*. Although I had never heard of Sai Baba, I was nevertheless interested in the life of Jesus Christ. So there and then, we decided to attend the viewing.

Viewing a short, pot-bellied, Indian man with an Afro hairstyle wandering among crowds of people at his ashram – Prasanthi Nilayam, Puttaparthi – not far from Bangalore, India, did not impress me. However, Sai Baba materialising Vibhuti ash and jewels for his followers drew my attention.

Before I left the home of the Baba devotee who had organised the films, I went to the bathroom. There, on my own, I was confronted by a vision of Sai Baba. He told me that I was to read a book about him and the cover would have a photo of him with his right hand raised. On reporting this to my host, she lent me the book.

Having recently built our new home, finances were not at an optimum. Within weeks money seemed to flow from the most unexpected sources. Visions of Sai Baba had started to come into my consciousness, so it was decided that I should be one of a party of twelve travelling to India in September. A family of six had moved onto our property and agreed to care for my daughter.

One week before the planned departure for India, I attended my doctor's surgery. His diagnosis: pleurisy. Medication was prescribed with a warning from my doctor that I should not travel, especially to India. But I had become inextricably drawn to what I felt was a spiritual destiny, a spiritual revelation, or the wellsprings where I would find answers to a spiritual quest that had been my life-long path.

Many of Sai Baba's devotees consider him to be one of the avatars of Lord Shiva, the most powerful deity of the Hindu religion. Sai Baba is said to have had two incarnations until now, his own and that of Shirdi Sai Baba.

Shirdi Sai Baba was born in 1838 and died in 1918. Before his death, he predicted that he would come again as a boy in eight years. Sai Baba was born in Puttaparthi, Andhra Pradesh on 23 November 1926. At age thirteen, he announced that he was the reincarnation of Shirdi Sai Baba. Sai Baba died on 24 April 2011, but before his death, he said he would be born again as Prema Sai Baba. Many believe Prema Sai Baba will emerge around 2023 or 2025.

Shirdi Sai Baba said he was an incarnation of Dattatreya – considered to be an avatar of the three Hindu gods, Brahma, Vishnu, and Shiva, collectively known as Trimurti.

The flight from Sydney to Mumbai, formerly known as Bombay, is approximately eighteen hours. This was followed by a domestic flight to Bangalore. During the flight, I was feeling far from well, but I was not the only one. Another member of the group was also suffering from a lung infection and being a compassionate person I shared some of my medication with her.

By the time we reached Bangalore, I was running out of antibiotics and praying for an answer. As I walked with the group down a narrow lane, a voice came into my consciousness: 'Turn right at the next corner, and you will find what you need.'

As the corner was reached, I was surprised to see a sign that read 'Herbalist' above the doorway of a small shop. Immediately after I had entered the shop, an Indian gentleman adjured me to please sit. In perfect English, he said, 'Madam, you are not well. You need antibiotics,' and instantly began to dispense antibiotics from a huge jar. Cough medicine was also offered to me and seeing the situation that just unfolded as something of a miracle, I settled down to a new experience.

As I walked from the Herbalist shop, I noticed a sign reading 'Jewel Merchant'. I was wearing the apported ring with the orange stone that had materialised a few years before. It was quite heavy and very ornate, but I loved it. With the Indian nod of the head, the jewel merchant took and studied the ring. Then a look of delight crossed his face as he remarked, 'Oh, madam. This is a rare Tibetan Cornelian.'

After a night at a hotel in Bangalore, we travelled by bus to Puttaparthi and Sai Baba's ashram, which was to be our home for two weeks. The sights and smells of India are unique! There is beauty, there is mystique, there is history, but there is also poverty. The heady smell of incense and the colour parade of women dressed in beautiful saris is a magnet to one's senses, but there are also smells that are an assault to one's senses.

By the early 1980s Prasanthi Nilayam had become quite a big ashram with a temple, Mandir (Baba's residence), canteen, rows of two-storeyed flats (one room with a small bathroom), and many large sheds used for accommodation. At the time of our arrival, there was a festival happening, no flats were available and our only alternative was to sleep in one of the big sheds along with maybe another 100 women. The toilets were squat-over pit-types with a cold water hose in place of toilet paper. My comfort zone had flown out of the window!

Twice daily I attended darshan – when Sai Baba would walk from his mandir (dwelling) and make a brief circuit of the surrounding grounds, pausing to produce Vibhuti for his dedicated devotees. I cannot say that Baba's presence invoked some kind of rapture within my senses. I persevered, hoping there would be some kind of spiritual revelation.

At 5 am, joining many others, we walked in circles around the temple, silent except for the shuffling of many feet. This was followed by finding a place to sit in the temple to meditate to the sound of chanting. I found it difficult to understand the Hindu custom of paying supplication to their various 'gods', especially Hanuman, the monkey god, and Lord Ganesha, symbolised by an elephant.

Returning to Australia, I continued to read books and watch videos about Sai Baba. More and more Sai Baba groups were springing up around the world. Politicians and movie stars made their way to India to visit the being who was touted as 'God on Earth', a title he is claimed to have expounded. Baba proclaimed that once he reached the age of ninety-six, he would walk into the Chivrati River and simply disappear. He passed in 2011 at the age of eighty-five, leaving his loyal followers distraught.

Although fraudulence and sleight of hand have been ascribed to the many miracles of Sai Baba, in a strange way, I do feel that there was a divine connection to a higher force, in spite of the eventual accusations of corruption, fraud, and sexual improprieties against young schoolboys in Baba's schools and young men in private interviews. An elderly Roman Catholic nun, the sister of a client of mine, returned from Bangalore, India, visiting me with very negative stories surrounding Sai Baba and a copy of a book detailing rather shocking incidents.

Sai Baba expounded that love is the only answer. 'Love is God. Live in love. Start the day with love, spend the day with love, fill the day with love and end the day with love. That is the way to God.' He encouraged devotees to seek their Atma-consciousness where there is no anger, no hatred, no envy, no jealousy, no hunger, no desire. Only complete Ananda. Only bliss, bliss, bliss. He did not ask that devotees relinquish their present religious beliefs, just advised them to become a better person. Sai Baba also insisted devotees practice unconditional love. It has been said that Sathya Sai Baba had up to 100 million followers in 134 countries around the world.

The logo of the Sai Baba Organisations is a six-petalled Lotus, with each petal portraying one of the main religions practised on Earth: Hinduism, Buddhism, Zoroastrianism, Islam, Christianity, and Judaism.

There is also a message of human values in truth, righteousness, peace, divine love, and nonviolence:

> *Just as the lotus plant lives in water but does not get contaminated by it, so we should live in the world but be untouched by it. Let the different faiths exist, let them flourish and let*

> *the glory of God be sung in all languages and in a variety of tunes. That should be the ideal. Respect the differences between the faiths and recognise them as valid as long as they do not extinguish the flame of unity.*
>
> Sathya Sai Baba.

Bhajans (devotional songs) were sung at Sai Baba's ashrams. As they were sung in a foreign language, possibly Hindi, I found it impossible to understand the meaning or feel inspired. I found the solution: I wrote lyrics encompassing not only Sai Baba but also Jesus Christ, Buddha, and Krishna 'as names of God that we can call on too'. Being a pianist and owning a large collection of well-known Western tunes, I set the words to Western melodies. I dutifully printed a stack of songbooks and took them to India along with a beautiful velvet cushion featuring the map of Australia with cities and the Australian native animals embroidered on it.

Al Druker, a long-time devotee of Sai Baba (devotees also addressed Sai Baba as Sri Sathya Sai Baba or Swami), wrote books and spoke at length on videos of how he first became aware of Sai Baba. As a young man, Al was piloting a small plane over the Sierra Mountains in the USA. A severe storm hit. The fuel gauge showed empty. Al cried out to God for help. Over the cockpit speaker, a calm loving voice guided him to safety and a landing at a private strip owned by a Sai Baba devotee. When Al travelled to India and had an interview with Sai Baba, Sai Baba related his knowledge and connection over the almost fatal plane trip.

A couple of years after my first trip to Sai Baba, I was approached by a woman I had known from the time I was an organist at a Brisbane Spiritualist church around 1978. She had become a devotee and organiser of groups travelling to India. For every ten paid bookings, she received one free trip. Being unable to travel herself at that time, I was offered the free trip in return for organising a party of twelve people.

My husband and fifteen year old daughter accompanied me on that trip, and we got to see a little more of the countryside of India. Money for their fares seemed to appear out of thin air as a friend and Sai Baba devotee we had assisted with buying property helped with the finances.

Prior to our departure, I was inspired to sew baby and toddler clothes for Mother Theresa's orphanages. Four boxes were packed with beautiful clothes and transported along with our luggage to the Madras Airport.

We arrived at the Madras Airport at night to find there was a problem with the lighting outside the terminal. Taxi drivers were operating by torchlight amid some confusion. The boxes of clothing were put on roof racks, and I was assured they would be secure. On reaching the hotel where we were to spend a night, our suitcases were placed before us but, alas, the boxes of clothing were gone!

My heart sank as I thought of the joy I felt, anticipating poor Indian children being dressed in pretty, new clothes and the despair I experienced at the loss. I prayed for an answer.

As I prayed, a vision came into my consciousness: the hands of God shuffling a pack of playing cards. Out from the pack flew the royal cards – the kings, the queens – and I was told the churches had money to buy clothes for the children. The hands of God once again shuffled the cards. In the vision before me lay the ten of spades and ten of clubs, and I was told that they were symbolic of the great numbers of poor people who could not afford beautiful clothes for their children. Spiritually, assurance was given to me that the clothes had gone to much-needed destinations.

In 1990, one of my clients, Kath, offered to pay my fare to India if I would accompany her to Sai Baba's ashram. I agreed.

On television, the story of a Brisbane Catholic nun in charge of an orphanage in Madras was featured. At that time, I was designing and manufacturing toddler clothing in a small home business and felt compelled to take some of my creations to help with the orphanage.

On the way to the airport, I crunched down on a sweet, breaking a tooth that painfully cut into my tongue. By the time Kath and I reached Madras, I was desperately seeking a dentist and found it hard to be understood at the hotel where we were staying.

Feeling very nonplussed, Kath and I got a taxi to the orphanage, delivered the boxes of clothes for the children, and were served cold tea by the kindly nun in charge. The children dressed in their new finery performed a special concert for us. Quite a few of the children were deformed. On questioning as to whether their condition was due to in-breeding, I was told that most were the result of unsuccessful abortion attempts.

An Indian man, wearing a lovely red shirt, came into the nun's office. She introduced him as a doctor. As I expressed admiration for his red shirt, she volunteered that he was the dentist at the orphanage. Of course, Kath immediately spoke up for my need, and within minutes, I was sitting in the dental chair having the broken tooth attended to. A miracle??

That third visit to India was not to Puttaparthi but to Sai Baba's ashram at Whitefield. There were vast crowds there, and we were told that there was no accommodation available. Within an hour of our arrival, I was greeted by Shirley, one of my clients who had heard of Sai Baba through me. Shirley had relinquished her all to live in India and teach and had transitioned from an elegantly coifed, well-dressed businesswoman to wearing a sari and sporting a white ponytail hairstyle.

With a little help from Shirley, Kath, another friend Sonia, and I were allocated a small room to be shared with an Indian lady and her daughter. Spartan as the ashrams were, shared bathrooms were down the hall. Blow-up mattresses we had brought were our beds, and I had sewn myself a mosquito-proof tent in order to sleep without attack from the mosquitoes.

Two days after our arrival at Whitefield, I was spiritually asked if I would agree to take a vow of silence and, apart from attending the bathroom, not leave the room for three days. As a prolific talker, that was a lot to ask, yet I agreed. My vow led to both serious and humorous incidents.

Before settling into the ashram at Whitefield, Kath and I had shopped in the many venues offering saris and Punjabi suits. As I have sewn for myself for most of my life, it is always a treat to buy a ready-made garment, so buying three Punjabi suits was a real bonus for me.

On the second day of my vow, I decided to get dressed in a beautiful orange Punjabi suit embroidered in black and white. The first problem I encountered was that although sewn, the buttonholes on the front of the garment had not been cut. Then, as I pulled on the pants of the suit, I found that the tie drawstring was missing. Immediately into my consciousness came the words, 'Now will you be like a good Indian wife – obedient – and let God be the boss?'

Towards the end of the third day of my vow, I was 'told' that I could go to the canteen for a meal and that I should offer myself for 'seva' (selfless service). Sonia had been bringing me food and coffee – serving me with love – and I felt my offer was compensatory to the universe.

Still in my vow of silence, I gesticulated to the sari-clad managers of the canteen in a bizarre charade-like way, offering to help make chapatis. Standing among some young girls and a few women, I began rolling balls of dough ready for others to flatten them out, ready for cooking. Suddenly a heap of walnut-sized balls of dough were thrown down before me with the retort, 'You Westerners do not know how to make chapatis! Please do them again.' Keeping to my silent vow, I had no other choice than to cop it sweet, knowing that the products thrown down before me were not of my making.

On my way back to my lodgings, I overheard a young Australian boy state that someone said I was crazy because I would not talk. Again, zealous to my vow, I could not defend myself.

On the fourth day at Whitefield I attended darshan. Sai Baba walked past me, then did a little back-step, stared intently at me, then walked on. Because of this, it was no surprise to me when I awoke the next morning to be told by Spirit, 'Go home to Australia. You have no need to be here. God is in your heart, in Australia, wherever you are. Travel light. Take only what you need to assist your journey.'

The fact we had planned to stay another two weeks at the ashram and that Kath had paid my fare to India really worried me. I offered her what money I could afford, trying to explain that I had to obey divine orders as I had done many times in my life, but my explanations could not assuage her disappointment in me. I told Kath that I was psychically told that Sai Baba was 'the Devil's Advocate' (Oxford Dictionary: a professional pleader in a court of justice).

I gave my suitcase and two of my beautiful Punjabi suits and saris to the Indian mother and daughter, along with my blow-up mattress and anything else dispensable. Then I got a taxi to the Bangalore airport carrying just my handbag, toiletries, and a plastic bag holding two shirts for Mike and one of the Punjabi suits.

Once at the airport, I sat meditating, processing, and planning, albeit a bit confused. The realisation hit me that Kath was in possession of both of our airline tickets. As I asked for an answer, into my consciousness came the words, 'You have the phone number of a taxi driver you have met a number of times. Phone him, and he can bring your ticket to the airport'. As I waited for the taxi to arrive, I was put to yet another test. Into my consciousness came the following dialogue: 'The taxi driver is a hard-working family man. His wife is a schoolteacher. The Punjabi suit you are carrying would make a lovely gift for this kind man to give to his wife.' So obediently, I parted with the lovely turquoise Punjabi suit, embroidered down one side with pink lilies edged with silver.

The year was 1990, the time of the Gulf War, and people were fleeing Kuwait in droves. Many were travelling through Madras, the airport transport halls packed and chaotic. I had travelled from Bangalore to Madras with only hand luggage. Had I been carrying baggage to check-in en route to Singapore, I would not have been able to get a seat on a plane.

As the plane lifted from the tarmac, I breathed a sigh of relief to be on my way back to Australia, unaware that my testing was far from over. The first test was as the aircraft flew over the Indian Ocean and became embroiled in a severe electrical storm. Out the window, I watched lightning strikes and felt the plane being tossed around like a feather in the wind. I surrendered myself to whatever the universe had in store for me.

By early morning, I had travelled by taxi from the Singapore airport to a hotel where I booked a room for two nights. My room was on the eighth floor. I showered then climbed into bed, expecting to find respite in sleep. My need for sleep was shattered as I began having precognition of an earthquake, so realistic that I questioned the safety of being in that multi-storeyed building.

With an overwhelming sense of urgency to get home, I returned to Singapore Airport. The words 'write a letter to Mary' kept repeating in my mind. Was it Mother Mary I was to pray to? Believe me, I was praying to whatever divine personage would hear my prayers.

An employee at the office of Air India was sympathetic to my plea and agreed to arrange a transfer to another airline company that would allow me to leave Singapore that afternoon. With the usual nod of the Indian head, he stated, 'I will write a letter to Mary', Mary being a contact at the airline company he was transferring me to.

I was psychically warned though, that there would be danger of a bomb threat on an airline, even being given a vision of the perpetrators. As I lined up to board, two men fitting the vision I'd had were in the line ahead of me. By the time I reached the counter, my heart was pounding. I guess it must have been obvious as the airline clerk asked whether I was okay. When I said I felt I was having a heart attack, she immediately called for help, and I was taken to a medical clinic upstairs in the airport. ECGs on two separate machines showed severe atrial fibrillation and a doctor suggested I become a patient in a Singapore hospital. I had no money to pay for hospitals, so I asked for sleeping pills to settle me down and left the clinic, intending to return to the hotel.

Again, I found myself thrust ahead in time, feeling the presence of an earthquake. Desperately I cried out to Spirit for help and was told to go out into a garden to sleep. Outside of the terminal lay a huge car park – acres of concrete. Where was the garden? My gaze was drawn to a raised freeway bordering the airport, separated from the car park by lawns and hedges. There, behind hedges, I lay exhausted and slept for a few hours.

It still amazes me to think of how I managed to chop and change my airline ticket between carriers. I eventually succeeded in getting my original flight from Singapore to Australia reinstated with Air India.

I found a few Australian dollars a friend had given me to buy Ayurvedic goods, cashed the money in for local currency and bought some breakfast: a croissant and coffee. A young Asian lady asked permission to share my table in the restaurant, and as she sat opposite me, I began to psychically tune in to her life. When I related some information pertinent to her, she was absolutely delighted. 'How do you know such things?' she asked. I answered that I was a clairvoyant-medium. The young lady was really excited at that news and asked if I would correspond with her as she had always wanted to meet someone like me. I agreed and was literally blown away when she said, 'Please write a letter to me. My name is Mary.'

My hunger appeased, I took advantage of free samples of perfume and hand cream at an airport chemist shop. Ensuites for hire at airports were unknown to me. So when Spirit told me to 'go have a shower', I totally disbelieved. Psychically, instructions were given to me, guiding me to another part of the huge Singapore Airport. As I turned a corner, I saw a sign advertising a facility for showers. I took a deep breath and felt deep down that I was being looked after.

By mid-afternoon, I was aboard the flight I had initially been booked on and tried to settle down and relax. But that was not to be. There was an urgent call to disembark, police and dogs swarming around the place. A bomb threat had been made on that plane!

Eventually, the plane was cleared for take-off, and I thanked God that at least I was now being carried home safely.

One of my clairvoyant clients was a brilliant portrait artist. Perusing a book about Sai Baba, she offered to execute two paintings to hang in my seminar centre. When an avalanche of adverse publicity about Sai Baba began to play out to the world, Mike promptly burnt the paintings. I suspect word of this got back to my client as I never saw her again and in no way blame her if she felt angry.

One of many spiritual tests I have faced involved the ring that was apported. One evening as Mike and I sat in front of a roaring fire, I was asked whether or not I was willing to throw the orange Cornelian ring and another ring I owned into the fire as an act of obedience to God. Of course, although I really loved the ring, I agreed. The next morning Mike and I sifted through the ashes in the fireplace. The man-made ring was molten, but there was no sign of either the metal or the Cornelian from the apported ring.

Revelations

There have been many times that Sai Baba has appeared to me both when he was in body and in spirit and also in many channelled writings. The one I value most, the one I find most pertinent to the cause I wish to attain, is the following received on 19 May 1989.

That cause is to establish a centre in a rural setting where people may visit to understand or find their spirituality, a re-establishment of the centre I managed for over twenty years.

There was movement at the station
For the word had got around
That a special Mountain Mission had begun.
All of those joined by Swami's Graces
One by one will take their place
And a new ground will soon be broken
By the way.
All the people from the city
Come to see what keeps them busy,
Bhajans sung along with song
To all creation.
As the soil is dug and weeded
And the future food is seeded
While the sounds of saws and hammers
Lend their ring.
Leave the theatres, leave the glamour
And the crazy folk who clamour
For a glimpse of something new
To please their taste:
For the work of farms and seva

Keeps the willing soul forever
On a forward path,
A path where there's no waste.
Karmic lives in many places
Have assured you all your bases
In a place that has been chosen for a few.
For the Hierarchy that guides you
Knows the size and fit of each shoe
And will watch each step
As each one holds their sway.
Little children on the mountain
I am proud to be the fountain
That you come to when you thirst
Or are in pain.
Just consider that the seasons
Are a changing for a reason
And the rains that fall
Are plainly not in vain.
Do not harbour mind confusion
To the soul that is contusion
Just pretend the mind's a boat
With swelling sails.
In the days ahead I'll give you
What the heart and soul aspire to
And I give my word
You'll have no need to bail.
All my children I adore you
And I really must implore you
To keep schedules tight
And projects underway.
For the Mighty Hand will never

Tell you when the past will sever
For to greet the dawning
Of a brand-new day.
You must give and take most freely
Of the Spirit and the Healing.
See the like of me
In all of those you meet.
What you'd give to your Dear Baba
You must give to one another
If you don't, the soul
The goal will never meet.
By the hand that gives Vibhuti
I bind all who're here to treaty
To abide by all the rules
And all the creeds.
For I walk with each and know you
And in time, Dear Ones, I'll show you
That your paths are blessed
When journey's end is reached.

Since I was a teenager, Revelation, the last book in the Holy Bible, has held somewhat of a fascination for me. It is very cryptic, to say the least, and open to many interpretations. Some modern scholars characterise Revelation's author as a person they call 'John of Patmos', dating the time of writing to the reign of the Roman emperor Domitian (AD 81-96). The chapter spans three literary genres: the epistolary, the apocalyptic, and the prophetic. The chapter culminates in the second coming of Jesus Christ.

In the final verses, the following words are purported to have been channelled to John from Jesus Christ: 'I am both

David's root and his descendant. I am the bright Morning Star. The Spirit and the bride say, "Come!" Let each one who hears them say the same, "Come!"'

The 'bright Morning Star' referred to is the planet, Venus. Lucifer, also known as Satan, is also referred to as 'lux-lucis' (light) and 'ferre' (to bring), referring to the Morning Star, the planet Venus that appears at dawn. Another woman I had introduced to Sai Baba refused to speak to me after I told her I had been 'told' that Sai Baba was 'the Devil's Advocate'. She insisted I had said he was 'the Devil Incarnate'.

My personal hypothesis is that duality is involved in the above interpretations, i.e., good/bad, hot/cold, spiritual/evil etc.; and that the part Sai Baba played in placing himself before literally thousands of people, whose personal responsibility it was to decide for themselves whether or not he was 'God come to Earth', was in fact duality playing out.

I now direct your attention to Revelation 13:11-14:

> *Then I saw another strange animal, this one coming up out of the earth, with two little horns like those of a lamb but a fearsome voice like the Dragon's. He exercised all the authority of the Creature whose death wound had been healed, whom he required all the world to worship. He did unbelievable miracles, such as making fire flame down to Earth from the skies while everyone was watching. By doing these miracles, he was deceiving people everywhere. He could do these marvellous things whenever the first Creature was there to watch him.*

As Jesus Christ is referred to as 'the Lamb of God', does the creature referred to above point to an Anti-Christ or an Ante-Christ, a 'false prophet' operating with the permission of Jesus

Christ in order to test people on Earth as to their vulnerability of persuasion?

In 1996, Jesus Christ and Sai Baba appeared to me and channelled the following verses:

Beloved: Cain and Abel
Are the bed, are the table.
Cain is the nightmares,
Abel the dreams.
Cain is the Thunder
And Abel Moonbeams.
Cain-man looks downward
And Abel looks up.
Cain-man will guzzle,
While Abel will sup.
Cain has a Heaven he cannot ascribe
For he killed his brother and wine did imbibe.
Abel has Heaven, can't comprehend Hell,
His life filled with loving,
His work done so well.
Cain lives in shadow
And Abel in light.
Cain is the black one
And Abel the white.

Cain is the sexual, the sordid, the sad.
Cain is the greedy, the guilty, the bad.
Abel is loving, and caring, and kind.
Abel has clarity of heart and of mind.
Both are in man as man is in God.
Lord Jesus is Abel and rules with a rod.

But Christhood can't meter a punishment true
So, the truth of the matter
I'll lay before you.
Sai Baba administers justice per se
As the planet's condition becomes 'Feet of Clay'.
But Sai Baba and Cain who strike with the rod
Only mete out justice if given the nod
Of Jesus and Abel who with heart see things clear
And whisper directions in Sai Baba's ear.
Sai Baba's the fulcrum upon which Mankind rests,
The Advocate true who administers tests.
But to cling to his robe and to follow his ways
Would mean you'd be tackled, surrender your days
To the will of The Serpent, the Ancient of Days,
The path of the Ida, Pingala and more.
The path of the Legends of Light and of Law.
Each soul in creation who follows this road
Can travel with Jesus if they cast off their load.
Then they will be Abel and they will be free
To eat of the fruit of the great Knowledge Tree.
And once having tasted the fruit sweet and ripe,
Will see as the Red Man with Peace and with Pipe.
He is really not Cain and he's really not Abel.
He's a cross between Truth and a very old Fable.
He's a bit of the Abel, a bit of the Cain.
A measure of joy and a measure of pain.
But then as man sees with this wisdom so rare,
The darkness will fade from his face and his hair
As Abel he is to become white as snow;
At the end of his journey
His Christ he will know.

Sai Baba appeared to me with tears in his eyes. He communicated to me that he was like the chimney sweep cleaning soot out of folks' chimneys in order that they might look up to the light of God and feel the warmth of God's Love. The following rhyme then was channelled:

I am the old, and you are the new.
You have the sweets, and I'm in the stew.
You have a Saviour, and I have Him not.
That is the story and, hereby, the plot.
I came from Heaven, and I took on birth.
I loved my ego; compounded my worth.
I look folks over, forlorn and in pain.
I seek adoration, and I seek gain.
You have the heart, and you have the mind.
And you are no longer spiritually blind.
I am a wonder to much of this world.
You will be known before comets are hurled.
You I've tormented, tested and more.
Christ gives you courage; it's Him you adore.
You are the mooring where ships run from storm.
You have the nest that is peaceful and warm.
You have Mount Warning, it tells you the truth.
My life is in danger – you'll soon see the proof.
For many of men who began life with me
Silently wish now that they could be free.
Fighting, frustration, foundations of sand,
That's now a picture of Sai Baba's Band.
News of an image alight in the sky
Will make you wonder, will make you cry.
For, in the Beginning, we melded as One.

But now I'm the Sweeper
And Jesus – God's Son.

Sai Baba claimed to be an Avatara – a living incarnation of the Divine. To his followers, he was a Living God, a claim he never disputed. He often talked of himself as being 'the Supra-worldly Divinity in Human Form' and 'the World Saviour'. When an American devotee asked Sai Baba directly whether he claimed to be God, Sai Baba is said to have replied, 'Let us say I am the switch'.

Although Sathya Sai Baba adjourned his followers to 'become a better one in whatever religion they followed', he was born into a Hindu family, and his ashrams were conducted on Hindu beliefs.

The Hindu pantheon consists of several gods and goddesses, believed to be the manifestations of the Supreme Being. Each deity has a specific dharma (duty) and purpose for taking a form. Among them, Lord Shiva is referred to as the most powerful. He, along with Brahma and Vishnu, makes the Trinity which takes care of the process of birth, sustenance, and death. Shiva is often referred to as the 'destroyer', but in reality, it is he who destroys the impurities that take refuge in the human mind. He rids a body of its shortcomings and makes it worthy of attaining moksha (release from the cycle of rebirth). Therefore, it is he who is in charge of destruction because unless the old perishes, the new wouldn't be able to take birth.

There is no doubt in my mind that we are at present living in the biblical times of 'tribulation' and 'resurrection'. Many souls on planet Earth at this time have earned their ascension through many incarnations of testing. A psycho-spiritual change is being felt by many people.

When asked about the Kingdom of God, Jesus Christ said, 'Most assuredly I say unto you, unless one is born again, he cannot see the Kingdom of God.' Once humans have developed a more evolved degree of consciousness, imbued with love for all creation, devoid of jealousies, greed, and negativity, a New Age will begin. Will this be the promised Kingdom of God?

And let us not forget the suffering of our Gaia, our Mother Earth. She has been the stage upon which vicious wars have been fought, and nuclear bombs have exploded. Oil and gas and coal have been leached from her body, and poisons dumped upon her land and in her seas. Like citrus fruit that has been juiced, her shell has become unstable, the livening up of volcanoes and the Ring of Fire sheer testimony to that fact.

Man and God are inseparable by virtue of 'the Higher Self' or Atma (eternal soul) – the Universal Divine spark which is in all beings.

In Genesis 1:26 in the Holy Bible it is written: 'Then God said, 'Let us make a man – someone like ourselves, to be the master of all life upon the earth and in the skies and in the seas.'

'So God made man like his Maker.

Like God did God make man;

Man and maid did he make them.'

The fact that God was talking in the plural sense has always held a fascination for me. This is a topic for a future book.

In mid-July 1986, I channelled the following text, which was described to me as 'an analogy of numbers.' The epochs listed hereunder are periods of time in which I had incarnations on Earth. I am no computer expert; however, I challenge any competent computer programmer to explain how these numbers came to be.

An analogy of numbers

The number of The Beast: 666

I was told to add the numbers of 24 July 1986 in separate quanta to find the 666 as beginning the year that would reveal the surfacing of the beast mentioned in Revelation, the Holy Bible. I queried the date as:

2 + 4 = 6

July = 7

1 + 9 + 8 + 6 = 24

2 + 4 = 6

I was told that Jesus Christ was not born on 25 December but on 15 February, which would set our calendar back by one month. The Gregorian calendar begins from the date of the birth of Jesus Christ, making February the first month of the year. Therefore:

2 + 4 = 6

July = 6

1 + 9 + 8 + 6 = 24

2 + 4 = 6

666

I was then told to check up on the date that Joan of Arc was burnt at the stake. I was told to deduce the number of years between that year, 1431, and 1986, which is 555.

I was next told to check up on which year Saint Patrick established his Archiepiscopal see at Armagh, Ireland. In 441, Saint Patrick travelled to Rome and received the pallium from Pope St Leo I. He established his Archiepiscopal see at Armagh in the year 444.

I was then told to look up King Darius III, who was a King of Persia and adversary of Alexander the Great. I was told to check the date he was defeated by Alexander when he invaded Persis (Persia). The battle of Issus was in the year 333 BC.

Next, I was drawn to the life of Ptolemy IV, Pharaoh of Ancient Egypt during the Ptolemaic dynasty. He had his mother, his brother, and his uncle killed. Ptolemy IV reigned from the year 222 BC.

I was told that the above eras were times when I had had an incarnation.

In late 2019 I was told to research the date that WWI began. I was then told to add the number 111 to that date to find the date that would change the world as we know it. WWI began on 28 July 1914.

$$28.7.1914 + 111 = 28.7.2025$$

Use of computers is a skill I have taught myself. Although I am not highly conversant with computer technology, I doubt the above triple numbers could have been arrived at physically.

While I am no exponent of Indian astrology, let me set out the following ideas so that you, dear reader, can research further.

It is written in Indian astrology that Kalki is the tenth avatar of the Hindu god Vishnu prophesied to appear at the end of the Kali Yuga age to punish the wicked, reward the good, and inaugurate the Satya Yuga age of sacrifice and dharma. Kalki is described in the Puranas as the avatar who rejuvenates existence by ending the darkest and most destructive period to remove adharma and usher in the Satya Yuga, while riding a white horse with a fiery sword.

In reference to the white horse, it may be noted that Sathya Sai Baba was born on 23 November 1926, meaning he was born under the sign of Sagittarius – the Archer on a white horse. Based on the Sagittarian sign, I also query the meaning of the following verse from Revelation in the Holy Bible. Revelation 19:11:

> *Then I saw Heaven opened and a white horse standing there, and the one sitting on the horse was named 'Faithful and True' – the one who justly punishes and makes war. His eyes were like flames and on his head were many crowns. A name was written on his forehead, and only he knew its meaning. He was clothed with garments dipped in blood, and his title was 'The Word of God'.*

The name Sathya means 'truth'. Sathya Sai Baba claimed to be an Avatar – in Hinduism, a manifestation of a deity or released soul in bodily form on Earth, an incarnate divine teacher. He dressed in red robes, and his devotees interpreted the 'many crowns upon his head' as his Afro hairstyle.

And the words 'the one who justly punishes and makes war'? I am inclined to view the words 'punishes' and 'makes war' rather loosely. Rather I see Sai Baba as the Devil's Advocate – his teachings adjuring one to look at and modify their behaviour in a more spiritual way.

And what have I learnt from my journeys, my searching? I have come to realise that there is no need to run hither and thither around the world seeking 'God'. For God is in all. Therefore, we must love and respect all, even they who differ from our way of thinking and living.

For almost thirty years, I was honoured to be ordained as a minister of the Spiritualist church and for many years officiated at Mitana Christian Spiritualist Church, performing marriages, baptisms, and funerals. Now I prefer not to wear a label of religion that would set me apart from others.

In 2020, the Statue of Belief – a statue of Lord Shiva standing 351 feet high – was constructed at Ganesh Tekri in Rajasthan's Nathdwara. This is the tallest statue of Lord Shiva, also known as 'the Destroyer', within the Trimurti, the Hindu trinity that includes Brahma and Vishnu. In the Shaivite tradition, Shiva is the Supreme Lord who creates, protects, and transforms the universe. Shiva is known as the Destroyer God because he removes all evil from the world. His wife is the Goddess Parvati. He has a blue neck because, according to Hindu legend, he swallowed a poison in order to save the universe.

In answer to my question, 'Why does Shiva carry a trident?' (a three-pronged spear), I received the following answer: tri meaning three and 'sula' meaning spear, the weapon held by Lord Shiva is of great significance. It is believed that Shiva's trishula destroys the physical world, which is illusion, the mental world, which is ego, and then takes us to the third world, which is spiritualism.

In answer to, 'What does the trident symbolise?' The trident is typically used to describe the weapon that characterises Poseidon as the god of the sea. The trident signified the domination of the seas across Roman, Greek, and Hindu mythologies. To the Romans, he is Mercury; to the Greeks, he is Poseidon; to the Hindus, he is Lord Shiva. In some schools, Poseidon is also known as the 'Greek god of the sea and earthquakes'.

Is it Sathya Sai Baba, Shiva, or Poseidon that is referred to in Revelation, when it speaks of the Creature from the sea? Or is it the concrete capped dome over the nuclear waste at Bikini Atoll, which I feel could rupture in the advent of the livening up of the Ring of Fire?

25 > MUSLIM PROPHECY FOR END DAYS

The Dajjal will appear. He is a false messiah, a liar.

A young man with a ruddy complexion. Short, with thick curly hair, a wide forehead, broad upper chest, blind or defective in the right eye (or metaphysically one-eyed). His left eye will have a thick piece of flesh growing at the edge (a mole?).

He will have no children. He will appear around thirty years of age and will reign for forty years.

He will appear to perform great miracles. He will be known worldwide.

He will claim to be God.

Allah will allow him to perform mighty wonders in order to test mankind. He will be a jinn.

Between his eyes will be a Kafir (something hidden); (a Bindi dot?).

BABA???

26   MY EXTRATERRESTRIAL EXPERIENCE

The year was 1980. Mike and I had been married for about eight months, during which time we had been living in a tent and shed. The intrusion of a snake into the tent was the end of my camping days, and with the generosity of a local farmer named George, we had moved into an old farmhouse.

One morning I awoke with the clear memory of being taken from the house by three little beings with large, black, almond-shaped eyes. I recalled Mike and myself sitting on metal benches in a room constructed of metal then a memory of myself lying on an operating table with large lights above me. As the strange beings were looking down at me, I was unable to move.

Relating the experience to Mike, he had no memories of the experience, either actual or a dream. It was very clear and real to me. And this was some years before stories about the Greys – aliens – extraterrestrials – were made public.

About eighteen months before, while still living in Brisbane, I bought a reconditioned lawnmower from an elderly man named Frank Howard. This dear man was spiritual, humble and an amazing spiritual channel. His book, *Journey into Space* with *Alizantil*, is composed of forty-eight pages, each page containing three columns. The dialogue is mainly between Alizantil and his partner Elanza; as aboard a cosmic liner, they discuss mankind, the state of our planet, Earthlings, and what they survey in their journey around planet Earth. The past history of planet Earth is discussed, as is their concern for the future of mankind and Mother Earth.

Before I left Brisbane, I read for Frank Howard, telling him that his best writings were still to come. Within the next year or so, Frank channelled two more books, *The Return of Alizantil* and *An Extraterrestrial Message to the Nations*.

The messages in Frank's writings warned how Earth is on a destructive course when viewed from the perspective of ecological devastation, war, greed and sickness. They speak of how the Brotherhood of Beings of the Great Galactic Order is saddened by the careless behaviour of mankind.

To quote Frank Howard:

> *Man must be awakened, and even the smallest candle lit may be comforting to the wanderer, yet may seem a feeble light to those who know already the brilliance of a Master's Presence. Nevertheless, if this work helps to guide but one soul towards the Light of Love and Service, then it shall have been worth the countless hours.*

I felt no fear of the Greys. Since that time, I have had meetings with the Great White Brotherhood and the Ascended Masters on a spiritual plane.

About ten years after my experience with the Greys, I began to experience their invisible presence, introduced by the smell of electrical wires burning. On discussing this with a friend, she invited me to attend a UFO conference in Brisbane where, among many other things, speakers were discussing abductions.

Whitley Strieber, a Canadian journalist, was a guest speaker. To this day, the author of more than forty books, Whitley Strieber spoke of his encounter with the Greys, becoming aware of their presence by the smell of burning cardboard. His book, *Communion*, tells of these experiences. It was comforting to me to know that others had had similar experiences to me.

In my fifties, during my studies with Dr Stan Grof, sessions of regression, recalling memories buried in the unconscious mind, were part of the workshops.

During one of these regression sessions, I recalled with clarity the night of my abduction years before. In my recall, I saw that Mike was not with me on what I came to realise was a spaceship. It appeared as though the beings had the power to dematerialise and rematerialise, taking me right through the walls of the bedroom. When I began to panic, they created a holographic vision of Mike to allay my fears.

The morning after a weekend workshop convened by Dr John Whitman-Ray, my eyelids refused to open. A fellow student, a well-qualified nurse, was staying with us at the time. In answer to my queries from Spirit as to this anomaly, I was told that a process was taking place in my brain that necessitated blocking the light. It was explained to me as equating to a film in the old box Brownie cameras, which had to be handled in a darkroom lest the photographs be ruined. Within twenty-four hours, my eyelids were back to normal.

Sometime later, the episode of eyelids refusing to open repeated but was accompanied by atrial fibrillation. Mike and

I decided to go to the local hospital, where I asked to see a local doctor who had been attending the workshops. She was on duty, and I was hoping that she would believe me. I believe she felt that I was in a state of paranoia. CAT scans were ordered for the next morning, at which time my eyes were open, and the atrial fibrillation had ceased.

Mike drove me from the hospital to the radiographer as, at that time, the hospital did not have the CAT scanner installed. As a young lady prepared me for the scan, I asked her if she had heard anything relating to extraterrestrials. Absolute fear filled her eyes as she refused to listen to what I had to say. The radiographer entered the room. When I asked him the same question, he retorted, 'Oh, you mean something like *X-Files?*' (a sci-fi series).

There have been no more repeats of my eyelids feeling as though they were glued together. However, there were other anomalies even stranger.

Following further attendances at workshops, my nurse friend again spent the night at our home. While sitting in our lounge room, I felt a pain in the right side of my brain. It felt rather like a red-hot needle piercing my skull. After explaining what was happening, my friend sat in the same chair, and she too had the experience.

Feeling rather freaked out at the red-hot needle experience, I decided to spend a few days at my friend's house. Something compelled me to make a bonnet of alfoil. Some years later, I saw a movie called *Signs* involving extraterrestrials, and one of the cast was wearing a hat made of alfoil.

The first night at my friend's home, my bed was on the bottom level of the bunks. As I began to fall asleep, a 'pinging' sound began as though an invisible force was hitting the wire mesh of the bunk above me. I called out to my friend, who also heard the pinging.

I loved the spiritual property and centre Mike and I had created. I was in awe of strange beams of light, unseen by the eye but appearing in photos, some resembling rays of sun emanating from about one o'clock high, even though taken at about 7.30 am. Together with a neighbour, we had witnessed what looked like searchlights moving across the cliff face of the mountains adjacent to our property. These lights were directed from a blind valley unable to be accessed by vehicles.

When I bought the property in 1979, I came across a large circle of burned grass near the boundary. At that time, I knew nothing of UFO circles or crop circles but on reflecting, feel it was indicative of a visitation. Governments of the world have for years professed ignorance of the existence of UFOs and extraterrestrials, and yet there has been evidence to the contrary.

In my late fifties, I attended Transpersonal workshops at Macquarie University in Sydney. One of the workshops was conducted by Professor John Mack, who had been head of the Department of Psychiatry at Harvard Medical School in the USA. Professor Mack completed his psychoanalytic training with honours and distinction and went on to win many awards.

For many years, Professor Mack had been a sceptic about extraterrestrials. In the early 1990s, his attitude drastically changed, much to the condemnation of many of his colleagues.

Professor Mack studied consciousness expansion with Dr Stan Grof and his late wife, Christina, at California's Esalen Institute. Through Holotropic breathwork, Mack later said he owed a lot to the Grofs (as do I). He stated, 'They put a hole in my psyche, and the UFOs flew in.'

He acquired a grant and travelled the world interviewing people who had made contact with or witnessed visitors from outer space. I viewed videos he made while interviewing a variety of people, from suburban dwellers to indigenous tribespeople.

Quite by coincidence, Glennys, the minister who ordained me, was also attending the workshop. And again, by coincidence, she had a copy of a photo taken at my property showing amazing rays. After Glennys had shown the photo to Professor John Mack, he asked to visit my property along with an Aboriginal elder.

In my library, I have two books written by John Mack: *Abduction* and *Passport to the Cosmos*. Sadly, in 1974, while in London lecturing, John was struck and killed by a vehicle operated by a man under the influence of alcohol.

There was no contact with the extraterrestrials for many years; however, lately, I have had a few brief visitations.

It would be very naïve of us to expect that planet Earth is the only habited planet in the universe. As the universe seems never-ending, there are probably many planets containing life, even if not by the same design as Earth.

As told in Part One, during my late twenties and early thirties, I lived in New Guinea. After I had become friendly with village people from the Huon Gulf area, they built me a holiday house on the beach in their village. They taught me their dialect, and in 1970, I wrote the first dictionary of the Yahapa dialect. During a visit to the village in 1998, I was presented with a copy of the first professional dictionary that was compiled by Dr Jeff Siegel from the University of New England, Armidale NSW.

Many years after returning to Australia, on a return visit, I was initiated into the tribe and given tribal papers. The inhabitants of the village were very intelligent, many of their youth leaving to train and accept positions necessitating high intellect.

In my late thirties, I contacted Erich von Däniken, who was speaking on a Brisbane radio station at the time. I discussed the above matter of the Yahapa dialect with him and was invited to a lecture he gave. Erich von Däniken has written many books, made many movies and, still today, promotes his theories of extraterrestrial visitations to planet Earth and their connections to this day.

In the 1970s, Erich von Däniken was invited to a secret speech at NASA where he met Josef F Blumrich. Following this meeting, Blumrich had an epiphany regarding Ezekiel's description in the Bible of a divine chariot of God. Blumrich was convinced it was, instead, a spacecraft. He went on to patent his own version of an omnidirectional wheel, according to Ezekiel's description.

To bring this result into context: in Ezekiel's day, crafts such as aeroplanes were not known. If, on Ezekiel's return home from tending his flocks, he asked his wife what news she had of the day, what would be her answer? 'Well, something that looked like my washing basket with fire around it and making a noise like thunder landed in the paddock.' In today's estimate, would we interpret that as a UFO or a spaceship?

I would like to put before you my hypothesis:

My theory is that the Labu people of New Guinea are descendants of the Lost Tribe of Israel. Tudor Parfitt wrote a book titled *The Lost Ark of the Covenant* in which he disputed a claim by New Guinean Sepik tribespeople that they were related to the Israelites.

Nevertheless, there are some anomalies you may wish to consider. It has been suggested to me that the Yahapa dialect may relate to Aramaic, but I feel more inclined to think it relates to an Akkadian language and ancient Mesopotamian culture. From the outset, I was impressed that the Yahapa dialect seemed too sophisticated to be primitive and that it appeared to make reference to extraterrestrials.

Following are some examples:

The transitive verb alters to six variants depending upon the person or persons involved.

I go…………………………Ai ndana

You go…………………......Je nana

He goes…………………….Eni nana

We two go………………....Alu lana

A group go……………….Maha mana

All go…………………….Esoha sana

The Yahapa word for God is 'Sapakwa'. 'Sapa' is the word for moon. 'Kwa' or 'gwa' is a craft. 'Ekato' is the word heaven. One of the young men from the village had a tattoo of a mermaid on his arm. When I questioned whether he had copied it from an ex-pat, he explained it was a picture of 'Henasekato' – the woman from Heaven. In the Yahapa dialect, the names of all fish start with the letter 'e'. Is it possible that there is a link to the Egyptian god Oannes?

The Yahapa methodology for counting appears to me to be relating to the Akkadian story of Gilgamesh and creation. It has been my belief for many years that the story of Adam and Eve has no relationship to a snake handing an apple to Eve. Show me where to find such a serpent, and I would be an instant millionaire! In Yahapa, counting appears to refer to creation in five days, not seven as in the Bible, and also with two people and a 'gwa'.

I believe the story has been misinterpreted from the story of the Anunnaki – Enlil and Enki. The Yahapa word for 'mother' is 'anna'. The word 'naki' means 'no'. Generally speaking, 'Anunnaki' interprets as 'no mother'. To me, this makes sense if the Anunnaki 'gods' altered the genetics of Earthlings by way of genetic engineering.

Genesis 3:16 in the Bible states that God said to Eve, 'I will make your pains in childbearing very severe; with painful labour, you will give birth to children.' With genetic engineering in mind, was there an alternative way to procreate?

To my thinking, the snake or serpent referred to in the Garden of Eden story is a metaphorical description of the Kundalini – the spiritual 'serpent' energy with a pathway up the spine. The apple, therefore, would represent a completed Kundalini arousal personified by 'the Tree of Life', a common motif throughout Mesopotamian mythology. With psychic insight recently imparted, a different version of the Garden of Eden is unfolding to me. This will be expanded on in the sequel to this book.

The native name for Labutali is 'Hapakakala', which literally translated means 'chickens or a flock carried in a container'.

There is an Akkadian myth of Etana, who, as a reward, was carried up into the sky. 'Metana' is the word for star in Yahapa.

'Maya' means shame or even dead. 'Mahano' means to die. As 'Ma' means spirit and 'hano' means house, is this a similar belief to the Parsees in India, where dead bodies are taken to the death-house to be prepared, then set out for the birds to eat?

There seems to be a correlation with the Hindu language in some of the words. As a matter of fact, the word 'hi' means to steer, and the word 'du' means people, i.e., 'Hindu' would mean one who steers the people.

In my research of ancient cultures, I travelled to Easter Island and found that the sacred Moai statues wore hats made of red stone. In Yahapa, 'mo' means old and 'ai' means first person. There has been evidence found of archaic beings, revered as gods, who had red hair.

The word for waterfall is 'pongala', which is the name for the Dalai Lama's palace in Tibet. The word for a Tibetan monk is 'lama'. In Yahapa, 'la' means brother and 'ma' means spirit.

Freddy Silva's book, *The Missing Lands,* is one of my recent acquisitions. This book is brilliant and a treasure trove of information to convince me that my research has validity. This is an ongoing project for me.

27 PROPHECIES

How many talented, enlightened souls — born psychics — have, in the early years of the Christian doctrines, been thrown into dungeons or burnt at the stake, labelled 'witches' by the ordinance of the church?

Joan of Arc — Jeanne d'Arc, circa 1412–1431, was a French heroine known as the Maid of Orleans. Guided by her voices, she led the French resistance that forced the English to raise the siege of Orleans in 1492. That same year, aged seventeen, she led an army of 12,000 to Rheims and had the dauphin crowned Charles VII. Sadly betrayed, she was captured and sold to the English by the Burgundians in 1430 and tried for heresy and sorcery. Joan was burned at the stake in Rouen in 1431. She was beatified in 1909, and canonised in 1920.

Mother Shipton was another notable psychic who saw many years into the future. Although she was burnt at the stake in Clifton, England circa 1449, some of her prophecies are still being borne out. Mother Shipton was born in Norfolk, England, circa 1386 – 1388 and forecast that she would die, burnt at the stake, in her seventies.

Some of her prophetic verses follow:

A carriage without horse will go.
Disaster fills the world with woe.
In London, Primrose Hill shall be
In centre hold a Bishop's See.

(This obviously refers to motor vehicles.)

Around the world, men's thoughts will fly
Quick as the twinkling of an eye.
And water shall great wonders do:
How strange. And yet it shall come true.

(This prediction was over 400 years before the telephone was invented!)

Through towering hills, proud men shall ride
No horse or ass move by his side.
Beneath the water, men shall walk,
Shall ride, shall sleep and even talk.
And in the air, men shall be seen
In white and black and even green.

(Again, a referral to motor vehicles, submarines, and aeroplanes.)

In water, iron then shall float
As easy as a wooden boat.
Gold shall be seen in stream and stone
In land that is as yet unknown.

(Ships built of iron and steel: the gold rushes in America, Canada, and Australia.)

For in those wondrous far-off days
The women shall adopt a craze
To dress like men and trousers wear
And to cut off their locks of hair.
They'll ride astride with brazen brow
As witches do on broomstick now.
And roaring monsters with man atop
Does seem to eat the verdant crop.
And men shall fly as birds do now
And give away the horse and plough.
There'll be a sign for all to see
Be sure that it will certain be.
Then love shall die, and marriage cease
And nations wane as babes decrease.
And wives shall fondle cats and dogs
And men live much the same as hogs.

(It was not until the twentieth century that women began to wear trousers. Short bobbed hair became the fashion in the 1920s.)

In nineteen hundred and twenty-six
Build houses light of straw and sticks.
For then shall mighty wars be planned
And fire and sword shall sweep the land.
When pictures seem alive with movements free,
When boats, like fishes, swim beneath the sea,
When men like birds shall scour the sky,
Then half the world, deep drenched in blood shall die.

(This obviously refers to movies, television, submarines, planes, and world wars still to come.)

TIME!! The elusive factor!

The factor of universal time differs greatly from our earthly time. Because of the fluidity of past, present, and future, it is very hard to place a precise time on events still to come. Many of my own prophecies from over twenty years ago are only now beginning to unfold.

During the 1990s, an American psychic, Gordon Michael Scallion, published many prophecies regarding Earth changes due to earthquakes, tidal waves, and volcanoes. I too have had visions of these happenings. Many are yet to take place, and I feel that there is a thirty to forty-year delay.

Edgar Cayce, also known as The Sleeping Prophet, made countless predictions. Some of them have occurred, but still, some of the Earth changes that he prophesied have not happened.

Michel de Nostredame, better known as Nostradamus, was a French astrologer and physician in the Court of Charles IX. He penned numerous quatrains titled *Centuries* in 1555, some obscure, some identifiable, and some yet to come.

Over the past years, I have channelled many prophecies but have been reticent to make them public. It has never been my wish to be a prophetess of doom. Many of my writings have to do with Earth changes, tidal waves, and wars. I have not made them public as I feel it serves no purpose to put fear into the minds of people, especially the elderly, who should be left to live out their lives in peace.

As with the abovementioned seers, correct timing of visions is very elusive. A few lines from channelling received on 26 June 1996 seem to have been borne out when Pope Benedict XVI retired from the Vatican. He was the first pope in 600 years to resign as leader of the one-billion-member church.

Pope Francis, the 266th vicar of Jesus Christ on Earth, elected in March 2013, appears to be revolutionising the edicts of the Catholic church. I feel most confident that the following verse channelled on 26 June 1996 is pertinent at this time.

The Ring of Fire takes on more power
As Middle East begins to sour.
A short and wiry race begins
To beat the drums of war to kings.
The shoes at last are left behind
As papal robes, he doth unwind.
Undaunted he who takes the key;
Relents and lets some secrets free.

Pope Francis has proclaimed that we are now in the 'judgement years', and I agree. Over the past few years, so much corruption has come to light. Political, corporate, sporting, and more have been under the spotlight and in the news because of corruption, deception, and downright lies. It sure bids one well to be on guard in all dealings.

With modern technology and DNA testing, proof of innocence or guilt is becoming more refined. Filing cabinets full of paper have been replaced with computer technology. Answers are literally at our fingertips.

Over a forty-four year career as a clairvoyant-medium, I have made many prophecies for clients. Although I cannot claim 100% accuracy, I am told I hold a good record. Many of my present clients have returned time and time again. I have never advertised.

Following are just a few prophecies on a worldwide scale.

In 2010 I was told that the pope would resign. Benedict XVI resigned in 2013. He was elected on 19 April 2005 following the death of Pope John Paul II. Pope Benedict announced his resignation in a speech in Latin before the cardinals, citing 'a lack of strength in mind and body due to advanced age.' His resignation became effective on 28 February 2013. He was the first pope to resign since Pope Gregory XII in 1415 and the first to do so on his own initiative since Pope Celestine V in 1294.

One prophecy, yet to come, also referred to a Catholic pope.

'Undaunted he who takes the key; relents and lets some secrets free.'

The last secret of the children of Fatima appears to be a vision of the Pope, along with other bishops, priests, religious and lay people, being killed by soldiers. Pope Benedict XVI cautioned against reading the third secret in a way that predicts a future event.

'In the city of marble, warnings to him will go unheeded. At the dawn of a September day, he will go down. Red coat beside him will also go but not in vain.'

Two years ago, I travelled throughout France and Italy, visiting many cathedrals. Twenty years before, I visited the Vatican. Although there is magnificence in construction, decoration, and contents of these venues, I nonetheless felt saddened at the grandeur and opulence displayed for the tourists.

On my return to Australia, I watched a movie called *The Two Popes*, gaining the impression that the present Pope Frances was an approachable soul. Searching the internet, I found that it was possible to write to the pontiff, instructions on how to address His Holiness being set down, and a statement that, in all probability, an answer would be received. My letter read as follows:

> *His Holiness Pope Francis,*
>
> *Most Holy Father and Brother in Christ,*
>
> *Last night I watched a movie, The Two Popes, which I am sure you must have seen. In the personification of yourself, I admired the humility and lack of ego shown to your followers.*
>
> *There is but one God – The Almighty – which we should all strive to serve in the best way we can.*
>
> *For over twenty years, I conducted a Spiritualist church in a rented Masonic hall, unpaid, and providing morning tea for all comers.*
>
> *I have recently returned from overseas, by the grace of God, being financed by a television quiz win. In Lima and Cuzco, I prayed in Catholic cathedrals. While travelling through France and Italy, I visited many magnificent Catholic cathedrals – all peaceful places to offer my prayers to God.*
>
> *Most Holy Father, I beg of you to hear my plea. According to the internet, you have 1.2 billion children of your faith, and those of other faiths are no less in need than the 'Catholic children'.*

While visiting Lyon, Bordeaux, Marseilles, Florence, and Messina in Sicily, I visited magnificent cathedrals and prayed in them. So beautiful to see, and yet I am sure God heard my prayers just as clearly when I lived among tribal brothers and sisters in New Guinea and had church services under the coconut trees beside the ocean.

I know your humility and dedication to reform, and I know that 'reform' by sharing the grandeur exhibited in the cathedrals and Vatican would warm the hearts of not only Catholics in the world but all who pray to their God.

Over twenty years ago, I visited the Vatican, the Sistine Chapel, and climbed the dome and prayed in Saint Peter's Basilica. As I prayed, my tears and sobs were unbearable. I had walked past women begging in Vatican Square, then past vast riches inside the Vatican.

In the museum attached to the cathedral in Messina, Sicily, I viewed gold, gems, and jewellery: of what service to God??

In my own country, at present, thousands of people are being affected by rampant bushfires. Homes and belongings burned away from them. I am sure many of them are crying out to God Almighty for help.

As the 'Earthly Ambassador for God' Holy Father, please hear my prayer. The time has come for sharing not just bread and wine but the proceeds of a 'garage sale' of goods that are seen but not used.

As a clairvoyant-medium for over forty years, I am sure that the world is very close to 'the day of reckoning' and the visions that were shown to the children of Fatima. Our Lord God turned the tide so that Moses and his followers could cross The Red Sea. Most Holy Father and brother, will you be the one to turn the tide and share not just bread and wine but accumulated wealth with the poor and needy of the world?

In closing, I offer you a poem that was channelled to me over forty years ago and offer the above not with criticism but to remind you of the lesson our Lord Jesus Christ taught with the serving of the loaves and fishes.

Yours sincerely from your sister in service to God.

The following prophecy was channelled to me in 1987:

The statues worshipped in the Church of Rome
Shall crumble, for they will be cursed.
The sharks shall swim among the ruins,
But sharks have trod for many moons.
The Vatican' held many rogues
Of scattered nations, many brogues,
But all pomposity shall be
Despatched beneath the deep, blue sea.
For Christ the Man of Nazarene
Preached God's words on hills of green
The words he spoke did not require
Cathedrals, music and a choir.
For Jesus Christ preached words of gold
Required not majestic bold.
These written words are prophecy.
Do not fear, they are not heresy.
For would I lie or kill a bird?
I'm here to teach you God's own word.

With the present climate changes of the world, with increasing volcanic eruptions, especially Mount Etna and Stromboli, I feel the above prediction is not far off.

Revelation in the Holy Bible foretells plagues in the end times. This past year has brought many plagues to the world. Locusts, jellyfish, ladybeetles, and mice. It unsettles me to see the current plagues affecting my beloved Australia. How impossible and frustrating it must be to live and work among such infestations.

Channelled October 2020:

The base of the pyramid is the fulcrum upon which energy is transmuted to light. Aligning the ascension process with the north, south, east, and west of the Great Pyramid of Giza will be a key to the Cosmic Transmutation. The Guardians of the Galaxy are aware of the dangers on planet Earth from those who seek to destroy by way of their folly of nuclear weapons.

2025 – Chinese Year of the Snake:

The Biosphere will collapse.

Before then, fingers of fire will enliven (volcanoes). A giant asteroid will cause the equilibrium of Planet Earth to falter.

By the year 2023, there will be danger of a nuclear winter. A culling of humanity will have taken place.

Scientists will release information that the shifting of the poles is affecting the equilibrium of the planet.

Channelled in 1990:

Scientists hold many clues
To many viruses and flues.

But up ahead, a ghastly plan
Will bring a plague to threaten man.
And AIDS will, as a droplet, be
To this plague with its adversities.
And no known cure will be found
To this plague that comes from underground.
[My note: 'Underground' - bat caves, or covert?]

(And now COVID-19 vaccinations are being touted as 'the safe way out'. I don't believe it! Past flu vaccinations have landed me in hospital for a month.)

Channelled 15 December 2019:

The world is standing on the edge of a precipice.
Governments are aware of this but doing little.
The melting of the poles is placing planet Earth in jeopardy as not only rising seas and flooding will occur, but also the equilibrium and rotation of the planet is becoming dire.

Channelled 6 July 1991 appertaining to the present:

July, then August, then begins
Upheavals that will threaten kings.
And arcane knowledge shall be shown
To tell the future as the phone.
[My note: advanced technology and off-planet radar are making it possible for 'arcane' (ancient) records to be found.]

During a meditation many years ago, I was taken spiritually to the Great Sphinx. I found myself inside this great edifice around the area of the Third Eye. Then I dropped down a very deep shaft. I was then told I was in the Hall of Records. This surprised me as I would have expected to see leather scrolls, papyri, or clay tablets full of inscriptions. There were none of these! The late Edgar Cayce also had a vision of a cavern inside the Sphinx.

As my spirit body stood in a vast stone chamber, a holographic image of the history of planet Earth began to play out around me. Past, present, and future were shown to me. I saw massive flooding, fires, tidal waves, and what appeared to be the ozone layer on fire.

When I lived in New Guinea in 1970, I wrote the first dictionary of the Yahapa language. The first official dictionary was written by professionals in 1997. I was told this language relates to the builders of the Sphinx, and it seems to relate to the time of Lemuria and Sumeria. The following is a poem that was channelled to me:

THE RIDDLE OF THE SPHINX

The readers of your epilogue
Will stand in silence, all agog
For you have found by your 'instincts'
The Riddle of the Cryptic Sphinx.
The Lion is masculine for sure,
But what is hidden 'neath the paws
Are documents: 'Adjourn ye not
Or else the form will turn to rot!'
The essence of this trilogy
Is common sense for you and me
That if a garden starts to grow,
Albeit vegetable or rose,
But midway through the growth process

The gardener takes his recess,
returneth not to tend the soil,
The plants therein will tend to spoil.
And so it is with human birth:
The soul encased in mortal girth
Begins its quest in Purity
Until around the age of three.
Exceptions to the norm exist
But from these now I will desist.
To further set the record straight,
An issue you can contemplate:
From education – school or church –
The soul can stand, the soul may lurch.
And so, with 'garden' of the home,
For child is not a garden gnome.
If child is nourished with pure love
And taught about the Pure White Dove,
The soul is nourished diligently
With produce fresh from garden, tree,
Then all attributes of God
Will follow as the plant in sod,
Will bloom with blossoms in due time.
There is a reason to this rhyme:
In time when Lion in form is strong,
Has learned to reason right from wrong,
The Lamb appears upon the scene
And brings to mind a world pristine.
The Lamb is meek and mild you know
And most Lambs with the flock will go
But tied to Lion the Lamb will see
The answer to this mystery.
For if the Lion who seeks its prey,

Who walks by night and sleeps by day,
Takes counsel naught from anyone,
Concedes that he is King bar none,
Were mated with a pure, white Lamb
In a serious marriage – not a sham,
The product of their Union be
A child of Pure Divinity.
The Lion that lays down with the Lamb,
Not Lioness and not the Ram,
If taught to child from early days
Will halt the errant of the ways.
Then as maturity enfolds,
The child will reach the Spiritual goal
Attendant with God's Spiritual Graces,
regardless of the Form or Faces.
A Lion, A Lamb, the Strength, the Mild,
No longer just a little child
But being of Strength – a True 'I AM':
At last, the Lion lays down with the Lamb.

The lessons Jesus Christ taught were most often delivered in parables. This is the manner in which many of my writings are received.

The parable of The Ten Virgins, as told in Matthew 25:1-13, appears to me to be very apt at this time in history. The story is based on a wedding ceremony in which ten bridesmaids were told to fill their lamps with oil before the bridegroom arrived. Five bridesmaids filled their lamps as told, but the other five ignored the instructions. When the bridegroom arrived, the tardy bridesmaids were locked out of the wedding ceremony.

COVID-19 has certainly woken many citizens of the world up with a jolt. There are also many who are not taking notice of the changing times. I am afraid there will be many 'bridesmaids' left with no oil!

Channelled to me:

The cattle a' lowing, the baby awakes:
The mother called Earth gives birth during the quakes.

There was no time frame given on the above, however, I have had graphic visions of tidal waves, earthquakes in New Zealand and east of there, causing tidal waves on the east coast of Australia. Being a fatalist, I am not at all perturbed by these visions. Although I live on high ground, I may be sitting on a beach when tidal waves happen. I do not fear death and believe in fate and karma.

In Luke 21, Holy Bible, Jesus warned of false messiahs, wars, nation rising against nation, 'great earthquakes, famines in many lands, epidemics and terrifying things happening in the heavens.'

Luke 21:25: 'Then there will be strange events in the skies – warnings, evil omens and portents in the sun, moon, and the stars; and down here on earth the nations will be in turmoil, perplexed by the roaring seas and strange tides.'

Luke chapters 23-24 tell of the crucifixion and resurrection of Jesus Christ. The fact that the body of Jesus Christ was not found in the tomb has always intrigued me. So too the fact that Jesus asked for food to eat with the two men from Emmaus before He went to Heaven. Isn't it feasible that Jesus's looks may have been altered by way of hair or beard change after he entered the tomb?

As a medium for many years, I see spirit people. They do not have a body, let alone a digestive system, to handle eating food. But this in no way denigrates the personage of the Lord Jesus Christ, whom I believe came into this world as a divine teacher for humanity.

Many people are not aware of the remains of nuclear testing that was carried out on Bikini Atoll by the USA between 1946 and 1958. Twenty-three nuclear detonations were carried out, and there are still ongoing concerns about potential radioactive spills. Bikini Atoll is situated in the Marshall Islands. They happen to be very close to the Mariana Trench, which is the deepest oceanic trench on Earth. This is also the area of the Ring of Fire, the line of territory prone to earthquakes.

For many years I have had visions of massive icebergs breaking off Antarctica and flowing towards Tasmania and mainland Australia. In May 2021, a chunk of ice called 'A-76' – bigger than the state of Rhode Island, USA – 4,320 square kilometres, 170 kilometres long and 25 kilometres wide, broke off and is floating in the Weddell Sea. It is currently the world's largest floating iceberg and has been named by some the 'Doomsday Glacier'.

Last year I channelled: 'Brute force will strike around the International Games.'

The recent 107th International Olympic Games were held in Tokyo, Japan. During the games (23 July to 8 August 2021), there were earthquakes and storms further north in Japan. On 29 July 2021, a magnitude 8.2 earthquake struck fifty miles south of the Alaska Peninsula. Also, during that time, there were massive, unprecedented floods in China, Germany, Belgium, Scotland, England, the USA, and many other countries.

Channelled about twenty years ago: 'America for all her might, goes down as in a single night, catastrophes ordained by God will purge from her power, purge from her might.'

Over the last two years, the USA has certainly had her woes. Fires, tornadoes, floods, earthquakes, and the scourge of the COVID-19 crisis with many deaths.

I recently watched a movie on the life of Marilyn Monroe, detailing some mysteries surrounding her death. Her involvement with President John F Kennedy and his brother Robert was discussed. Also, a plan to deflect a nuclear attack from Cuba, that country being supplied with weapons from Russia.

According to the script, the plan was to have a submarine get close to the Cuban coast, from where it would project an image of Jesus Christ onto the clouds. The idea was that as Cuba has a majority of Catholics, the utter astonishment of the image would delay a war. Preposterous? Well, it got me thinking about my fascination with Revelation in the Holy Bible, the most cryptic chapter of that book.

Once again, one of my prophecies from around thirty years ago seems to be taking place at this time. Prophecies are mostly received by me in verse.

At this moment, as I write, I have been told about troubles in the Middle East. Verses channelled by me in 1996 are as follows:

A wicked cup of brew there boils
Inside the kingdom built on oils.
And dastardly the deeds and debt
Of USA. They will regret
The information gained from clones

In satellites that spy on thrones.
With some of this they've been mislead
Enticed into a 'fickle bed'.

The dykes that edge the sands will come undone
As Potentates unlock their plans to put an end to history's wars
In one short moment overruled by 'Thor' (the God of Thunder)
The ground will shake as Tehran shows force with troops to bring alarm.

Received 6 November 1994. I believe, as many prophecies I have received thirty years ahead of time, the time frame for the following is 2024:

The twenty-third psalm will be sung
By many as the year is done.
The 'Dance of Death' now holds the score
Awaiting for the mid-East war.
Los Angeles, 'The Queen of Coast',
Within mere weeks will be the host
Of more upheavals, more ague
As close to home, volcanoes spew.

The Ring of Fire readies now
As 'Wise Men' watch and wonder how
To put an end to history's wars,
In one sharp moment stilled by Thor (the God of Thunder).

During the year 1986, I channelled many poems. Spirit now adjures me to quote the following as a timely reminder to one and all:

IF GOD CAME TO VISIT

If God came to visit the Earth that he made
Not in Heavenly body but in flesh form arrayed,
Would you beckon Him in, and a table arrange?
Or be fearful of Him and feel terribly strange?
Would you try to excuse the mistakes that you've made?
Or beg His forgiveness and hope guilt would fade?
Would the knowledge that He knows you outside and in
Make you much more wary when it comes to sin?
If the Governments who make all the bombs to explode
Were called to a meeting in God's Heavenly Abode
Do you think they'd explain all that monetary waste
When there's millions of children with no food to taste?
If God went to visit the President's men
When they opened their office at quarter to ten
Would they give Him a hearing?
Say 'Please take a seat till the President comes'?
He'd arrive looking neat.
Would the President sit and on subjects demur?
Or say, "My Dear Lord, on Your Peace I concur!'
Or else could he say – with a smile on his face –
'To touch that red button means no Human Race.'
If the rich and the famous who sail 'round in their yachts
Could help sick, little children as they lay in their cots,
I'm sure God would excuse all the bourbon and gin
And when they went to Heaven, would welcome them in.
Friend, I give you fair warning to be on your guard
And to try to be good: 'Tho it's terribly hard.
For God will not tell you when He will appear.
He needs no appointments,

Friend: ALREADY HE'S HERE!

And as for Biblical prophecies, Revelation chapter 13: 14-18:

> *And he ordered the people of the world to make a great statue of the first Creature, who was fatally wounded then came back to life. He was permitted to give breath to this statue and even make it speak. Then the statue ordered that anyone refusing to worship it must die.*
>
> *He required everyone – great and small, rich and poor, slave and free – to be tattooed with a certain mark on the right hand or on the forehead. And no one could get a job or even buy in any shop without the permit of that mark, which was either the name of the Creature or the code number of his name.*
>
> *Here is a puzzle that calls for careful thought to solve it. Let those who are able, interpret this code: the numerical values of the letters in his name add to 666.*

In my chapter on Sai Baba, I drew a comparison with the 'strange animal, this one coming up out of the Earth, with two little horns like those of a lamb but a fearsome voice like the Dragon's'. I also hypothesised that Sathya Sai Baba could have been the Anti-Christ, the 'strange animal' mentioned.

Over the years, many have conjectured that Vicarius Filii Dei, Vicar of the Son of God, had a numerical value of 666. Vicarius Filii Dei is the papal title. In light of the idea of projecting images in the sky, I am looking in that direction for clues.

In a poem channelled to me from Sai Baba after his passing, the following lines occur. The full channelling can be read in the previous chapter on Sai Baba.

News of an image alight in the sky,
Will make you wonder; will make you cry.
For in the Beginning, we melded as one
But now I'm the Sweeper
And Jesus's – God's Son.

The first bank card produced in the 1980s sported three 6s on the surface. With the world health threat from COVID-19, there is talk of a vaccination passport being placed on mobile phones. That idea may even move to a plastic card to provide entry to buildings, similar to the door keys used in resorts.

There are many third world countries where people do not own a mobile phone. Those same countries have a large populace who follow the Catholic religion zealously. An image of their Christ telling them to get vaccinated or they will die may do the trick! Is my imagination linked to my psychic abilities running riot on me? Let us wait and see.

Many years ago, I read a statement that 'When man becomes as clever as God, the world will come to an end.' This feels to me a little like computer games, i.e., *Game Over*.

Since childhood, I have been a seeker of truth. On any given subject, there will always be different opinions or interpretations. My advice to my students has always been the following: 'Ye with ears – listen. Ye with eyes – look closely. Ye with a voice – speak up. And you with a brain and spirit – seek the truth yourself !'

Scientists, to humanity's benefit, have mastered cloning, stem cell proliferation and even the manufacturing of human parts. In-vitro fertilisation has become commonplace these days. Public figures such as the late, great Stephen Hawking and well-known Elon Musk have expressed concern that full Artificial Intelligence (AI) could result in human extinction. The consequences of the singularity and its potential benefit or harm to the human race have been intensely debated.

Although I have always strived to be as honest as I possibly can with Readings, I do not want to be labelled a prophet of doom. I have discreetly communicated with some authorities, warning them of dangers. I believe in fate and do not want to spread fear among the populace.

I LIVE IN THE NOW.
I REMEMBER THE PAST.
I DREAM OF THE FUTURE.

EPILOGUE

My love and gratitude go out to all who have deigned to share my journey. And for those of you who have been able to relate in any way and have found my words helpful or encouraging, I bless the path ahead of you.

Love for my five children burns deep within my soul. During some of my darkest days, my love for them became the anchor, the catalyst that saved me from drowning in a sea of despair. And to my 'surrogate children' who love and support me in many ways, you have my Eternal love.

I also send out my love and gratitude to Mike. I bear him no ill will and wish only the best for him in life. We worked hard and for long hours, turning a cow paddock into a paradise. What we created can never be lost. I hold to the good memories of the times we had together. Unhappy memories are like poison to the soul. I prefer to hold on to the happy memories. They are like delicious chocolate!

Undaunted, I have chosen to bare my soul. My spirit guides call me 'Teacher', and as such, I have shared my education in The University of Life. Lessons are not always found in classrooms and books but in practice. For it is only when you have fallen down and hit the road that you can see and realise what the road is made of and perceive where it will lead you.

To the people who have tormented, tested, cheated on, and judged me, I give my unmitigated love and gratitude. Although not appreciated or understood at the time, the part you played on the stage of Life has manifested in the material for this book. May it help many!

Today, in my eighty-fourth year, I enjoy a peaceful life. I have laid to rest ghosts from the past, handle unfathomable obstacles with 'que sera sera', love the being that is me, and do not suffer fools gladly.

My life has been very full. Boredom and idleness are unknown to me. My wide and varied interests and care for humanity fill my days. With the rapid changes of energy on planet Earth, I feel the need to expedite the truth.

Confucius said, 'He who learns but does not think is lost. He who thinks but does not learn is in danger.'

To the above, I will add, 'He who has knowledge but does not share it willingly is comparable to a greedy person.'

The world is changing rapidly! Although there is much suffering and upheavals, there are also amazing breakthroughs in science and technology. The younger generation has the opportunity to literally reach the stars.

And although I have to turn to my younger friends to explain the more intricate workings of the net, the new technology really excites me. We have come a long way since I pounded on the keys of a Royal or Remington-Rand typewriter!

I have faith that a Brave New World is waiting just down the track, and it is my wish to be a part of the birthing of a new Gaia; the woman clothed in the sun with the moon at her feet and a crown of stars on her head, as described by John the Divine in Revelation.

In any university, there are many faculties and diversities. And this is also the case with The University of Life. Accept and enjoy the lessons, be they good or bad, for they will eventually lead you to The Peace that Passeth All Understanding.

A DOVE OF PEACE

A Dove of Peace at home within itself
Flew down and sat with others on a shelf
And though its cooing sounds it tried to teach,
The black and brown birds seemed beyond its reach.
'Come fly with me, and in the currents of the wind there let us play.'
Bespoke a bird with feathers brown as clay.
'I'll listen to the wind around my beak
But cannot hear the words you long to speak!'
A Raven, wings of midnight, head as black as coal,
Soared high, then higher, beauty to my soul;
So high, so lofty that it could not hear
The words so sweet I wished to whisper in its ear.
Should Dove of Peace then turn to Dove of War
Because the brown bird plays, the black bird soars?
The Dove of Peace has losses naught
If other birds are overwrought.
Two wings can keep one bird on high
But with two wings two birds can't fly;
Why then surrender to the ground
And Dove be sacrificed for black and brown?
Maybe in former lives passed by
The Dove of Peace screamed Ravens cry.

Perhaps white wings of Dove were clay
And in that time cried 'Come and play!'

PEACE, LIGHT, AND LOVE.

To the academics who feel drawn to read my stories, I in no way wish to demean the psychiatric profession. My studies have not been in universities but have entailed many workshops, researching, reading and, most importantly, experiences.

My terminology may seem rash at times, although the main focus of my book is to assist the layperson and guide them to find a spiritual path and the peace that passeth all understanding.

'I' am as a tree that has been striving to reach the heavens since the time of my birth. There have been many times when heavy birds have landed on my branches, weighing me down. The storms of life have shaken me, stripped me of my leaves and blossoms and left my branches bare.

The heavy birds of worries, fears and people who have taken advantage of my good nature and gifts have been shaken off my branches by the winds of spirit. The chill of the frosts has been melted by the warmth of the Creator God.

Life is Good! In what would normally be the winter of my life, I have found spring. The branches of my tree are bursting with new leaves and blossoms. The sun shines down on me and draws me towards the heavens. Sweet songbirds alight on my branches, bringing joy to my heart with their sweet songs.

The compost of decayed past nourishes my roots and feeds me. And the thought that my words can be the compost to help other trees to grow warms my heart.

I am alive! I am well! I am blessed!

ABOUT THE AUTHOR

This book is a baby whose gestation period has extended across thirty years. The ideas, notes, channelled poems, and prophecies have lain on the shelf of consciousness awaiting 'the right time'.

Joan Miller is an eighty-four year old clairvoyant-medium whose extraordinary life has led her to bare her soul in order to help others. From the depths of despair, near-death experiences, and physical and psychological pain, she has fought back to gain equilibrium and wholeness in her life.

Over a forty-four year period, Joan has been the spiritual support for countless people, many of whom have become staunch friends and supporters. They too have been waiting a long time to welcome this baby.

Joan describes her life as a rich tapestry. The bright, vivid colours can only be appreciated in contrast with the darker shades – and this only in retrospect, when we look back at our University of Life and the lessons we had to learn to satisfy our soul's journey.

Having attained dux in high school and denied further education in her teens, Joan went on to marry and give birth to five children. In mid-life, Joan undertook studies in Hypnotherapy, Transpersonal Psychology, and Body Electronics.

Joan is a believer in inherited skills from past lives and encourages others to believe and seek out this facet of themselves. She enjoys an array of her own skills, mostly self-taught and including writing, playing piano, dressmaking, upholstery, art, cooking, and cake-decorating. Joan finds joy in her gardening – floral, vegetables, and herbs.

www.ingramcontent.com/pod-product-compliance
Lightning Source LLC
Chambersburg PA
CBHW052011070526
44584CB00016B/1711